THE LETTERS OF

JOHN STUART MILL

Volume II

Elibron Classics
www.elibron.com

Elibron Classics series.

ISBN 1-4212-6383-1 (paperback)
ISBN 0-543-68676-0 (hardcover)

This Elibron Classics Replica Edition is an unabridged facsimile
of the edition published in 1910 by Longmans, Green and Co., London, etc.

THE LETTERS OF
JOHN STUART MILL

By permission of Fredk. Hollyer

John Stuart Mill

from the portrait by G. F. Watts

THE LETTERS OF JOHN STUART MILL

EDITED, WITH AN INTRODUCTION, BY

HUGH S. R. ELLIOT

WITH A NOTE ON MILL'S PRIVATE LIFE, BY

MARY TAYLOR

VOL. II

WITH PORTRAITS

LONGMANS, GREEN AND CO.
39 PATERNOSTER ROW, LONDON
NEW YORK, BOMBAY, AND CALCUTTA
1910

CONTENTS

LIST OF ILLUSTRATIONS

THE LETTERS OF
JOHN STUART MILL

CHAPTER IX

1864–1865

TO W. E. GLADSTONE,

on the *Alabama* case.

ST. VÉRAN, *22nd January* 1864.

MY DEAR SIR,—When I took the liberty of sending you Mr. Loring's pamphlet, nothing was further from my thoughts than to engage you in a controversy of any sort. I am much honoured by your having spared time to write to me so fully on the subject, and am very glad to find, in the view you take of it, nothing from which I differ in principle. I did not mean to identify myself with all Mr. Loring's sentiments; I think him decidedly unjust to our Government, which has shown itself throughout in a far more favourable light than the predominant portion of our public. But he seemed to me to be often right, and when wrong, only in a manner in which it is most natural and scarcely unreasonable that an American should be so. I thought that his statement would interest you, and that your being acquainted with it might perhaps be of use.

1864 — Aetat. 57.

In addition to the two important points touched on in your letter, it seems to me that several others are raised by Mr. Loring. I pass over those which are evidently untenable, or which have a moral but not a jurisprudential value. But he argues—

1st. That a State which, professing itself neutral, does

1864 — Aetat. 57. not make all reasonable exertions to enforce the obligations of neutrality upon its own subjects, gives to the belligerent who is prejudiced by their acts just ground of complaint, and in certain cases lays itself open to a demand of indemnity, and that the Government of the United States has faithfully acted on this principle at times when we were belligerents and they were neutrals.

2nd. That the use of neutral territory as a place where an expedition may be fitted out, and from which it may issue and execute warlike operations without having acquired the right to do so in the country of the belligerent whom it serves, is, by international law, not a commercial operation but a hostile act.

3rd. That the *Alabama*, &c., in burning their prizes before condemnation by any prize court, are acting in a manner forbidden by international law, and which deprives them of any claim to the privileges or immunities which distinguish regularly commissioned cruisers from pirates.

4th. That those cruisers have made use of the British flag in a manner which brings them within the provisions of the Merchant Shipping Act, 17 and 18 Vict., chap. 104.

As to the argument which Mr. Loring founds on the fact that the ships were built by contract, his reason for insisting so strongly on that point probably is that it makes the precedent of the *Santisima Trinidad* so far inapplicable. He would no doubt be very glad to get rid of that case altogether, and to have it ruled that ships of war must not be sold at all by a neutral country to a belligerent. This opinion—which I hope I am not mistaken in thinking that you are not far from agreeing in—is forcibly maintained in an article by Professor Cairnes in *Macmillan's Magazine* for the present month, which seems to me one of the ablest and most valuable papers which this controversy has called forth. But to return to Mr. Loring. He regards the building by contract as intrinsically important simply as evidence of intent. You think that the intent of the Confederate agents may admit of proof, but not that of the builder. Doubtless it is in general neither provable nor probable that the *motive* of the builder was one of hostility or was any other than the profit of the transaction, but his *intention*, I apprehend, depends only upon whether or not he *knew* that he was selling the ship to an agent of a belligerent. I presume that on the general principles of law any one would be held to have intended all such consequences of his actions as he foreknew or expected.

I should be much to blame in replying to your letter by so long a one as this did I not add my sincere hope that you will not consider it necessary to make the smallest answer to it.

I thank you heartily for your kind invitation to your breakfasts, and I promise myself to make use of the privilege. I do not expect to be in England for the first two months after Easter, but shall be there in June.—I am, my dear sir, very truly yours, J. S. MILL.

To Alexander Bain.

BLACKHEATH PARK, 18*th March* 1864.

DEAR BAIN,—I was much delighted by receiving your new edition.[1] You must have worked very hard to get it out so soon. I have not yet come to much of the new matter as I am reading the book regularly through from the beginning, but the remaining portion of my task with Hamilton will soon be plain sailing. I am very glad the additions are considerable, as they will all tend to the clearing up of difficulties.

I have read your Grammar with considerable care and attention. It is a great improvement on any other grammar that I have seen, and as far as I can judge, I think you right on all the questions of theory. Nobody has so completely got to the bottom of shall and will. As to minute details, I found myself every now and then differing from you—chiefly, though not always, in cases where you seemed to me to draw grammatical principles too tight, to the exclusion of modes of speech which have a real *raison d'être*. But all these are points open to

[1] [Of "The Senses and the Intellect."]

1864 — Ætat. 57. discussion, and I should not have such confidence in my own impressions if you did not agree with them when stated. I have not written them down, but I have made references by which I can recall them if wanted.

In consequence mainly of your last letter, I have been reading Spencer's "First Principles" over again. On the whole I like it less than the first time. He is so good that he ought to be better. His *à priori* system is more consistent than Hamilton's, but quite as fundamentally absurd; in fact, there is the same erroneous assumption at the bottom of both. And most of his general principles strike me as being little more than verbal or at most empirical generalisations, with no warrant for their being considered laws. As you truly say, his doctrine that the Persistence of Force is a datum of Consciousness is exactly Hamilton's strange theory of Causation. But how weak his proof of it. We cannot, he says, conceive a beginning, because all consciousness is consciousness of difference, and when the true terms of the comparison are Something and Nothing, one of the two is not a possible object of consciousness at all. This is merely a play on the word Nothing, very like one which Hamilton shows up in his discussion of the different theories of Causation. "Nothing" cannot be an object of consciousness, but the *absence of Something* may be. We can be conscious of x, and conscious of the universe minus x, and of ourselves minus x, and the difference between these two states is the difference required by the law of Consciousness.

Neither does Spencer, any more than Tyndall, remove any of my difficulties about the Conservation of Force. The law of Conservation, as exhibited in the cases which go farthest to prove it, consists in this, that one form of force only ceases to manifest itself when a force equivalent in quantity, but of a different form, manifests itself instead. When a ball strikes another ball, the force which the first ball loses does not become latent; the motion lost is either transferred entire to the other ball, or, if any of it is lost sight of, the corresponding amount of force reappears in an increase of temperature. As, however, we know that there is latent heat, I can conceive that force in general might become latent and remain unmanifested even for many geological periods, reappearing identical in quantity at their close. But I have not seen the formulæ of the theory so expressed as to place such a fact as this in a rational and comprehensive light. I require a great many explanations respecting the molecular motion which is supposed to be the material antecedent of the phenomenon heat. Force may be latent, but what is the meaning of latent motion? Is the molecular motion supposed to continue during the period of latency? When an object is at a fixed temperature, is there a fixed degree of molecular motion always taking place in it? Spencer's doctrine, as a connected theory, fails entirely if there is not. Yet surely all that can be proved is that a molecular motion takes place at every *change* of temperature, and surely it is contrary to all our knowledge of material forces to suppose that a motion either of bodies or of particles can be perpetually going on for a cycle of ages in a resisting medium without diminution.

With regard to the theory as a whole, difficulties multiply round me the longer I consider it. Spencer says, "Just that amount of gravitation force which the sun's heat overcame in raising the atoms of water is given out again in the fall of those atoms to the same level," thus implying that the force of gravity is not acting all the while and kept in equilibrium by a counter force, in the cessation of which it again manifests itself, of course neither increased nor diminished in amount; but is actually (so to speak) absorbed and again restored by the annihilation of an equivalent quantity of heat. Now, if this be so, none of the heat can be expended as heat, for if the agent which destroys the heat has its own temperature raised by the process (which it surely has), there remains so much the less heat to be reconverted into gravitation, and the body will not fall, as I apprehend it does, with a force exactly equal to that which was overcome in raising it.

Again, Spencer says, "The investigations of Dulong,

1864 — Aetat. 57.

Petit, and Neumann have proved a relation in amount between the affinities of combining bodies and the heat evolved during their combination." I should much like to know the numerical law of this relation, as it could not fail to enlarge our conception of the meaning of the negative sign. It would be interesting to know what strength of the affinity corresponds to the "heat evolved" by a freezing mixture.

Again, I do not understand how the theory adjusts itself to the ordinary phenomenon of accelerating force. If the earth were falling into the sun it would, when it had passed through half the distance, be acted upon by four times the original force to begin with, and, in addition, by the enormous momentum generated by the acquired velocity. In what antecedent form did this enormous additional force exist? Is it all acquired at the expense of heat? and would its development be attended by an inconceivably great amount of diminution of temperature? If these are not difficulties to you, their being so to me can only arise from my ignorance of the subject; but as I desire very much to understand it, I warn you of the demand which will be made upon your didactic faculties when we have the opportunity of discussing it together. . . .

To Alexander Bain.

Blackheath Park, 10*th April* 1864.

. . . I have finished your new edition.[1] I have not compared it minutely with the old, but I think you have greatly improved the book; both as to the thoughts and the mode of exposition. The only point on which I find much matter for comment is the account you give of Association by Contrast. No doubt, the relativity of all Consciousness (in your sense of relativity, which is not the same as Hamilton's) accounts for part of the phenomena, and seems to be the real explanation of some cases which you have very successfully analysed. But I do not

[1] [Of "The Senses and the Intellect."]

think it will do as a general explanation, nor do I think it fits your leading instances. According to the law of relativity the correlative which should be suggested by large is not small but ordinary. If a thing is only large relatively to what is small we do not call it large simply. I am myself inclined (I speak under correction) to solve the question of Contrast as a source of Association by denying its existence. I cannot find in myself that present suffering has any tendency to recall my idea of former happiness. On the contrary, it tends, I think, as one might suppose beforehand, in the way of obstructive association, to exclude that idea. What is real in the case is, I think, that during the state of suffering the idea of previous enjoyment may be recalled by something which is associated with it in the way of resemblance or contiguity, and that then the clashing of the two simultaneous emotions arrests the attention upon them, intensifies the consciousness of them both, suggests the additional idea of change or vicissitude, and the painful one of change for the worse, and all this being intimately mixed up with the state of present suffering, people fancy it is the suffering which suggested the remembrance when, in truth, it was an obstacle to it.

1864 — Aetat. 57.

I have also read through Spencer's "Principles of Psychology," which is as much better than I thought as the "First Principles" are less good. He is, no doubt, a great deal too certain of many things, and on some he is clearly wrong, but much less so than I fancied (barring the Universal Postulate, on which he now tells me that my difference from him is chiefly verbal, but I do not think so). He has a great mastery over the obscurer applications of the associative principle. As you say, he is particularly good on the subject of resistance and extension. Still, his argument against Hamilton does not thoroughly satisfy me. There seems to be an occult *petitio principii* in it. He argues that we cannot acquire the idea of extension from sight alone, because that idea involves muscular feelings, which last is just the point to be proved. Of course the idea *such as we now have it* involves muscular feelings, and any idea

1864 — Aetat. 57. we could have got from sight must have been very unlike our *present* notion of extension; but that distinction is perfectly well drawn by Reid, in his "Geometry of Visibles." What I want to know is, exactly what idea of one thing as outside another we could have obtained by sight; whether merely the vague feeling of two simultaneous objects, or what more than this. A similar question arises as to touch: if two distinct parts of the skin came simultaneously into passive contact with objects, should we, apart from other experience, distinguish two sensations or only one mass of sensation; and if we should distinguish two simultaneous sensations, is this simultaneous consciousness of a plurality of sensations what we mean by outness; as if so, we might acquire that idea from the simultaneity of a taste or a smell.

I cannot quite make out why you advised me to read the Fichte. I find nothing at all in it. It is a fanciful theory to account for imaginary facts. I do not see how his preconscious states can have had the merit even of suggesting to you or Spencer the first germ of what both of you have written, with a real science and philosophy to connect our conscious with our purely organic states. . . .

To Earl Grey,

on his "Essay on Parliamentary Government with Reference to Reform."

St. Véran, 13*th May* 1864.

My dear Lord,—I am much obliged by the opportunity you have given me of reading the new chapters of your "Essay on Parliamentary Government" in the present stage of their progress. As you have added to the honour of a very flattering mention of what I have written on the subject, that of inviting any remark which occurs to me, I readily avail myself of the invitation, though much of what I have to say has probably presented itself to your own mind.

You already know, as well as I could state, and better

than I could state in few words, in what respects we agree and differ on the general principles of the question. I presume that my principles being such as you are aware of, what you are desirous of knowing in the present case is the impression made on me by your practical suggestions. I entirely agree with you that Parliamentary Reform is a subject which can only be usefully considered as a whole; since the unobvious consequences of political changes being still more important than the obvious ones, a change in only one part of a political system, though in itself desirable, may do as much harm as good, while several changes made at once, and well adapted to one another, may secure all the good and guard against the harm.

In your various proposals you have been guided by this just idea, and it seems to me that they have been suggested by a more enlarged conception than is at all common among politicians, both of the evils which exist, and of those which there might be danger of introducing by the remedies.

To some of your proposals I attach great importance. The first place among these I give to the representation of minorities, which would be obtained, to a very useful extent, by the cumulative vote. Mr. Hare's plan, however, seems to me vastly superior both in the direct and in the indirect benefits it would produce; and the supposed difficulty of working it would, I am almost certain, in a great measure disappear after a little experience.

The plan has been several times discussed in the legislatures of the two principal Australian colonies; and, though not yet adopted, I have been struck by the proof given in the debates how perfectly the great majority of the speakers, both Conservative and Radical, understood it, and how generally the best of them on both sides supported it. I feel confident that it would require nothing for success but a real desire in the public to make it succeed. This does not yet exist in England, but in a colony there is less prejudice against novelties. In Australia, Conservatives favour the plan as a check to the absolute power of numerical majorities, and Democrats because it is a direct and obvious corollary from the democratic principle.

1864 — Aetat. 57. Your proposal for allowing the House of Commons to join to itself by co-optation a certain number of members I am more doubtful about, though quite alive to the inconvenience which it is intended to meet, that of governments with so small a majority that they cannot carry and dare not propose anything disliked by even a very small number of their supporters. But it does not seem likely that a plan, even if adopted, would be permanent, of which the avowed object would be that a government or a policy might have a considerable majority in the House for the remainder of a Parliament, though it had ceased to have a majority in the constituencies. This would scarcely, I think, be accepted unless combined with a great reduction in the duration of Parliaments—perhaps even to annual. But there is another mode of co-optation which, though it would not attain so completely the particular object, would probably attain it partially, and would be much less objectionable in other respects: viz., that the House should elect a certain number of members, not by lists, but by a modification of Mr. Hare's principle, in the mode which I have recommended for a portion of the House of Lords, and which you yourself propose in another case. This would add a very valuable class of members to the House, while it would effect the object you have in mind in your proposal for the election by Parliament of fifteen life members; a proposal open to objections both apparent and real which cannot have escaped your notice.

The objections I have urged against two stages of election are certainly considerably weakened (though not removed) by your suggestion, that the election of electors should take place in the regular course of affairs without waiting till Parliament is dissolved, or a vacancy occurs in the representation. But if there is to be indirect election, an idea occurs to me which may be worth bringing under your consideration. I attach great importance to giving a vote of some sort to *every* person who comes up to such an educational standard as can be made accessible to all. But as long as manual labourers are a separate class I do not wish them to have the complete command of the

House. You, again, think it desirable to admit that class to a considerable, though not a preponderant, influence. Might not these desirable conditions be all realised, at least for some time to come, by such an arrangement as this? The present electoral qualification, with the improvements it admits of, to remain in force for direct votes, but all non-electors who can read, write, and calculate to be allowed to choose electors, say one in ten or one in five of their number, who should form, along with the direct electors, the Parliamentary constituency? By this plan the working classes would obtain a substantial power in Parliament but not the complete control, and this is perhaps the only shape in which the attaching of unequal value to the votes of different electors, which I have proposed in the form of plural voting, would have much chance of being adopted.

The only remark of a non-practical character which I will make on any part of your two chapters is that, though there are many great faults in the working of democratic institutions in America (some of which the salutary shock that the American mind is now undergoing will have a tendency to correct), I do not think that the protective tariffs can justly be laid to the charge of democracy, for I believe that Protectionism is the creed in America of the majority, both of the wealthy and of the literary classes, involving even the political economists; and though I am far from thinking that they are in the right, there are some things to be said for their opinion in the circumstances of America which are inapplicable to the old countries of Europe.

To Alexander Bain

St. Véran, *2nd December* 1864.

. . . When I last wrote to you I believe I had not yet read Professor Tait's articles on the Conservation of Force. They have made some parts of the theory much clearer to me than before. I now understand better what is meant by potential energy, and how the force may be said to be constantly preserved even when not acting in its usual way;

1864 — Aetat. 58.

but I am not sure that my way of comprehending it fits all the cases. When air is compressed a reaction equal to the compressed force exists in the form of pressure against the sides of the vessel; when a projectile is thrown into the air, the force of gravity which ultimately brings it to the ground exists all the while though counteracted, for it shows itself in retarding and finally stopping the upward motion before it begins to determine the downward one, and it is calculably the same amount of force all the time. But the force said to be latent in coal, being that which would be generated by its chemical combination with oxygen, does not manifest itself by any pressure, or tendency to motion, or neutralisation of counter force for ages on ages. Still, if it can be shown that a force was lost, or used up, in making coal out of the carbonic acid gas of the atmosphere, equal to that which is generated by the reconversion of an equal quantity of coal with carbonic acid gas, I admit that there is a virtual conservation of force, though as force it was non-existent during the long interval: but so, you will say, is the latent heat of the water in the ocean, and of the gases comprising the atmosphere; therefore, though I do not know how the equality of the force lost and that reproduced is in this case ascertained, I can understand that it may be so. But I complain of a great want in Tait as well as in Tyndall, of proper clearness in making out what it is that is conserved. They speak as if the case of the compressed air or the projectile were exactly like that of the coal, when in reality it is extremely different. They would probably say that the force in the coal is alive all the time, creating molecular motion. But this unprovable hypothesis is just the part of the theory which I cannot swallow.

There is a difficulty, to my comprehension, in the old theory of heat, which I have long intended to mention to you, but have always forgotten, and I do not know whether the new theory takes it away. It relates to the common mode of explaining the law by which objects of unequal temperature tend to equalise their temperature by radiation. The theory is, namely, that all bodies are constantly radiating heat, and, if of equal temperature, radiate it in equal

1864 — Aetat. 58.

quantity; but every body radiates in proportion to its temperature, so that, all bodies constantly exchanging heat, the hotter give more than they receive, and the colder receive more than they give. On this theory it seems to me that if two bodies at the temperature of the atmosphere are placed in the foci of opposite parabolic mirrors they ought both to rise in temperature; for there is nothing to make them give out less heat than previously, and they certainly receive more. Even if one of the bodies is a lump of ice it ought even then to raise the temperature of the other body instead of cooling it, as it does, for even the ice sends out some heat which would not have reached the other focus if it had not been collected and concentrated by the mirrors. There is probably an answer to this, but none given in the usual explanation of the apparent radiation of cold.

The Association Psychology is decidedly getting into France. Seeing a short newspaper article of an "Etude sur l'Association des Idées," by a writer named P. M. Mervoyer, written as a thesis for the degree of Docteur ès Lettres, we sent for the book and found that it was in great part composed of translated extracts from your writings, for which he professes warm admiration, and has very well mastered a great many of the thoughts. He is a complete disciple of yours, and I may say also of mine, and will do good, though not apparently a person of great vigour of mind, his own part of the exposition contrasting not advantageously, in clearness and precision, with his translations from us, which are very well done. I wish it may come into his mind to translate you into French. I will bring the book with me to England, as you will, I think, be interested, as I have been by it.

The writer in the *North American Review* has followed up his article on "Time and Space" by one on Hamilton, the most severe one I have seen, but a striking contrast to my controversy with him, being a judgment of him from the opposite point of view; wherever Hamilton is right the reviewer contrives to be wrong, and when Hamilton is wrong, he is still more wrong himself.

I am glad you are to lecture at the Royal Institution,

1864 though your time of lecturing will probably fall during our
— absence. The managers of the Institution seem laudably
Aetat. 58. desirous of recruiting their staff with fresh notabilities. They have invited over Jules Simon to lecture, fortunately not on metaphysics. . . .

To Robert Harrison,

concerning John Black, former editor of the *Morning Chronicle.*

St. Véran, *12th December* 1864.

Dear Sir,—Your estimate of Black's character is true to the letter, and such as all who were intimate with him would confirm.

I do not know how soon after his coming to London he knew my father. I was a child at the time, and up to the beginning of 1814 my father lived so far from the north-east side of London that I suppose they did not often meet. All I know is that when Black became editor of the *Chronicle*, in the autumn, I think, of 1821, they were already old friends. After that time he constantly frequented my father, and no doubt often expressed opinions imbibed from him; but he was far from being a mere follower of any one. As an example of this, Black, as I well remember, changed the opinion of some of the leading political economists, particularly my father's, respecting Poor Laws, by the articles he wrote in the *Chronicle* in favour of a Poor Law for Ireland. He met their objections by maintaining that a Poor Law did not necessarily encourage over-population, but might be so worked as to be a considerable check to it, and he convinced them that he was in the right.

I have always considered Black as the first journalist who carried criticism and the spirit of reform into the details of English institutions. Those who are not old enough to remember those times can hardly believe what the state of public discussion then was. People now and then attacked the constitution and the boroughmongers, but none thought of censuring the law or the courts of justice; and to say a word against the unpaid magistracy was a sort of blasphemy. Black was the writer who carried the warfare into these subjects, and introduced Bentham's opinions on legal and judicial reform into newspaper discussion. And by doing this he broke the spell. Very early in his editorship he fought a great battle for the freedom of reporting the Parliamentary investigations of the police courts, in which Fonblanque, who just at that time began to become known, occasionally helped him, but he had little other help. He carried his point, and the victory was permanent. Another subject on which his writings were of the greatest service was the freedom of the press in matters of religion. His first years as editor of the *Chronicle* coincided with the prosecutions of Carlile and his shopmen, and Black kept up the fight against those prosecutions with great spirit and power. All these subjects were Black's own. Parliamentary Reform, Catholic Emancipation, Free Trade, &c., were the Liberal topics of the day, and on all of these he wrote frequently, as you will see by any file of the *Chronicle*. One of the remarkable things is that nearly all the leading articles, at least in those early years, were his own writing. He now and then had an article sent to him by a friend, but there was, I believe, for a long time no one regularly associated with him as a writer of leaders. This, I believe, is not generally known. He was constantly bringing into his articles curious passages and scraps of recondite information from old books which people thought must have been furnished by a host of friends behind him; but they all came from his own great miscellaneous reading. He used to walk about London, stopping at all the bookstalls, and got together a large collection of books not generally known, from which he had a knack of picking out and using whatever they contained that was interesting or instructive.

1864 — Aetat. 58.

Why Cobbett attacked him I do not remember, and it is scarcely worth knowing. Somebody said of Cobbett, very truly, that there were two sorts of people he could not endure, those who differed from him and those who agreed with him. These last had always stolen his ideas. I do

1864 — Aetat. 58. not know that he selected Black for a very special object of attack. If he had a controversy with him about anything he was sure to load him with comical abuse.

I shall be happy to give you any further information I have, and to answer to the best of my ability any questions, but the real source of the information you want is the *Chronicle* itself. He poured out his whole mind into it, as indeed he had much need to do considering how many volumes yearly he wrote in it.

To Max Kyllman, of Manchester.

BLACKHEATH, 15*th February* 1865.

1865 — Aetat. 58. DEAR SIR,—It is pleasant to hear from you again. Your letters, besides being interesting on your own account, almost always contain some valuable piece of intelligence. What you tell me about the progress of Mr. Hare's system among the working classes of Manchester is pre-eminently so. I know very well to whose indefatigable exertions it is owing. But it confirms me in the opinion that the working classes will see the true character and the importance of Mr. Hare's principle much sooner than their Parliamentary allies. The speeches made by these to their constituents lately have very much disgusted me. The proverb "Il vaut mieux avoir affaire à Dieu qu'à ses saints" is true of the demagogues and the Demos. The demagogues never dare admit anything which implies a doubt of the infallibility of the majority. The Demos itself makes no such pretensions, and can see the utility of taking precautions against its own mistakes. I shall make use of your letter to convince some of the dress-coated democrats that there is no need to be "plus royalistes que le roi."

With regard to the other subject of your letter; I quite agree with you that no Reform Bill which we are likely to see for some time to come will be worth moving hand or foot for. But with respect to the manhood suffrage movement, and the question of my taking part in it, I have long been determined that I would on no account whatever aid any attempt to make the suffrage universal to men, unless the inclusion of women were distinctly and openly proclaimed as a substantive part of the design. There are only two things worth working for—a practical result or a principle; if a practical result, it should be one which is attainable; if a principle, not to go the whole length of it is to sacrifice it. I look upon agitation for manhood, as distinguished from universal suffrage, as decidedly mischievous. The exceptionally enlightened leaders mentioned in your letter may not intend, in claiming half, to deny the whole; but such is the power of words, that every time the phrase "manhood suffrâge" is publicly pronounced, save in contempt or execration, an additional rivet is added to the chain of half the human species. It is to be remembered, too, that universal suffrage was the expression formerly used by all Radicals, and it was withdrawn and manhood suffrage substituted precisely because the wider expression had been criticised as including women. To adopt a phrase which has no other reason of existence than that it excludes them, would be, in my opinion, to betray the principle, and, at the same time, to make a retrograde step.

When any portion or body of the working classes chooses as its programme a reading and writing (or rather writing and ciphering) qualification, *adult* instead of manhood suffrage, and Hare's system, I will gladly give to such a noble scheme all the help I possibly can. Do not suppose that my opinion about plural voting would be any obstacle. I put that in abeyance, first because I would accept universal suffrage, and gladly, too, without it (though not without Hare's system), and next because Buxton has smashed plural voting for years to come by associating it with property, a thing I have always protested against and would on no account consent to. Plural voting by right of education I should not mind defending to any assemblage of working men in the kingdom. But though I would always speak my mind on it, it would be no bar to my co-operating. But on *adult* suffrage I can make no compromise.

1865 — Aetat. 58.

I must therefore defer the pleasure of an introduction to Mrs. Kyllman till she or you happen to be in London, when it will increase the pleasure I am sure of having from seeing yourself.

The Baden minister whom I referred to must be well known to you—Professor Mohl of Heidelburg, who advocated Hare's plan by articles in the *Zeit* of Frankfort. Mr. Hare has the papers.

The two French authorities whom I mentioned are Louis Blanc (of course) and Laboulaye.

P.S.—I have the greatest regard and respect for Louis Blanc, but I think it would be fatal to the success of any political movement in this country to put him forward in it, as his name is associated in the vulgar English mind with everything that can be made a bugbear of.

To James Beal,

in reply to a letter asking whether Mill would allow himself to be nominated as Parliamentary candidate for Westminster, if a circular to the electors should bring to light a general desire on their part for his nomination.

Blackheath Park, *7th March* 1865.

Dear Sir,—Your note, I am sorry to say, did not reach me till yesterday evening owing to a mistake at the post-office.

To be the representative of Westminster is an honour to which no one can be insensible, and to have been selected as worthy of that honour by a body like that in whose name you write, not only without solicitation, but without my being personally known to them either in a public or private capacity, is a very signal one indeed. While it must ever command my sincere gratitude, it is a proceeding which nothing but the truest public spirit could have dictated. And the mode in which you propose to ascertain the sense of the electors cannot be too highly applauded. It is an example deserving to be imitated by all popular constituencies, and worthy of the rank which belongs historically to Westminster as the head and front of the Reform party. 1865 — Aetat. 58.

In answer, therefore, to your question, I assent to having my name submitted to the electors in the proposed manner, if, after the explanations which it is now my duty to give, the committee should still adhere to their intention.

I have no personal object to be promoted by a seat in Parliament. All private considerations are against my accepting it. The only motive that could make me desire it would be the hope of being useful; and being untried in any similar position, it is as yet quite uncertain whether I am as capable of rendering public service in the House of Commons as I may be in the more tranquil occupation of a writer. It is, however, certain that if I can be of any use in Parliament, it could only be by devoting myself there to the same subjects which have employed my habitual thoughts out of Parliament. I therefore could not undertake the charge of any of your local business; and as this, in so important a constituency, must necessarily be heavy, it is not impossible that my inability to undertake it may in itself amount to a disqualification for being your representative.

Again, my only object in Parliament would be to promote my opinions; and what these are, on nearly all the political questions in which the public feel any interest, is before the world: and until I am convinced that they are wrong, these, and no others, are the opinions that I must act on. I am ready to give any further explanation of them that might be wished for, and should I be elected I would freely state to my constituents, whenever desired, the votes I intend to give, and my reasons for them. But I could give no other pledge. If the electors are sufficiently satisfied with my opinions as they are, to be willing to give me a trial, I would do my best to serve those opinions, and would in no case disguise my intentions or my motives from those to whom I should be indebted for the opportunity.

1865 — Aetat. 58.

Lastly, it is neither suitable to my circumstances nor consistent with my principles to spend money for my election. Without necessarily condemning those who do, when it is not expended in corruption, I am deeply convinced that there can be no Parliamentary reform worthy of the name so long as a seat in Parliament is only attainable by rich men, or by those who have rich men at their back. It is the interest of the constituencies to be served by men who are not aiming at personal objects, either pecuniary, official, or social, but consenting to undertake gratuitously an onerous duty to the public. That such persons should be made to pay for permission to do hard and difficult work for the general advantage, is neither worthy of a free people, nor is it the way to induce the best men to come forward. In my own case, I must even decline to offer myself to the electors in any manner; because, proud as I should be of their suffrages, and though I would endeavour to fulfil to the best of my ability the duty to which they might think fit to elect me, yet I have no wish to quit my present occupations for the House of Commons, unless called upon to do so by my fellow-citizens. That the electors of Westminster have even thought of my name in this conjuncture is a source of deep gratification to me, and if I were to be elected I should wish to owe every step in my election, as I should already owe my nomination, to their spontaneous and flattering judgment of the labour of my life.

Whatever be the result as regards myself, allow me to express the hope that your recommendation to the electors will not be limited to two names. To obtain the best representative, and even if only to ensure success against the powerful local influence which is already in the field, it seems plainly desirable to give the electors the widest possible choice among all persons willing to serve, who would worthily represent the advanced Liberal and reforming party. Several eminent persons have been mentioned, whom it would be highly desirable to give the electors an opportunity of selecting if they please. Sir J. Romilly is in the number of these, and would, in every way, do

honour to your choice. Mr. Chadwick would be one of 1865
the most valuable members who could be chosen by any —
constituency; and besides the many important public Aetat. 58.
questions on which he is one of the first authorities, he is peculiarly qualified to render those services in connection with your local business which it would not, in general, be possible for me to perform. The admirable mode of selection which you have adopted will not have fair play unless you bring before the consideration of the electors the whole range of choice, among really good candidates, which lies within their reach. It will not be inferred from your placing any particular person on the list that you consider him the best. Some will prefer one and some another, and those who are preferred by the greatest number of electors would alone be nominated.

In requesting you to lay this matter before the committee, I beg to assure yourself and them that, whatever may be their decision, I shall never cease to feel the proposal they have made to me as one of the greatest compliments I have ever received.—I am, dear Sir, very sincerely and respectfully yours, J. S. MILL.

To the Secretary of the Co-operative Plate-Lock Manufactory, Wolverhampton.

BLACKHEATH PARK, *22nd March* 1865.

SIR,—I beg to enclose a subscription of £10 to aid, as far as such a sum can do it, in the struggle which the Co-operative Plate-Lock Makers of Wolverhampton are maintaining against unfair competition on the part of the masters in the trade. Against fair competition I have no desire to shield them. Co-operative production carried on by persons whose hearts are in the cause, and who are capable of the energy and self-denial always necessary in its early stages, ought to be able to hold its ground against private establishments—and persons who have not those qualities had better not attempt it. But to carry on business at a loss in order to ruin competitors is not fair com-

1865 — Aetat. 58. petition. In such a contest, if prolonged, the competitors who have the smallest means, though they may have every other element of success, must necessarily be crushed through no fault of their own. Having the strongest sympathy with your vigorous attempt to make head against what in such a case may justly be called the tyranny of capital, I beg you to send me a dozen copies of your printed appeal, to assist me in making the case known to such persons as it may interest in your favour.

To James Beal,

in which Mill makes a declaration of his political opinions, on receiving official intimation from Beal that he had been adopted as candidate for Westminster.

19th April 1865.

Dear Sir,—I beg leave to acknowledge your communication of the 12th inst., informing me that at a meeting of Westminster electors it has been resolved to adopt me as a candidate on the terms of my letter of 7th March, and to invite subscriptions to defray the expenses of my election.

On the subject of this resolution it would not become me to say anything, except what might equally be said by one who had no personal interest in the matter: that if the electors of Westminster return to Parliament as their representative any one, either myself or another, who has no claim whatever on them except their opinion of his fitness for the trust, and if on that sole ground they elect him without personal solicitation and without expense, they will do what is as eminently honourable to themselves as to the object of their choice, will set an example worthy to be, and likely to be, imitated by other great constituencies, and will signally raise the character of the popular party and advance the cause of Reform.

On this part of the subject, I have only to express the earnest hope, that in accepting me on the terms of my letter, the meeting intended to include in their adhesion the principle of an individual appeal by circular to every elector, laying other names before him as well as mine, and requesting him to select from among them or from any others the person or persons whom he would wish to be brought forward as candidates. 1865 — Aetat. 58.

I am also invited to state, for the more full information of the electors, my opinions on various political questions of general interest. Such a call can only be properly answered by the most complete openness. I hold decided opinions on all the subjects on which my sentiments are asked, and whether those opinions may serve or injure me in the estimation of the electors it is equally incumbent on me to state them plainly.

1. With regard to Reform Bills: I should vote at once both for Mr. Baines' bill and for Mr. Locke King's, and for measures going far beyond either of them. I would open the suffrage to all grown persons, both men and women, who can read, write, and perform a sum in the rule of three, and who have not, within some small number of years, received parish relief. I would not vote for giving the suffrage in such a measure that any class, even though it be the most numerous, could swamp all other classes taken together. In the first place, I think that all considerable minorities in the country or in a locality should be represented in proportion to their numbers. What other adjustments of the electoral system to an universal or nearly universal suffrage might prove practically the best adapted to secure to every portion of the community its just share of influence, while preventing any class from acquiring an unjust degree of preponderance either by means of property or of numbers, is a question which may be answered in many different ways, and which will require much sifting and public discussion before the best can be selected. In the meanwhile I should be prepared to support a measure which would give to the labouring classes a clear half of the national representation.

2. I prefer a mixed system of direct and indirect taxation to either alone. If the attempt were made to raise so

1865 — Aetat. 58. large a revenue, as ours, after all due retrenchments, would still be, exclusively by direct taxation, I do not know of any taxes, in themselves just, which, under such strong pecuniary temptation, would not be successfully evaded: the evasions of the Income Tax are already a disgrace to the national morality. I would in no case tax any of the necessaries of life; but if even a working man expends in luxuries for himself, and especially in stimulants, what is required by the necessities of his family, I think it perfectly just that he should be taxed on such expenditure.

3. Every civilised country is entitled to settle its internal affairs in its own way, and no other country ought to interfere with its discretion, because one country, even with the best intentions, has no chance of properly understanding the internal affairs of another. But when this indefeasible liberty of an independent country has already been interfered with; when it is kept in subjection by a foreign power, either directly, or by assistance given to its native tyrants, I hold that any nation whatever may rightfully interfere to protect the country against this wrongful interference. I therefore approve the interposition of France in 1859 to free Italy from the Austrian yoke, but disapprove the intervention of the former country in 1849 to compel the Pope's subjects to take back the bad government they had cast off. It is not, however, a necessary consequence that because a thing might rightfully be done, it is always expedient to do it. I would not have voted for a war in behalf either of Poland or of Denmark, because on any probable view of consequences I should have expected more evil than good from our doing what, nevertheless, if done, would not have been, in my opinion, any violation of international duty.

4. Respecting the disabilities of Dissenters, my answer may be brief. There ought to be no disabilities whatever on account of religion.

5. Voting for a member of Parliament is a public and political act, which concerns not solely the elector's individual preferences, but the most important interests of the other electors, and even of posterity; and my con-

viction is that in a free country all such acts should be done in the face of and subject to the comments and criticisms of the entire public. I wish that the elector should feel an honourable shame in voting contrary to his known opinions, and in not being able to give for his vote a reason which he can avow. The publicity which lets in these salutary influences admits also, unfortunately, some noxious ones; and if I believed that these were now the strongest—if I thought that the electors of this country were in such a state of hopeless and slavish dependence on particular landlords, employers, or customers, that the bad influences are more than a match for the good ones, and that there is no other means of removing them—I should be, as I once was, a supporter of the ballot. But the voters are not now in this degraded condition; they need nothing to protect them against electoral intimidation but the spirit and courage to defy it. In an age when the most dependent class of all, the labouring class, is proving itself capable of maintaining by combination an equal struggle with the combined power of the masters, I cannot admit that farmers or shopkeepers, if they stand by one another, need despair of protecting themselves against any abuse now possible of the power of landed or other wealth.

6. As regards retrenchment, it is certain that chiefly through unskilful management great sums of public money are now squandered for which the country receives no equivalent in the efficiency of its establishments, and that we might have a more useful army and navy than we possess at a considerably less expense. I expect little improvement in this respect until the increased influence of the smaller taxpayers on the Government, through a large extension of the suffrage, shall have produced a stricter control over the details of public expenditure. But I cannot think that it would be right for us to disarm in the presence of the great military despotisms of Europe, which regard our freedom, through its influence on the minds of their own subjects, as the greatest danger as well as reproach to themselves, and might be tempted

1865 — Aetat. 58.

to pick a quarrel with us, even without any prospect of ultimate success, in the mere hope of reviving the national antipathies which so long kept apart the best minds of England and the Continent.

7. I am decidedly of opinion that landed property should be subject to the Probate Duty, and that property in settlement should pay succession duty on its full value, and not, as at present, only on the value of the life interest.

8. Purchase is the very worst way but one, in which commissions in the army could possibly be appropriated. The one, which is still worse, is jobbing and favouritism. I would support any mode in which the one evil can be got rid of without replacing it by the other. That there is such a mode I am fully satisfied, and that it would put an end to what is justly called in your letter, the monopoly by certain classes of the posts of emolument.

9. I am entirely opposed to flogging, either in the army or out of it, except for crimes of brutality. In some of those it seems to me a very appropriate punishment.

10. The differences between employers and workpeople which give rise to strikes are, it appears to me, a subject which wholly escapes the control of legislation. I see nothing which law can do in the matter, except to protect from violation the equal liberty of all to combine or to refrain from combining. After a sufficient trial of each other's strength, both sides will probably be willing to refer their disputes to arbitration; but even then I do not think that the arbitrators should have power to enforce their decisions by law; because, in such cases as they would usually have to decide, it is impossible to lay down rules of justice and equity which would suit all cases, or would obtain universal assent, and the adjustments must generally be of the nature of compromises, not acting on fixed principles, but each side giving up something for the sake of peace. I do not presume to say that a better rule may not be arrived at in time, but it would be quite premature to act as if it had been already arrived at.

To W. E. Hickson, the educational writer, on the death of Cobden.

St. Véran, *24th April* 1865.

. . . Death has indeed been busy lately, and one is continually reminded, if at our age we needed reminding, of our own mortality. Cobden was perhaps the most perfectly honest man among all English politicians of his time and of anything like his celebrity, for he meant every word that he said. . . .

1865 — Aetat. 58.

To Henry Soden, of Melbourne; making clear Mill's position on the subject of Protection in young countries.

Avignon, *2nd May* 1865.

Dear Sir,—I have just received your letter, dated 25th February.

It is a great compliment to me that my supposed opinions should have had the influence you ascribe to them in Australia. But there seems to have been a considerable degree of misunderstanding about what they are. The fault probably lies with myself, in not having explained them sufficiently. I have entered rather more fully into the subject in the new editions published this spring. But, not to give you the trouble of referring to them, I can have no difficulty in saying that I never for a moment thought of recommending or countenancing, in a new colony more than elsewhere, a general protective policy, or a system of duties on imported commodities, such as that which has recently passed the representative assembly of your colony. What I had in view was this. If there is some particular branch of industry, not hitherto carried on in the country, but which individuals or associations, possessed of the necessary capital, are ready and desirous to naturalise; and if these persons can satisfy the legislature that after their workpeople are fully trained, and the difficulties of the first introduction surmounted, they shall

1865 — Aetat. 58. probably be able to produce the article as cheap, or cheaper, than the price at which it can be imported, but that they cannot do so without the temporary aid either of a subsidy from the Government or of a protecting duty: then it may sometimes be a good calculation for the future interests of the country to make a temporary sacrifice by granting a moderate protecting duty for a certain limited number of years, say ten, or at the very most twenty, during the latter part of which the duty should be on a gradually diminishing scale, and at the end of which it should expire. You see how far this doctrine is from supporting the fabric of Protectionist doctrine, in behalf of which its aid has been invoked.

. . . . . .

You are at full liberty to make any use you please of this letter.

To W. E. Hickson,

on the assassination of Abraham Lincoln.

St. Véran, *3rd May* 1865.

Dear Hickson,—The universality of the feeling occasioned by Lincoln's catastrophe is a good sign of our common humanity—for it is, in most cases, genuine feeling of the bitterness of losing such a man. He himself may be considered happy in his death—quite otherwise than if he had died before the decisive triumph. There cannot be a more glorious fate than to die so mourned by a whole people—to have become so dear to them through the best part of their character exclusively. I agree with you in having no fear of public mischief from his loss. It will perhaps, on the contrary, prevent a great deal of weak indulgence towards the slaveholding class, whose power it is necessary should be completely and permanently broken at all costs. Meanwhile the effect is admirable in Continental Europe (England does not need that particular lesson) of the example of power passing by course of law, without a dream of opposition, in the freest country in the world. . . .

To J. F. D. Maurice,

in reply to a letter acknowledging a presentation copy of the "Examination of Hamilton."

St. Véran, *11th May* 1865.

Dear Mr. Maurice,—I was already so well aware of your kind feelings towards me, that even such a letter as I have just received from you hardly increases my sense of them. I most sincerely feel towards you and your work in life, the full equivalent of all which you so kindly express. I never voluntarily leave unread any of your writings, and if I have not more frequently offered you any of mine, it was because I seldom felt confident that what you would approve in them, would outweigh what you would disapprove. I knew, however, that there was much in my new book with which you would fully sympathise, greatly as I know you differ from the metaphysical doctrines contained in it. You were continually in my thoughts when I wrote the chapter against Mansel, and your controversy with him contributed much towards stirring me up to write the book. 1865 — Aetat. 58.

I sympathise with the feeling of (if I may so call it) mental loneliness, which shows itself in your letter and sometimes in your published writings. In our age and country every person with any mental power at all, who both thinks for himself and has a conscience, must feel himself, to a very great degree, alone. I should think you have decidedly more people who are in real communion of thoughts, feelings, and purposes with you than I have. I am in this supremely happy, that I have had, and even now have, that communion in the fullest degree where it is most valuable of all, in my own home. But I have it nowhere else; and if people did but know how much more precious to me is the faintest approach to it, than all the noisy eulogiums in the world! The sole value to me of these is that they dispose a greater number of people to listen to what I am able to say to them; and they are an admonition to me to make as much of that kind of hay as I

1865 — Aetat. 58. can before the sun gives over shining. What is happening just now is the coming to the surface of a good deal of influence which I had been insensibly acquiring without knowing it; and there are to me many signs that you are exercising a very considerable influence of the same kind, though you yourself seem to think the contrary.

To Emile Littré.

St. Véran, *le* 11 *mai* 1865.

Cher Monsieur,—La second partie de mon travail sur M. Comte ne sera publiée que le 1er juillet, mais on m'a promis de me donner bientôt les exemplaires séparés. Il vous en sera expédié cinq, destinés comme auparavant pour vous-même, pour le traducteur, pour Mme Comte, pour M. de Blignières et pour M. Taine. Il est très naturel que vous n'approuviez pas sans réserve tout ce que j'ai dit dans la première partie. Ce que votre livre a montré d'accord entre nos jugements est encore plus que je n'osais espérer. Une critique de ma critique, faite de votre point de vue, m'intéresserait grandement, et ce serait une bonne fortune pour moi si vous pouviez avoir le temps de vous en occuper.

Quant au livre sur Hamilton c'est en grande partie une œuvre de circonstance, comme le doit être tout livre de polémique, mais avec quelques chapitres de psychologie positive. Ce que ce livre a de mieux c'est qu'il porte la guerre dans le camp ennemi. Aussi je crois que les métaphysiciens de l'école éclectique et allemande ne me pardonneront pas.

Si un journal a dit que je sollicite des électeurs, ce journal se trompe; ce sont des électeurs qui m'ont sollicité; on m'a porté candidat presque malgré moi. J'ai refusé de rien faire de ce que font ordinairement chez nous les candidats. Je n'ai fait que ce qu'ils ne font guère, c'est à dire, une profession de foi parfaitement sincère. Au reste je pense avec M. Comte que, sauf des circonstances exceptionnelles et transitives, la place des philosophes n'est pas dans le gouvernement; et malgré mes 35 ans de fonctions administratives je ne me regarde pas comme une exception. Vous savez que dans l'idée que je me fais des assemblées délibérantes, elles doivent être un lieu de discussion plutôt que d'action, et si je consentais à y siéger, ce serait pour n'y exercer qu'un pouvoir spirituel. P. L. Courier disait que, presque seul parmi les Français, il ne voulait pas être roi : si l'on me nommait à la chambre, j'y serais probablement le seul deputé qui ne voudrait pas être ministre.

1865 — Aetat. 58.

To Parke Godwin,

on the assassination of Abraham Lincoln, and the end of the American civil war.

Avignon, 15*th May* 1865.

Dear Sir,—I had scarcely received your note of 8th April, so full of calm joy in the splendid prospect now opening to your country and through it to the world, when the news came that an atrocious crime had struck down the great citizen who had afforded so noble an example of the qualities befitting the first magistrate of a free people, and who in the most trying circumstances had gradually won not only the admiration, but almost the personal affection of all who love freedom and appreciate simplicity and uprightness. But the loss is ours, not his. It was impossible to have wished him a better end than to add the crown of martyrdom to his other honours, and to live in the memory of a great nation as those only live who have not only laboured for their country but died for it. And he did live to see the cause triumphant and the contest virtually over. How different would our feelings now be if this fate had overtaken him, as it might so easily have done, a month sooner!

In England, horror at the crime and sympathy with your loss seem to be almost universal, even among those who have disgraced their country by wishing success to the slaveholders. I hope manifestations which were instantaneously made there in almost every quarter may be received in America as some kind of atonement or peace-

1865 — Aetat. 58.

offering. I have never believed that there was any real danger of a quarrel between the two countries, but it is of immense importance that we should be firm friends. And this is our natural state; for though there is a portion of the higher and middle classes of Great Britain who so dread and hate democracy that they cannot wish prosperity or power to a democratic people, I firmly believe that this feeling is not general even in our privileged classes. Most of the dislike and suspicion which have existed towards the United States were the effect of pure ignorance; ignorance of your history, and ignorance of your feelings and disposition as a people. It is difficult for you to believe that this ignorance could be as dense as it really was. But the late events have begun to dissipate it, and if your Government and people act as I fully believe they will, in regard to the important questions which now await them, there will be no fear of their being ever again so grossly misunderstood, at least in the lives of the present generation.

As to the mode of dealing with these great questions, it does not become a foreigner to advise those who know the exigencies of the case so much better than he does. But as so many of my countrymen are volunteering advice to you at this crisis, perhaps I may be forgiven if I offer mine the contrary way. Every one is vaguely inculcating gentleness, and only gentleness, as if you had shown any signs of disposition to take a savage revenge. I have always been afraid of one thing only, that you would be too gentle. I should be sorry to see any life taken after the war is over (except those of the assassins), or any evil inflicted in mere vengeance; but one thing I hope will be considered absolutely necessary, to break altogether the power of the slaveholding caste. Unless this is done, the abolition of slavery will be merely nominal. If an aristocracy of ex-slaveholders remain masters of the State legislatures they will be able effectually to nullify a great part of the result which has been so dearly bought by the blood of the Free States. They and their dependents must be effectually outnumbered at the polling-places, which can only be effected by the concession of full equality of political rights to negroes and by a large immigration of settlers from the North, both of them being made independent by the ownership of land. With these things in addition to the constitutional amendment (which will enable the Supreme Court to set aside any State legislation tending to bring back slavery in disguise) the cause of freedom is safe, and the opening words of the Declaration of Independence will cease to be a reproach to the nation founded by its authors. 1865 — Aetat. 58.

To Edwin Chadwick,

on the Westminster election campaign.

St. Véran, *15th May* 1865.

Dear Chadwick,—I have been so very busy, and have had besides so many letters to write, that I am very tardy in replying to your interesting letter of 29th April. We were greatly amused by the election humours which it communicates, and by the comments you report on the injudiciousness of my second letter. I do not wonder that people should think it injudicious if they suppose that my grand object in the whole matter is to get myself elected. But as the only purpose for which I care to be elected is to get my opinions listened to, it would have been very injudicious in me to forego so good an opportunity of that, for fear that it should damage my election. I have gained this by it, that what are thought the most out-of-the-way of all my opinions, have been and are discussed and canvassed from one end of the country to the other, and some of them (especially women's voting) are obtaining many unexpected adhesions. I reckon this a good stroke of practicality, whether I am elected for Parliament or not.

As to the election itself, I had much rather you were elected than I; and if I could transfer my supporters in a body to you I would do so instantly. I suspect, however, that the thing will be taken out of our hands. The appearance in the field of the illustrious man whom the Tories have put forward as the representative of the intelligent

1865 — Aetat. 58. classes against popular ignorance as embodied in me, will probably produce a general demand that one of the professedly Liberal candidates should be withdrawn; and perhaps the appeal to the individual elector by circular, which we have contended for, will be made for the inferior purpose of ascertaining who ought to retire. I do not think the Tories expect their man to come in; otherwise some more considerable person would have started in that interest. But they are glad when anybody with money to spend is willing to venture it on the chance.

I feel for Sir Edward Lytton,[1] who expected to get some credit from my friends by the expression of his good wishes (which were very likely sincere), but found he had come across a man who had the peculiarity of expecting that people should act up to what they say. I should have thought more highly of him if he had said plainly, "These are my private sentiments, but I must go in with my party," a feeling which, as men go, is very excusable. Lord Amberley, I am glad to see, has a higher standard. It is really a fine thing in him to have withdrawn from Grosvenor's committee and come over to me.

It is an agreeable surprise to me that Mr. Westerton has been so favourably impressed by the "Liberty." I give him very great credit for it. It shows that his view of religion is a much higher and better one than is at all common. Had I listened to common-sense notions of "practicality" I should never have published that book, yet its publication does not seem to do me any practical harm.

As to the application you have received about having my likeness taken for publication, I have a real difficulty about it, owing to having refused my photograph to friends who much wished for it. If it should be necessary, however, there is a cameo likeness of me from which a copy could be taken, but it cannot be till we return.

P.S.—I have just received your packet of printed documents. The list of the committee is very good: there are some names on it which I am glad to see, but was afraid would be wanting.

[1] [Bulwer-Lytton.]

To Edwin L. Godkin, of New York,

acknowledging a copy of the *North American Review*, containing an article by him on "Aristocratic Opinions of Democracy."

Avignon, *24th May* 1865.

Dear Sir,—I thank you very sincerely for your article in the *North American Review*—not merely for sending it to me, but for writing it. I consider it a very important contribution to the philosophy of the subject—a correction from one point of view of what was excessive in Tocqueville's theory of democracy as my review of him was from another. You have fully made out that the peculiar character of society in the Western States, the mental type formed by the position and habits of the pioneers, is, at least in part, accountable for many American phenomena which have been ascribed to democracy. This is a most consoling belief, since it refers the unfavourable side of American social existence (which you set forth with a fulness of candour that ought to shame the detractors of American literature and thought) to causes naturally declining, rather than to one which tends to increase.

1865 — Aetat. 59.

But if any encouragement was required by those who hope the best from American institutions, the New England States, as they now are, would be encouragement enough. If Tocqueville had lived to know what those States have become thirty years after he saw them, he would, I think, have acknowledged that much of the unfavourable part of his anticipations had not been realised. Democracy has been no leveller there as to intellect and education, or respect for true personal superiority. Nor has it stereotyped a particular cast of thought; as is proved by so many really original writers, yourself being one. Finally, New England has now the immortal glory of having destroyed slavery; to do which has required an amount of high principle, courage, and energy, which few other communities, either monarchical or republican, have ever displayed. And the great con-

1865 — Aetat. 59.

cussion which has taken place in the American mind must have loosened the foundations of all prejudices, and secured a fair hearing for impartial reason on all subjects such as it might not otherwise have had for many generations.

It is a happiness to have lived to see such a termination of the greatest and most corrupting of all social iniquities which, more than all other causes together, lowered the tone of the national, and especially the political, mind of the United States.

It now rests with the intellect and high aspirations of the Eastern States, and the energy and straightforward honesty of the Western, to make the best use of the occasion. And I have no misgiving as to the result.

Do not trouble yourself to send me the *North American Review*, as I already subscribe to it. But I shall always be glad to be informed of any article in it which is of your writing, and to have your opinion on any American question.

To Dr. Whewell,

in reply to a letter from him acknowledging a gift by Mill of his "Examination of Sir William Hamilton's Philosophy."

Avignon, *24th May* 1865.

Dear Sir,—It gave me great pleasure to receive your note of 15th May. It was, in the first place, very agreeable to hear that you go along with my book, so far as it is directed against Sir W. Hamilton; which is fully as much approbation as I could hope for; and it was pleasant to be told that there are other points which could have been made against Sir W. Hamilton, but which I had omitted—fearful as I was of being charged, on the contrary, with having pursued him *à toute outrance.*

But a still greater cause of satisfaction to me from receiving your note, is that it gives me an opportunity on which, without impertinent intrusion, I may express to you, how strongly I have felt drawn to you by what I have heard of your sentiments respecting the American struggle (now drawing to a close) between freedom and slavery, and between legal government and rebellion without justification or excuse. No question of our time has been such a touchstone of men, has so tested their sterling qualities of mind and heart as this one, and I shall all my life feel united by a sort of special tie with those, whether personally known to me or not, who have been faithful when so many were faithless.

To Edwin Chadwick,

on the Westminster election campaign.

St. Véran, 28*th May* 1865.

Dear Chadwick,—You have indeed a fine list of occupations for anyone to carry on *pari passu* with his election to Parliament. But your power of work seems unlimited.

The request of the committee places me in a considerable embarrassment. What they propose is in itself perfectly reasonable, and anyone who comes forward and proposes himself as a candidate ought to be willing to meet the committee and the electors in the way they propose, as often as they think desirable. But I have never from the beginning been in the position of one who offers himself as a candidate. In my first letter I disclaimed doing so; I said that my personal inclination was against going into Parliament; but that if the electors of Westminster, nevertheless, did me the great honour of choosing me, I would do my best to serve them, and in the meantime would answer unreservedly any number of questions respecting my political opinions which might be put to me by or in behalf of any body of electors. My candidature went forth to the public on this footing, and this declaration seemed to be one of the causes of the feeling so widely expressed in favour of the candidature. If I have now to attend meetings and make speeches to the electors in the usual, and, in most cases, very proper manner, it would seem as if there had been no truth in my declaration that I did not personally ask to be in Parliament; as if I had merely been

1865 — Ætat. 59. finessing to get myself elected without trouble and expense, and having found more difficulty than I expected, had at last shown myself in my true colours rather than run the risk of losing the election.

If you will kindly represent these things to the committee they will, I hope, enter into the difficulty I feel. If they think that any further explanation of my opinions would be desirable they have only to ask for it. If Mr. Beal, or Mr. Westerton, or any other member of the committee will write to me asking my opinion on any new points, or the reasons and justification of my opinion on any of those on which it has been already asked and given, I shall have the greatest pleasure in satisfying them.

In the same manner I shall be happy to reprint any of my articles which the committee may propose. I cannot, however, remember any that would be much to the purpose, as the political articles are mostly on gone-by politics. I should be very happy to reprint the article on "Enfranchisement of Women," but it must be as my wife's, not as mine.

I am glad to hear what you tell me concerning Mr. Maclean. In addition to his very handsome subscription he has lately sent me two polite invitations in his capacity of president of the Institute of Civil Engineers, and I was desirous to know how I had acquired so much of his goodwill.

Any writing by Tories, nominally in my favour, is of no consequence. The Tories prefer anybody to a regular Government man, as they suppose Grosvenor to be. Anyone who is not a pledged member of the Ministerial party, they hope may now and then give them a stray vote. But if I were elected I should hope to be a much greater thorn in their side than a member of the old Whig connection can be.

This letter, of course, is not for publication, but it may be shown to any members of the committee.

To Max Kyllman, of Manchester

St. Véran, 30*th May* 1865.

Dear Sir,—I have not written to you since I came here, having from various causes been so overwhelmed with letter-writing that I was obliged to adjourn all of it that admitted of postponement. I now write though I have not anything very particular to say, except that I am going to leave Avignon for a tour in the Cevennes and Auvergne, and though letters will be sent to me from here they will not reach me so soon or so certainly as at present. It seems to me that discussion on the fundamental points of representative government, and especially on the points raised in my Westminster letters, is going on very satisfactorily at present. Numbers of country papers are sent to me in which Hare's system, representation of minorities, in all its shapes, and women's suffrage are mooted—sometimes with approbation, and often (especially as to women's suffrage) with much less hostility than was to be expected. You have probably seen Mr. Hughes' declaration in favour of Hare's system, and Francis Newman's commendation of me for adhering to it. The cheap editions also are going off at a wonderful rate, and even the dear ones are increasing in sale. These are substantial advantages derived from the Westminster contest, whether it succeeds or not. I think it hardly possible that it should succeed. Though it has brought to light a most unexpected amount of good feeling by isolated individuals towards me personally, there is no *set* of political men who wish to have me in Parliament; neither Whigs nor Tories, nor the Bright Radicals (though I hear that Bright himself speaks in my favour), nor any other set of Radicals, except perhaps the co-operative section of the working classes. Look at the list of subscribers for the election expenses; next to none of them are representative men. They are people from here, there, and everywhere who have happened to like my books. Many even who for personal reasons might have subscribed, hold back, evidently because their sets are

1865 — Aetat. 59.

1865 — Ætat. 59. hostile to me. This is what I always said would be the case. As Comte says, "tout ce qui est aujourd'hui classé" is sure to be hostile to really new ideas—a little shuffling of the cards is all they want.

But enough of this. I am full of joy and spirits for the glorious future of America. The catastrophe of Lincoln, though it was a great shock, does not cloud the prospect. How could one have wished him a happier death? He died almost unconsciously in the fulness of success, and martyrdom in so great a cause consecrates his name through all history. Such a death is the crown of a noble life.

To the Hon. and Rev. W. H. Lyttelton,

in reply to a letter from him thanking Mill for that portion of the "Examination of Hamilton" in which he attacks Mansel's doctrine that there is a difference in kind between human and divine morality.

Blackheath Park, *21st July* 1865.

Dear Sir,—I thank you most sincerely for your tract, which I have read with very great pleasure and sympathy. Though I had read several papers belonging to the same series, and was well acquainted with your name and character, I had not happened to see this tract. You had a strong case, and you have stated it well and effectively, and, above all, like one who feels its importance. I cannot conceive how any other view than that which you take of the question raised by Mr. Mansel, can be deemed religious or Christian; and I felt sure that in maintaining, from my own point of view, the same conception of religious duty, I should be in complete sympathy with the best part of the religious world, using that phrase in its literal and not in its slang acceptation. Accordingly, the manner in which so many of the greatest ornaments of the Church of England lately came forward to share the responsibility of a doctrine which, coming from me, was called atheistic and satanic, did not cause me half as much pleasure from its connection with myself as because it so fully justified the perfect confidence I had in their high feelings and principles. It causes me no surprise, but additional pleasure, that you so fully participate in the same convictions and sentiments.

I return, as desired, your letter in the *Guardian*, with thanks for the pleasure it has given me.

To a Correspondent,

on a point raised in the "Liberty."

BLACKHEATH PARK, 21*st July* 1865.

DEAR SIR,—I have been prevented by much occupation from sooner acknowledging your letter dated the 14th.

The difficulty which you feel I understand to be this: How is the opinion that Christianity might have been extinguished by persecution compatible with the belief that God intended and pre-ordained that Christianity should subsist? I conceive there is no inconsistency between the two opinions. If Christianity would have perished had it been persecuted in a certain manner, and if God had pre-ordained that it should not perish, the reasonable inference is that God pre-ordained that it should not be persecuted in that manner. The preservation of Christianity thus brought about would be no "accident," but part of the Divine plan.

The relation between means and ends is quite compatible with a providential government of human affairs. It is only necessary to suppose that God, when he willed the end, willed the means necessary to its accomplishment. If the Maker of all things intended that a certain thing should come to pass, it is reasonable to suppose that provision was made in the general arrangements of the universe for its coming to pass consistently with these arrangements.

To Richard Congreve, on Mill's book on Comte.

Blackheath Park, *8th August* 1865.

1865 — Ætat. 59.

Dear Sir,—It is precisely because I consider M. Comte to have been a great thinker that I regard it as a duty to balance the strong and deeply felt admiration which I express for what I deem the fundamental parts of his philosophy by an equally emphatic expression of the opposite feelings I entertain towards other parts. It is M. Comte himself who, in my judgment, has thrown ridicule on his own philosophy by the extravagances of his later writings; and since he has done so, I conceive that the mischief can only be corrected if those who desire to separate the first from the last show that they are as much alive to the ridiculous side of his character and speculations as those are who are unable to appreciate his greatness. Unless this separation can be effected, either the absurdities will weigh down the merits, or the merits will float the absurdities, since many of those last are, in my estimation, of such a kind that, if it were impossible to laugh at them, it would be necessary to denounce them seriously and severely. I am glad that the former side of the alternative is possible. Forgive the freedom with which I express what I know must appear to you not only error and prejudice, but want of due modesty and reverence. But any weaker terms would not put you in full possession of what I feel in the matter, on which feeling must rest the justification of the tone of the article. In saying that the offence I feared I might give would be unintentional I did not mean that it would be unforeseen, but only that such a consequence of my free speaking on the subject would be one which I should sincerely regret. I earnestly disclaimed, near the beginning of the second article, any feeling but that of respect towards M. Comte's persistent disciples, and I am bound to acknowledge the extreme courtesy of your letter in circumstances which would have excused in my eyes some vehemence of language.

To Professor T. H. Huxley,

in reply to a letter in which he invited Mill to join an educational society, promoted for the purpose of creating "a system of education in which Modern Literature and Science on the one hand, and Theology on the other, shall occupy their proper places."

Blackheath Park, *18th August* 1865.

Dear Sir,—From what you say of the projected school I feel no doubt that it will be a good thing, and deserving of support, but I do not see how, with my opinions, I could publicly associate myself as a special supporter and recommender with any school in which theology is part of the course; for assuredly I do not think that theology ought to be taught in any school; and there are even at present schools (the Birkbeck schools) in which none is taught, though I am not aware of any schools of that sort for the higher and middle classes, unless it be the London University College School, which is, I believe, only a day school. It might be useless in the present state of the public mind to propose such schools, and it may be quite right to support others, but I do not feel that that justifies me in holding myself forth as appearing, and partly founding, schools in which a principle I wholly condemn is even partly recognised and acted on. I must wait therefore to know more of the actual plan of the institution in this respect before I can judge how far and in what way I can join in promoting its establishment. 1865 — Aetat. 59.

When I said that our educational system needs other modifications still more than it needs the due introduction of modern languages and physical science, what I had strongly in view was improvements in the mode of teaching. It is disgraceful to human nature and society that the whole of boyhood should be spent in pretending to learn certain things without learning them. With proper

1865 — Aetat. 59. methods and good teachers boys might really learn Greek and Latin instead of making believe to learn them, and might have ample time besides for science, and for as much of modern languages as there is any use in teaching to them while at school. And if science were taught as badly as Greek and Latin are taught, it would not do their minds more good.

To J. Boyd Kinnear,

in acknowledgment of his book, "Principles of Reform, Political and Legal."

Blackheath Park, 19*th August* 1865.

. . . The chief points on which I differ from you are—1st, I think you ascribe too great influence to differences of race and too little to historical differences, and to accidents as causes of the diversities of character existing among mankind.

2nd, I cannot join with you (glad as I should be to do so) in thinking that the wages-receiving class, if universally enfranchised, would have no class feelings or class opinions as such. The fact that the operative classes are divided on many questions of politics and legislation is equally true of the higher or the middle class of landholders or of capitalists, and is as consistent in the one case as in the other with their holding together as a compact body in cases in which their joint interest is or seems to be involved, or in which any bias arising from their common social position is liable to operate.

I am heartily glad to welcome you as an adherent of a reading and writing qualification. We agree in thinking that this, combined with independence of public charity, should entitle to a vote. I do not find any notice in your book of the principle of representation of minorities, or rather, representation of all instead of a number of local majorities. I cannot help wishing that your attention were drawn to a principle which, besides its inherent justice and manifold expediency, would be the most important corrective, as I think, of the inconveniences liable to arise from universal suffrage even subject to the condition of reading and writing. . . .

To J. Boyd Kinnear,

a further letter on the same subject.

MUNICH, 25*th September* 1865.

DEAR SIR,—Many thanks for your long and interesting letter. It is well that those who agree as much as we do should occasionally discover their points of difference, if only for the sake of suggesting to each other matter for further thought. I will therefore add a few words by way of rejoinder, confining myself at present to your third point, the extension of the suffrage.

My experience agrees with yours as to the greater mental honesty, and amenability to reason, of the better part of the working-classes, compared with the average of either the higher or middle. But may not this reasonably be ascribed to the fact that they have not yet, like the others, been corrupted by power? The English working classes have had no encouragement to think themselves better than, or as good as, those who are more educated than themselves. But once let them become the ascendant power, and a class of base adventurers in the character of professional politicians will be constantly addressing them with all possible instigations to think their own crude notions better than the theories and refinements of thinking people, and I do not deem so highly of any numerous portion of the human race as to believe that it is not corruptible by the flattery which is always addressed to power. The vertical divisions of opinion which you speak of seem to me to belong to the past, and to be almost wholly the effect of bad laws, now mostly removed. Who ever thinks of opposition of interests or feeling between the agricultural and the trading classes now that

1865 — Ætat. 59.

the Corn Laws have been repealed? But the division between labourers and employers of labour seems to me to be increasing in importance, and gradually swallowing up all others, and I believe it will always be widening and deepening unless, or until, the growth of Co-operation practically merges both classes into one. And if either of the two powers is strong enough to prevail without the help of an enlightened minority of the opposite class, it seems to me contrary to all experience of human nature to suppose that it will not abuse its power. There is no considerable opposition of apparent interest among the different kinds of manual labourers. Even if there be any kind of them whose wages do not admit of being raised, which I for one do not believe (much less would they), they would still, I apprehend, vote for a law which they thought would raise the wages of others, since the rise would not be at their expense. Neither is it only on the question of wages, or hours of labour, that the poorest and most numerous class would feel a common interest as against the propertied classes; might they not be tempted to throw all taxes on property—or even on realised property—and to make the taxes heavy, in order, by their outlay, to benefit, as they might think, trade and labour? Does anyone think them sufficiently enlightened to have outgrown these fallacies? I am expressing all this very crudely for want of time and space, but "I speak as to wise men—judge ye what I speak." . . .

To a Correspondent in Southport, Connecticut,

in reply to a letter from him, indulging in very vulgar abuse of the British people.

AVIGNON, *25th October* 1865.

DEAR SIR,—Your letter dated 29th September has been forwarded to me here. For the good opinion and good will which it expresses as regards myself I am duly thankful. You will scarcely be surprised that the bitter hostility it declares against my country and (with a few individual exceptions) against the whole of my countrymen, produces in me a very different sentiment. 1865 — Aetat. 59.

No one disapproves more, or is in the habit of expressing his disapprobation more strongly than I do, of the narrow, exclusive patriotism of former ages, which made the good of the whole human race a subordinate consideration to the good, or worse still, to the mere power and external importance, of the country of one's birth. I believe that the good of no country can be obtained by any means but such as tend to that of all countries, nor ought to be sought otherwise, even if obtainable. If my country were peopled, as you seem to think, by the scum of the earth, and if its existence were a standing nuisance to all other nations, I for one would shake the dust from my feet, and seek a better country elsewhere. But, speaking as one who has never kept any terms with national vanity, nor ever hesitated to tell his countrymen of their faults, and who has especially censured the feelings and conduct of an influential portion of them on the occasion of your late glorious contest, I do not admit the charges brought against them in your letter. England is to the populations of Europe the representative, by no means perfect but still the representative, of the same principles of social and political freedom which Americans so justly cherish. Any weakening of her influence would be simply so much additional discouragement to popular institutions and to liberty of thought, speech, and action throughout the old continents, and strengthening of the hands of despotism, temporal and spiritual, all over the world.

A war between Great Britain and the United States, were such a calamity possible, would give a new lease to tyranny and bigotry wherever they exist, and would throw back the progress of mankind for generations. Let me remind you that what you say about the grasping disposition and aggressive spirit of the English Government and people, is exactly and literally what the ignorant and prejudiced part of the higher and middle classes of Great Britain sincerely think and say concerning America. In

1865 — Aetat. 59.

neither of the two cases is the accusation true; but the profound ignorance of each other which it exhibits in both countries, is a most serious danger and evil to the world, which all who wish well to mankind must earnestly desire to cure, and which can only be aggravated by the indulgence of such feelings as you express.

To a Schoolboy of Fourteen,

in reply to a letter asking Mill's opinion on the question, "Is flogging good or bad for boys?"

AVIGNON, *13th November* 1865.

SIR,—To give a proper answer to your question would be to write the essay which you are intending to write. But if you wish for a mere opinion, expressed in few words, I would say—

1. Severe punishments of some kind are often necessary for boys, but only when they have been negligently or ill brought up and allowed to acquire bad habits.

2. Assuming severe punishments to be necessary, any other method of punishment that would be effectual is preferable to flogging. In the case, however, of certain grave moral delinquencies, chiefly those which are either of a cowardly or brutal character, corporal punishment in that or some equivalent form may be admissible.

To Dr. MacCormac, of Belfast,

on restrictions on marriage.

AVIGNON, *4th December* 1865.

DEAR SIR,—In answer to your letter of 29th November, I would say, that restrictions on marriage, or on any other human action, when so conducted as to be directly injurious to others than the agents themselves, do not appear to me objectionable on the principle of liberty. For all our actions which affect the interests of other people I hold that we are morally, and may without violation of principle be made legally, responsible. I have, however, expressly guarded myself against being understood to mean that legal restrictions on marriage are *expedient*. That is an altogether different question, to which I conceive no universal and peremptory answer can be given, and in deciding which for any particular case due weight ought to be given to the probability of consequences of the kind you mention, as well as of any other kinds.

1865 — Aetat. 59.

I am glad that you agree with me on the subject (much more urgent in this country) of compulsory education.

To Horace White, editor of the *Chicago Tribune*, in reply to a letter from him.

Avignon, *15th December* 1865.

I hardly know any point in Political Economy which it is more difficult to treat popularly, and so as to carry persuasion to those who have not studied the subject, than that one, of the influence of high and low wages on foreign trade. To understand the matter it is necessary to realise the fact that all trade is in reality barter—that the question is not whether the home capitalist shall produce or not, but whether he shall produce one thing or another—cotton fabrics, for instance, or wheat; and that the high wages which must equally be paid in either case, cannot place one of these two modes of employing his capital at any disadvantage by the side of the other. If it was only in cotton-spinning that American wages were higher than English, while in agriculture they were equal, then indeed the high wages being peculiar to one employment would really make it more difficult, and perhaps impossible, to carry it on without a protecting duty. But in that case it would clearly be an employment unsuited to the country, since labour employed in it would require to be remunerated more highly than the general rate of wages in the country.

It is very difficult to make this argument popular. What one might do is to ask, If high wages are sufficient

1865 — Aetat. 59. to make the American cotton manufacturer unable to compete with the English, how is it that the same high wages do not prevent the American farmer from underselling the English, unless because farming is an industry suited to the country and cotton-spinning not?

HELEN TAYLOR

CHAPTER X

1866–1867

FROM this date onwards, Mill received much assistance from Helen Taylor in the transaction of his correspondence. In many cases his letters were written entirely by Helen Taylor; and occasionally by Helen Taylor and Mill together: but in every case the letter was subsequently copied by Mill, and despatched in his name, with no indication of its true authorship. Wherever Helen Taylor was either the sole or the part author of a letter, I have notified the fact at the head of the letter.

TO HENRY FAWCETT,

acknowledging his book, "Economic Position of the British Labourer."

ST. VÉRAN, *1st January* 1866.

DEAR MR. FAWCETT,—I have delayed long to thank you for your book, having been very busy writing, and unable to read it with proper attention until within these few days. 1866 — Aetat. 59.

I think the essays must have been very interesting as lectures, and will be very useful as a book. The subject of the land laws and laws of inheritance is very well treated, and is one of which few feel the importance. You have broken ground very usefully on it. The considerations you have brought forward will be much needed in the discussions we shall soon have on Irish affairs, and the whole subject will become much more practical after

1866 — Ætat. 59. any considerable Parliamentary reform. One of the most important consequences of giving a share in the government to the working classes is that there will then be some members of the House with whom it will no longer be a maxim that human society exists for the sake of property in land—a grovelling superstition which is still in full force among the higher classes.

I need hardly say how highly I approve your chapter on Co-operation, and the restatement of the ideas of your *Westminster Review* article respecting strikes. On all these subjects you have strengthened yourself by new thoughts and illustrations; and the speculations in the concluding chapter, on the possibilities of the future, open a class of considerations both new and very necessary to be thought of.

The chapter which, on the whole, I least like is the one on wages, though it will probably be more praised than any of the rest: but I think I could show that an increase of wages at the expense of profits would not be an impracticability on the true principles of political economy. It might doubtless send capital to other countries, but we must recollect that the movement for higher wages and shorter working hours is now common to all the industrious nations.

There is one mistake in a matter of fact which I saw with regret in the book, and which I hope a new edition may soon give you an opportunity of correcting. You have entirely misunderstood the *ateliers nationaux*. They were not advances to co-operative societies, but direct payment of wages for work mostly nominal, from the public purse; and so far were they from having any connection with Louis Blanc or his opinions, that he has always bitterly complained of them, as having been set up not for but against him and his plans. The member of the Provisional Government principally responsible for them was, he says, M. Marie. The advances to associations of workmen were quite another matter, and did none of the harm which the *ateliers nationaux* did—probably even some good; at all events the Government could not have refused such experimental aid when the associations thought that they could not get on without it. I am not certain that such advances (resembling those the Crédit Mobilier makes to a richer class) would not sometimes be useful even now, though it is one of the lessons of the experience of that time that in most cases the associations which did without subsidies prospered the most.

1866 — Aetat. 59.

We shall now soon meet on our common field of battle. The two great topics of this year will be Jamaica and Reform, and there will be an immensity to be said and done on both subjects. I have just seen with great pleasure that Lord Hobart has come out decidedly (in *Macmillan's Magazine*) for Hare's system. It is gradually taking hold of one after another of the thinking men, of whom Lord Hobart is decidedly one. I shall perhaps invoke your aid on the metropolitan government question, of the burthen of which I shall probably have to take a considerable share.

To Judge Chapman,

who had left Australia for New Zealand, where he was now acting as Judge of the Supreme Court.

Avignon, *7th January* 1866.

Dear Chapman,—Your letter of 18th June reached me just before leaving England for Avignon, where I have been during the whole time which, as you mentioned, Mrs. Chapman and your younger children were to pass in London. I consequently have not seen them, but I shall hope to see your son who is to remain in England, as well as his brother who was already there. I have had less intercourse with your eldest son than I had hoped and intended to have, owing to the great engrossment of my time when in England by occupations which you can well appreciate—and now there is more on my hands than ever, and I have so many calls upon every moment

1866 — Aetat. 59.

of time that I am obliged to seem negligent of old friends and almost to avoid making new ones. But I am not the less desirous to be of use to any one connected with you, and if I seem inattentive it is not owing to indifference.

It must be very interesting to you to renew your knowledge of British New Zealand after an interval which bears so considerable a proportion to its short history. England has heard much of New Zealand these few years—and in a manner far from agreeable. Thoughtful people have found it hard to make up their minds on the New Zealand aspect of the universal colonial question—what to do with the aborigines. It was hoped that this would be a less desperate difficulty in New Zealand than elsewhere, on account of the higher qualities and more civilisable character of the Maoris. But the eternal source of quarrel, the demand of the colonists for land, has defeated these hopes, and it seems as if, unless or until the progressive decline of the Maori population ends in their extinction, the country would be divided between two races always hostile in mind, if not always in actual warfare. Here then is the burthen on the conscience of legislators at home. Can they give up the Maoris to the mercy of the more powerful and constantly increasing section of the population? Knowing what the English are when they are left alone with what they think an inferior race, I cannot reconcile myself to this. But again, is it possible for England to maintain an authority there for the purpose of preventing unjust treatment of the Maoris, and at the same time allow self-government to the British colonists in every other respect? How is that one subject to be kept separate, and how is the governor to be in other things a mere ornamental frontispiece to a government of the colony by a colonial cabinet and legislature, and to assume a will and responsibility of his own, overruling his cabinet and legislature whenever the Maoris are concerned? If the condition of colonial government is to keep well with the colonial population and its representatives, there is no hindering the colonists from making their co-operation depend on compliance with their wishes as to the Maoris. I do not see my way through these difficulties. Nor do I feel able to judge what would be the consequence of leaving the colonists without the aid of Queen's troops, to settle the main difficulty in their own way. Perhaps the proofs which the Maoris have given that they can be formidable enemies may have produced towards them in the colonists a different state of mind from the overbearing and insolent disregard of the rights and feelings of inferiors which is the common characteristic of John Bull when he thinks he cannot be resisted. On all these questions I am now under a special public obligation to make up my mind, and I hope to be helped to do so by your knowledge and experience. The information your letters are always full of will be often valuable to me now.

Your account of the Middle Island and its impassable range of high Alps is very attractive to me, and if New Zealand were an island in the Northern Atlantic would speedily send me on a visit there. The very idea of anything impassable and impenetrable is almost too charming now when every nook and corner of our planet has got or is getting opened to the full light of day. One of the many causes which make the age we are living in so very important in the life of the human race—almost, indeed, the turning-point of it—is that so many things combine to make it the era of a great change in the conceptions and feelings of mankind as to the world of which they form a part. There is now almost no place left on our own planet that is mysterious to us, and we are brought within sight of the practical questions which will have to be faced when the multiplied human race shall have taken full possession of the earth (and exhausted its principal fuel). Meanwhile we are also acquiring scientific convictions as to the future destination of suns and stars and the whole visible universe. These things must have ultimately a very great effect on human character. You have read Buckle's remarks on

1866 — Aetat. 59.

the effect of the aspects of nature in different parts of the earth upon the moral characteristics and thence on the social development of the different nations. One begins to see a long vista of effects of analogous origin, but of very different kind, on the future generations of mankind. Even without looking to anything so distant, or going beyond the proximate effects of social and commercial causes already in operation, some thinkers are beginning to speculate on what will happen when the agricultural labourers of England shall have followed those of Ireland to America, and are asking themselves whether we shall have to import Chinese to supply the vacancy. The most certain result that I foresee from all this is that English statesmanship will have to assume a new character and to look in a more direct way than before to the interests of posterity. We are now, I think, standing in the very boundary line between this new statesmanship and the old, and the next generation will be accustomed to a very different set of political arguments and topics from those of the present and past.

To the Secretary of the Commons Preservation Society, on the formation of that body.

AVIGNON, *22nd January* 1866.

DEAR SIR,—I regret that the extreme proximity of the date at which the meeting of the Commons Preservation Society is to be held makes it impossible for me to be present. I have all my life been strongly impressed with the importance of preserving as much as possible of such free space for healthful exercise and for the enjoyment of natural beauty as the growth of population and cultivation has still left to us. The desire to engross the whole surface of the earth in the mere production of the greatest possible quantity of food and the materials of manufacture, I consider to be founded on a mischievously narrow conception of the requirements of human nature. I therefore highly applaud the formation of the Commons

Preservation Society, and am prepared to co-operate in the promotion of its objects in any manner which lies in my power. 1866 — Aetat. 59.

To the Speaker's Secretary.

By Helen Taylor and Mill.

22nd February 1866.

Sir,—I have had the honour of receiving an invitation to dine with the Right Hon. the Speaker on Wednesday next, 28th February, but beg that I may be allowed to excuse myself from accepting it, as I think it desirable that those members of the House of Commons who do not approve of the regulations in respect to dress at present in force should make their objection known to the Speaker, who, I do not doubt, will give to it whatever weight is justly due. I sincerely hope that in taking this mode of expressing the objection which I entertain to the practice hitherto followed, I shall not be considered to be wanting in that respect and deference to the Right Hon. the Speaker which it is as much my wish as my duty invariably to observe.

To F. Milnes Edge,

London representative of the *Chicago Tribune*, on Protectionism in the United States.

Blackheath Park, *26th February* 1866.

Dear Sir,—I have to acknowledge a letter from you dated 15th February, asking me to explain a passage of my "Principles of Political Economy" in which I express the opinion that a protecting duty, for a limited space of time, may be defensible in a new country as a means of naturalising a branch of industry in itself suited to the country, but which would be unable to establish itself there without some form of temporary assistance from the State. This passage, you say, has been made use of

1866 — Aetat. 59.

by American protectionists as the testimony of an English writer on political economy to the inapplicability to America of the general principle of free trade. The passage has been used for a similar purpose in the Australian colonies, erroneously in my opinion, but certainly with more plausibility than can be the case in the United States, for Australia really is a new country whose capabilities for carrying on manufactures cannot yet be said to have been tested; but the manufacturing parts of the United States, New England and Pennsylvania, are no longer new countries; they have carried on manufactures on a large scale and with the benefit of high protecting duties for at least two generations, and their operations have had full time to acquire the manufacturing skill in which those of England had preceded them; there has been ample experience to prove that the inability of their manufactures to compete in the American market with those of Great Britain does not arise merely from the more recent date of their establishment, but from the fact that American labour and capital can in the present circumstances of America be employed with greater return and greater advantage to the national wealth in the production of other articles. I have never for a moment recommended or countenanced any protecting duty except for the purpose of enabling the protected branch of industry in a very moderate time to become independent of protection. That moderate time in the United States has been exceeded, and if the cottons or iron of America still need protection against those of the other hemisphere it is in my eyes a complete proof that they ought not to have it, and that the longer it is continued the greater the injustice and the waste of national revenues will be. . . .

To John Campbell, of Liverpool.

Avignon, *4th April* 1866.

Dear Sir,—The supposition that I approve of the Bill empowering Government to make loans for the improvement of the dwellings of the working classes is quite correct. If I thought that such a measure would injure the independence of the working classes or encourage their improvidence, I should strenuously oppose it. But the case seems to me to be one of a class of cases in which people require artificial help, to enable them afterwards to help themselves. The taste for better house accommodation has still to be created; and until it is created, private speculation will not find its account in supplying that improved accommodation. The aid of Government is often useful and sometimes necessary to start improved systems which, once started, are able to keep themselves going without further help. I support loans from the public for the purpose in question (which is still more important morally than even physically), as I would support similar loans for the purpose of creating peasant proprietors, or (if necessary for the purpose) in aid of colonisation. I think, however, that the loans ought not to be accessible only to Town Councils, but also to building companies or private capitalists under strict conditions and on proper security; and the Bill introduced by the Government gives, I believe, the power of making such advances.

1866 — Aetat. 59.

From J. A. Roebuck to Edwin Chadwick,

stating the impression made in the House of Commons by Mill's maiden speech, on the Reform Bill.

19 Ashley Place, *14th April* 1866.

My dear Chadwick,—Thinking you would like to hear from me the fortune of Mill last night, I write you my opinion of his speech; and I can give you not only my own estimate of its worth, but that also of Mr. Speaker, who asked me to send Mill to him, so that he (the Speaker) might be able to express to him personally his high admiration of his address. And assuredly that address did deserve all the eulogy which the Speaker bestowed on it—it settled for ever the position Mill is to hold in the House, and I believe lays open to him the highest offices in the

1866 — Ætat. 59. administration of the country. Bulwer-Lytton spoke immediately before Mill, and never was there a more remarkable contrast than that offered by the two speakers. Lytton's was a mere House of Commons party *ad captandum* oration—full of House of Commons wit and sparkle, telling epigrams and personal thrusts, but as to instruction nothing; there was no deep thought, no high and exalting feeling. But this was just what distinguished Mill's address—so much so, that I consider this speech an epoch in Parliamentary oratory. It was the outpouring of a great, honest, yet modest mind; the vigorous expression of well-considered and accurate thought. The manner, too, was attractive; as regards his voice, he seems to have taken and well used my hints. A very little pains and exercise will give him confidence and power, and make him one of the great speakers in Parliament. I hardly know whether the suggestion I am about to make is wise or useful—*that* will depend very much on his habit of composition and thought. I myself never use a note, but this has been brought about by long training expressly to that end; but it seems to me, that if he made the very slightest skeleton of his intended speech and put the heads on a card, which card he might openly hold in his hand, he would find his memory aided, his confidence increased, and (now don't laugh) the carriage of his body improved. He has a habit of joining his hands behind him, and rolling from side to side, looking like a schoolboy saying his lesson. Now I would suggest to him, to stand for some minutes every day before a cheval glass, with a card in his hand; to make a little speech, and watch carefully his own demeanour. Now I think you must be tired of me and my advice, so I will end.—Yours very truly,

J. A. R.

To Mrs. Caroline Liddell,

in reply to a letter from her advocating Women's Suffrage, but saying that she was "no strong-minded female, and should never dream of going to the hustings."

By HELEN TAYLOR.

6th May 1866.

MADAM,—I am happy to hear that you and other ladies are disposed to assert your just claim to be represented in the body that taxes you, and I recommend to you to lose no opportunity of doing so. When men who wish to remove the invidious distinctions under which you labour offer arguments founded on the evident justice of your cause, we are constantly met by the reply that ladies themselves see no hardship in it, and do not care enough for the franchise to ask for it. I am glad to be able to say that I know several members of Parliament who wish to grant the franchise without distinction of sex, but I know many more who would be ashamed to refuse it if it were quietly and steadily demanded by women themselves. I am sorry to find that you disclaim being strong-minded, because I believe strength of mind to be one of the noblest gifts that any rational creature, male or female, can possess, and the best measure of our degree of efficiency for working in the cause of truth. But such mental powers and energies as we any of us do possess, ought to be employed in striving to remove the evils with which circumstances have made us acquainted; and a woman who is a taxpayer is the most natural and most suitable advocate of the political enfranchisement of women. I hope, therefore, that you will endeavour to strengthen the hands of those (and I know more than one) who have devoted their lives to working in your cause, by protesting against the injustice you suffer, whenever and wherever you can, both in society, and when occasion offers in public. If you could yourself write a petition (almost in the terms of your letter to me), and procure as many signatures to it as you can, I should be happy to present it to Parliament.

1866 — Aetat. 59.

To Darby Griffith, M.P.

Blackheath Park, *9th June* 1866.

1866 — Aetat. 60. Dear Sir,—I am happy that, as I infer from your note of yesterday's date, you are not indisposed towards the extension of the electoral franchise to women within the limits expressed in the petition.

The notice which I gave in the House yesterday goes as far as I think it prudent to go, on this subject, in the present session. As there is no chance that we can succeed in getting a clause for admitting women to the suffrage introduced with the present Reform Bill, it seems to me and to other friends of such a proposal desirable merely to open the subject this year, without taking up the time of the House and increasing the accusation of obstructiveness by forcing on a discussion which cannot lead to a practical result. What we are now doing will lay the foundation of a further movement when advisable, and will prepare for that movement a much greater amount of support in the country than we should have if we attempted it at present.

To the Rev. James Martineau,

in reply to a letter in which he requested Mill's support of his candidature for the chair of Mental Philosophy and Logic in University College.

Blackheath Park, *6th July* 1866.

Dear Sir,—It would be very discreditable to any Englishman who watches the progress of opinion, and is capable of understanding the vast importance of speculative philosophy, to have remained ignorant of your contributions to it, or of the influence you have exercised over the mode of thought of a considerable proportion of the few and scattered metaphysical students in this country. It would always give me much pleasure to bear testimony to your knowledge, both special and general, your abilities, and your candid appreciation of opponents, of which I have had a striking instance in my own case. Unfortunately, however, if I were to volunteer that testimony on the occasion of the vacancy in University College, and if when given it were of any value to you, it could only be so by being prejudicial to another candidate who, though I have no reason to think his claims superior to yours in any other respect, would certainly teach doctrines much nearer than yours to those which I myself hold on the great philosophical questions. Now, though this in itself is far from being a paramount consideration with me, the opportunities are so few and unfrequent of obtaining for opinions similar to my own their fair share of influence in the public teaching of this country, that if I myself had a vote in the disposal of the professorship, I should think myself bound, in the general interest of philosophical thought no less than of my own form of it, to give the preference to a candidate otherwise sufficiently qualified, who would teach my own opinions, in one of the very few chairs from which those opinions would not be a peremptory exclusion. You are perfectly capable of entering into this feeling even if you do not approve of it, and I can only add that I do not think I have ever in any instance regretted so much my inability to support a similar candidature.

To Robert Pharazyn, of New Zealand.

St. Véran, 21*st August* 1866.

Sir,—The great occupation of my time in the latter part of the session has prevented me from more promptly acknowledging your letter of 14th April. I am glad to find that a student and thinker, such as you evidently are, finds so much in common between me and himself. The author of the article in the *Westminster Review* from which you quote (who is not, as you suppose, Mr. Lucas) is quite right in saying that I have thrown no light on the difficulty of reconciling the belief in a perfectly good God with the actual constitution of Nature. It was not my business to

1866 — Aetat. 60.

do so, but if I had given any opinion on the point it would have been that there is no mode of reconciling them except the hypothesis that the Creator is a Being of limited power. Either he is not all-powerful or he is not good, and what I said was, that unless he is good I will not call him so nor worship him. The appearances, however, of contrivance in the universe, whatever amount of weight we attach to them, seem rather to point to a benevolent design limited by obstacles than to a malevolent or tyrannical character in the designer, and I therefore think that the mind which cherishes devotion to a Principle of Good in the universe, leans in the direction in which the evidence, though I cannot think it conclusive, nevertheless points. I therefore do not discourage this leaning, though I think it important that people should know that the foundation it rests on is a hypothesis, not an ascertained fact. This is the principal limitation which I would apply to your position, that we should encourage ourselves to believe as to the unknowable what it is best for mankind that we should believe. I do not think it can even be best for mankind to *believe* what there is not evidence of, but I think that, as mankind improve, they will much more recognise two independent mental provinces, the province of belief and the province of imaginative conjecture, that they will become capable of keeping them distinct, and while they unite their belief to the evidence, will think it allowable to let their imaginative anticipations go forth, not carrying belief in their train, in the direction which experience and study of human nature shows to be the most improving to the character and most exalting and consoling to the individual feelings. . . .

To Mr. John Morley,

on an article written by him in the *Fortnightly Review* condemning the annexation of Mysore.

26th September 1866.

Dear Sir,—I am much obliged to you for your article though I do not altogether agree with it. I presented the petition, not because I concurred in its sentiments, but because it came from people who were entitled to be heard, and on the last day of the session they could not find any other member whom they thought suitable. I approved of all Lord Dalhousie's annexations except that of Kerauli, which never took effect, having been at once disallowed from home, and indeed Lord Dalhousie himself gave it up before he knew of its having been negatived. My principle was this. Wherever there are really Native States, with a nationality and historical traditions and feelings, which is emphatically the case (for example) with the Rajpoot States, there I would on no account take advantage of any failure of heirs to put an end to them. But all the Mahomedan (Rampore excepted) and most of the Mahratta kingdoms are not of home growth, but created by conquest not a century ago, and the military chiefs and office-holders who carry on the government and form the ruling class are almost as much foreigners to the mass of the people as we ourselves are. The Scindia and Holkar families in Central India are foreign dynasties, and of low caste too. The home of the Mahrattas is in the South, and there is no really native Mahratta kingdom now standing except Kolapore. In these modern states created by conquest I would make the continuance of the dynasty by adoption not a right nor a general rule, but a reward to be earned by good government and as such I would grant it freely.

All this, however, was changed by Lord Canning's promise, which I thought at the time and still think most ill-advised. And even if right otherwise, I think it ought to have excepted States actually created by our gift, as Mysore was. In such cases we are by right the sole interpreters of our own deed of gift. All arguments grounded on vague phrases of that most plausible and successful of political humbugs, Lord Wellesley, count with me for nothing. He would have taken the whole country outright had he dared, but Parliament had then very recently made a solemn declaration against territorial acquisitions in India, and his object was to throw dust in the eyes of Parliament and take the country as far as it could be

1866 — Aetat. 60.

done while pretending not to do it. The only practical question with me is, Does Lord Canning's promise to the native princes which revived our right of escheat, fairly and reasonably include this particular case? Opinions among experienced Indians are divided on the point, and I have not yet thoroughly examined the documents. I therefore have not made up my mind, though I much fear our faith is committed beyond recall.

In one thing I fully agree with you, that whenever we sanction an adoption we ought to undertake the education of the young successor and train him to public business under a judicious and experienced resident. This has been done in a good many instances and often with very considerable success. Travancore, which you mention, is only one of a number of cases in point (if we did educate the chief himself, which I forget); and though the princes so trained usually degenerate more or less in the lapse of years, they almost always remain much better than the miserable creatures brought up in the zenana.

To C. Gavan Duffy,

in reply to a question as to how far it is justifiable in politics to compromise on minor matters, in order to secure victory on matters of greater importance.

St. Véran, *2nd October* 1866.

Dear Sir,—I feel it a very high compliment that you should wish to know my opinion on a point of conscience, and still more so that you should think that opinion likely to be of any assistance to you in the guidance of your own political conduct.

The point mentioned in your letter is one which I have often and carefully considered, for though my own course in public matters has been one which did not often call on me to co-operate with anybody, I have reflected much on the conditions of co-operation among the requisites of practical public life. The conclusion which I have long come to is one which seems rather obvious when one has got at it, but it is so seldom acted on that apparently most people find it difficult to practise. It seems to me, in the first place, that a conscientious person whose turn of mind and outward circumstances combine to make practical political life his line of greatest usefulness, may, and often ought to be, willing to put his opinion in abeyance on a political question which he deems to be, in the circumstances of the time and place, of secondary importance; which may be the case with any question that does not in one's own judgment involve any fundamental principle of morality. But in consenting to waive his opinion, it seems to me an indispensable condition that he should not disguise it. He should say to his constituents or to the world exactly what he really thinks about the matter. Insincere professions are the one cardinal sin in a representative government. If an Australian politician wishes to be in the Assembly for the sake of questions which he thinks much more important, for the time being, than that of protection, I should hold him justified in saying to a constituency, "I think protection altogether a mistake, but since it is a *sine qua non* with you, and the opposite is not a *sine qua non* with me, if you elect me I will not oppose it." If he conscientiously thought that the strong feeling of the public in its favour gave them a right, or made it expedient to have it practically tried, I should not think him wrong in promising to support it; though it is not a thing I should lightly or willingly do. He might even, for adequate public reasons, consent to join a protectionist ministry, but only on condition that protection should be an open question, and that he should be at liberty to speak his mind publicly on the subject.

The question of expediency in these matters each must decide for himself. The expediencies vary with all sorts of personal considerations. For instance, if he has considerable popular influence, and is, in all other respects than this, the favourite candidate, it will often be his most virtuous course to insist on entire freedom of action, and make the electors feel that they cannot have a representative of his quality without acquiescing in his voting

1866 against some of their opinions. The only absolute rule I
— would lay down is, not to consent to the smallest hypocrisy.
Aetat. 60. The rest is matter of practical judgment on which all that can be said is, Weigh all the considerations and act for the best.

To David Urquhart, the diplomatist,

in reply to a letter from him supporting Mill's action in the prosecution of Governor Eyre; and enclosing subscriptions from various persons, to assist in that object.

St. Véran, *4th October* 1866.

My dear Urquhart,—I am really obliged to you for the sight of Mrs. Urquhart's letter. I wish it were read by every person in the British Isles. Let me also beg you to thank your two friends, if they are still with you, both for their subscriptions and for their letters. I feel a real respect for men who not only have a conscience, but whose conscience makes them feel that they are personally responsible for their actions, and cannot shift off that responsibility upon the shoulders of superiors.

It is a real pleasure to me to find you and myself in thorough and hearty co-operation, even were it only on one subject. But the principle which actuates both of us on that subject is progressively important, and extends far beyond the particular case. You approve of my speech because you see that I am not on this occasion standing up for the negroes, or for liberty, deeply as both are interested in the subject—but for the first necessity of human society, law. One would have thought that when this was the matter in question, all political parties might be expected to be unanimous. But my eyes were first opened to the moral condition of the English nation (I except in these matters the working classes) by the atrocities perpetrated in the Indian Mutiny, and the feelings which supported them at home. Then came the sympathy with the lawless rebellion of the Southern Americans in defence of an institution which is the sum of all lawlessness, as Wesley said it was of all villainy—and finally came this Jamaica business, the authors of which, from the first day I knew of it, I determined that I would do all in my power to bring to justice if there was not another man in Parliament to stand by me. You rightly judge that there is no danger of my sacrificing such a purpose to any personal advancement. I hope I should not be so base even if I cared for personal advancement, but, as it happens, I do not. . . .

To David Urquhart

St. Véran, *26th October* 1866.

My dear Urquhart,—I thank you sincerely for your letter. The actual experience of one who has had so much of it, and of so unusual a sort, is sure to be worth having, and worth meditating on.

Your letter makes me wish to give you an equally explicit statement of my own way of thinking, so far as it is different from yours. And I think I can trust myself sufficiently not to be afraid that my having done so will raise any obstacle of *amour propre* in my own mind to prevent me from changing any part of that way of thinking which can be shown to be wrong. I feel as strongly as you the absence of control over the executive in matters of foreign policy, and the absolute inutility and nullity, as far as that is concerned, of any change of Ministers. I should never dream of telling the working or any unrepresented classes that they have no power unless they can get the suffrage, and I do not ascribe the prodigious superiority of their moral sentiments on such matters as Eyre, the Indian Mutiny, &c., over the classes socially above them, to any intrinsic superiority of moral excellence. But I do not believe that the bad feelings, or absence of good feelings, in the others, arises from their having votes. I ascribe it to the sympathy of officials with officials, and of the classes from whom officials are selected with officials of all sorts. I ascribe it also to the sympathy with authority and power, generated

1866 — Aetat. 60. in our higher and upper middle classes by the feeling of being specially privileged to exercise them, and by living in a constant dread of the encroachment of the class beneath, which makes it one of their strongest feelings that resistance to authority must be put down *per fas et nefas*. I do not believe that feelings of these kinds would exist where there was no privileged class, and where no one had more political influence of a direct kind than his mere vote gave him. There is much in American politics that is regrettable enough, but I do not observe that there is a particle of the English upper-class policy that authority (meaning the persons in authority) must be supported at all costs; and American foreign policy is all above-board and in broad daylight. So, I believe, would that of England be, if the working classes had votes. I am no worshipper of those classes, and they know it. I have written and published harsh truths of them, which were brought up against me in meetings of the working classes during my election, and I never was so much applauded by them as when I stood to what I had written and defended it. They are not yet politically corrupted by power. I doubt not that they would be corrupted like other classes by becoming the paramount power in the country, though probably in a less degree, because in a multitude the general feelings of human nature are usually more powerful and class feelings proportionately less so than in a small body. But I do not want to make them predominant. I see the country under the leadership of a higher and a middle class who, by very disuse of attempting or wishing to do their duty as managers of the national affairs, have become incapable of doing it, and I am hopeless of any improvement but by letting in a powerful influence from those who are the great sufferers by whatever evil is done or is left uncorrected at home, and who have no personal or class interests or feelings concerned either in oppressing dependencies, or in doing or conniving at wrong to foreign countries. I could write at great length on all this, but it is not my object to defend my view of existing English politics; my object is to enable you, whom I respect, to understand the source from which that view proceeds in my own mind. As for those whom I do not respect, a category which includes the great majority of public men and public writers, I should never take the trouble to give any other explanation of myself to them, than that which I hope my conduct will give. 1866 — Aetat. 60.

To George Grote,

in which Mill declines a proposal to allow himself to be nominated for the Senate of London University.

St. Véran, *12th November* 1866.

It is very desirable that there should be some one in the Senate who would give you a more effective backing than you have at present. But there are others besides me who could do this. Bain being unattainable, have you ever thought of Herbert Spencer? He is as anti-clergymanish as possible; he goes as far as the farthest of us in explaining psychological phenomena by association and the "experience hypothesis"; he has a considerable and growing reputation, much zeal and public spirit, and is not, I should think, more *suspect* on the subject of religion than I am. I think he would be of great use in the Senate on the subjects on which you most need to be supported, and a very valuable acquisition otherwise. I do not know whether the duty would be agreeable to him, but from the little I know of his tastes and habits I should expect that rather than the contrary. . . .

To George Grote,

concerning the suggested nomination of Herbert Spencer for the Senate of London University.

St. Véran, *2nd December* 1866.

My dear Grote,—I am very happy that you think my objection to being proposed for the Senate fair and reasonable. With regard to Spencer, Bain's judgment will

1866 — Aetat. 60. be a great help to you in the matter. I have not seen very much of Spencer, but what I have seen adds to the favourable side of the impression his writings make on me. I am not inclined, from anything I know, to consider him as on the whole disposed to magnify his differences from others whose philosophical opinions are allied to his own. He did so in the case of Comte, whom he knew very imperfectly. But in his controversies with me it is rather I who have magnified the differences, and he who has extenuated them. With regard to his reputation, no doubt it has not yet reached its height, but it is constantly growing. His is the rising philosophical name at the present, and will probably stand very high ten years hence; and it is rather with a view to the future than to the present that additional thought is wanted in the Senate. . . .

To Edwin Chadwick.

St. Véran, *29th December* 1866.

. . . I have, as you know, always agreed with you as to the importance of introducing military drill into schools. though I should be a little frightened at it if I thought it would do what in your present paper you say it sometimes does—make the majority of the boys wish to be soldiers. There can be no doubt also that by this means the purposes of an efficient reserve would be attained without either the expense or the loss of productive power or any other of the evil consequences of increased armaments. But for that very reason it will not be listened to by any of the Continental governments, except possibly Italy. Those governments do not want a real defensive force; they want an aggressive force; they want to have the very largest body of adult soldiers ready for service anywhere whom they can afford to pay, and your arguments will be of no avail, except to the French and Prussian Liberals to use against their governments. In that respect they may be very useful. . . . The idea of employing the soldiers in civil work is not new in France, and it has been much discussed; you will find many minds prepared for it. I do not at present see any service that I can be of in the matter, at least by writing. I do not understand military subjects, and can carry no authority upon them. But I will most willingly move for your paper, and may take that opportunity of speaking my mind on the matter as a question of education. 1866 — Aetat. 60.

To H. S. Brandreth,

on the utilitarian basis for veracity.

Blackheath Park, *9th February* 1867.

Dear Sir,—Your question respecting the obligation of veracity on the utilitarian view of ethics seems, if I understand it rightly, to proceed on a misapprehension of the utilitarian standard. The test of right as the happiness principle is not the pleasure of doing the act which is declared to be right, but the pleasurable or painful consequences to mankind which would follow if such acts were done; and these, in the case you put, could not be enunciated as any general rule, because they depend on varying circumstances. There are cases in which martyrdom is a useless self-sacrifice, and a sacrifice of other means of doing good. There are other cases in which the importance of it to the good of mankind is so great as to make it a positive duty, like the act of a soldier who gives his life in the performance of what is assigned to him. There are cases again where, without being so necessary as to be on the utilitarian ground an absolute duty, it is yet so useful as to constitute an act of virtue, which then ought to receive the praise and honours of heroism. The duty of truth as a positive duty is also to be considered on the ground of whether more good or harm would follow to mankind in general if it were generally disregarded, and not merely whether good or harm would follow in a particular case. 1867 — Aetat. 60.

To the Rev. T. W. Towle,

in reply to a letter asking Mill's opinion on the subject of teaching the Bible in schools.

Blackheath Park, *9th February* 1867.

1867 — Aetat. 60. Dear Sir,—I agree entirely with the general principles and spirit of your letter received yesterday. I think it highly desirable that the New Testament, and those parts of the Old which are either poetical or properly historical, should be taught *as history* in places of education; and so far my only difference with you would be that nearly all teachers, both churchmen and dissenters, being as yet far short of the enlightened views which you entertain on the subject, would at present be sure to teach and inculcate all that is contained in those books not as matter of history but of positive religious belief. There are, however, other parts of the Old Testament, viz., those which scientific knowledge or historical criticism have shown not to be, in any proper sense of the word, historical, the book of Genesis for example; and I do not think it right to teach these in schools even as history, unless it were avowedly as merely what the Hebrews believed respecting their own origin and the early history of the world.

To Dr. W. G. Ward,

concerning an article by him in the *Dublin Review*.

Blackheath Park, *14th February* 1867.

Dear Sir,—I have read your article with very great interest. You are the clearest thinker I have met with for a long time who has written on your side of these great questions. And I quite admit that your theory of divine premovement is not, on the face of it, inadmissible. Your illustration of the mice inside the piano is excellent. The uniform sequences which the mice might discover between the hands and the phenomena inside would not negative the player without. But you only put back the collision between the two theories for a certain distance. It comes at last. At whatever part in the upward series the unforeseeable will of the divine musician comes in, there the uniformity of physical sequence fails; the chain has been traced to its beginning; a physical phenomenon has taken place without any antecedent physical conditions. Now what would be asserted on the other side of the question is, that the facts always admit of, and render highly probable, the supposition that there were such antecedent physical conditions, and that there has been no ultimate beginning to that series of facts, short of whatever beginning there was to the whole history of the universe.

We do not pretend that we can disprove divine interference in events, and direct guidance of them. All our evidence is only negative. We say that as far as known to mankind everything takes place as it would do if there were no such divine guidance. We think that every event is abstractedly capable of being predicted, because mankind are in such case as near to being able actually to predict what happens as could be expected, regard being had to the degree of accessibility of the data, and the complexity of the conditions of the problem.

I cannot perceive in your article any errors in physics. But I am not a safe authority on matters of physical science. Astronomers now think that they can predict much more than eclipses and the return of comets, and their predictions reach even to the dissipation of the sun's heat and the heaping up of the solar system in one dead mass of congelation. But I hold all this to be at present nothing more than scientific conjecture. All that is required by your argument is, that the possibility of absolute and categorical prediction should be as yet confined to cosmic phenomena. This, I believe, all men of science admit, and I endorse everything on that subject which is said by Mansel in your note. Scientific prediction in other physical sciences is not absolute but conditional. We know certainly that oxygen and hydrogen brought together in a particular way will produce water, but we cannot predict with certainty that oxygen and

1867 — Aetat. 60. hydrogen will come together in that way unless brought together by human agency. The human power of prediction at present extends only to effects which depend on a very small number of causes, and consequently can be predicted. Most other physical phenomena can be predicted with the same certainty, provided we are able to limit the causes in operation to a very small number. *This* power of prediction you have not, I think, allowed for in your Essay. Yet it surely is all-important. For if the effect of any single cause, or of any pair or triad of causes, can be calculated, the joint effect of a myriad of such causes is *abstractedly* capable of calculation. That we are unable practically to calculate it is no more than might be expected, at least in the present state of our knowledge, however calculable it may in itself be.

With regard to free will, you have not said much that affects my argument: I am not aware of having ever said that preknowledge is inconsistent with free will. That knotty metaphysical question I have avoided entering into, and in my "Logic" I have even built upon the admission of the free-will philosophers that our freedom may be real though God preknows our actions. You simplify the main question very much by your luminous distinction between the spontaneous impulse of the will, which you regard as strictly dependent on pre-existing mental dispositions and external solicitations, and what the man may himself do to oppose or alter that spontaneous impulse. The distinction has important practical consequences, but I see no philosophical bearing that it has on free will; for it seems to me that the same degree of knowledge of a person's character which will enable us to judge with tolerable assurance what his spontaneous impulse will be, will also enable us to judge with almost an equal degree of assurance whether he will make any effort, and (in a general way) how *much* effort he is likely to make, to control that impulse. Our foresight in this matter cannot be certain, because we never can be really in possession of sufficient data. But it is not more uncertain than the insufficiency and uncertainty of the data suffice to account for.

To W. R. Cremer,

in which Mill withdraws his support from the Reform League, on account of some inflammatory speeches made by representatives of the League.

Blackheath Park, *1st March* 1867.

Dear Sir,—I am sorry to say that the proceedings at the meeting of delegates reported in the *Star* of 28th February, a meeting promoted by the Reform League, and at which members of its Council were the chief speakers, make it necessary for me to withdraw the paper which I had expressed my willingness to sign; because I can no longer say with sincerity that an agitation conducted in the manner proposed at that meeting could be beneficial to the cause of Reform.

1867 — Aetat. 60.

The speeches delivered at the meeting were characterised by two things; a determined rejection beforehand of all compromise on the Reform question, even if proposed by the public men in whose sincerity and zeal as reformers you have repeatedly expressed the fullest confidence; and a readiness to proceed at once to a trial of physical force if any opposition is made either to your demands or to the particular mode, even though illegal, which you may select for the expression of them.

It is best that I should express my opinion plainly and unreservedly on both these points. My conviction is that any Reform Bill capable of being passed at present and for some time to come must be more or less of a compromise. I have hitherto thought that the leading minds among the working classes recognised this, and though frankly declaring that nothing less than the whole of what they think required by justice will finally satisfy them, were aware that such ultimate success can only in this country be obtained by a succession of steps, and that a large portion of the middle and some portion of the higher classes may be carried with them in the first step, and perhaps in every successive step, but would certainly resist a passage

1867 — Aetat. 60. all at once from the present distribution of political power to one exactly the reverse, the effects of which they feel quite unable to foresee. All this the speakers at the meeting on Thursday either forgot or entirely disregarded. But even if I thought them right on this point I should think them utterly and fatally wrong in the course they adopted, of directly instigating the mass of reformers to seek the attainment of their object by physical violence. One of the leading speakers proclaimed superiority of physical force as constituting right, and as justifying the people in "riding down the ministers of the law"; and the speaker who followed him emphatically expressed concurrence in his treatment. I do not impute to the meeting the monstrous doctrine of these two speakers. But unless misreported, the general tone was that of a direct appeal to revolutionary expedients. Now, it is my deep conviction that there are only two things which justify an attempt at revolution. One is personal oppression and tyranny and consequent personal suffering of such intensity, that to put an immediate stop to it is worth almost any amount of present evil and future danger. The other is when either the system of government does not permit the redress of grievances to be sought by peaceable and legal means, or when those means have been perseveringly exerted to the utmost for a long series of years, and their inefficacy has been demonstrated by experiment. No one will say that any of these justifications for revolution exist in the present case. Yet unless the language used was mere bravado, the speakers appear to have meant to say that the time has already come for revolution.

I do not wish to exaggerate the importance of these things; I believe them to be the result of feelings of irritation, for which there has been ample provocation and abundant excuse. But however natural irritation it may be, things done or said under its influence are very likely to be repented of afterwards. This is human—it is for you to judge of. I do not claim the smallest right of offering advice to you or to the League; but you have asked me to express, in a written document, approbation of the general character and efforts of your agitation, and as it is impossible for me to do this when it has assumed a character of which I decidedly disapprove, I have thought it best to explain candidly the reasons why I must now decline to comply with your request.

To R. Russell,
on Woman Suffrage.
By Helen Taylor.

6th March 1867.

Dear Sir,—I do not see that the fact that it may become expedient at some future time to admit women to the House of Representatives can be any bar to admitting their claim at present to be electors. Any objections to the meeting of persons of both sexes for the purposes of legislation are such as naturally tend to diminish with a higher state of civilisation. In some countries the sexes are still separated at church; in the East the influence of sex is so strong that even family life is rendered impossible by it, and brothers and sisters, fathers and daughters, are separated, and men and women can only associate together in the single relation of husband and wife. But we have proved by experience that exactly in proportion as men and women associate publicly together in a variety of relations not founded on sex, their doing so becomes safe and beneficial, and raises the tone of public morality. I am disposed to think that no legislation is needed to prevent women from becoming members of Parliament, for that before any woman is likely to be chosen by a sufficient number of electors, public opinion will ensure sufficient propriety of sentiment in the House of Commons to make her presence there perfectly harmless.

As to the objection that men and women might on some occasions differ collectively, and that the women might have their own way, it has much less force than the similar objection to the working classes, because men and women are much more likely to be evenly balanced in number

1867 — Aetat. 60. than the poor and the rich. I cannot see how arranging that men shall always have their own way in everything can in justice be the proper way to prevent women from occasionally having theirs. There is a more even balance between men and women than between any other two classes, and therefore the attainment of justice through equal representation may be more easily trusted to the reason and right feeling of the best among each, acting as a check to violence or party feeling on either side.

I should object to the plan of a subordinate house of representatives for women just as I should object to any such plan for working men, and just as I should object to placing the House of Commons in any such subordination to the House of Lords. I dislike all merely class representation, and I still more disapprove of all class subordination. Moreover, one of the useful functions of a House of Representatives is discussion, and the representation of women's point of view, whether through male or female representatives, is part of what would be gained by admitting women to the suffrage. And it is not merely in the House of Commons, but also even in the tone of electioneering and popular politics, that the admission of new elements to the national life is of importance. New topics get discussed, and old ones from new points of view. Different classes of electors are aroused to interest, and to influence one another. Shutting their representatives up separately, even if with equal powers, would be to weaken the educational influence of political contests, and at the same time to intensify their bitterness.

To R. Russell.

By Helen Taylor.

2nd April 1867.

Dear Sir,—I am glad to find that you agree with me in thinking that there is no sufficient evidence that women are morally or intellectually or essentially inferior to men. But in that case I am afraid I no longer think your theory reasonable so far as it goes and complete in itself.

I do not think it indisputable that the physically strongest must necessarily be dominant over the physically weaker in civilised society, since I look upon it as the fundamental purpose of civilisation to redress as much as possible all such natural inequalities, and I think the degree to which they have been redressed one of the best tests of civilisation. 1867 — Aetat. 61.

Nor is superior physical strength invariably even at present the ground of political supremacy, for I suppose there can be little doubt that negroes are physically stronger than white men. But superiority whether of physical strength or of intelligence, having once given any sub-division of humanity an advantage over another, it is always difficult for the dominant class to see that their own particular superiority does not justly entitle them to limit the freedom or check the development of those who chance to be inferior to themselves in some respects. To see this it is necessary to admit in some form or other the law of justice or of the general good as the final test; but I do not at all despair of mankind as a whole becoming capable of recognising it as such, as I understand you yourself to do. I must beg you to excuse the brevity with which I am obliged to write.

To Archdeacon John Allen, on Woman Suffrage.

BLACKHEATH PARK, *27th May* 1867.

DEAR SIR,—I do not anticipate that women would be made less valuable in the home by having their minds directed to the great concerns of mankind, but quite the contrary wherever men's minds are employed as much as they ought to be on those great concerns.

Neither do I think that the adaptation of the work of each person to his or her special endowments and position is a thing to be preappointed by society. I believe that perfect freedom will adjust these things far better than any general regulation can.

1867 — Ætat. 61.

Perhaps I do not differ so much from you as you suppose as to what is likely to be permanently the main occupation of a very great majority of women. But I do not think that the majority should give laws to the individual action of the minority.

I do not undervalue "what teachers of religion can effect," I rate it most highly; but what they *do* effect I rate very low. An example of what they might do has been given lately by the Independent Church at Totnes in severely rebuking those of its members who have been implicated in bribing, and only not expelling them from communion because they expressed the deepest penitence and determination never to offend in that manner again. This gave me the rare satisfaction of finding an existing Church, or branch of a Church, who are actually Christians.

To G. W. Sharp,

who had written to Mill to remonstrate with him on a speech he had made with reference to the Fenians, in which he had laid down the doctrine that revolts were only justified when they had "a reasonable prospect of success."

Blackheath Park, *1st June* 1867.

Sir,—In answer to your letter of 27th May I beg to say that the passage you refer to in my speech at St. James's Hall was correctly reported. And I do not know how anyone could express himself otherwise who believes, as all Englishmen do, that insurrections and revolutions are sometimes justifiable. I will only mention, as cases about which there is in this country scarcely any dispute, the resistance to Charles I., our own Revolution of 1688, the Polish insurrections, and the Italian revolutions by Garibaldi and his friends.

I did not mean that all insurrections, if successful, stand exculpated; the rebellion of the American slave-holders would have been equally guilty and even more detestable if it had succeeded. What I was arguing for was that even those revolutionists who deserve our sympathy ought yet, for the general good, to be subject to legal punishment if they fail. 1867 — Aetat. 61.

To William Wood,

a working man of Hanley. Mill carried on a correspondence with various working men in different parts of the country; and the following is given as a specimen.

Blackheath Park, *1st June* 1867.

Dear Sir,—Your letter of 20th May has interested me very much, as the preceding ones did. You seem to have profited much by your really solid reading, and to have made excellent use of your powers of thought, and I shall be most happy to hear from you on the other subjects you mention. My immediate object in writing is to say that though it is very honourable to you to have relinquished your intention of going to the Paris Exhibition, it is really desirable that you should go, as there is much to be learnt in that way also by a thinking person like yourself; and to make up for the delay it may cause in stocking your bookcase, I would with the greatest pleasure lend you, say for six months at a time, any standard books I have in my library which may be interesting or useful to you, and which I am not immediately using. If you would let me know the subjects which you would like to study at present, I could perhaps recommend to you some of the best books there are in it.

To Dr. W. W. Ireland,

who had written to thank Mill for his moderate attitude during the Indian Mutiny.

Blackheath Park, *22nd June* 1867.

Dear Sir,—I am very glad to receive so favourable an account of your health, and to know that you fully share the feelings I expressed respecting the monstrous

1867 — Aetat. 61. excesses committed and the brutal language used during and after the repression of the Indian Mutiny. It is a duty to speak one's mind openly concerning these things when there is a proper opportunity, and the abusive attack made by some of the military officers in the House on a petition which referred in a very mild manner to these horrors, not only gave the opportunity, but would have made the omission to use it a disgraceful piece of cowardice.

To a Bond Street tradesman,

who had written to ask Mill's support for a movement which it was proposed to inaugurate, for the purpose of bringing "to the notice of Her Majesty the social and political evils attending upon her continued retirement from public life."

By HELEN TAYLOR.

3rd July 1867.

DEAR SIR,—I should certainly endeavour to find time for assisting any movement among my constituents which I think of public importance, and with which I am able to sympathise.

But any movement for attempting to interfere with the full liberty of the Sovereign in the disposal of her private life, so long as the example given is not mischievous, I should look upon with the very strongest disapproval.

I can conceive nothing more likely to be immoral and mischievous in its whole influence on society than any attempt to exact luxurious expenditure as a duty from those placed in high station; and I believe I am not expecting too much from the morality, the public spirit, and the patriotism of those tradesmen who make an immediate profit from such expenditure, in believing that they will be content to live by ministering to the store of luxury and pleasure which is a strong and universal principle in human nature, without seeking to stimulate artificially what, if not kept within close bounds, is the ruin of public and private happiness and morality.

I do not hesitate to say that from the point of view of political economy, the notion entertained by many that such artificial stimulus is good for trade, is founded in error. All which it really does is to transfer gains from some dealers and tradesmen to others; while, by encouraging expenditure which is not reproductive, it tends to diminish instead of increasing the employment for labour and the general wealth of the country.[1]

And even if my convictions on these points were different from what they are, I should still think that the private affections—I will go further, and say the personal tastes—of a constitutional sovereign are entitled to the respectful acquiescence of the people, and ought never to be interfered with until at least they lead to conduct which would excite moral disapprobation, or entail legal penalties on private individuals.

To the Rev. Stephen Hawtrey,

acknowledging two books which he had written on education.

Blackheath Park, 10*th August* 1867.

Dear Sir,—I thank you for your two little books, and regret that until within the last few days I have been prevented from reading them by mere want of time, and by no means through indifference to their contents.

You have not misunderstood my meaning in the St. Andrews address, though the very concise manner in which I was obliged to express everything in that paper may probably have given you a partially incorrect impression of my opinions on education generally. There is much in your view of the subject with which I heartily agree. Your strictures on the system of French schools, by which the boys are never for an instant out of the sight or far from the direct control of a master, I entirely agree

[1] [This paragraph was inserted in Mill's handwriting.]

1867 — Aetat. 61.

in, and I have long thought that while French schoolboys, on the average, are better taught and learn more than English boys, the freer system of the English schools has much to do with the superiority of England over France in the love and practice of personal and political freedom. I also agree to the full in your and Dr. Hook's principle, that real education depends on the contact of human living soul with human living soul. But I am entirely sceptical as to the possibility of accomplishing this in any very considerable degree in a numerous school. Even the family, if it consisted of two hundred or three hundred boys, could not possibly accomplish it. A wise and zealous master may no doubt acquire a certain amount of beneficial moral influence over the boys, and may come into really close contact with the minds and characters of a few among them. In the former of these points, if not in both, St. Mark's School appears to have been singularly successful; and the principles on which it appears to be conducted are well calculated to attain whatever such success is attainable. But while I applaud both your theory and your practice, I have the less hope of finding my opinion radically altered by them, because you seem to me to regard Eton as a favourable specimen of what a school can do in the way of moral and religious training; an opinion from which all that I know of the kind of article turned out annually from Eton into the higher walks of life in this country, leads me strongly to dissent.

To R. W. Emerson,

introducing Lord Amberley.

Blackheath Park, *12th August* 1867.

My dear Sir,—I give this letter to my friend Lord Amberley, not so much for his sake, for he would easily obtain abundant introductions to you, as to make use of the privilege of writing to you which was kindly conferred on me by the letter I had the pleasure of receiving from you last year. Few Englishmen, especially few Englishmen in political life, are more worthy of the privilege of knowing you than Lord Amberley, who, while he is one of the very best of our rising politicians, is even more interested in the intellectual movement of mankind than in the political. He is likely to keep always in the front rank of his contemporaries, and I fully share the general hope of his friends that he will be as useful to the coming generation as his father has been to that which is past.

I wish I could share with him the pleasure and benefit of hearing from your lips your commentary on the present state and prospects of mankind. To me it seems that our two countries, on the whole the two most advanced countries of the world, have just successfully emerged from a crisis, essentially similar though by much the gravest and most trying in the United States, which has shaken up and dislocated old prejudices, set the stagnant waters flowing, and the most certain consequence of which is that all the fundamental problems of politics and society, so long smothered by general indolence and apathy, will surge up and demand better solutions than they have ever yet obtained. To those who like me regard stagnation as the greatest of our dangers and the primary source of almost all social evils, this is a very hopeful and promising state of things, but it will make a most serious demand upon the energies of all cultivated minds, to obtain for thoughts which are not obvious at first sight their just share of influence among the crowd of notions plausible but false or only half true.

To W. T. Thornton,

on an article by him in the *Fortnightly Review*.

Avignon, 19*th October* 1867.

Dear Thornton,—I have just finished reading your chapter in the *Fortnightly*, and I put down my observations while my mind is full of its contents. In execution I think it excellent, and of good augury for the success of the book, for, beginning with so luminous a statement of principles

1867 and going on as it probably will do afterwards to important practical recommendations, it bids fair both to make a more than ordinary impression on those who read it at first, and to be permanently distinguished from other writers on the subject as a systematic treatise. I expect that the subsequent chapters will be equally well executed, and that I shall agree with all or most of your practical conclusions. But in its principles the chapter does not carry me with it. I find in it what I always find where a standard is assumed of so-called justice distinct from general utility and supposed to be paramount whenever the two conflict, viz., that some other standard might just as well have been assumed. Not only do I not admit any standard of right which does not derive its sole authority from utility, but I remark that in such cases an adversary could always find some other maxim of justice equal in authority but leading to opposite conclusions. A great many rules of morality of everyday application are habitually classed as principles of justice. You have selected one of these; Louis Blanc, against whom you are arguing, would select others. You say, the rich are not bound to give employment and subsistence to the poor because they had nothing to do with bringing the poor into the world. Louis Blanc would or might say that the riches and often the very subsistence of the rich would not exist for them if the poor had not been brought into the world, and that to return good for good and the product to the producer is a duty of justice. Again, when he says that the raw material of the earth was not given to a few or to one generation but to the human race, you answer: Admitting this, the vast majority of the poor could never have been born if the earth had not been appropriated; and compensation is only due to them for their share of what the earth could have produced if it had remained unappropriated. To this Louis Blanc might answer, Compensation is due to them not for that only, but for not allowing them to appropriate their share of the soil and to obtain what they by their labour can make that share produce. Again you argue throughout that no question of justice can arise as to the amount for which A hires the labour of B,

Aetat. 61.

because A is not bound to hire B at all. Is not this assuming that what the jurists call a duty of imperfect obligation, *i.e.*, not owed to an assignable individual, is no duty? A may not be bound to hire B, but if he is bound to hire or to benefit some person or persons at his choice, the amount of the benefit may be an essential condition to his fulfilment of the duty. You carry your adherence to one particular view of moral obligation so far as to pronounce a person blameless in point of duty (however odious otherwise) who refuses to save the life of another without an exorbitant payment; I conceive, on the contrary, that it is a serious question whether a person who can save another's life and does not do it even without any hope of reward, ought not to be amenable to the universal law. For these reasons I think that the chapter, though as I said impressive, and though likely to be provocative of thought, will probably not convince a single person. All who did not already agree with you will find maxims of justice equally plausible, and in my estimation quite equally strong, in support of contrary conclusions.

What you may perhaps effect is to make some of the poor, or of their friends, think they ought not to be severe on the rich as men for using the advantages which their position gives them. But the more they are persuaded of that the more determined will they be to upset the social system which gives a few persons these advantages. They may say, It is not A's fault that he is rich; but they will be not the less likely to say, Let us oblige him to divide his riches equally among all and start afresh; and they will never be persuaded by the principles of justice which you have laid down to think this unjust. They would say, it may have been right to allow appropriation as long as unappropriated land was to be had by all, but when all is appropriated, and some are left without, there ought to be a redivision, the γῆς ἀναδάσμος of the Greeks. Nor can they be met, as far as I see, by any arguments but those of expediency—which, once let in, would open the whole question of the rights of the poor and the obligations of the rich, and would, I think, lead to consequences very

1867 — Aetat. 61. different from those which you draw from your theory of justice, though probably not very different from what you would practically recommend.

I have stated strongly the fault I find with your chapter. It would take me a considerable space to set out all the good I find in it. To mention only one thing, the book will be very serviceable in carrying on what may be called the emancipation of political economy—its liberation from the kind of doctrines of the old school (now taken up by well-to-do people) which treat what they call commercial laws, demand and supply for instance, as if they were laws of inanimate matter, not amenable to the will of the human beings from whose feelings, interests, and principles of action they proceed. This is one of the queer mental confusions which will be wondered at by-and-by, and you are helping very much in the good work of clearing it up.

We arrived here a few days ago, and I am settling down to the winter's work, which will not be political or economical but psychological. I am going to prepare, in concert with Bain, a new edition of my father's "Analysis of the Mind," with notes and supplementary matter. This will be not only very useful but a very great relief, by its extreme unlikeness to Parliamentary work and to Parliamentary semi-work or idleness. I hope your health has greatly benefited by your holiday and goes on improving.

To Mr. Oscar Browning.

Mill's letter of 10th August to the Rev. Stephen Hawtrey was shown by him to Mr. Browning, from whom it called forth a remonstrance. The following is Mill's rejoinder:—

Avignon, *26th October* 1867.

Dear Sir,—I was glad to receive your letter, because it is important to know what an Eton master (especially one who admits defects in the institution) says in vindication of Eton. Your defence, however, is mainly directed to other points than those which I have attacked. I have never, I believe, expressed any opinion as to the merits or defects of Eton in comparison with our other public schools. As the one of highest pretensions, I took it as the representative of them all. Nor in what I said of moral results had I particularly in view the grosser and more disreputable vices. I look upon the general moral state of the educated classes of Great Britain, taken in the mass, as essentially low and mean—a mean standard, and a contemptible falling short even of their own standard. You will not expect that I should, in such a letter as the present, enter into a discussion as to the truth of this opinion, or show how it is verified in our whole social state and in the manifestations which proceed from those classes on all public occasions on which the moral aspect of the facts is the predominant one. But if this opinion or anything approaching to it is justified by the fact, I cannot be wrong, as you seem to think, in visiting the shortcomings or vices of a class upon the school (or schools) which chiefly educates that class, not as the authors or primary causes of the evil, but as having at least been signally unsuccessful in counteracting it. The teachers, I apprehend, are only entitled to wash their hands of the shortcomings or vices of their pupils when they acknowledge and deplore them and show that their utmost efforts are steadily exerted in the contrary direction.

When you say that so many of your best boys go into the Guards, you say what amounts to an acknowledgment of utter failure in educating them morally either for the special responsibilities of a governing class or for the universal duties of a man.

I am not called on to deny that Eton, as well as other schools, is far more successful in individual specimens than it is in the mass; and the peculiarities which you mention in its system, the less rigid confinement to a single curriculum and the more intimate association of every boy with his tutor, afford facilities for this, which I have no doubt are often taken good advantage of. But the use made of these facilities depends on what the tutors

1867 — Aetat. 61.

are, and that their general quality should be high is hardly consistent with what you say in your letter of the nepotism, favouritism, and general unfitness of the body who possess "the patronage" of the chief school appointments. From this evil you call on Parliament to relieve you and on me to do what I can to help, and you may rely on my doing so. The Public Schools Bill has been passed over in the House of Commons in the last two sessions not from neglect, but from the incessant occupation of the House with the Reform Bill, and I look forward to its occupying much of the attention of the House in the session next to come.

To Alexander Bain.

St. Véran, *4th November* 1867.

Dear Bain,—I thank you very much for your letter, and for the promise of matter so soon for the edition of the "Analysis." I myself have not begun writing yet, but see my way more and more clearly to the work; I have been reading through Laromiguière, and Maudsley. The first I read chiefly to know what he makes of the active department of human nature (that being his strong point) from the psychological side without the physiological. On that and on other subjects he is meritorious as far as he goes, but too easily satisfied. In the higher departments he leaves everything unexplained, or smuggles the explicandum into its own explanation. His acute remarks sometimes, however, anticipate the thoughts which others have worked out. I was surprised to find in him a complete anticipation of my father's important remark on the ambiguity of the copula. He also anticipated Hamilton's view of abstraction as distinct from generalisation, and his notion of the substantial identity of Nominalism and Conceptualism. From Maudsley I have learnt more; but (as with most of the physiologists) his theories seem to me to go far beyond the evidence. I observe, by the way, that he takes Carpenter's view that *ideation* is the special function of the cerebral hemispheres, sensation (or rather something ill-defined which he calls a residuum) being packed up there by nerve force to be manufactured into idea. If I am not mistaken, you consider this to be obsolete and false theory. Is it not so? *À propos*, why does Maudsley charge me with disparaging physiology either in itself or in its application to mind? It is like Matthew Arnold enumerating me among the enemies of culture. 1867 — Aetat. 61.

Besides these I have been toiling through Stirling's "Secret of Hegel." It is right to learn what Hegel is, and one learns it only too well from Stirling's book. I say only too well, because I found by actual experience of Hegel that conversancy with him tends to deprave one's intellect. The attempt to unwind an apparently infinite series of self-contradictions not disguised but openly faced, really, if persisted in, impairs the acquired delicacy of perception of false reasoning and false thinking which has been gained by years of careful mental discipline with terms of real meaning. For some time after I had finished the book all such words as *reflection*, *development*, *evolution*, &c., gave me a sort of sickening feeling which I have not yet entirely got rid of.

Mansel's article is very poor. It is a satisfaction to know that he could find nothing better to say. It will cost me only a few sentences in another edition. It is tolerably good-tempered, however—much more so than his last.

I am obliged to you for discouraging the idea of my lecturing for University College. I have so little time now that I must keep it for the few things which it is my special duty to do before the night cometh when no man can work. I wonder how you find time to do all you do. I look forward to your new book with much pleasure.

I am glad that Mr. Hunter has done so well with the article for Chambers. That question is making way in a wonderful manner. In the United States the so-called Radical party seems to be taking up in a body the equality of women as it has that of negroes. At least, all the leaders seem to be doing so, Chief Justice Chase among the rest. The Governor of Kansas is said to be actually

1867 — Ætat. 61. canvassing the State for the sanction by popular suffrage of the constitutional amendment which has passed both Houses admitting women to the franchise.

We are very well, and hope to return three months hence in good condition.

To Edwin Chadwick.

Avignon, *4th November* 1867.

Dear Chadwick,—Thanks for sending me a bulletin of your progress. What you say about the effect of your address is encouraging; but it is disheartening to see that in the constituencies generally the only power which seems capable of making head against money is local influence. The great question of next session will be the promised bill against electoral corruption. The advanced Liberals must have *their* rival bill, and I am anxious that all who have thought on the subject, and particularly that you, should put down as heads of a bill all that has occurred to them as desirable on this subject. When all suggestions have been got together the most feasible may be selected, and the best Radicals in and out of the House may be urged to combine in forcing them on the Government.

Whenever you think the time has come to form a committee and raise a subscription for your return to Parliament I beg you to put me down, as I said before, for £50, and I am ready to serve on any London or general committee. I suppose that for the University the committee must consist of members of the constituency, which I am not; but if any others are eligible, I should be glad to be one.

I have read and been duly edified by the paper you mention in the *Journal of the Society of Arts*. I think there is a chance that Ireland may be tried as a *corpus vile* for experimentation on Government management of railways and telegraphs, as well as of other things. Certainly there is little to spoil there; the worst that could happen would

but be one more failure, and there is no necessity to fail. 1867 — Aetat. 61.
Your first paper read at the Academy I have lately received and *will* read, as well as the one which is yet to come. There is no difficulty of principle in legislating for trade unions, but a great deal in detail. For example, on that question of picketing. The principle is that they may persuade, but must not intimidate. But who is there to be persuaded in case of a strike but those who have accepted work, and how are they to be got at except by watching to see who they are? and if persuasion is permitted, can the persuader be withheld from expressing disapprobation, and strongly too? while, as we all know, this expression of disapprobation easily degenerates into illegitimate intimidation. But how or where is the line to be drawn? Can more be done than to prohibit threats? And not even that, if the mischief threatened is not physical, but mere ill will, with its natural expression? Hardly any one who has written on the practical question seems to have faced this difficulty.

To R. W. Emerson,

introducing Mr. John Morley.

AVIGNON, *6th November* 1867.

DEAR SIR,—A few months ago I took the liberty of introducing Lord Amberley to you. I now venture to give an introduction to another friend of mine, of great capacity and promise, Mr. John Morley, one of our best and most rising periodical writers on serious subjects—moral, social, and philosophical, still more than political—and at present editor of the *Fortnightly Review*. I should not thus presume did I not feel confident that you would find Mr. Morley worthy of your attention and interest, both as man and as a thinker.—I am, dear Sir, very truly yours,

J. S. MILL.

To E. W. Young,

in reply to a question concerning a passage in the "Utilitarianism."

Avignon, *10th November* 1867.

1867 — Ætat. 61.

Dear Sir,—I beg to acknowledge your letter of the 23rd ultimo.

I do not claim any greater latitude of making exceptions to general rules of morality on the utilitarian theory than is accorded by moralists on all theories. Every ethical system admits the possibility, and even frequency, of a conflict of duties. In most cases the conflict occasions no great difficulty, because one of the duties is in general obviously paramount to the other. The difficulty arises when the choice is between a very great violation of a duty usually subordinate and a very small infringement of one ordinarily of more peremptory obligation. In such a case the former, I cannot but think, may be the greater moral offence. When I mentioned, as a case of this kind, the case of stealing or taking by force the food or medicine necessary for saving a life, I was thinking rather of saving another person's life than one's own. A much stricter rule is required in the latter than in the former, for the obvious reason that there is more probability of self-deception or of dishonesty. But I am far from saying that the rule should never be relaxed, even when the case is one's own. A runaway slave by the laws of slave countries commits a theft: he steals his own person from his lawful owner. If you say this is not morally theft, because property in a human being ought not to exist, take the case of a child or an apprentice who runs away on account of intolerable ill usage. There is in the doctrine I maintain nothing inconsistent with the loftiest estimation of the heroism of martyrs. There are times when the grandest results for the human race depend on the public assertion of one's convictions at the risk of death by torture. When this is the case martyrdom may be a duty; and in cases when it does not become the duty of all, it may be an admirable act of virtue in whoever does it, and a duty in those who as leaders or teachers are bound to set an example of virtue to others, and to do more for the common faith or cause than a simple believer. I do not know whether what I have written will do anything towards removing your difficulty, but I have not leisure to enter further into the subject.

1867 — Aetat. 61.

To Alexander Bain.

Avignon, *6th December* 1867.

. . . I am very thankful to you for having found, and indeed made, time to do so much for the "Analysis." I like all your notes very much, and they all supply valuable matter, most of which I could not have made out by myself. The only case in which we have gone over the same ground is the case of Association by Resemblance, on which I have also written, to the same general effect as you; and I propose to retain both, as they do not repeat, but enlarge and strengthen one another, and yours is, I think, one of the very best of the present batch. I also have been working pretty vigorously, and have exactly got through the first volume. I have written (as far as regards the rough draft) a great number of minor notes and several long ones, the two longest being on the subjects that you particularly recommended to me, Belief and Nominalism. I have no doubt that I shall get through the second volume in the same manner by the meeting of Parliament. What will remain for the next recess will be the rewriting, which will probably involve much enlargement as well as improvement. But I shall not commence this until your part of the work is finished and before me. I shall be particularly glad of any notes on the chapter on Memory, as that phenomenon is still to me the great unresolvable fact of psychology. It seems to me that it and the problem of Belief are in fact the same, viz., that which I have stated in the chapter on the Ego in my book on Hamilton—the distinction between

1867 — Aetat. 61. recognising something as a mere thought and as an actual fact.

There are two subjects which my knowledge is unequal to, and on which I hope you will give me further assistance. One of them is the direct relation between ideas and states of the nerves. You must have observed that the source of some of the chief imperfections of the "Analysis" is the author's steady refusal to admit any production of ideas by physical causes except through the medium of sensations raising up ideas already associated with them. He carries this so far, as to explain the fact that chronic indigestion excites feelings of anxiety by the circumstance that anxiety disorders the digestion. You have just touched this topic in one of your notes, but in a very summary manner. The other point is one which I could, if necessary, get up from your grammar without troubling you; it is the distinctive characters of the subordinate parts of speech. Your view of the adjective, I believe, coincides with my father's, that it serves for making cross divisions. You could, however, help me very much if you had time to annotate those sections. There is one point which I am quite unequal to. The philology of the "Analysis" on the subject of prepositions, conjunctions, &c., though right in principle, is now obsolete in detail, and I do not know who is the best person to ask to amend it. Can you suggest the right person?

I have not found any help in [Samuel] Bailey for dealing with Nominalism, though he objects to the same parts in my father's exposition which I object to. I have, however, derived some benefit from reading again Bailey's four volumes; but how very very shallow he is! He not only cannot seize any of the less obvious applications of the principle of Association, but he is unfeignedly unable to make out what the writers who speak of such things can possibly mean. Yet at the same time, how plausible! He has scarcely his equal in skimming over the hollow places in philosophy, and putting a smooth face on unsolved difficulties. If he had been in the Forum at the time of Curtius he would not have leaped into the gulf, but would have thrown a platform over it, by which people might walk across without noticing it. When he attempts to confute those who are trying to resolve difficulties which he does not see, he usually does it by formally stating and developing at great length some elementary truth which he fancies to be all there is in the matter. As elementary truths are very often lost sight of, these elaborate enforcements of them are in many cases useful, but are seldom at all germane to the particular controversy. The best thing about him (excepting his chapters on the moral sentiments) is that he is a decided supporter of the "experience hypothesis"; but he is so in a way, and in a sense, peculiarly his own. What used to be called the *mundus intelligibilis*, consisting of all the obscurer notions which have wearied and divided metaphysicians, he disposes of by maintaining that the intelligible world is all perceived through the senses. Why puzzle ourselves about the *necessity* of any of our beliefs? Necessity is a quality of outward parts, and can be seen. We *see* that the theorems of geometry are necessary. How absurd to seek for an explanation or a definition of Cause! We *see* one thing cause another.

How different Herbert Spencer, whose "Psychology" I have been reading for the third time! The second of his four parts is admirable as a specimen of analysis. It is a great satisfaction to find how closely his results coincide with ours. I hope he will not make the book worse instead of better in the projected rewriting, as I am afraid he is going to do with his "Social Statics."

The long miscellaneous chapter with which the second volume of the "Analysis" commences will give us a great deal of occupation, for under the guise of explaining names it contains the author's solutions of most of the great questions of metaphysics proper. I shall hope by-and-by for a full note from you on the Will, whether I write one myself or no. The original generation of Will, which Hartley had the first glimpse of, but which you have been the first to understand thoroughly, will be

1867 much better treated by you than by me. I may perhaps add something of my own on the polemics of the subject.

Aetat. 61.

To Miss Florence Nightingale,

in reply to a letter from her, in which she declined to join the Woman Suffrage Society, though expressing sympathy with its objects.

By Helen Taylor.

Avignon, *31st December* 1867.

Dear Madam,—You will readily believe that only the pressure of constant occupation has prevented me from replying earlier to the interesting letter I received from you in August. If you prefer to do your work rather by moving the hidden springs than by allowing yourself to be known to the world as doing what you really do, it is not for me to make any observations on this preference (inasmuch as I am bound to presume that you have good reasons for it) other than to say that I much regret that this preference is so very general among women. Myself (but then I am a man) I cannot help thinking that the world would be better if every man, woman, and child in it could appear to others in an exactly true light; known as the doer of the work that he does, and striving neither to be under nor overvalued. I am not so "Utopian" as to suppose that bad people will readily lend themselves to this programme; but I confess to considerable regret that good women should so often be almost as fond of false appearances as bad men and women can be; seeking as much to hide their good deeds as the others do to hide their bad ones; forgetting probably the while that they are putting somebody—more or less willing—in the position of a false pretender to merits not his own, but belonging legitimately to the lady who delights to keep in the background.

I know that it often appears, in practical matters, that one can get a great deal of work done swiftly and apparently effectually, by working through others; securing, perhaps, in this way their zealous co-operation instead of their jealous (or perhaps only stupid) obstruction. In the long run, however, I doubt whether any work is ever so well done as when it is done ostensibly and publicly under the direction or at the instigation of the original mind that has seen the necessity of doing it. Whether this is the fact or not, I am quite certain that were the world in general to know how much of all its important work is and always has been done by women, the knowledge would have a very useful effect upon it, and I am not certain that any woman who possesses any talent whatever could make a better use of it in the present stage of the world than by simply letting things take their natural course and allowing it to be known just as if she were a man. I know that this is not pleasant to the sensitive character fostered by the present influences among the best women; but it is to me a question whether the noble and, as I think, heroic enthusiasm of truth and public good ought not in this age to nerve women to as courageous a sacrifice of their most justly cherished delicacy as that of which the early Christian women left an example for the reverent love and admiration of all future time. I have no doubt that the Roman ladies thought them very indelicate.

1867 — Aetat. 61.

In regard to the questions you do me the honour to ask me: first, Are there not evils which press much more hardly on women than not having a vote? Second, May not this, when attained, put women in opposition to those who withhold from them these rights, so as to retard still further the legislation necessary to put them in possession of their rights? Third, Could not the existing disabilities as to property and influence of women be swept away by the legislature as it stands at present?

To answer these questions fundamentally would require only to state fundamental principles of political liberty, and to reiterate that debate so nobly carried on in our own history, whether social happiness or dignity, commercial liberty, religious freedom, or any form of material prosperity, is or is not best founded on political liberty.

It may be granted in the abstract that a ruling power,

1867 — Aetat. 61. whether a monarch, a class, a race, or a sex, could sweep away the disabilities of the ruled. The question is, Has it ever seemed to them urgent to sweep away these disabilities until there was a prospect of the ruled getting political power? More than this, it is probably a question whether it is in human nature that it ever *should* seem to them urgent.

In the same way it may often be a question whether painful symptoms do not press more hardly upon a patient than the hidden disease which is the cause of them. And undoubtedly if the symptoms themselves are killing, the physician had better address himself to them at once, and leave the disease alone for a time. But if the oppressions and miseries under which women suffer are killing, women take a great deal of killing to kill them. God knows I do not undervalue these miseries, for I think that man, and woman too, a heartless coward whose blood does not boil at the thought of what women suffer; but I am quite persuaded that if we were to remove them all to-morrow, in ten years new forms of suffering would have arisen, for no earthly power can ever prevent the constant, unceasing, unsleeping, elastic pressure of human egotism from weighing down and thrusting aside those who have not the power to resist it. Where there is life there is egotism, and if men were to abolish every unjust law to-day, there is nothing to prevent them from making new ones to-morrow; and moreover what is of still greater importance, new circumstances will constantly be arising for which fresh legislation will be needed. And how are you to ensure that fresh legislation will be just, unless you can either make men perfect, or give women an equal voice in their own affairs? I leave you to judge which is the easiest.

What, however, constitutes an even more pressing and practical reason for endeavouring to obtain the political enfranchisement of women, instead of endeavouring to sweep away any or all of their social grievances, is, that I believe it will be positively easier to attain this reform than to attain any single one of all the others, all of which must inevitably follow from it. To prefer to sweep away any of these others first, is as though one were to prefer to cut away branch after branch; giving more labour to each branch than one need do to the trunk of the tree. 1867 — Aetat. 61.

The third question, whether there is not danger of political partisanship and bitterness of feeling between men and women, is also a question which I think has been asked and answered in other departments of politics. It has been asked and answered too, though the answer has been different from that which we most of us approve of in politics, in some cases of marriage. To prevent quarrels, it has been thought best to make one party absolute master of both. No doubt if women can never do anything in politics except for and through men, they cannot be partisans against men. No doubt, where you have death, you have none of the troubles of life. But if women were to prove possessed with ever so great a spirit of partisanship, and were they to call forth thereby ever so intense partisanship on the part of men, and were they, as the weakest, to be drawn to any extremities, I don't see that the result could be very different from what it is at present, inasmuch as I apprehend that the present position of women in every country in the world is exactly measured by the personal and family affections of men, and that every modification for the better in women's absolute annihilation and servitude is at present owing not to any sense of abstract right or justice on the part of men, but to their sense of what they would like for their own wives, daughters, mothers, and sisters. Political partisanship against the mass of women will not among civilised men diminish the sense of what is due to the objects of their private affections. But I believe on the contrary, that the dignity given to women in general by the very fact of their being able to be political partisans, is likely to be itself a means of raising men's estimation of what is due to them. So that if men come to look upon women as a large number of unamiable but powerful opponents, and a small number of dearly loved and charming persons, I think men will think more highly of women, and will feel less disposed to use badly any superior power that after all they them-

1867 — Aetat. 61. selves may still possess, than if they look upon women, as I think men generally do at present, as a few dearly loved, pre-eminently worthy, and charming persons, and a great number of helpless fools.

On the whole, then, I think, firstly, that political power is the only security against every form of oppression; secondly, that at the present day in England it would be easier to attain political rights for such women as have the same claims as enfranchised men, than to obtain any other considerable reform in the position of women; thirdly, I see no danger of party spirit running high between men and women, and no possibility of its making things worse than they are if it did.

Finally, I feel some hesitation in saying to you what I think of the responsibility that lies upon each one of us to stand steadfastly, and with all the boldness and all the humility that a deep sense of duty can inspire, by what the experience of life and an honest use of our own intelligence has taught us to be the truth. I will confess to you that I have often stood amazed at what has seemed to me the presumption with which persons who think themselves humble set bounds to the capacities of improvement of their fellow-creatures, think themselves qualified to define how much or how little of the divine light of truth can be borne by the world in general, assume that none but the very *élite* can see what is perfectly clear to themselves, and think themselves permitted to dole out in infinitesimal doses that daily bread of truth upon which they themselves live, and without which the world must come to an end. When I see this to me inexplicable form of moderation in those who nevertheless believe that the truth of which they have got hold really is the truth, I rejoice that there are so many presumptuous persons who think themselves bound to say what they think true, who think that if they have been fortunate enough to get hold of a truth they cannot do a better service to their fellow-creatures than by saying it openly; who think that the truth that has not been too much for themselves will not be too much for others; who think that what they have been capable of seeing, other people will be capable of seeing too, without a series of delicately managed gradations. I even go so far as to think that we owe it to our fellow-creatures and to posterity to struggle for the advancement of every opinion of which we are deeply persuaded. I do not, however, mean to say that there is any judge but our own conscience of how we can best work for the advancement of such truths, nor do I mean to say that it may not be right for any of us endowed with special faculties to choose out special work, and to decline to join in work for which we think others better qualified, and which we think may impede us for our own peculiar province. Therefore, while I have seen with much regret that you join in so few movements for the public good, I have never presumed to think you wrong, because I have supposed that your abstinence arose from your devotion to one particular branch of public-spirited work.

CHAPTER XI

1868

To the Rev. L. J. Bernays,

showing Mill's view of the form which State-education ought to take.

Avignon, *8th January* 1868.

1868 — Aetat. 61.

Dear Sir,—I thank you for the opportunity of reading the little pamphlet on education. All that the author says against centralising the education of the country in the hands of Government is very just, and I entertain the strongest objections to any plan which would give a practical monopoly to schools under Government control. But I have never conceived compulsory education in that sense. What I understood by it is that all parents should be required to have their children taught certain things, being left free to select the teachers, but the efficiency of the teaching being ensured by a Government inspection of schools, and by a real and searching examination of pupils. The actual provision of schools by a local rate would not necessarily be required if any schools already existed in the locality which were sufficient for the purpose, or which could be made so by aid from the local funds and by inspection. Moreover, a mere consolidation of the already existing school endowments, now mostly jobbed or, at best, very insufficiently applied, would probably enable good instruction to be provided in all localities in which it is not already afforded by private exertions. Of course there must be a Government Department to control the employment of these funds, but it does not follow that the teachers need be appointed or directly controlled by any public office. The control might rest in a school committee chosen from the locality itself, perhaps by a mixed system of election and nomination, and entrusted with considerable latitude as to all details. These are all points for mature consideration; but a thorough system of instruction for the whole country we must have; and I do not see anything short of a legal obligation which will overcome the indifference, the greed, or the really urgent pecuniary interest of parents.

To Charles Hayes, a storekeeper of Leeds,

in reply to a letter from him suggesting the imposition of a tax of 6d. per ton on coal, to be used for paying off the National Debt.

Blackheath Park, *15th February* 1868.

Dear Sir,—I should be happy to support almost any feasible plan which would ensure the appropriation of a surplus revenue to the reduction of the National Debt. The mode you propose of effecting this is strongly recommended by the close connection of the subject with the limitation of our coal supply, and plans similar to it have sometimes been suggested. For my own part I am unable to see the force of the strong objection which many public men entertain to any tax on coals. As for the iron manufacturers, Mr. Plimsoll has shown in his letters to the *Times* that the coal they waste amounts to as great a quantity as their Belgian rivals consume altogether, and it would do good instead of harm to compel them by a tax to be more economical. No plan for reducing the Debt has a better claim to consideration than yours, but until it has been more discussed it is impossible to come to a positive opinion in favour of it.

To Lindsey Aspland,

who retired from the Jamaica Committee on account of the decision to prosecute Governor Eyre.

Blackheath Park, *23rd February* 1868.

Dear Sir,—I am sorry that the resolution adopted by the Jamaica Committee should deprive them of the benefit

1868 — Aetat. 61. of your co-operation. But the fact that it does so reveals a fundamental difference of opinion between you and the majority of the Committee as to the mode in which a struggle like that which they have undertaken should be carried on. This is not like a contest for some political improvement, in which the only question is whether it shall be obtained a little sooner or a little later. Ours is, morally, a protest against a series of atrocious crimes, and politically an assertion of the authority of the criminal law over public delinquents. This protest and vindication must be made now or never; and to relinquish the effort while a single unexhausted chance remains would be, in my estimation, to make ourselves to some extent participants in the crime. Suppose it to be certain that we shall fail in bringing the criminal to justice, still there will be a portion of the nation that will have held out to the last and refused to condone the guilt, and it is better for the future that even one person should have done this than that the national judgment should go in favour of the criminal with universal, at least passive, acquiescence. You talk of leaving Eyre to contempt. What he would be left to is boastful triumph, followed by the fruits of victory in the shape of lucrative Government employment, probably with power to do again what he has done, and with undiminished if not increased disposition to do it. He has, after years of skulking, come over and defied us doubtless for this express purpose, and were we not to accept his challenge we should be justly reproached for our past conduct towards him, since we should shrink from meeting him before the tribunal which we have been invoking as the proper judge of his guilt or innocence.

To Nicholas Kilburn,

in reply to a letter asking whether it was true that Mill believed in Spiritualism.

By Helen Taylor.

Blackheath Park, 18*th March* 1868.

Dear Sir,—I have to thank you for your enclosure and inquiry. It is the first time I have ever heard that I was a believer in Spiritualism, and I am not sorry to be able to suppose that some of the other names I have seen mentioned as believers in it are no more so than myself. 1868 — Aetat. 61.

For my own part, I not only have never seen any evidence that I think of the slightest weight in favour of Spiritualism, but I should also find it very difficult to believe any of it on any evidence whatever. And I am in the habit of expressing my opinion to that effect very openly whenever the subject is mentioned in my presence.

You are at liberty to make any use you please of this letter.

To James Trask,

on compulsory insurance.

Blackheath Park, *22nd April* 1868.

Dear Sir,—I beg to acknowledge your letter of the 20th instant and its enclosures.

Even labourers who have the means of saving from their wages (which cannot be said of the first person mentioned in your letter) must, if they have not done so, be relieved at times of temporary inability to work; but there ought to be legal means of recovering the amount from their wages as soon as they are again able to earn. By the Poor Law of 1834 power was, I believe, given to Guardians to grant temporary loans to persons in distress; certainly this power was given in the original Bill, and I am not aware of its having been struck out, though I am surprised at never having heard of its being used.

I do not think it beyond the competence of a Government to compel all its subjects to insure against the various evils of life—which is the principle of your proposed National Friendly Society. But I think it much better simply to afford them facilities for doing so without employing compulsion, and I do not believe that a compulsory measure would be carried, unless long and thorough previous discussion had led the working classes themselves to demand it. Neither, I think, would it even be

1868 felt to be just to take compulsory measures against the improvidence of the labouring classes, leaving that of all other classes free.

— Aetat. 61.

To Peter Deml, a journalist of Vienna.

Blackheath Park, *22nd April* 1868.

Dear Sir,—I beg to acknowledge your letter of the 14th instant.

Your purpose of endeavouring to improve the popular discussion of the remedies for poverty by substituting reason and science for vague declamation is most laudable, and commands my strongest sympathy. You will render a great service by diverting the attention of thinkers and of the working classes to the close connection between the rate of wages and the ratio of population to the means of subsistence and employment. At the same time you doubtless agree with me in thinking that this is only one of several causes which conspire to determine the good or bad material condition of the labourer. It would not be a correct view of my opinions to suppose that I think everything wrong in the doctrines of Socialism; on the contrary, I think that there are many elements of truth in them, and that much good may be done in that direction, especially by the progress of the co-operative movement, now so successfully commenced in most of the leading countries of Europe. Since you do me the honour to be a reader of my writings, I may be permitted to refer you, on this subject, to the chapter of my "Principles of Political Economy" entitled "The Probable Future of the Labouring Classes," which expresses in a sufficiently distinct manner the position I take up with regard to this class of questions.

During the Jamaica episode, and the prosecution of Governor Eyre, popular feeling ran very high in this country. Mill received a number of abusive letters, threats of assassination, &c., which he pre-

served with his other letters. As may be supposed, 1868
they bear the signs of having been written by ignorant Aetat. 62.
and illiterate persons. One begins, "The Mill atheist of Westminster, lately M.P., but now a dog." Another begins, "John, your conduct is extremely vindictive, malicious, and disgraceful." A third threatens to stab him the next time he entered Westminster. But these abuses and threats had very little effect upon him.

To Mr. Goldwin Smith,

at the time of the prosecution of Governor Eyre.

Blackheath Park, *28th May* 1868.

My dear Goldwin Smith,— . . . It would be difficult to find any one less likely to be discomposed by the abuse heaped upon him than myself, or, I believe, than Taylor. The worst of all this is the indication which it gives of the spirit of our higher classes and of a considerable portion of the public.

À propos, I receive abusive letters at the rate of three or four a week, and the other day I received one threatening me with assassination. They are all anonymous, and as ineffably stupid as one might expect.

To W. S. Pratten,

one of Mill's constituents, who wrote to remonstrate with him on his action in the case of Governor Eyre.

By Helen Taylor.

Blackheath Park, *9th June* 1868.

Dear Sir,—I regret deeply that any one who has ever done me the honour to vote for me can ever disapprove of the course I thought it my duty to take in regard to Mr. Eyre's proceedings in Jamaica, because I have never

1868 — Aetat. 62.

in the whole course of my life felt myself called upon to take practical action on any matter on which I felt more clear as to the course indicated by the principles which I hold and have always endeavoured to promulgate. In regard to Mr. Eyre personally, my feelings towards him, so far as I can be said to have had any, before I knew of his conduct in Jamaica, were favourable, inasmuch as I knew of him only as a traveller whose narrative I had read with interest. Neither has anything ever occurred, directly or indirectly, in the whole course of my life to arouse the smallest personal feeling of any sort in me towards Mr. Eyre as a private man. But I cannot say that it is possible to me as a man to regard Mr. Eyre's conduct in Jamaica without the deepest indignation, or as an Englishman without a sentiment of humiliation: nor can I pretend that I can regard without abhorrence and contempt the man who, knowing himself to be guilty, in the eyes of many disinterested persons, of the wanton torture and death of many hundred men and women, can be content to shelter himself under any shield whatever against a judicial examination, and does not eagerly challenge and earnestly invite the closest possible scrutiny into whatever justification he thinks that he can urge. To me it appears that the conduct of Mr. Eyre since his return to England shows a callousness to human suffering and a contempt for his fellow-men which alone go far to show his total unfitness for any station of authority over them. Yet if all human sympathies could be laid aside altogether, the importance of instituting a judicial inquiry into the proceedings in Jamaica would still be paramount in the eyes of all thinking persons who look upon law and justice as the foundation of order and civilisation. If the majority of any nation were willing to allow such events to pass unquestioned, I have no hesitation in saying that all the ties of civil society would in that nation be at the mercy of accident. There would be no principle in the minds of men to bind civilised society together. Happily, I am fully convinced that the great majority of the English nation does desire judicial inquiry into these events. Were I not so convinced I should be ashamed of my country. Nevertheless, even if I were not convinced of this, I should think it my duty to express in the clearest, the most public, and the most practical way in my power my opinion of the importance of checking the lawlessness of which Mr. Eyre's conduct in Jamaica appears to my humble judgment a flagrant example. I believe from a perfectly calm and disinterested examination of the subject that Mr. Eyre has either been guilty of, or has tolerated under his authority, crimes of violence and cruelty which no man of even ordinarily tender conscience or good heart could be capable of. The detestation of the right-judging among his fellow-creatures might, however, in some cases be a sufficient punishment for this. At all events, while the world is as full of crime as it is, I do not suppose that, however strong my feelings about it, I should have considered myself as peculiarly called upon to interfere against him. But I do so consider myself as an Englishman called upon to protest against what I believe to be an infringement of the laws of England; against acts of violence committed by Englishmen in authority calculated to lower the character of England in the eyes of all foreign lovers of liberty; against a precedent that could justly inflame against us the people of our dependencies; and against an example calculated to brutalise our own fellow-countrymen. Nor would any amount of declamation, public or private, political or literary, have been to my mind a proper mode of chastising what I believe to be the offence committed, so long as it was uncertain whether the laws of England are not impotent to restrain such lawless proceedings for the future or punish them in the past. The humblest or obscurest English man or woman, animated with that respect for law and love of liberty on which the greatness of England has been founded in past times and depends in the future, ought in my opinion to contribute his part towards a calm and legal settlement of this question. And it is at once amazing and humiliating to me that any one who has done me the honour to read, much

1868 — Aetat. 62.

1868 — Aetat. 62. less to approve, of any of my writings, could for one instant doubt that I should think so. I can understand that any one might doubt what might be my opinion of Mr. Eyre's conduct. I can understand that those who have not examined it as carefully as I have done might expect me to approve of it. But I cannot understand that any one should expect me not to desire an examination of it, conducted in the fairest and most open manner that could be attained. That the real or supposed crimes of men in authority should be subject to judicial examination is the most important guarantee of English liberty; and I am not aware that any reason has ever yet been brought forward why Mr. Eyre should be the sole and solitary exception to this liability.

In regard to the petition concerning which you ask my opinion (that of one of the Foreign Affairs Committees against the Abyssinian war), I did not present it because I agreed in it, but because I think members of Parliament should extend as widely as possible the limits within which they accept petitions to present. The power of petitioning is very important, especially to all unrepresented citizens, and as it can only be exercised through members of Parliament I think they should throw as few obstacles as possible in the way. Those who approve of my little book on "Liberty" can scarcely think me inconsistent in this opinion. I have always thought and often said that this country was bound to recover its envoy even by war if necessary, and the manner in which the war has been carried on by Sir R. Napier does honour to him and to our country. Its success is probably owing in great measure to the spirit of law and order which reduced the sufferings of war to the lowest possible point amongst the people in whose country it was carried on. The continuance of hostilities after the prisoners had been surrendered is the one point which requires and which will probably receive explanation.

To a Correspondent,

who asked Mill's assistance in obtaining him a post as teacher. This he found difficult to obtain on account of his religious views.

All but the last paragraph by HELEN TAYLOR.

BLACKHEATH PARK, *13th June* 1868.

DEAR SIR,—I should be most happy were it in my power to further your wishes in regard to independent employment, in which I most heartily sympathise: but there are few persons less able than myself to do so, and although I can sincerely say that I shall not forget your name should any occasion offer itself to me, yet I cannot hold out any hope that I am likely to meet with one. 1868 — Aetat. 62.

In regard to the points on which you say that the convictions in which you were brought up have been shaken, I fully agree with you that it would not be right for you to attempt to inculcate those convictions. I think, however, that you will find them, at least as stated in your letter, as difficult to disprove as to prove: except, indeed, in the case of prayer. I think you have omitted to mention one effect that prayer may reasonably be said to have on the mind, and which may be granted to it by those who doubt as well as by those who admit divine interposition in answer to it; I mean the effect produced on the mind of the person praying, not by the belief that it will be granted, but by the elevating influence of an endeavour to commune and to become in harmony with the highest spiritual ideal that he is capable in elevated moments of conceiving. This effect may be very powerful in clearing the moral perceptions and intensifying the moral earnestness. It may be so powerful as to leave it open to question whether it is produced solely by the internal action of human nature itself or by a supernatural influence, and this question will have to be resolved by

1868 — Aetat. 62. each individual from his personal experience. I know of no proof sufficient to entitle psychologists to assert it as *certain* that the whole of this influence is reducible to the known elements of human nature, however highly probable they may think it. As to the other two points, the existence of a Deity and the immortality of the soul, it would be still less possible to bring negative proof to bear upon such questions that would be conclusive to all minds. You might perhaps find much to interest you on these matters in Mr. Herbert Spencer's "First Principles" and in Mr. Grote's work on Plato.

As to the sentence you quote from my "Utilitarianism"; when I said that the general happiness is a good to the aggregate of all persons I did not mean that every human being's happiness is a good to every other human being; though I think in a good state of society and education it would be so. I merely meant in this particular sentence to argue that since A's happiness is a good, B's a good, C's a good, &c., the sum of all these goods must be a good.

To G. K. Holden, Member of the Legislative Council of New South Wales.

Blackheath Park, *5th July* 1868.

Dear Sir,—I hope you will pardon me for the delay in acknowledging your letter, dated as long ago as February. Parliamentary business is so exacting, and I receive such a multitude of letters which require an immediate answer, that I am often obliged to put aside for a time those which admit of delay.

Your impression is quite correct that I was applied to from Victoria in consequence of the use made by protectionists of the passage in my "Political Economy" which speaks of the occasional benefit in a young country of aiding the naturalisation of an industry suited to the circumstances. I did, at that time, return an answer, which was published in a Victoria newspaper, to the effect that if this encouragement took the form of a protecting duty, it should be strictly limited to a moderate number of years, and not continued beyond. I have not altered the opinion that such encouragement is sometimes useful, and that in many cases the most just mode in which it could be given is that of a temporary protecting duty, on condition that it should be known and declared to be merely temporary, and of no very long duration. But I confess that I almost despair of this general understanding being ever practically established. I find that in Australia, protection is not advocated in this form or for this purpose, but that the vulgarest and most exploded fallacies are revived in its support. As far as I can perceive, those who contend for protection in Australia mean it to be as permanent as any other legislative arrangements; and hold to all the false theories on the subject, of which Europe is rapidly ridding itself, and which are declining even in America. In such a state of opinion as this I should resist, with my utmost strength, any protection whatever, because it is far easier to withstand these false and pernicious doctrines before they have been carried into practice to any serious extent, than after powerful protected interests have been allowed to grow up under their influence.

Allow me to express my high sense of the ability and effectiveness of your letter, signed H., on this question. Such clear expositions of the principles of the subject are what can alone be trusted to for combating any natural prejudices in a free and popularly governed country.

I well remember your exertions for the adoption of Mr. Hare's system in the election of the Legislative Council, and the very valuable report in which you discussed the subject. The debates in the British Parliament which have since occurred may well have struck you by the amount of ignorance they disclosed; but great and daily progress is making in the correction of that ignorance, and many political men, including some of the most active and intelligent leaders of the working classes, are

1868 — Aetat. 62. now converted to Mr. Hare's system, in principle at least, and frequently even in its detail. The doctrine of personal representation is making the same rapid progress among thinking minds on the Continent and in America. But as you are probably in correspondence with Mr. Hare, you have access to the best source of information on this subject.

To the Secretary of the Society for the Prevention of Cruelty to Animals.

BLACKHEATH PARK, *26th July* 1868.

DEAR SIR,—I am much honoured by the wish of the President and Committee of your Society to include me in the list of its Vice-Presidents; but though I think the Society very useful, and have been for many years one of its members and subscribers, I do not feel it consistent with my principles of action to identify myself to any greater extent with the management, while it is thought necessary or advisable to limit the Society's operations to the offences committed by the uninfluential classes of society. So long as such scenes as the pigeon-shooting exhibitions lately commented upon in the newspapers take place under the patronage and in the presence of the supposed élite of the higher classes, male and female, without attracting the notice of your Society, this respect of persons, though it may be prudent, is too foreign to my opinions and feelings to allow of my sharing in any, even indirect, responsibility for it.

I cannot help thinking that anything of the sort is peculiarly to be regretted, because the Society really includes so many of the upper classes (and does them so much honour) that an attack upon the cruelty of the less enlightened among themselves would come with the best possible grace from them, who cannot be accused of class-feeling.

To James Henderson, of Glasgow,

recommending Edwin Chadwick as a candidate for Parliament.

Avignon, *22nd August* 1868.

Dear Sir,—I have heard with much gratification that it is under the consideration of some of the advanced Liberals to put forward my old friend Mr. Chadwick for one of the districts of Scottish boroughs; for not only do I deem Mr. Chadwick eminently qualified for a seat in the House of Commons, both for the work he would himself do and for that which he would be the cause of in others, but I should consider his absence from the next Parliament as a public misfortune. Any constituency that returns him to Parliament will, in my opinion, be doing a public service of great value, and would do itself still further honour if he were to be returned free of expense.

1868 — Aetat. 62.

I have known Mr. Chadwick with considerable intimacy from the time when both of us were very young men. He was then quite unknown to the public, but was already active in a quiet way, in standing up against jobbing and oppression; and it is within my knowledge (for I was aware of every step in the proceedings) that within a very short interval he had the principal share in defeating two different attempts to commit great public and private wrong. He had even then bestowed much thought and study on the details of administration, and some papers which he wrote on administrative subjects attracted the notice of Mr. Senior,[1] who appointed him an Assistant-Commissioner under the original Commission of Poor Law Inquiry, in which capacity he displayed such superior ability that he was made a member of the Commission itself, for the express purpose of assisting in drawing up the new Poor Law. No one, except Mr. Senior, had so great a share as Mr. Chadwick in originating all that was

1 [W. Senior, one of the Poor Law Commissioners.]

1868 — Ætat. 62. best in the Poor Law of 1834, and had his counsel been taken in all respects, as it was in some—had his clauses respecting the education of pauper children not been rejected in the House of Lords—had his plans been accepted for the separation of the sick, the lunatic, the old, and the young from one another and from the able-bodied, and their distribution in different houses with a view to totally different modes of treatment, not only would the vast expense of administrating the Union Workhouses have been in a great measure saved, but the greatest blots upon our present Poor Law administration would have been effectually provided against.

The next of Mr. Chadwick's great public services was as a member of the Factory Commission, which proposed and carried the limitation of the labour of children in factories to six hours. From that time Mr. Chadwick has never ceased to occupy himself with the improvement of the conditions of factory operatives. He was the proposer, and has been the indefatigable apostle of the half-time school system, by which the education of the children of the operative classes has been made compatible with the necessities of the family. He proposed but did not succeed in carrying a measure for the protection of the operatives by making masters pecuniarily responsible for accidents. He has been from the beginning the leading mind of the sanitary movement which has done so much, and will do much more to improve not only the health, but the moral and economical condition of the working population generally, and especially of its most neglected portions. Almost as much of his time and thoughts has been employed upon the great question of public education, in its most difficult department, its business details; and I know of no one capable of being of so much use to our future ministers and legislators in forming an organised plan by which the most efficient education can be given to the whole people at the smallest sacrifice either to the public or to individuals. I have touched only on main points, for to go through all the minor but important matters of public interest which he has helped forward would take up far too much time and space. I may say in brief that he is one of the contriving and organising minds of the age; a class of mind of which there are very few, and still fewer who apply those qualities to the practical business of government. He is, however, one of the few men I have known who have a passion for the public good; and nearly the whole of his time is devoted to it in one form or another.

With respect to political questions in the narrower sense of the word, I may say that Mr. Chadwick was highly esteemed by Mr. Bentham, the father of enlightened Radicalism; that throughout life I have seldom had occasion to differ from him on subjects of that nature; and should we be returned to Parliament, there are few whose vote I should expect oftener to agree with mine on all subjects involving the principles of popular government.

You are at liberty to make any use you think well of this letter.

To CHARLES GILPIN, Liberal M.P. for Northampton, in reply to a letter in which he had mildly protested against Mill's support of Bradlaugh against himself and Lord Henley.

By HELEN TAYLOR.

AVIGNON, *12th September* 1868.

DEAR SIR,—I should be sorry indeed if your election could be perilled, but I do not think it can be. I understood from Mr. Bradlaugh not only that he had no intention of standing against you, but that he considered your election certain; and I hope you will not allow yourself to be persuaded that one of the mere rank and file Liberals can be as valuable in the House of Commons as yourself. But (although for totally different reasons) I think Mr. Bradlaugh also would be a very valuable member of Parliament. He also holds opinions not cut after the pattern of some three hundred or so other Liberal members of Parliament,

1868 — Aetat. 62.

and I think him able to sustain them with ability which would give them effect. This is what we want in the House of Commons, and while it is most important to uphold honest and honourable men, faithful supporters of our own party like Lord Henley against Tories and lukewarm Liberals, I do not think that their claims ought to be allowed to prevail against the claims of exceptional men. Where there are two men to sustain one opinion and only one man to sustain another, the one is a more valuable man than either of the two; and after all, the men willing to vote against the Irish Church are at least two hundred to one as against men holding original opinions of their own like yourself and Mr. Bradlaugh. Moreover, the good average Liberal, especially if he is a man of rank, is likely to have a better chance for a larger number of constituencies than such a man as Mr. Bradlaugh; you will see that I urged upon Mr. Bradlaugh the importance of not allowing a Tory to step in, and this seems to me the only important consideration in the matter. You will perhaps let me add that I could scarcely forbear smiling at the modesty which could let you suppose that *you* were the candidate against whom Mr. Bradlaugh's efforts are likely to have the greatest effect, even if he did oppose you, which I sincerely believe he would not do.

To Charles Eliot Norton.

Avignon, 24*th September* 1868.

. . . There is no doubt that the feeling of the mass of the working classes in England is very much alienated from the propertied classes. They are very strongly imbued with a sense of the opposition of interest between the receivers of wages and the payers of them. But I do not think that this feeling has reached the point of personal hatred between classes. I think that the operatives have confidence in the goodwill towards them of many persons in the higher and middle ranks, and that experience has taught them to expect that the others will be brought round gradually by the joint influence of conviction, persuasion, and prudence. The intelligent, who are the politically active part of the working classes, are not impatient; they have a sincere dread of the mass of brutal ignorance behind them, and have consequently set themselves to demand very vigorously a real national education. This they will soon obtain, and it will alter, in an incalculable degree, all the bad elements of the existing state of things. Already the aspirations of the workmen to the improvement of their physical condition are pointing not so much to anything to be done directly by the State as to what they can do for themselves by co-operation. Revolution and civil war will not come from their side of the question, for when their minds are sufficiently made up the existing political institutions are sufficient to carry into execution their will.

The political enfranchisement of women, whenever it takes place, will further strengthen the influences opposed to violence and bloodshed. The only question which may possibly become dangerous is that of the land. There are signs of a rapidly growing conviction in the operative classes that the land ought not to be private property but should belong to the State. This opinion, which has always seemed to me fundamentally just, may perhaps come to maturity before the landholding classes are prepared even to listen to it; and in that case there will be bad blood and violent class animosities: but even then, as far as I am able to anticipate the future, it seems to me that the probabilities are in favour of the settlement of the question by a succession of compromises without coming to blows.

TO THOMAS BEGGS, a member of Mill's election committee at Westminster,

in reply to a letter of protest about Mill's subscription to Bradlaugh's election expenses.

AVIGNON, *27th September* 1868.

DEAR SIR,—I am exceedingly sorry that you should have had any trouble or annoyance in consequence of my

1868 — Ætat. 62.

subscription for the election of Mr. Bradlaugh. In giving him this aid I did not take at all into consideration his religious opinions, with which, as practical politicians, we have nothing whatever to do. Though, like yourself, I know his early career only by report, I have understood that he was formerly violent and intemperate in his language, a defect which it is to be hoped may disappear with time, but which, if it does not, he will share with some of the best-known men in the House of Commons; for there are several members of Parliament whom few working men at all events would be disposed to consider models of temperance in speech, yet whom all parties are willing to see in the House because they are forcible exponents of a particular point of view. It may be said for Mr. Bradlaugh in palliation that persecution naturally provokes violence, and at the time when he commenced men were still put in prison for expressing his opinions; indeed, if I remember right, he himself has been imprisoned for them.

But with regard to Mr. Bradlaugh's political opinions and conduct all that I know is greatly in his favour. No one who is active in politics on the Radical side seems to me less open than he is to the much-launched accusations of being a demagogue or a panderer to popular prejudice. He seems to me a thinking man, who forms his opinions for himself, and defends them with equal ardour whether they attract or alienate those whom he seeks to influence. I may mention as one example, that he is a strenuous supporter of representation of minorities, which, whether right or wrong (a thing I do not now discuss), at least proves him to be no friend to the despotism of the greater number; and as a second example his earnest Malthusianism, which places him in opposition to a vast mass of popular prejudice, supposed to be particularly rife among the Radicals of the working classes. If the capability of taking and the courage of maintaining such views as these is not a recommendation, to impartial persons, of an extreme Radical politician, what is?

With regard to his standing against Liberals, or rather against a Liberal, for to my excellent friend Mr. Gilpin he disclaims all opposition, I am extremely desirous that you should fully understand my opinion on that subject. Undoubtedly the point of first importance at the present juncture, is to return to Parliament supporters of Mr. Gladstone and of the disendowment of the Irish Church. This object ought not to be sacrificed to any other, and a member whose vote can be relied on for this purpose ought not to be opposed at any risk of bringing in a Tory. You are aware that I have cautioned Mr. Bradlaugh on this point, as I do everyone to whom I give any advice about the approaching elections. But the importance of the immediate struggle ought not to make us forget that the Parliament we are going to elect has much other work to do besides this—that we are looking to it for a general revision of our institutions and for making a commencement of effort against the many remediable evils which infest the existing state of society. Already the too exclusive attention to one great question has caused it to be generally remarked by friends and enemies, that there will be very little new blood in the future Parliament, that the new House of Commons will be entirely composed of the same men, or the same kind of men, as the old one. Now I do not hesitate to say that this is not what ought to happen. We want, in the first place, representatives of the classes now first admitted to the representation. And in the next place, we want men of understanding whose minds can admit ideas not included in the conventional creed of Liberals or of Radicals, and men also of ardent zeal, even if not always according to discretion, for it will all be wanted to make any impression against the force of at least negative resistance of those who are satisfied with their own position in life, and without meaning any harm are careless of evils because they do not feel them. Were Mr. Bradlaugh in Parliament, his zeal and ability would be of great use, and his violence, if he were still violent, could do no harm except to himself; and he is a much less able man than I take him for, if he ever again repeats such errors of violence as those he is accused of.

These are the reasons why I should be glad to see Mr.

1868 — Ætat. 62. Bradlaugh in the House of Commons, and why, though I should have preferred to see him displace a Tory, I still desire his success even against Lord Henley, who, moreover, would probably have much less difficulty than Mr. Bradlaugh in obtaining another seat. And I hope to stand acquitted, even if not justified in your eyes, and in those of the friends whom you mention. I can say most sincerely that no one more thoroughly disapproves than I do any conduct or expressions needlessly offensive to the reverential feeling of any one, even if I had less sympathy of feeling with him than I have with many pious minds.

To a Westminster Voter,

in reply to a letter asking whether Mill's subscription to Bradlaugh's election expenses was a fact.

By HELEN TAYLOR.

AVIGNON, *9th October* 1868.

DEAR SIR,—The letter of which you enclosed a copy was written by me. I believe there can be no doubt that Mr. Bradlaugh is a very fair representative of the opinions of a very large and important portion of the working men of England. I, who have always maintained that the working classes do not form a homogeneous mass all exactly like one another, as we have been often told they do by their opponents, of course admit most readily that Mr. Bradlaugh is no fair representative of other large and important sections of the working class. But as there are in the House of Commons, and ought to be, representatives of the Quakers, the Roman Catholics, many of the various Dissenters, as well as of the Church of England and the Jews, so I do not see why the working classes may not have one representative of opinions which are indisputably extensively rife among many of them, however distasteful these opinions may be to many others.

I say all this as regards what, if I understand rightly, is the main objection to Mr. Bradlaugh, because I would fully face the most serious difficulty; and I do not hesitate to say that if Mr. Bradlaugh chooses to take his stand upon what are called secularist principles in religion, and can succeed nevertheless in inducing any constituency to send him to Parliament, he ought not to be prevented from doing so by want of funds; for in that case it is plain that he must represent a class of opinions sufficiently considerable to have a right to be represented. But I am not aware that Mr. Bradlaugh does take his stand upon these principles. I understood him to come forward as a representative of purely political opinions, and in that case I do not think that any one is entitled to object to him on the ground of religious opinions; for to do so is contrary to the principles we follow when Jews, &c., are admitted to Parliament. If Mr. Bradlaugh were a rich man, I should not have taken any steps to forward his election; had he been a rich man, I think no one would have blamed me if I had taken any such steps. As a matter of fact, I have done nothing whatever to forward Mr. Bradlaugh's election except to help to remove in a very small degree whatever obstacle poverty may be to his chances. I pronounce no opinion upon his merits, but leave them to be judged by those who are better qualified to judge them than I can profess to be myself.

1868 — Aetat. 62.

To Edwin Chadwick.

Chiefly by Helen Taylor.

Avignon, *9th October* 1868.

I think it is a mistake to suppose that my support of Mr. Bradlaugh at all diminishes my weight. The sort of people with whom it does so have had to put up with my women's suffrage, Jamaica committees, representation of minorities, and other "crotchets," and probably have long ago given me up, or more properly speaking have never taken me up at all. You know that my Malthusian and religious heresies, and my accusing the working people of not speaking the truth, were all brought up against me at the Westminster election, and all increased my popularity: I

1868 am quite convinced that nothing more increases a man's

Aetat. 62. influence than his having decided opinions of his own and sticking to them, provided he has got good reasons to give for them. No doubt they will give handle to his enemies to laugh at him, attack him, or abuse him as the case may be. But people's enemies will always have something to say against them, and those who side with you in some things are delighted to see that you have the pluck to stand to your colours even when they do not altogether agree with you. See how great has been the influence of mere pluck even in such a case as Roebuck's; surely this should be a lesson to men not to be afraid when they are sure they are in the right. Working men in particular hate hesitation and anything approaching to smoothing away differences, and have so much of it from Tories and Whigs that nothing makes them more sure that a man is what they think "of the right sort" than his speaking and acting plainly and decidedly with them when he is with them and against them when he is against them. I doubt whether my opposition to the ballot will cost a single vote at Westminster, and I believe that what I have done in the matter of Bradlaugh is likely to gain quite as many as it will lose, although this had nothing whatever to do with my doing it.

To the Right Hon. E. P. Bouverie, M.P.

This letter was written in reply to a protest from Bouverie, who had been for twenty-five years the Liberal member for Kilmarnock, against Mill's action in recommending Edwin Chadwick to the electors. The publication of this and other letters at the time was considered by many to have cost Mill his seat at Westminster.

Chiefly by Helen Taylor.

Avignon, *19th October* 1868.

Dear Mr. Bouverie,—Though a great deal surprised I am far from dissatisfied at seeing our correspondence up to this point in the paper, as I had not thought myself at liberty to publish it without your previous consent. 1868 — Aetat. 62.

Your observation that choosing the best men to be had "would be fatal to the mutual confidence between represented and representative" is a misanthropical sentiment which I should scarcely have expected to hear from you, since I can see no meaning in it unless it be that the constituencies so seldom get a good man that they can scarcely ever be expected to be faithful to the man they have got: I do not look upon the matter from so cynical a point of view. It seems to me that in this, as in other matters in life, the more particular people are in choosing, the less likely they are to change their minds after they have chosen. In the particular case also in which you deprecate inconstancy, it would appear that the constituency of Kilmarnock has been constant for the last five-and-twenty years, from whence one may fairly infer that they made a very good choice five-and-twenty years ago. But five-and-twenty years and a new Reform Act make a great change in men and in politics, and if the constituency of Kilmarnock makes as judicious a choice now as it did when it last changed its representative, I sincerely hope it will be five-and-twenty years before it changes again. Still, with the fullest regard to the consideration due to past services, one must admit that there ought to be some limit to it. You would not, I presume, maintain that a seat in Parliament ought to be a seat for life unless the member has given some violent offence to the constituency. The urgency of an infusion of new blood is as good a reason for making a new choice, as dissatisfaction with an existing representative; and there is no time at which giving the preference to a new candidate is so little of a reflection on the former member as when a change has been made in the constitution, admitting new electors often much more numerous than the old.

I am sorry that the occasions on which people have asked my advice or help in their electioneering affairs should have caused me so often to incur your disappro-

1868 — Aetat. 62.

bation by expressing opinions so very different from yours as to the sort of men that would be of most use in the House of Commons. But I do not see that the fear of being disagreeable to one class of candidates ought to prevent me from giving my opinion, when asked, in favour of another class, or that there is anything presumptuous either in answering questions that are addressed to me, or in giving testimony which I am told will be of use to those in whose favour it is given, and which, if as you say it has no weight, will at least be innocuous to their rivals.

I have no objection to receiving the advice you tender in the last sentence of your letter, although I did not invite it by opening up any communications between us. For my part I never presumed to give you any advice, nor did I "incite" you to retire in Mr. Chadwick's favour, because I had no idea that you were in the least likely to do so; I merely, in reply to a communication from yourself, showed how very public-spirited a proceeding I should consider it if you did. I should not, however, have troubled you with this opinion if you had not been the first to write to me.

Writing to yourself, what at the time I wrote it I supposed was to be a private letter, I did not think it necessary to raise the question how far the present member for Kilmarnock is entitled to claim the support of Liberals on the ground of fidelity to the Liberal party. But to the public or to the constituency I have no hesitation in saying that no untried man can be looked upon as less a member of the Liberal party than the man who at the beginning of this present year called the Liberal party a rabble, and declared that their leader was incapable of leading. I do not know that any one is likely to do more than this to sow dissension among the Liberal party, nor do I see what possible claim this gentleman can have upon party fidelity, or what pledge he can give his constituents that he will not at a critical moment turn round again upon this same "leader who cannot lead," and show himself even more a conspicuous example of a "follower who will not follow." Whatsoever claims he may have upon his constituency can only be those of his own individual personal merits; he is the last man who has a right to the sympathy of his whilom party, or who can appeal against me on the ground of his high sense of the claims of party organisation.

1868 — Aetat. 62.

Even in the most ordinary circumstances, the efficiency of representatives can only be kept up by a keen rivalry, and a probability that if they fall below the standard they have ever attained, their constituents will look out for new men who come up to it. But we are not now in ordinary times. There are not only new electors to be represented, but new questions to be decided, requiring men deeply impressed with the wants of the country, and who have exercised their minds on the means of remedying the most pressing existing evils. The Liberal electors have a right to a choice between their present members and any others who may seem to them better qualified in this respect, and such choice is denied them if it is regarded as treason against Liberalism for a new Liberal candidate to offer himself in competition with an old member.

I am keenly sensible of the importance of not dividing the Liberal party, but it is not a very hopeful way of keeping the party united for the representatives of the old electors to engross all the representation, leaving none for the new; and if a reasonable number of men of advanced opinions, and possessing the confidence of the working classes, are not to be included among the recognised candidates of the party, they cannot be blamed if they sometimes stand against those who are. Just as we are often told that to secure the unity of a married couple what is the man's is his own, and what is the woman's is the man's, so now we are being told every day that to secure the unity of the Liberal party, which is threatened by a division between the old men and the new, the old men should be represented by themselves and the new men by the old. With the solitary exception of the advice which you suppose me to give to yourself, I have not heard of any instance in which it has not been proposed to resolve the difficulty by the new men retiring and the

1868 — Aetat. 62.

old men magnanimously accepting their retirement. And this in many cases is very naïvely put upon the ground that as the old men will not consider the public interest and retire, for fear of letting in a Tory, the new must.

The real danger, in my opinion, of the Liberal party, is not what you consider it to be. It is in the renewal of the tactics which made the last House of Commons a spectacle of dissension and want of principle, showing us representatives trying to slip out of the engagements their constituents conceived them to be bound by, and others yielding a shameful obedience when called to order by the dread of losing their seats; while in cases where this powerful motive was not in operation, men elected under the same banner proved by their conduct that there was as irreconcilable a variance in their intentions and political feelings as if they had sat on opposite sides of the House. What gave this deplorable character to the last House of Commons was that its so-called Liberal members were rallied under the cry of supporting Palmerston, as we are now told they ought to be rallied under the cry of disestablishing the Irish Church. Now, I am not one of those who think that the political progress of England has but one step more to make before reaching its summit, where it may rest and be thankful, and that if a man is ready to vote for the disestablishment of the Irish Church, he is ready to do all that the staunchest Liberalism can demand of him. But I would remind those who differ with me as to the all-sufficiency of this particular step, that our power to make even that step next session may depend upon our getting men into the House of Commons who are not merely certain to vote for that step, but who will follow their leaders loyally through all the Parliamentary tactics with which our skilful opponent will try to impede the way. Days, weeks, and months may be lost if Mr. Gladstone's majority is composed of men who will keep their word in voting for the disestablishment of the Irish Church, but will thwart and embarrass their leader in every previous step by which that desirable consummation may have to be led up to.

It was not the Tories, but the Adullamites, who weakened the Liberal party in the last Parliament; and if a similar result should befall it in the next, there will be cause for bitter regret that the Liberal party did not fight out its battles at the polling booths rather than in the lobby of the House of Commons. There does not appear to be any danger that Mr. Gladstone's nominal majority will not be greater than in the last Parliament. What the country has to look to is that his majority shall be more steadfast to genuine Liberal principles. We do not want men who cast reluctant looks back to the old order of things, nor men whose Liberalism consists chiefly in a warm adherence to all the Liberal measures already passed, but men whose heart and soul are in the cause of progress, and who are animated by that ardour which in politics, as in war, kindles the commander to his highest achievements, and makes the army at his command worth twice its numbers; men whose zeal will encourage their leader to attempt what their fidelity will give him strength to do. It would be poor statesmanship to gain a seeming victory at the poll by returning a majority numerically large, but composed of the same incompatible elements as the last, even if we put political principle aside, and look at nothing but the exigencies of the fight we are going to sustain against a politician renowned for his skill in availing himself of the disunion of his opponents.—I am, yours very faithfully, J. S. MILL.

1868 — Aetat. 62.

To a Correspondent,

who wrote to ask Mill's advice on the education of his children.

By HELEN TAYLOR.

AVIGNON, *29th October* 1868.

DEAR SIR,—I beg to acknowledge your letter of the 26th inst.

Your difficulties and anxieties are such as the extreme imperfection of our public arrangements for education

1868 — Aetat. 62. (though I am happy to say they are at last showing some signs of improvement) imposes on all parents who are at once thoughtful and conscientious, especially when, as is the case with the greater number, circumstances compel them to rely [more] on others than themselves for a great part of the education of their children.

In regard to religion, I do not think it right either oneself to teach or to allow any one else to teach one's children, authoritatively, anything whatever that one does not from the bottom of one's heart and by the clearest light of one's reason believe to be true. It seems to me that to act otherwise, on any pretext whatever, is little if at all short of a crime against one's children, against one's fellow-creatures in general, and against abstract truth in whatever form it appears most sacred to one's eyes. One has assuredly no right to encumber the reason and entangle the conscience of one's children; one has no right to send citizens out into the world to play their various parts for or against their fellow-creatures furnished with anything less than the most honest truth that one can give them. Nor can I see that the plea of worldly interest is the smallest valid excuse, although I am well aware how many people think it so. But, in the first place, he would be a wise man indeed who can foresee the state of society fifteen or twenty years hence. In the second place, the clear intellect and the sturdy conscience which are acquired in a household where truth is reverenced above all things are as valuable to men and women pushing their way in the world as any supposed conformity with popular prejudice. In the third place, if there is one thing to which we all ought to give our allegiance irrespective of consequence it is truth, and here I look upon the ancient Christian teaching as the highest the world has yet known, and should regard it as a misfortune indeed if this noble spirit were to die out with the prejudices which have overlaid it. But I do not believe it will, and the immense value attached to worldly prosperity by the bulk of so-called Christians is to me the best proof that their doctrine is hollow and effete.

But I do not think that there should be any *authoritative* teaching at all on such subjects. I think parents ought to point out to their children when the children begin to question them, or to make observations of their own, the various opinions on such subjects, and what the parents themselves think the most powerful reasons for and against. Then, if the parents show a strong feeling of the importance of truth, and also of the difficulty of attaining it, it seems to me that young people's minds will be sufficiently prepared to regard popular opinion or the opinions of those about them with respectful tolerance, and may be safely left to form definite conclusions in the course of mature life. 1868 — Aetat. 62.

There is one other point in which a mother may, I believe, be of immense use to her children which is apt to be too much overlooked, in my opinion, in modern education, but on which there is a great deal of good sense in Miss Edgeworth's stories for children, in "Sandford and Merton," and in Miss Martineau's "Household Education"; and this is, teaching children (more especially, if they are not going to be rich) to respect, to enjoy, and habitually to practise manual and domestic labour. The love of this, and the sense of moral dignity in doing it, are, next to the love of truth, the very most valuable possessions with which to begin life, whether we consider happiness or the power of getting on.

To cultivate the intelligence, nothing perhaps is of so much value as a love of reading, and to secure this it is essential to let young people read whatever they may come across and are disposed to read. Moreover, if careful selections are to be made for them, it becomes a most embarrassing question at what age are they to begin to be allowed to know any of the realities of life? and in many respects such knowledge is likely to be more mischievous if it comes startlingly upon them when they are of an age to understand it than if it is taken for granted in what they read when it has no particular interest for their childish minds.

I know of no schools so good as the Birkbeck schools,

1868 — Ætat. 62. and if there is one within reach I should think both boys and girls could receive an excellent education at it. I do not know precisely up to what point the education is carried on at them, nor what amount of education you contemplate giving to your children. I imagine that some of the best education to be had now, of a more advanced sort, at no great expense, is to be had by following the classes at the Working Men's College or at one of the Scotch universities. Either of these, however, are, of course, not for children, but I believe that the Birkbeck school would be a fit preparation for either of these. You are no doubt quite aware that I consider it a duty to give girls as solid an education as boys, and doubly so if they are likely to have to earn their own living; and the progress now making in the education of girls is so considerable that it is not likely that twenty years hence any young woman will be able to earn by teaching who has not some solid instruction herself.

To a Westminster Voter,

who had asked Mill's view as to the limit of the income tax.

BLACKHEATH PARK, *5th November* 1868.

DEAR SIR,—As a good opportunity did not present itself at the meeting yesterday evening for answering your questions, I now answer them by letter.

The first question you ask raises a difficulty which will exist at whatever sum we fix the limit to the income tax, for whether the tax begins at £100, at £200, or at £500, that sum will represent a larger real means of support in some places than in others. But I am very much disposed to think that the limit of £100 is too low; and that it would be an improvement to make the income tax begin at £150 (as it did at first), if not higher. If all taxation were direct it ought to come down to the limit of income just sufficient for the necessaries of life, and everyone ought to pay in proportion to the surplus

of income he possesses beyond those mere necessaries. 1868
But so long as the larger part of our revenue is raised by Aetat. 62.
indirect taxation on articles of almost universal consumption, and of which the poor consume more in proportion to their small means than the rich, so long I think that the incomes between £50 and £150 or £200 pay more than their fair share of indirect taxation, and this requires to be made up to them by levying a tax on the higher incomes, from which they should be exempt.

In answer to your second question, my opinion is that in justice the same amount of income should pay the same amount of tax, whether it be a fixed annual income or a variable sum paid weekly. But it would be extremely difficult to check fraudulent concealment of income in the latter case.

To a Westminster Voter,

who wrote to ask Mill whether it was true that he was an atheist.

BLACKHEATH PARK, *5th November* 1868.

DEAR SIR,—When I was first proposed as a candidate for the representation of Westminster, an attempt was made to raise the same religious cry against me, which, you inform me, is now being repeated. But I publicly announced my determination, on principle, to answer no questions respecting my religious belief, because I would not give any encouragement to a practice the effect of which would be that, when no objection could be made to a candidate either on the ground of character or of political opinions, his opponents would endeavour to extract from himself materials for raising a religious prejudice against him. You will, I hope, pardon me for adhering to the resolution I then declared. But if there really are persons who, in good faith and honesty, conclude me to be an atheist because I subscribed to the fund for the election of Mr. Bradlaugh, such persons merely show that they are ignorant or regardless of the principles I have openly proclaimed, especially in my book on "Liberty," viz. that atheists, as well

1868 — Ætat. 62.

as the professors of any, even the worst religions, may be, and often are, good men, estimable and valuable in all the relations of life, and are entitled like all other persons to be judged by their actions ("By their fruits ye shall know them" are the words of Christ), and not by their speculative opinions. My subscription was not given for Mr. Bradlaugh as an atheist, but for Mr. Bradlaugh as a politician; just as we may presume that the working men of Northampton selected him as their candidate, and the Reform League as a member of its Council, not as an atheist, but as a politician.

P.S.—You are at liberty to make any use you please of this letter.

To J. H. Fletcher, of Northampton,

who wrote to inquire on what grounds Mill had subscribed to Bradlaugh's election expenses, in opposition to the other Liberal candidates.

Blackheath Park, *5th November* 1868.

Dear Sir,—In answer to your letter dated yesterday, I beg to say that Mr. Gilpin is a distinguished and valuable member of the advanced Liberal party, no opposition to whom I should for a moment countenance, and that Lord Henley has always been faithful, and I have no reason whatever to doubt that he will remain faithful to the party and to Mr. Gladstone. In subscribing, therefore, towards the expenses of another candidate, I was not influenced by any hostility to either of the present members. The motive by which I was actuated was a strong sense that the working classes have a just claim to a fair number of the men of their choice in the reformed House of Commons, which fair share, I regret to say, there is from present appearances extremely little prospect of their obtaining. I am also of opinion, and in this I hope you will agree with me, that the Liberal electors have a right to be allowed to decide which, among any number of candidates who are willing to offer themselves, they prefer to be represented by. After they have had time to weigh the pretensions of the various candidates, and to make up their minds whom they intend to support, then if a Tory has offered himself, and the division among Liberals renders at all probable his return, my opinion is that some means should be adopted of deciding which two of the Liberal candidates are the strongest, and that the remainder should withdraw. I may add that Mr. Bradlaugh is aware that this is my opinion.

1868 — Aetat. 62.

TO CHARLES BRADLAUGH,

in reply to a letter from him expressing the fear that the subscription to his election expenses had been the cause of Mill's defeat at Westminster.

BLACKHEATH PARK, *19th November* 1868.

DEAR SIR,—I may have lost some votes by my subscription for you, but neither that nor any one thing is the cause of my losing the election. Many things have contributed to it, and I should very likely have been defeated if my name had never been coupled with yours. In any case it was a right thing to do, and I do not regret it.

I am very sorry that you, as well as all other candidates who would have especially represented the working classes, have been unsuccessful. But their time will come. Your perseverance at Northampton is fully justified by the result, as, notwithstanding the large number who voted for you, you have not, as was predicted, brought us a Tory.

TO A LADY,

who wrote to ask Mill to tell her "in a few lines" what Bradlaugh's principles were.

BY HELEN TAYLOR.

AVIGNON, *28th November* 1868.

DEAR MADAM,—Mr. Bradlaugh is a man who has been guilty of the very great fault of using insulting language towards those who differ from him in religious opinions;

1868 — Aetat. 62.

a fault which he appears to share with your friend the clergyman, who calls Mr. Bradlaugh "the prince of scoundrels" in a country abounding in murderers, thieves, &c., &c. I am not aware that any accusations are made against Mr. Bradlaugh's moral character, while I am quite certain that no such accusations could be substantiated, as if they could they would have been brought forward against him in the bitterness of the recently contested elections. The violence of the language which has been made use of by Mr. Bradlaugh has been very greatly exaggerated by his opponents, and I believe that it was in his younger days that he made use of it, but at the same time I have no excuse to offer for that. I myself know nothing of him except that he has put himself very boldly forward to advocate with considerable ability a great number of unpopular opinions; some of them unpopular among the upper classes, such as religious scepticism and democracy, others unpopular among working men, such as representation of minorities and the equality of women. If you will do me the honour to read my little book on Liberty, you will at once understand why I think such men as Mr. Bradlaugh ought to be allowed to say what they have got to say, nor be abused for their opinions so long as they do nothing wrong.

I cannot easily express to you, and I will not take the trouble to try to express, the contempt I feel for a man who, calling himself a Christian, can call another man the prince of scoundrels, because of differences on religious opinion. If Mr. Bradlaugh is wrong, a clergyman ought to be the first to pity him, the first also to recognise with humility that men with such opinions as Mr. Bradlaugh can behave honourably and uprightly, while men who call themselves Christians are daily guilty of any crime against the laws of their country, of religion, and of the human conscience. Let such clergymen apply themselves to the improvement of their own flocks, and they will have neither time nor energy to spare for abusive language.

To Alfred Steinthal, Secretary *pro tem* of the Manchester Women's Suffrage Committee.

By Helen Taylor.

Avignon, 1*st December* 1868.

Dear Mr. Steinthal,—The result of the new elections, now that they are complete, appears to be on the whole unfavourable to the cause of women's suffrage. The new members in favour of it are but few, and there have been losses among both its Tory and Liberal supporters. It appears therefore improbable that any efficient stand can be made on this subject in the House of Commons this session; and I have long been of opinion, and expressed myself strongly to that effect last year, that it would be injurious to the cause if a division should take place leaving us with smaller numbers than in the former division. It would be doubly injurious, first by seeming to show a reaction in public opinion against us, and secondly, by depriving us, as it very probably would, of the prestige of Mr. John Bright's name, which at present we are able to boast.

1868 — Aetat. 62.

Shortly before the late elections I received (and I suppose other expected Members of Parliament received also) a circular which I enclose, which was addressed to me in a blank cover. The announcement it contained seemed singularly injudicious at a moment when it was quite unknown what would be the character of the new House, and the question ill timed, being addressed to men who might not be, and some of whom have not proved to be, in it. I cannot help thinking that you will agree with me that the most judicious way of bringing the subject before the House of Commons is by petition, and if possible, by a petition on a far greater scale than has been yet attempted. A really extensively signed petition on the part of the women of the kingdom, with those men who desire with them an alteration of the law in their favour, is the proper reply to the authoritative decision

1868 — Aetat. 62. that the law is now against them. Indeed, if it were a good occasion for bringing forward a Bill in the House of Commons, and if all promised favourably for an influential increase of the votes on our side, it would still be most desirable to show that out of the House as well as in it, and among women as well as men, there exists a strong desire for their representation. And while the feeling is still fresh among those women who have been disappointed of the power to vote, is the time for asking them to petition. It would show but little perseverance in women if they cannot go on year after year asking for this change of the law, when we remember with what patience these sorts of petitions are continually renewed for the various political objects which men desire. If we compare the amount of petitioning that women have yet had patience for, with the numbers sent up year after year on the comparatively small grievance of Church rates, it would almost seem to justify the assertions of those who say that women are not yet fit for political rights if they are already wearied out. The desire to produce *éclat* and great results with small means, and effects that should tell at once rather than that should prepare the way silently for the future, are indeed what we have to fear from inexperienced politicians. If seems very advisable to show women that they have a means in their own hands of quietly and steadily pressing their claims upon the legislature, and encourage them to begin that great lesson of steady, silent, persevering effort by which every class and nation has to be fitted for freedom.

To Thomas Dyke Acland, M.P.,

in reply to a letter of condolence on Mill's defeat at Westminster.

Nearly all by Helen Taylor.

Avignon, *1st December* 1868.

Dear Mr. Acland,—There are few if any of my friends in the House of Commons from whom such an expression of good opinion and of kind and friendly feeling as your letter contains, would have given me greater pleasure. I have been in strong sympathy with you on most or all of the subjects in which you have shown a special interest during the time I was in the House, and I am heartily glad that you are still there to continue working for them.

Among those subjects, that of the most just and fair mode of raising taxes for local purposes is one of the most difficult and puzzling. It is quite true that Lopes was playing, to a great extent, a landlord's game, and in my speech on his motion I contended that the peculiar pressure of the local rates on the rent of land was, as to a considerable part of it, just. At the same time, I believe we (you and I) agree in thinking that money is wanted for important local purposes now neglected or insufficiently provided for; that the difficulty of putting further pressure on the ratepayers is at present a serious obstacle to important public objects; and that the pecuniary resources required will have to be sought, entirely or partially, at the expense of kinds of property and income which now, in the main, escape from local rates. Your suggestion of transferring the assessed taxes wholly or partially to local purposes, amounts in fact to allowing taxes on male servants, and on horses and carriages, in aid of local rates; for the house-tax falls entirely on the present ratepayers, and the minor assessed taxes are not worth taking into account. I do not think that taxes on male servants, or on horses and carriages not employed in business, are at all objectionable on grounds of political economy. They are fair taxes on luxuries, and the luxuries of all classes are fit objects of taxation. *E contra*, I would not tax any kind of public conveyance, post-horses, stage coaches, railways, &c., nor horses nor carts used in trades; nor perhaps the carriage of a medical man; and even a private carriage is, to many persons in weak health, a luxury so nearly amounting to a necessary, that I would tax the *first* carriage much more lightly than the second, or any greater number. And the same reason applies in some circumstances to the first man-servant. It must be re-

1868 — Aetat. 62.

membered in abatement from the efficacy of such taxes in affording relief to the rates, that they would be, in a large proportion, paid by the same persons. But falling impartially on all who expend large incomes in the ordinary way, they would be in themselves a mode of raising money unobjectionable as to fairness.

What you say about the growing intelligence of the yeomen and the younger tenant farmers is one of the most gratifying things I have heard for a long time. If that improvement is general in the rural districts, political and social progress are safe, even where the obstacles to them are strongest.

What you say of the possibility of reaction arising from religious feeling is very true, and it has long been a subject of grief to me that those feelings of religion which belong to the best parts of human nature should not only be turned to mischief by their association with dogmas confusing to the intellect and very often, I am sorry to say, perverting to the moral sense, but that they should actually be themselves the cause of dissension between the very persons who are most deeply imbued with them—those who feel them most strongly disliking most just those who also feel them most strongly, with whom they ought to be the firmest allies. Thus the most genuinely pious among the Catholics are often the most bitter against Protestants, those among the Church of England against Dissenters, those among the Dissenters against Deists, &c., &c. This is comparatively speaking an old evil, and one which it is comparatively difficult to remove, because when people hold very strongly particular dogmas it is natural that they should specially dislike those who hold with equal intensity to other dogmas specifically contradictory to their own.

But I have long thought that what we now want in the present stage of the world is a union among all those men (and women) who are deeply impressed with the fundamental essence of religion, *in so far as religion affects this world.* To you I need scarcely point out that the special characteristic of Christianity as opposed to most other religions is that it insists that religion does affect this world, making charity to our fellow-creatures and good actions the criterion of a good man. Now this is also the fundamental doctrine of those who are called Atheists, as well as those whose religious opinions are founded on individual convictions, and are not therefore altogether in accordance with any of the sects. Honesty, self-sacrifice, love of our fellow-creatures, and the desire to be of use in the world, constitute the true point of resemblance between those whose religion, however overlaid with dogmas, is genuine, and those who are genuinely religious without any dogmas at all. I have often been amazed that there are not more Christians who perceive that Christianity (I do not myself think, however, that any Christian sect comes up to this ideal) forms a point of union for all men in this point of view. Now, if those men who from any peculiarities of mental constitution—whether superiority or inferiority to the general average—find themselves unable to accept any dogmatic religion whatever, not even the dogmas of natural religion, are to continue to wrap up their doubts in mystery, to be afraid to speak out, and to be the object of abuse whenever they do, a strong premium is put upon dishonesty on their part, and those among them who have a great deal of natural energy of character are drawn into a violence of language which hurts the feelings of other people, and arouses in themselves something of that very intolerance from which they are sufferers. They are led to speak without respect and without tolerance of the religious convictions they do not share. In doing so they excite just resentment on the part of genuinely religious people, who would be the best qualified to sympathise in their honesty and disinterestedness, and those who really profit by the result are the hypocrites of all parties. Those who make religion a matter of worldly success and profit take care to draw the moral from all this, that if a man once gives up the formal dogmas there can be no unison of feeling between him and pious men; those who have not a trace of religious feeling or religious conviction of any kind whatever, but

1868 — Aetat. 62. who have not the smallest wish to sacrifice a particle of worldly consequence or success, are confirmed in the opinion that if they allowed the world in general to know the true state of their mind on religious matters they would become objects of opprobrium and deep-seated dislike, such as they see the outspoken men of their own opinions to be.

Now you will see how all this applies to Bradlaugh. Few people feel more dislike than I do to anybody who can use insulting expressions to that which excites the respect of their fellow-creatures, or who treats with ingratitude those influences to which the world owes so much. A tender respect for every worthy and pious feeling and a pious tenderness towards the past constitute to my mind important elements of the religious character, without which no character can be complete or altogether worthy of respect. But a courageous willingness to face opprobrium, an urgent need to speak the truth, a kind of necessity to fight against all falsehood and hypocrisy, are no less important elements of true religion. Some men will excel in some of these elements, some in others. "A diversity of gifts, but the same spirit." I do not doubt in my own mind that many Ritualists who are or who fancy themselves ready to go to the stake for the cause of smart dresses in church, Dissenters who will go to prison rather than pay Church rates, Church of England missionaries who distribute Bibles among the Chinese, are the true brothers in spirit of Mr. Bradlaugh. Like him, they rush to excess in following out their opinions, but, like him, they act upon the principle that there are other things in this world better worth exertion than this world's goods. I myself know very little of Mr. Bradlaugh, but I do happen to know that he has taken up several points of opinion which it is to be supposed are obnoxious to the working classes, although it is from the working classes alone that he can look for support and influence. I know that he offends the upper classes by his democracy, the middle classes by his atheism, and the working classes by Malthusianism, not to speak of the representation of minorities and of women—not very popular ideas, either of them. How far Mr. Bradlaugh supports any of these opinions in the same manner or on the same grounds that I should do myself I have not watched his career sufficiently closely to know. I do know that he supports some of them very differently from the way I think right. But I do not see how one can escape from the conviction that he is a brave man, and nobody can have heard him speak without believing him to be a clever one, so that he could probably push his way by more commonplace means if he chose to give up his opinions. I cannot say that I volunteered to support him as I did Odger (the only man I have volunteered to support); but when I was asked to do so, it seemed to me that it would have been fundamentally irreligious, because fundamentally cowardly and self-interested, to shrink back. We want now to establish a bond of union—public spirit and practical good deeds—between all disinterested men. They ought all to stand by one another, whatever their opinions, on this ground, and on this ground alone. Again and again, since this doctrine was taught in the parable of the Good Samaritan and in the Epistle of St. Paul to the Romans, the battle has had to be fought for it; it is not half so bitter a struggle now as it was in former times, but there is a good deal of bitterness left, most of which bitterness, however, is imported into it by the hypocrites, who use it as a weapon for their own purposes.

1868 — Aetat. 62.

To George Grote.

By Helen Taylor.

AVIGNON, *1st December* 1868.

MY DEAR GROTE,—I am extremely obliged to you for your kindness about the note on Aristotle's theory of Universals, to which I look forward with great pleasure, and which will be a contribution to the value of the book such as no one but yourself could give. I am very grateful also for the kind things you say about my defeat in Westminster.

1868 — Aetat. 62. Except as a part of the general rout of men of brains or of strong opinions at these elections, I doubt if my rejection is to be regretted even on public grounds, and on private it is most heartily to be rejoiced at. I do not gather from my friends in Westminster any very clear accounts of the cause of my defeat, but I put it down myself mainly to three causes: the inferiority of the organisation directed by a committee to that which is pushed by one individual, the immense influence of money, and the dislike of the vestries to the Metropolitan Bill. With such good causes as these, every little helps to swell the general result, and with Disraeli for a leader, the Tories are better fitted to take advantage of every possible chance than they have been for a long time. Of course if my own rashness cost the seat I should not the less have done what I have done, for after all, Gladstone can better afford to lose one vote than I and those who care for me can afford that I should not act up to my principles. But as a matter of fact, I greatly doubt whether Bradlaugh, Bouverie, &c., are at all accountable for my defeat.

Helen thanks you very much for your kind mention of her in your letter. But she feels the relief, if possible, with even more pleasure than I do. Her health suffers very much from the English climate, and she is very deeply imbued with the conviction that one true principle set afloat in the world does more for progress than one hundred points of practical detail. I am not sure whether she does not dislike my being in Parliament more than I did myself, as she certainly suffered more from it in health; but she would not give in, and made it a point of pride to encourage me to stay at the post as long as there seemed any chance of my doing anything at it. On the whole, we both feel that circumstances have decided well for us. We think I was able to do some good work while I was in the House, and we look forward with delight to being able now to work in a much pleasanter manner. I shall soon have the "Analysis" ready for the press, and have other projects in view.

With our kind regards to Mrs. Grote, whose health, we hope, continues to improve.

To Archibald Michie, of Victoria.

Avignon, *7th December* 1868.

Dear Sir,—I am much honoured by your thinking it worth while to write so long and interesting a letter for the purpose of convincing me that the people of Victoria are not so far gone in Protectionism as they are thought to be. I have never laid stress on anything contained in the article in the *Westminster Review*, which did not, to my judgment, look like a fair representation. I need not say how glad I should be to believe that the Victoria Protectionists are Protectionists only within the limits of my excepted case, *i.e.* that they only wish for temporary Protection to try the experiment of naturalising foreign branches of industry. Unfortunately the writings I have seen on their side of the question—I admit that they are not numerous—make no reservation of the kind, but advocate the general theory of Protection on the old ignorant grounds, and support it by the old stock fallacies, and refer to the stupidest authorities —British, American, and Continental—as a sanction for it. All this is very natural. The Protectionist theory appears plain common sense to persons thoroughly ignorant of the subject; and industries artificially fortified, even though it be professedly for a time only, raise up private interests which combine, as they have done in the United States, but too effectually, to convert what was intended as a temporary expedient into a permanent institution (though the thick end of the wedge seldom follows the thin end at so short an interval as three years). These considerations have greatly shaken the opinion I expressed in my book; and though I still think that the introduction of a foreign industry is often worth a sacrifice, and that a temporary protecting duty, if it was sure to remain temporary, would probably be the best shape in which that sacrifice can be made, I am inclined to believe that it is safer to make it by an annual grant from the public treasury, which is not nearly so likely to be continued indefinitely, to prop up an industry which has not so thriven as to be able to dispense with it.

1868 — Aetat. 62.

1868 — Aetat. 62.

I can readily believe that the Free Trade party in Victoria is swelled by the private self-interest of importing merchants, but a cause seldom triumphs unless somebody's personal interest is bound up with it. It would have been long before the Corn Laws would have been abolished in Great Britain if, besides the public interests concerned, those laws had not been contrary to the private interests of nearly the whole of the manufacturing and mercantile classes.

It gives me extreme pleasure that you approve of what I have said and done to promote the admission of women to the political franchise. If your important and rising community could be induced to adopt this great social improvement (if I am rightly informed, it is adopted already at your municipal elections) it would not be the first time that a colony has outstripped the Mother Country in the introduction of improved principles of legislation. . . .

To John Candlish, M.P.,

in reply to a letter of condolence on Mill's defeat at Westminster.

AVIGNON, *7th December* 1868.

DEAR MR. CANDLISH,—A thousand thanks for your kind and warm-hearted letter. It is not altogether a selfish pleasure to be so glad to be regretted; for the assurance that friends like you think after trial that my presence was really useful in the House of Commons is an evidence I could ill spare that I did not commit an error of judgment when I exchanged another mode of usefulness for the far less congenial one of a seat in Parliament. In returning to my older and more natural mode of activity I shall not lose the feeling which my three years in Parliament have given me, of brotherhood in arms with those who are still there fighting the battles of advanced Liberalism, and I shall always be happy and proud to co-operate with them out of the House, either by my pen or otherwise.

To the Hon. General Secretary of the Chelsea Working Men's Parliamentary Electoral Association,

in reply to a letter of condolence on the defeat at Westminster.

AVIGNON, *7th December* 1868.

DEAR SIR,—The earnest and kindly letter which I have just received from the Committee of the Chelsea Working Men's Parliamentary Electoral Association gives me very great pleasure. That the *élite* of the working classes should think so kindly of me, and should attach so much importance to my political services, I feel to be a subject of just pride, since it has been given to me not in spite of, but, as I believe, partly in consequence of, my having made no sacrifices of my honest convictions to obtain it. It is because I have never concealed from the working classes, any more than from any other class, my differences of opinion with them, and my determination not to be the organ in Parliament of any opinions not my own, that they have had confidence in my sincerity when I professed to agree with them, and have never failed to give me a patient, a respectful, and even a sympathetic hearing on the points on which we differed.

1868 — Aetat. 62.

If the electors of the working classes continue to guide themselves in the choice and treatment of their representatives by the same principles and feelings which have governed their conduct towards me, the progress of democracy will soon cease to give uneasiness to any sincere and reasonable minds.

There is much which is gratifying and something which is disappointing in the result of the General Election. It has decided, thoroughly and irrevocably, the question of religious equality in Ireland in the only way which could be tolerated in the present age, the impartial disendowment of all sects, and has to that extent lightened the burthen of the reparation due to the people of that ill-treated country for centuries of misrule. It has also raised to the place of highest power the one English

1868 — Aetat. 62.

Minister of past or present times who has best deserved, and has obtained in largest measure, the confidence of the labouring classes. On the other hand, those classes, though to their votes the Liberal party principally owes its victory, are far from having had their just influence in the selection of the members who represent the party in the new House of Commons. No working man has been a successful candidate; even so distinguished a member of the working class as Mr. Odger, the ignorant attacks on whom have only served to bring forth from all sides additional tributes to his worth, has found, even in your metropolitan borough, that the zeal of his supporters could not compete with the greater wealth and superior organisation of other candidates, and when this was ascertained he honourably consented to withdraw. Those new candidates who, though not working men, possess the special confidence of the working classes, or who combined high education and culture with advanced opinions, have in general been equally unsuccessful.

It was not to be expected that there could be much organisation and concert among voters who, when the election took place, had only just been put on the electoral roll. But if these things happen a second time, the new electors will have themselves chiefly to blame.

Public opinion will in time demand the only complete remedy, the adoption of Personal Representation, by which the electors would be enabled to group themselves as they pleased, and any electors who chose to combine could be represented in exact proportion to their number by men of their own personal choice. But as this great improvement in representative government is not yet ripe for adoption, what should be done now is that the working classes should assert their right to an equal voice with the Liberals of the higher and middle classes in the choice of Liberal candidates. Where a place returns two members, one of these should be a candidate specially acceptable to the working classes: where there is but one, he should be selected in concert by both sections of Liberals. Thus much the working classes are fairly entitled to, and thus much if they insist they will obtain, for Liberal candidates can in most places no more be elected without their co-operation than elected by them alone without the co-operation of others.

1868 — Aetat. 62.

There is one thing more which demands the most strenuous efforts of the working classes, and of all who wish the recent change in our representative institutions to be more than nominal. The real cause of the failure of working-class candidates and of so many of the advanced Liberals in the late contests is the inordinate expense of elections. In a great majority of these cases, if money had had no influence, or if the expenditure of it had been equal on both sides, the popular candidate would in all probability have succeeded. If the working classes ever wish to be more genuinely represented than they are, they should make a united and energetic appeal to Parliament to clear away this obstacle to their representation. They should demand that the necessary expenses of elections be made a public charge, and that the useless and noxious expenses be made illegal and punishable. Some of their best friends vainly exerted themselves to extort measures for this purpose from the last Parliament, but Tories and lukewarm Liberals were too strong for them. Mr. Gladstone, however, made known both by speech and vote his approbation of the attempt; and we may feel confident that if properly supported by the people he will be no reluctant leader in the accomplishment of this, one of the most urgent as well as essential of remaining Parliamentary reforms. But when there is so great a mass of interested or timid resistance to be encountered, a reform is not properly supported unless it is strenuously urged.

Once more thanking your committee for their gratifying expression of feeling towards me, I am, &c.,

J. S. MILL.

To a Minister of New Zealand.

In this letter Mill indicates his withdrawal of the opinion expressed in the "Political Economy," that Protection is justifiable in the case of young countries.

11th December 1868.

1868 — Aetat. 62.

DEAR SIR,—When I had the honour of receiving your letter of 4th September my time was so fully occupied with our great electoral struggle and other things that I have been obliged to defer answering it till now.

I have had a rather extensive correspondence with various persons in Australia respecting the sanction supposed to be given by the passage which you quote from my "Political Economy" to the Protectionist doctrines there afloat. One of my most recent explanatory letters, which was addressed to Mr. Holden, Member of the Legislative Council of New South Wales, has been printed in the newspapers of that colony, and it is not unlikely that since writing your letter you may have seen it.

The Protecting duties, which I thought might sometimes be advisable in a young country for the purpose of ascertaining by experiment the suitability of its circumstances for the naturalisation of foreign branches of industry, are duties expressly imposed for a limited time, not exceeding a few years (say from five to twelve or thereabouts, according to the case), and to cease peremptorily at the end of the period unless it could be conclusively shown that the facilities given by the duties had been fairly used, but required some further and still more strictly limited time to make the experiment a fair one.

Some Australians have assured me that the Australian Protectionists do not carry *their* Protectionist proclivities beyond this point. I observe, however, that the Protectionist interests which are fostered by the Protecting duties are raising up, as they have always done elsewhere, Protectionist theories of the old type, and that the most exploded fallacies of the mercantile system are revived, with a simple ignorance of all that has been written and proved against them, which is strange to minds accustomed to the subject as usually discussed in Europe. 1868 — Aetat. 62.

There is great danger that the duties, even if imposed ostensibly for a time only, would at the expiration of the time, or before it, have been made permanent. But they were not, I believe, in any case imposed as temporary duties, but were as permanent as any Acts of the Colonial Parliaments.

I am now much shaken in the opinion, which has so often been quoted for purposes which it did not warrant; and I am disposed to think that when it is advisable, as it may sometimes be, to subsidise a new industry in its commencement, this had better be done by a direct annual grant, which is far less likely to be continued after the conditions which alone justified it have ceased to exist.

To Thomas Beggs.

By Helen Taylor.

11th December 1868.

Dear Sir,—Pray excuse my long delay in answering your letter. I have no doubt that, as you say, our defeat in Westminster is owing to the good organisation and discipline of the Tories; to their lavish expenditure, much of which, according to your account, must have come within the legal penalties of treating; and to their having on their side a large number of practised electioneers, and perhaps some of them vestrymen, offended by the Municipal Bills. It is of great importance that Westminster should redeem itself, and I heartily wish you success in your endeavours. At the same time, if we take a large view of the subject, it appears to me that it is more conducive to the growth of high political principle in the electors, and consequently to the permanent political progress of the nation, that the Liberal party in any constituency should occasionally suffer defeat from the scrupulous purity of the means it employs, than that it should

1868 — Aetat. 62.

practise tactics unworthy of a good cause, and thereby win a seeming success by means subversive of the principles to which the party owes its life. It is very painful to all true Liberals to see their own constituency represented by a Tory in Parliament, yet I think that this sometimes may be a wholesome humiliation if it stimulates them to redoubled efforts to arouse the political energies of the constituency by all morally legitimate and honourable means. The true humiliation is when honourable men become, in the words of the Psalm, "emulous of evil doers," and, despairing of serving a good cause by good means, fancy that a temporary discomfiture is a permanent defeat, and have recourse to methods of achieving success which are quite as humiliating as, and infinitely more mischievous than, defeat itself. It is much to be hoped that the advanced Liberal party, which has to a certain extent—owing partly to its want of organisation and partly to the results of its scrupulous adherence to perfectly honourable means—sustained a comparative defeat all over the country, will not despair of future success by such means, but will remember that so great and so important a reform as purity of election cannot be won at once nor until after having sustained many partial reverses.

I must take this opportunity of thanking you and the other kind friends who supported me in Westminster for their zealous support, and for the thorough manner in which they carried out the principles on which I stood: and I can assure you that although I had not personally any desire to be in the House of Commons, I did not on that account neglect anything that I thought it right for me to do or not to do for the purpose of securing my election. I can sincerely say (and it is due to the electors of Westminster that it should have been so) that I acted in all things as I should have done had my career been dependent upon my success. Whatever I did that might seem to have perilled my return, I did not do because I was indifferent to my return, for as an honourable politician I could never be indifferent to the return of any Liberal candidate, and as candidate for Westminster I was doubly bound in honour to exert myself for the Liberal representation of the constituency: which motive, I am sure you will do me the justice to believe, was fully as strong in my mind as the desire to be in Parliament could be in the mind of any ambitious young politician. . . .

To the President of the Edinburgh Women's Suffrage Society,

in reply to a letter of condolence on the defeat at Westminster.

By HELEN TAYLOR.

AVIGNON, *12th December* 1868.

DEAR MADAM,—Few things could be more gratifying to me than the letter with which I have been honoured by you and your committee, and I beg you to accept and to convey to the committee my warmest acknowledgments.

Of all my recollections connected with the House of Commons, that of my having had the honour of being the first to make the claim of women to the suffrage a Parliamentary question, is the most gratifying, as I believe it to have been the most important, public service that circumstances made it in my power to render. This is now a thing accomplished, and the cause has a sufficient number of supporters among the best men in the House of Commons to carry on as much of the contest as can be conducted there. It remains for the intelligent women of the country to give their moral support to the men who are engaged in urging their claims, and to open the minds of the less intelligent to the fact that political freedom is the only effectual remedy for the evils from which most women are conscious that women suffer. Whatever power I may have to promote this cause outside the House of Commons, I shall not fail to exert to my utmost.

Your expressions of sympathy with my feelings and approbation of my conduct on the subject of the Jamaica

1868 — Aetat. 62.

atrocities are peculiarly grateful to me, for it has been with especial sorrow that I have seen so many women cold and unmoved at the recital of sufferings which it might have been supposed would at least have caused some womanly pity, and generous indignation against the perpetrators. It is peculiarly among women, who are not aware that it is their duty to use their intelligence on matters of politics, that the severest condemnation of Mr. Eyre and his instruments should have been found, for if such women had possessed the warmth of heart which all women ought to have, their feelings would have been revolted at the tortures inflicted, and they would have considered the reasoning by which they were attempted to be palliated as beyond their province. As it is, the conduct of so many among them has afforded one more evidence that the renunciation of masculine intelligence gives no security for womanly kindness.

To an Elector of Westminster,

who had written to Mill, saying that he would not vote for him on account of his subscription to Bradlaugh's election expenses, Bradlaugh being "celebrated for his open blasphemy."

By Helen Taylor.

AVIGNON, 13*th December* 1868.

DEAR SIR,—I beg to say that in the first place to wish for a man's success as a Parliamentary candidate is not to identify oneself with him; if it were, how could a Catholic vote for a Protestant, a Churchman for a Dissenter, or a Christian for a Jew? In the second place, I did not go out of my way to subscribe to Mr. Bradlaugh's expenses (expenses for which, had my own and Mr. Fawcett's amendments to the Bribery Bill been carried last session, no subscription would have been needed), but I did not consider myself justified in refusing when asked to lighten the iniquitous expenses which would have prevented an otherwise eligible man from even taking the sense of the electors of Northampton concerning him, merely because either I or other people did not approve of his being, as I have been told he has been, as violent towards Christians in general as excellent Christians have often been towards one another. If you think that the man who will vote for the perpetuation of the oppression of one sect of Christians by another, as Mr. Smith will do, represents you better than I could have done, you did your duty. If not, you must excuse my saying that you appear to me to have allowed an unreflecting displeasure at an unpractical evil to overcome your sense of what as an elector you owe not only to your own country, but to a nation which your countrymen have long oppressed.

If Mr. Bradlaugh is only generally known for blasphemy, it must be because the facts concerning him are not generally known. I, who do know that he has stood forward as the advocate of many other opinions, the advocating of which must be contrary to his interests, was bound to act upon my better knowledge, and if a long-established character is worth anything, those who have done me the honour to approve of my general line of conduct and my published writings for thirty years or more might fairly be expected to suppose that I was not likely to support any man for no other reason than that he had made himself remarkable by blasphemy.

The fact that you approved my conduct in the proceedings against Mr. Eyre makes me hope that, on further reflection, you will see that I was not so much to blame as you imagine about Mr. Bradlaugh.

To James Beal,

in reply to a letter in which he had asked Mill's view on the reform of the London Police Force.

Chiefly by Helen Taylor.

AVIGNON, *14th December* 1868.

DEAR SIR,—I have not gone deeply into the subject of the treatment of prisoners, tickets-of-leave, &c., but from

1868 — Aetat. 62.

all that I have seen and heard upon it, I am under the impression that I should place great reliance upon the opinion of Sir Walter Crofton.

There are, however, some points respecting criminals and the police on which I have formed a decided opinion of my own, which in each case, were it necessary, I think I could support by a very wide induction. I will not go at length into any of these, but I will just note them down.

1. I observed with satisfaction that one point was judiciously insisted on by Mr. Edwin Hill at the meeting at which you attended. It is that there should be a great increase of efforts to root out the receivers of stolen goods. The receivers are the solid support and foundation of all professional theft, and without them a criminal class, as a class, could not exist. If there were no receivers there could be no professional or habitual thieves, but only casual acts of theft from necessity or temptation, with which it is comparatively easy to deal. Receivers being persons of some pecuniary means and permanent habitation, it is possible to make them accountable. I am not in a condition to say what means should be adopted for making receivers of stolen goods more amenable to justice; it requires some one more familiar than I am with the criminal law and with the practice of the criminal courts to say at what point the failure now takes place, but I am satisfied that this is a direction in which the law requires either to be strengthened or to be more vigorously enforced.

2. A great effect in checking crime would be produced by simply abrogating the rule of our criminal procedure which forbids putting questions to the prisoner. I doubt if public opinion is yet prepared for abolishing this rule, yet it might be done without any danger of introducing the evils of the French criminal procedure, which mainly arise from making the judge instead of the counsel the interrogator of the prisoner and witnesses.

3. I am clearly of the opinion that to place criminals who have worked out their sentences under the permanent

surveillance of the police is wrong in principle, and would not work well in practice, necessarily carrying along with it a number of abuses which it would be impossible efficiently to control, besides involving the decision of some other large questions, for the decision of which the time is not yet ripe. The difficulty of dealing with those who pick up a livelihood by odd jobs, and with those whose employers know their antecedents but whose fellow-workmen do not, would be in its own nature very great, while it would give great scope either for connivance or for oppression by the police. It would be necessary to decide what are lawful means of livelihood, and the law would either have to recognise prostitution as a legitimate profession or to put it down by force. I believe many of those who wish for the permanent surveillance of criminals are desirous also of establishing prostitution on a legitimate basis. I think them completely wrong in principle, and mistaken as to the practical benefits which seem to arise from such a plan; but, whether or no, the one change cannot be made without the other, and I believe that a more efficient police force, greater vigour against receivers, greater certainty of conviction, and greater steadiness and uniformity in the treatment of convicts, would be much more efficient in reducing crime than any surveillance that it is humanly possible to practise over criminals.

4. The first, the most obvious, and the most important condition of an efficient police is an exceedingly simple one, which, while it recommends itself at first sight to every impartial person, has been of late years totally neglected among ourselves, although the insisting upon it alone, without any other reform, would, I believe, do more to improve the character of the force than all other measures put together.

This condition is that no person in the police force be permitted to receive money or gifts of any sort whatever from any private individual. This rule should be absolute, and inflexibly applied. No services of any sort, whether within or without the routine of regular duty, should be permitted to receive any reward, either honorary or pecu-

1868 — Aetat. 62. niary, openly or privately, from individuals or from public bodies, except from the superior authorities of the force itself, and then in the way only of avowed promotion and increase of pay. Also the mere acceptance of food or drink or shelter, while on duty, from any person whatever should be *ipso facto* sufficient to ensure expulsion from the force.

It is obvious that employing policemen for private purposes must draw off their time, their attention, and their interest from their public duty. It is a mere sophism to say, for instance, that if you give a man whose duty it is to watch over the safety of a whole street a few pounds a year to watch more peculiarly over the safety of a few houses in it, it only quickens his zeal for them without diminishing his zeal for the rest. The work for which he receives no extra pay is certain to be considered of minor importance, and to be neglected in favour of that for which he expects special remuneration.

The insidious working of the system of perquisites is even more mischievous than its direct and obvious effects. It may be laid down as a rule of political economy that what people get by way of gifts connected with their profession or mode of earning their living comes in the end to be counted as part of their earnings. Hence, however little they themselves may desire such a result, perquisites invariably have the effect of lowering men's legitimate and regular pay. This has been found both in higher and lower examples than that of the police force. The working of this rule is well known to all political economists with regard to the agricultural labourers under the old Poor Law system; it is well known to all reforming politicians with regard to the perquisites of public servants of the highest ranks; and I believe it to have acted injuriously upon the moral character of the police force.

The fall in the value of money, which should be met by increase of pay, is apt to be—I believe has actually been—chiefly met by the increased urgency and ingenuity of the men in eking out their pay by perquisites. This is a natural tendency which can only be combated by liber-

ality in pay on the part of the employers, accompanied 1868
by inflexible severity in putting down the perquisite system. — Aetat. 62.
This combined liberality and severity is essential precisely in proportion to the responsibility of any employment and the importance of honesty in it. When the perquisite system is allowed to prevail, the best men get the fewest gifts, for they neither are so impudent in putting themselves in the way of gifts nor so willing to neglect their proper duty for the sake of them. Hence the best men get the worst pay, are disgusted with the force, gladly take other places when they can get them, and leave only the worst men behind. The same reasons apply, of course, to the enlistment of new men, and step by step the men get worse and worse, carry on the system of favour more openly and impudently year by year, until the disgraceful state of things of the Haymarket is arrived at, while the increasing difficulty of the superiors in finding trustworthy men to replace the untrustworthy causes them to go on tolerating abuses, the toleration of which in its turn makes the men more encroaching, and creates a vicious circle which nothing but a complete change of system can break through.

I am glad to hear the Tory is not to sit for Westminster without at least an attempt to protest against it, and I hope the attempt will result in opening the way for a Liberal. I can say this the more freely as I am no longer a party concerned.

To Dr. E. L. Youmans,

who had sought permission from Mill to publish some favourable expressions of opinion on Herbert Spencer, which Mill had made use of in a private letter.

AVIGNON, *20th December* 1868.

DEAR SIR,—Owing to the peculiar sensitiveness which both of us are aware of in Mr. Spencer, it is to be feared that he would be displeased at anything that would look like an advertisement or a testimonial; and it would be well if the purpose you have in view, and which I greatly

1868 — Aetat. 62.

wish to promote, could be attained by something written ostensibly for a different purpose. Your suggestion of putting something quotable into the book I am now editing is of this nature, and there are already passages in it respecting Mr. Spencer that would serve for quotation; but they refer to the "Psychology," not to the "First Principles" or the "Biology," and it would be difficult to find a good occasion for referring to either of these in a book exclusively psychological. There is in the thirteenth chapter of my "Examination of Sir William Hamilton's Philosophy" the following sentence: "This last extract is from Mr. Herbert Spencer, whose 'Principles of Psychology,' in spite of some doctrines which he holds in common with the intuitive school, are on the whole one of the finest examples we possess of the Psychological Method in its full power." Mr. Spencer is mentioned with honour in several other parts of the same work. If some of these passages will serve the purpose, or if you think it desirable in addition to have something from me in which the "First Principles" and "Biology" are spoken of to the same effect as in my letter to Mr. Spencer, I think the best way would be for you, or some one else, to write me a letter asking my opinion on those works, as if for private satisfaction. . . .

To W. T. Malleson, Hon. Sec. of Mill's Election Committee,

on the defeat at Westminster. The letter to M. Esquiros, referred to, was published without Mill's consent in the *Revue des Deux Mondes*. In it he gave an account of the causes which led to his defeat.

By Helen Taylor.

Avignon, *25th December* 1868.

Dear Sir,—When I received your letter I was on the point of writing to you to say that when I wrote to M. Esquiros I had not the remotest idea that my letter would be published; for had I intended it for publication, as perhaps you supposed I did from the manner in which it was inserted in the *Star*, I should not have omitted to make honourable mention of your name. I was greatly surprised to see it, and still more to see the manner in which it was inserted in the *Star*. I do not know how my friend M. Esquiros came to consent to its publication, for I am sure he would not have done so had he known my feeling against the publication of *private* letters without the permission of the writer. I certainly did infer from your published letter that you thought me wrong, not in the things I did, but in doing them without sufficient consideration for my constituents. I am therefore very glad to hear from yourself that that was not your feeling. 1868 — Aetat. 62.

Although I think it is to be regretted that you thought it necessary to give publicity to any difference of opinion between us, I might have been tempted to reply publicly to your letter myself, but I think it better to abstain than to give a handle for those who would be delighted to see anything like apparent dissension.

If I have not written to you before now, thanking you for your exertions in the election, it has been from the tendency to say least to those in whom one feels the fullest confidence. I felt so sure of your public spirit that I have thought you could not possibly doubt my esteem nor care for any expressions of gratitude from me for services to the cause in which we are fellow-workers.

I had occasion some little time ago to write to Mr. Beggs in reply to a letter from him, and in doing so I said what I would have been far more willing to see published than anything else I have written on the subject, inasmuch as I assured him that I had omitted nothing that conscience and sense of public duty would allow me to do to secure my return for Westminster. However little I personally wished to be returned, I felt that I owed it to my constituents to do all that lay in my power to succeed; but I did not feel that I owed it either to them or to myself to go against the very principles upon which I was standing. Those for whose sake I most cared to succeed, among the

1868 — Aetat. 62.

foremost of whom was yourself, would not have had a true representative in me if I had after all succumbed to that temptation to time-serving, the very prevalence of which, and my protests against which, were their original reason for choosing me. It is better to have a man who has never made any pretence of disliking it, than one who, after having protested strongly against it, has finally fallen a victim to the many temptations to practise it. In fine, I thought that my constituents as well as myself would rather have Mr. Smith as he is, than myself false to my professions. It is, of course, a subject of regret to all who feel as you and I do that absolute purity of principle in electioneering, and perfect independence on the part of candidates, cannot be made to succeed better than it generally does at present, yet I think I have done more to draw attention to the need of it by my failure than I could have done if I had allowed it to be possible to reproach me with the smallest tergiversation. The slightest example of anything of the kind would of course have been eagerly seized by our opponents, and nothing that they can say now can be so mortifying to you or myself as such accusations would have been had they had a shadow of foundation. Could it have been said that I turned my back upon old friends or shrunk from any associations that were not likely to be popular with the mass of my constituents, neither society nor the press would have failed to say it.

P.S.—As I have very unexpectedly seen so many of my letters lately in print, may I beg you to consider my letters as not intended for the public. Pray excuse my making this request to you, with whom I have every reason to believe it unnecessary.

To Philip H. Rathbone,

in reply to an invitation to come to Liverpool to the annual dinner of the Philomathic Society.

Avignon, *26th December* 1868.

Dear Sir,—I am much honoured by the renewal of the invitation from the Philomathic Society, and could I be sure of any definite result, more particularly of any definite political result, that could be obtained by my acceding to it, I would not hesitate to come to England for the purpose, and to undertake the labour of preparing something for the occasion, although to do so would require me to put aside avocations in which I am now engaged, and which I expect will fully occupy my time for some months to come, so that my present plan is not to be in England until the beginning of March. But I am very distrustful of the good that can be effected, or at all events, of my own power to effect much good, by merely social means, or even by eliciting sympathies, chiefly literary or scientific. Knowing as I do how many of the slaveholders approved of and admired my writings, I know how little any practical political results need necessarily follow from this sort of approval; and although I am aware that the enthusiasm produced by oratory is among many, perhaps among the majority of men, warmer than that felt for any literary works, still I doubt whether it is more lasting, and I am quite sure that it is not within my own power to excite so much of it. Could I within the compass of an after-dinner speech, carefully calculated to touch upon no points which could hurt the feelings of any who differ from us most radically both in principles and in their applications, produce any appreciable effect in reuniting and stimulating the Liberal political opinion of Liverpool? Were you proposing to discuss any especial political topics, for example, such as the representation of minorities, which I have made the subject of study, the case might be different, for it might then be in my power to advance arguments and to put them in a point of view not usual. But from what you say I imagine that you think politics should be eschewed, and even the political aspect of such subjects as education avoided. Nor am I quite sure whether just at present my views on personal representation, on the applications of endowments, on the land laws, on trades-unions, and other topics partly politico-economical and partly political, might not be somewhat too startling for those who shrink even from the disendowment of the Irish Church. . . .

To George Howell,

to whose election expenses in contesting Aylesbury Mill had subscribed. Howell's letter ended: "I wish I had been successful, to have had the honour of placing the seat at your disposal."

Avignon, *27th December* 1868.

1868 — Ætat. 62.

Dear Sir,—I cannot leave unacknowledged the concluding sentence of your letter of the 19th inst. If you had been returned for Aylesbury and had made the public-spirited offer of retiring in my favour, I could not possibly have accepted it. I attach far too much importance to the representation of the working classes, in some cases at least, by the *élite* of themselves, to have consented to put myself in the place of one of them if he had fortunately been elected. The defeat of all the working-class candidates, and of most of those of any other class in whom the working classes took special interest, would have made my presence in the House of Commons of far less use than it might perhaps have been if I had been one of a phalanx of men of advanced opinions. I hope the working classes will learn from their present failure a lesson of organisation, and, as the Liberal party can never succeed at a general election without their active support, will henceforth make such support conditional on being allowed an equal voice in the selection of the Liberal candidates, so that, whenever a constituency returns two members, one of these may be a man designated by, and especially acceptable to, the Liberals of the working classes.

CHAPTER XII

(1869)

To Henry (afterwards Sir Henry) Maine, on the Indian land question.

Avignon, *1st January* 1869.

My dear Sir,—The painfully interesting papers which you kindly forwarded to me have impressed me with a very strong sense of the degree in which official opinion has retrograded in India since I ceased to be a regular reader of Indian official correspondence. When I left the India House the feeling that the actual cultivators had claims upon us which we could not ignore was leading to plans for revising in their favour, so far as was still possible, even the system established by Lord Cornwallis in Bengal proper. Act 10 of 1859, with the provisions of which I am very imperfectly acquainted, was, I believe, the fruit of this movement. Now, however, there seems to be a reaction towards landlordism of the present English type, at the very time when in England opinion is, though slowly, beginning to turn the contrary way. And what is most of all deplorable, this reaction seems to be chiefly among the younger men. I do not maintain that the evil is to be ascribed to the constitutional change made in 1858, for it is very probable that the Mutiny and its consequences would have wrought the same change for the worse if the old organ of government had continued. The greater fear of the natives, and desire of conciliating the natives, which have existed since the Mutiny ("the natives" being, as usual, a mere synonym for the powerful classes, the great landholders), have discredited the ideas of protection to the interests of the great mass of the population, which in a more or less enlightened shape had been the animating

1869 — Aetat. 62.

1869 — Aetat. 62.

principle of Indian government for a whole generation. The Talockdars of Oude, the very men whose atrocities were the defence pleaded for the annexation of the country, have been made by us greater men than they ever were; and now everybody, even though a peasant, on whom it is possible to fasten the name of a proprietor, is, in the opinion of an apparently powerful party, to be treated as if the land and its inhabitants only existed for his benefit. These notions, which I am afraid are ruling the local administration of the Central Provinces as well as the Punjab, naturally find warm support from the ignorant, *arriéré*, prejudiced, and bigoted Toryism of Sir W. Mansfield. Until now the strong contrary convictions of Sir John Lawrence have moderated the mischief, but India has now got an Irish landlord to rule over her; and it is quite uncertain whether his official superior, the Duke of Argyll, will be any check upon his landlordism. There has been no more determined defender than the Duke of the evictions, in utter defiance of customary and traditional ideas of rights, which have depopulated the North of Scotland.

To look at the matter on another side: is it not monstrous that young settlement officers should have had it in their power, without express authorisation or instructions from the Government, to reduce to the condition of mere tenants at will in a single district 46,000 out of 60,000 cultivators who had been declared at the former settlement to have rights of occupancy? and that, too, when they had been so declared on the ground, equitable enough under the circumstances, of continuous occupation for a minimum period of twelve years, which ten or fifteen years additional occupancy under our rule had increased to a quarter of a century. All this disturbance of recognised rights and authorised imputations, so great an evil anywhere and one of the greatest in India, is incurred for the sake of a retrograde step in economics and social organisation! I hope I am not wrong in collecting from the discussion in Council that these divisions of the settlement officers will not be upheld unless when they would have been valid divisions under the Act just passed. A great part of these, however, would have been valid under the Act, especially in the case of tenants who have at any time made an admission of their having no rights of occupancy, which I perceive they did in 19,000 out of the 46,000 cases, and I agree with you in profoundly distrusting these admissions; not only for the very sufficient reasons stated by you in Council, nor only from the great probability that the admissions were often obtained by unfair means, but also from the little value which the natives of India habitually attach to admissions against their own interest, because they have not been accustomed to expect that they will be held bound by them.

Except the exclusion of so large a number of cases from its benefits, I do not see much to complain of in the terms of the compromise established by the new Act. The distinction between Khoodkaust ryots and Pyekaust ryots is familiar to all administrators of Northern India, the former being understood to have an inherited right of occupancy of ancient date, while the latter belong to families who have arrived at a comparatively late period and remained on tolerance; though I am not sure that the Pyekaust ryots are always strictly tenants at will. Supposing, then, that all are allowed rights of occupancy who have a just claim to them, then, when there is no evidence of a right to hold at a fixed rent, it seems as much as they could expect that their rent should be fixed by law at 15 per cent. less (your letter by a *lapsus calami* says 15 per cent. more) than the rent paid by tenants who have no right of occupancy. It is, however, a defect that while there is a power given to the proprietor to buy out, on certain terms of compensation, the rights of the tenant, the Act gives no power to the tenant to buy out the rights of the landlord. As was well said in the discussion, this is as if the English Copyhold Commission, instead of enabling the copyholder to redeem the legal claim of the lord of the manor, had empowered the lord to turn out the copyholder for a compensation. This omission in the Act admits of being corrected by subsequent legislation. But

1869 unless it is done this year you will not be there to do it,

— Aetat. 62. and who can tell how your place may be filled?

It has given me great pleasure that your health does not seem to have suffered from your residence in India. You will find abundant work for one like you in England, much of it such as few have anything like your qualifications for performing. I hope that such personal acquaintance with you as I have ever had the good fortune of enjoying will be not only renewed but greatly improved after your return to Europe.

To Parke Godwin,

in reply to a letter congratulating Mill on his release from Parliamentary duties.

Avignon, *1st January* 1869.

Dear Mr. Godwin,—It gave me great pleasure to hear from you, and especially to receive a letter showing so fundamental an agreement in our modes of thinking on the great questions of the future. The emancipation of women and co-operative production are, I fully believe, the two great changes that will regenerate society. But though the latter of these may grow up without much help from the action of Parliaments and Congresses, the former cannot. I have always thought with you that the abstinence of many of the best minds in America from political life was to a great degree accounted for by the fact that America, as a rule, needs very little governing. But the present is surely a time in which, even in America, the action of legislation and administration is of transcendant importance; and in the old and complicated societies of Europe the need of political action is always, more or less, what exceptional circumstances make it in America at present. Moreover, a place in Parliament is, in England, a vantage ground from which opinions can be promulgated to a larger audience and with a far greater probability of being listened to, than from any other position, except perhaps that of an editor of a widely circulated daily paper. It was with this hope principally that I accepted a seat in Parliament, and on one subject at least, the political enfranchisement of women, the results have far exceeded my expectation. It is doubtful whether there remains anything of the first importance which I could more effectually help forward by being in Parliament. Personal representation—the greatest political improvement, after women's suffrage, which remains to be made—I can help, perhaps as effectually, by my writings. I am, therefore, quite content, on public grounds, to be no longer a member of the House, while on private, my release justifies, and more than justifies, your congratulations.

If you are in England in March or April I shall hope to see you and to compare notes with you on many subjects, both American and general.

To D. McLaren, M.P.,

on the publication by him of one of Mill's letters without having previously asked permission from Mill.

Avignon, *3rd January* 1869.

Dear Mr. McLaren,—I need hardly say that I am very much gratified by your kind letter. I know that you and Mrs. McLaren acted for the best, and I agree with you that the publication of my letter to her may do some good. As a rule, however, I prefer that my letters should not be made public unless they were written with a view to the contingency of their being so, and I have seen with regret several recent instances in which publicity has been given to them without my consent: not that I shrink from exposure to criticism, which any public man, even any writer, ought to welcome, from however hostile a quarter, but because, when writing confidentially to friends who feel as one does oneself, one takes many things for granted which would require explanation to general readers, and one does not guard one's expressions as prudence and courtesy would require one to do in addressing oneself

1869 — Aetat. 62.

to those who differ from one. All the letters of mine which have lately been published have been treated by the newspapers exactly as if they had been written for the public and sent to the editors by myself.

It is, as a general rule, best, I think, to ask the writer's consent before publishing a letter. This is so flattering a thing to do that there can never be any difficulty in doing it.

I am particularly pleased at your approbation of the last sentence of my letter, because I can share in it myself, for it was dictated to me, as I wrote it word for word, by my dear daughter. We always agree in sentiments, but she sometimes can find better words to put them in than I can myself.

To George W. Smalley,

who had sent Mill two copies of the American *Tribune*, in which an account was given of the defeat at Westminster.

Avignon, *6th January* 1869.

Dear Sir,—I am much obliged to you for sending me the *Tribunes.* I need hardly say that your letters are most gratifying to myself personally, and that I have read with great interest the picture of the elections as they presented themselves to your mind. In regard to the Westminster election, I think your first impression of the cause of my defeat was more correct than your subsequent one. I may have lost a good many votes by the Bradlaugh business, but not so many as to account for the great difference between Smith's number at the poll and mine.

On one point I ought to correct your impression. You say it is reported that I spent a great deal of money, some £1100, on my first election, and was expected to spend as much more on the second. I was not aware that such things had been said or thought by any one. It is a literal fact that neither of my contests has cost me one penny, directly or indirectly. You are right in thinking that I both could and would have paid the expenses had I thought it desirable on public grounds to do so; but, having said that I would not, I thought it right to adhere to my word, for nothing does more mischief than high-flown professions, which are only intended to be taken *cum grano salis* by the initiated. 1869 — Aetat. 62.

Republican opinions certainly seem to have a much greater number of partisans in Spain than was supposed, and the number is likely to increase as the prospect becomes more familiar to people's minds in the absence of any generally acceptable candidate for the throne. But it strikes me that it would be a great mistake on the part of the Republicans to include a President in their programme. They should have a mere Prime Minister, removable by the Cortes. Even in America the inconvenience is very great of having a President and a Congress who, if hostile to one another, cannot either of them get rid of the other for what may be several years; and in any Continental European country the almost certain consequence of discord between the two authorities would be a *coup d'état* by the one which has the troops under its command. There is nothing in Prim's career which gives me the smallest confidence in his being, that rarity among Spanish politicians, a man of principle; and if he becomes President of a Spanish Republic it will be very likely with the full intention to take the first opportunity of playing the game of Napoleon the Third, after which Spain will be a Republic after the fashion of those of Spanish America—a perpetual succession of military dictators, each supplanting his predecessor by a pronunciamento or a civil war. That at least is my impression, grounded no doubt on very imperfect knowledge.

To W. T. Thornton.

Partly by Helen Taylor.

Avignon, 16*th January* 1869.

Dear Thornton,—I have to thank you again for one of your pleasant letters. I congratulate you on having

1869 — Ætat. 62. brought your book to a happy termination, and most heartily wish it the success with the public which I am sure it deserves. Your description of your feeling of recovered liberty after the completion of your book would seem to describe my feeling at having recovered the free disposal of my time. I also, like you, have a great arrear of miscellaneous reading to bring up, and this is not yet getting itself done very quickly in consequence of other arrears. The printer is making good progress with the "Analysis," and I hope to succeed in the attempt to get it published by or soon after the 1st of March. From what you say I hope to have read your book before that time. I have a good deal to read and study before I next revise my "Political Economy" for another edition.

What you say of Sir Stafford Northcote's weakness of character, giving up good reasons of his own to bad ones of other people, explains to me much of his political life; how the more vigorous will of Sir Charles Trevelyan kept him true to his convictions as to competitive examinations; and how his honesty of purpose did not hinder him from going all lengths with Disraeli, though Disraeli did not convince his reason. I do not know what sort of a Minister the Duke of Argyll will turn out, but I am glad you have not got Bright, who would have had much to unlearn, and very little disposition to unlearn it. The two members of Council you mention are not good average specimens, having been selected by the old body out of their own number in consequence chiefly of their personal popularity, which was in itself not undeserved.

We are glad you share in our estimate of our terrace, which, so far from being suppressed, has been nearly doubled in size, we having increased the part of the house of which it is the roof, and added a bathroom thereto. Moreover, Helen has carried out her long-cherished scheme (about which she tells me she consulted you) of a "vibratory" for me, and has made a pleasant covered walk some 30 feet long, where I can vibrate[1] in cold or

[1] [Mill doubtless adopted this word from Bentham, who had a similar covered walk at Ford Abbey. *Vide* Bain's "Life of James Mill," p. 133.]

rainy weather. The terrace, you must know, as it goes round two sides of the house, has got itself dubbed the "semi-circumgyratory." In addition to this, Helen has built me a *herbarium*—a little room fitted up with closets for my plants, shelves for my botanical books, and a great table whereon to manipulate them all. Thus, you see, with my herbarium, my vibratory, and my semi-circumgyratory, I am in clover, and you may imagine with what scorn I think of the House of Commons, which, comfortable club as it is said to be, could offer me none of these comforts, or, more properly speaking, these necessaries of life. Helen says *your* room is not finished yet, because, as she is architect and master mason all in one, she is carrying on the improvements very slowly, not letting the attention to them interfere too much with her other work. But you may be sure we have not altered the outward aspect of our dear little cottage, which looks as small as ever, and you may be equally sure that I am lost in wonder and admiration of the ingenuity with which Helen has contrived to manage it all. You will not be surprised to learn that among the other additions there is a puss-house. Altogether we are very comfortable, and only wish everybody could be as comfortable as we are. The weather this year, though cloudy and wet, is still so delightfully mild that we can still spend hours upon the terrace.

1869 — Aetat. 62.

To Standish O'Grady,

in reply to a question about Mill's discussion of Miracles in the "Logic."

Avignon, 16*th January* 1869.

Dear Sir,—The reason why I think that a miracle could not prove supernatural power to any one who did not already believe in the existence of some such power, is this, that we never can know that any seeming miracle implies supernatural power. The achievement of apparently impossible results by strictly natural means is a fact,

1869 — Aetat. 62. not only within experience, but within common experience. It is not even necessary to suppose the employment of a law of nature not previously discovered. It is sufficient to bear in mind the innumerable and truly wonderful exploits of jugglers, and, supernatural power not being proved by the miracle, *à fortiori* it would not be proof of a God.

If, however, any man possessed the apparent power of controlling not some particular laws of nature, but all laws of nature—if he actually stopped the course of the sun, arrested the tides, changed the water of the sea instantaneously from salt to fresh, and so on without limit; then indeed he would prove by the direct testimony of sense that there existed a supernatural power, and that he was possessed of it. The fact is, that this would be an experience as complete as, and the exact counterpart of, that which we should have of creation if we had ocular demonstration of worlds similar to our own called into existence by a Will.

But if the apparently supernatural power only manifests itself in the seeming supersession of a limited number of natural laws, the hypothesis of its being done by means of other natural laws would be, as it seems to me, intrinsically so much more probable, that nothing but the proved impossibility of this could warrant the conclusion that the power was supernatural. And this proof of impossibility it is evident could never be obtained, in the existing or very probable future state of human knowledge.

To E. Jones,

in acknowledgment of a pamphlet by him on Orthography.

AVIGNON, 19*th January* 1869.

DEAR SIR,—I thank you for your pamphlet. It is truly a frightful consideration that the annual number of pupils who pass the highest grade in the schools aided by Government, *i.e.* who leave the schools able to read a newspaper with understanding, is less than the number of teachers (including pupil teachers) employed in the schools. To remedy such a state of things as this requires a most earnest devotion of the administration, and probably of the legislative mind to the purpose. There is no doubt that, as you say, a simplification of English orthography would facilitate considerably the task of learning to read. A language which, like the Spanish of the present time, has reduced its spelling to a perfectly uniform system, has a great advantage over others. But it would take a much longer time to effect a change in orthography than would be required to teach every child in the United Kingdom to read with facility. There certainly is no necessity that it should take "seven years of the best learning period of a child's life" to teach him to read. So great a waste of time only proves the wretchedness of the teaching. I, myself, cannot remember any time when I could not read with facility and pleasure; and I have known other children with whom this was the case. Such essays as yours, however, do good, both by causing discussion, and by promoting useful though gradual changes. The Commission you propose would be useful in a similar manner, but the Government may perhaps not think that a subject which does not come within the province of direct legislation is a suitable subject for a Government inquiry.

1869 — Aetat. 62.

To the Secretary of the American Social Science Association,

in reply to an invitation to come over to America. The Association undertook to pay the whole of Mill's expenses, both of travelling and living in America; to send a representative to England to escort him over and attend to his comfort; and if he felt in-

1869 — Ætat. 62. clined to lecture while in America, to pay him three hundred dollars for each lecture.

AVIGNON, 19*th January* 1869.

DEAR SIR,—I have had the pleasure of receiving your letter of the 21st ulto., proposing on the part of the American Social Science Association that I should visit the United States as their guest, and make a lecturing tour through the Northern States under their auspices.

Few things could be more flattering to me than the high honour of such an invitation from such a body; and your letter also contains proposals of a pecuniary nature on such a scale of liberality, as to convert a visit to the United States from an expensive pleasure into a source of great personal profit.

The shortness, however, of life, and the numerous unexecuted literary projects which the public duties, on which the greater part of my life has been occupied, have left on my hands, and which require all the leisure of my remaining years for their fulfilment, admonish me of the necessity of dividing such time as I am able to dispose of between those undertakings, and a rest more complete than would be afforded by a journey such as that to which I am so flatteringly invited.

These are the considerations which compel me to decline an invitation so honourable, and which, if I had more leisure and a greater number of years of life in prospect, would have been so welcome to me.

Allow me in conclusion to express to yourself personally my sincere acknowledgments of the friendly and courteous terms in which you have communicated to me the proposal of the Association.

TO HEWETT C. WATSON,

acknowledging the gift of his book "Cybele Britannica."

AVIGNON, 30*th January* 1869.

DEAR MR. WATSON,—I am much obliged to you for your kind present. You are right in thinking that my absence from Parliament will give me more time for botany; I am now looking through my herbarium for the first time since the winter of 1864–65. But the scientific interest of your book gives it a value to me beyond the purely botanical. 1869 — Aetat. 62.

In regard to the Darwinian hypothesis, I occupy nearly the same position as you do. Darwin has found (to speak Newtonically) a *vera causa*, and has shown that it is capable of accounting for vastly more than had been supposed; beyond that it is but the indication of what may have been, though it is not proved to be, the origin of the organic world we now see. I do not think it an objection that it does not, even hypothetically, resolve the question of the first origin of life, any more than it is an objection to chemistry that it cannot analyse beyond a certain number of simple or elementary substances. Your remark that the development theory naturally leads to convergences as well as divergences is just, striking, and as far as I know, has not been made before. But does not this very fact resolve one of your difficulties, viz., that species are not, by divergence, multiplied to infinity? since the variety is kept down by frequent blending. The difficulty is also met by the fact that the law of natural selection must cause all forms to perish except those which are superior to others in power of keeping themselves alive in circumstances actually realised on the earth.

To a Youth of Fifteen,

who asked Mill's opinion on the subject of predestination. The youth wished to become a sailor, but was opposed by his parents, lest he might be drowned.

AVIGNON, *3rd February* 1869.

DEAR SIR,—I do not believe, nor I fancy does any one in the present day, except Mahometans and some other Orientalists, believe, that there is such a thing as destiny in the sense in which you understand it. The only necessity in events is, that causes produce effects, and means accom-

1869 — Aetat. 62. plish ends. Effects never come but through their causes. By avoiding, to the utmost of one's power, all the causes of an effect, one greatly increases the chances of one's avoiding the effect. And if one desires an end, one greatly increases one's chance of obtaining it by adopting some known means. It is true, what we desire sometimes comes to pass without any effort of ours, and what we dislike sometimes happens in spite of all we can do to avert it; but our conduct has on the average many times more effect on the fate of such of us as are not under the control of other people, than all other circumstances put together. There is no doubt that if you adopt a sailor's life you have a greater chance of being drowned than in most other occupations, because the causes which operate in that direction occur oftener and are less (though still very much) under human control. It is not, therefore, by any argument founded on destiny that you can hope to overcome the scruples of your parents, but rather by urging that all occupations are exposed to some evil chances, that one may be too much afraid of death, and that if persons of good health and strength were to avoid a really useful employment like that of a sailor because of its dangers, the world's affairs could not be carried on.

To James Beal,

on London Municipal Administration.

AVIGNON, *8th February*, 1869.

DEAR SIR,—I certainly do think your original plan of municipal government in London preferable to that of a single municipal government for the whole metropolis. When I first heard of your plan, it at once struck me as that which best met the real difficulties of the case, while it had also the advantage of being less open to unreasonable as well as reasonable objections; and this opinion has been confirmed by the additional consideration which since the receipt of your letter I have given to it. I will endeavour to put down what occurs to me, for any use you like to make of it except sending it to the press. I rather regretted that you published the letter I sent you about police; not that there was anything in its substance that I could wish to withhold from publicity, but because in a mere memorandum for a friend, with whom one agrees generally in opinion, intended to be used by him for what it may be worth as materials for forming his own judgment, the same things are said in a different manner from that in which one would address the public. Accordingly, though you used the precaution of stating that the letter was to a private friend, the newspapers took no notice of that, but judged the letter exactly as if it had been written for the public, and charged it with dogmatism, arrogance, and what not. These accusations are not a very great evil, but there are so many purposes for which one is bound to risk them that it is better not to court such occasions unnecessarily, and in the case of the letter I am now writing there are special reasons against communicating it to those who are not to be taken into practical council, which will appear in the very first things I have to say.

It is to my mind certain that Parliament will not tolerate the existence in its immediate vicinity of another assembly resting on a broad basis of popular election, wielding the power and disposing of the great amount of revenue which would belong to a single body carrying on every branch of local administration for the whole of London. The idea excited would be that of the "Commune de Paris" during the Revolution. If, therefore, the plan adopted is that of a single assembly, one of two things will happen. Either, first, the power of the body will be extremely curtailed. This may be done in one or both of two ways: by leaving much of the administration in the hands of the parochial bodies, the vestries and local boards, whom it is a great object to extirpate, root and branch; or by withholding many of the most important parts of the local administration from the Council, and either leaving those parts in their present state of general neglect, varied by fitful parliamentary activity, or turning them over to a department of the central Government. These are modes in which the

1869 — Aetat. 62. *powers* of the municipal body may be brought within what Parliament would tolerate. The other course which may be adopted is that of spoiling its constitution, either by adopting a high electoral qualification, or by joining to the elected members a certain number of members nominated by the Government, or by making the assent of a Minister necessary to their more important acts. All these systems would be more intolerable to you and me, and to most of those who think with us in general politics, than even the present irregularity and want of system, and would be far more likely to last. These prudential reasons should, I think, prevent our friends from encouraging, or consenting to support, any plan for a single municipality.

But even in itself, a single municipality in so enormous a city seems to me unlikely to work well. There is far too much work to be done; and the mass of details affecting only particular neighbourhoods, would leave too little time or energy to the Council for maturing and carrying out general plans of improvement, and would, moreover, require it to be more numerous than is quite consistent with that purpose. Those who hold up as an example the local administration of Paris do not know what that administration is. Letting alone the fact that every single person connected with it is a Government nominee, it is not the fact that all Paris is under a single municipal administration: there is indeed but one Council, but there are twenty mayors, each of whom administers one of the twenty arrondissements. It is as much a double administration as that which would be given by our two bills, except that, England being a free country, our mayors must have councils, and properly elected ones, to assist and control them. I confess also I should not like to restrict to a single popular body all that exercise of the business faculties on public concerns which does take place under the present local institutions with all their imperfections, and which in England, and still more in America, trains many men of no great ability or reach of thought to be quite capable of discharging important public functions and of watching and controlling their discharge by others. This is one of the great differences between free and unfree countries—practical intelligence in public affairs not confined to the Government and its functionaries but diffused among private citizens. Our vestries are bad schools, but yet those who organise public movements, and bring the people together for an object, have mostly gained their first experience in the capacity of vestrymen, and it might easily happen that the too great concentration of municipal action might leave London without a sufficient number of such persons.

1869 — Aetat. 62.

To the President of a Committee,

formed for the purpose of securing an amnesty for political prisoners.

AVIGNON, *8th February* 1869.

DEAR SIR,—Your letter and the proposed Address enclosed in it reached me several days after the meeting to which you invited me.

I do not think I could go to the full length of what is claimed in the Address. I am very doubtful if the Government ought to release all who may be in prison for being connected, for instance, with the Clerkenwell outrage, or for having joined in the Fenian invasion of Canada. To those political prisoners who have shed no blood, or have shed it in the way of what may be called fair or legitimate insurrection on Irish soil, I would, simultaneously with a great act of justice to Ireland, grant a full pardon, with a public declaration that it is done from the hope that the willingness practically shown to redress Irish injuries by legislation would induce the Irish in future to seek for redress only in that way, and would thus render legal punishment unnecessary. But in rebellion, as in war, it seems to me that a distinction should be made between fair weapons or modes of warfare and foul ones. And a good deal of thought would be required to decide exactly where the line should be drawn.

To T. Cliffe Leslie.

Avignon, *8th February* 1869.

1869 — Aetat. 62.

Dear Mr. Leslie,—I have read your first letter in the *Economist* with great pleasure, and your paper on La Creuse with much interest and instruction. It is very important to put such points as it contains before the conceited Englishmen who fancy they understand all that relates to the land and politics of France, when they do not know the first rudiments of it, much less the many important matters you discuss. I look forward with great expectation to the other papers which you announce as in prospect, and shall not fail to weigh well what they say on political economy.

Many thanks for the trouble you have taken for M. Chauffard's Mittermaier.[1] I agree with you in going the complete length with Bentham as to the admissibility of evidence. There are, I believe, frequent cases like that you mention of practical mischief both to the accused and to others from his not being examined as a witness. The one point on which alone Bentham seems to me to be wrong is in allowing the judge to interrogate. But I have recently seen it stated that the prodigious abuse of this power which takes place in France is, in part, owing to the fact that men are almost always made judges from having been public prosecutors, *i.e.* persons the whole business of whom it has been to find evidence of guilt; and not, as with us, from among barristers, who have equally often had the duty of finding evidence of innocence. The reason is that the salaries of judges are not worth the acceptance of an advocate in good practice, and the salaries are small because, in France, there are everywhere courts of five judges or more, where a much smaller number and, in general, one judge would suffice; thus does a single error in a system engender a series of others.

The physical illustrations in my "Logic" were all reviewed and many of them suggested by Bain, who has a

[1] [Mittermaier's "Traité de la Procédure criminelle, &c.," translated from German into French by A. Chauffard. Paris, 1868.]

very extensive and accurate knowledge of physical science. 1869
He has promised me to revise them thoroughly for the —
next edition, and to put them sufficiently in harmony with Aetat. 62.
the progress of science; which I am quite aware that they have fallen behind.

To Sir Charles Dilke,

on his book "Greater Britain."

AVIGNON, *9th February* 1869.

My dear Sir,—Ever since reading your book, which a variety of occupations prevented me from doing until very lately, I have felt desirous of expressing to you the very high sense I entertain of its merits, and the great pleasure which, as one who has turned much of his attention to the same subjects, I have felt at seeing such a number of sound judgments, and such a sustained tone of right and worthy feeling, sent forth to the world in a style so likely to command attention, and by one who has the additional vantage-ground of a seat in Parliament. It is long since any book connected with practical politics has been published on which I build such high hopes of the future usefulness and distinction of the writer, showing, as it does, that he not only possesses a most unusual amount of real knowledge on many of the principal questions of the future, but a mind strongly predisposed to what are (at least in my opinion) the most advanced and enlightened views of them. There are so few opinions expressed in any part of your book with which I do not, as far as my knowledge extends, fully and heartily coincide, that I feel impelled to take the liberty of noting the small number of points of any consequence on which I differ from you. These relate chiefly to India; though on that subject also I agree with you to a much greater extent than I differ. Not only do I most cordially sympathise with all you say about the insolence of the English, even in India, to the native population, which has now become not only a disgrace, but, as you have so usefully shown, a danger to

1869 — Aetat. 62. our dominion there; but I have been much struck by the sagacity which, in so short a stay as yours must have been, has enabled you to detect facts which are as yet obvious to very few; as, for instance, the immense increase of all the evils and dangers you have pointed out, by the substitution of the Queen's army for a local force, of which both men and officers had at least a comparatively permanent tie in the country; and, again, that the superior authority in England, having the records of all the Presidencies before it, and corresponding regularly with them all, is the only authority which really knows India, the local Governments and officers only knowing at most their own part of it, and having generally strong prejudices in favour of the peculiarities of the system of government there adopted, and against those of the other parts. I observe that your preferences seem to be, as mine are, for the systems which give permanent rights of property to the actual cultivator, which is best done in the modern Bombay ryotwar system. I am sorry to say that there is at present a strong reaction in favour of setting up landlords everywhere, and, what is worst, I am told that this prevails most among the young men (the hide-bound Toryism of Sir W. Mansfield assisting), and there is great mischief of this kind in progress, both in the Punjaub and in the Central Provinces, notwithstanding the contrary predictions of Sir John Lawrence; what will happen under the Irish landlord who is now Viceroy,[1] I dread to think.

But have you not, on the questions which concern the English planters, leant too much to their side? You have yourself stigmatised their treatment of the natives, and what better can be expected in a country where a station-master kicks and cuffs the passengers, and a captain of a steamer kicks the pilot round the deck whenever the vessel runs aground? If it could be right to make the breach of a contract to labour for the planters, under habitual treatment of this sort from them and their low nigger-drivers, a penal offence, the evil could not be so flagrant as your book shows it to be, and as it undoubtedly is. Another thing

[1] [Lord Mayo.]

to be considered is that either a most unjust advantage would be given to European over native landholders and employers of labour, or the same legal remedy must be granted to both; and I suppose even those who think that an English indigo planter and his underlings would not suborn witnesses to depose falsely in a criminal court, will admit that a native landowner would. 1869 — Aetat. 62

In your plan for the improvement of the organ of Indian government in England, you show a just and enlightened appreciation of the necessity of making the organ a permanent one in the sense of not going out with the Ministry: but this will not and cannot be, if the organ is a Secretary of State, or any member of the Cabinet. No one who does not go out when the majority in Parliament changes will, or ought to, have a voice in the Cabinet which decides the general policy of the country. Neither is it likely to be thought right, nor indeed would it be right, that the Government of the empire should have no voice, not even a negative one, on the administration of its greatest dependency. If, then, the head administrator of India were not to be in the Cabinet, we should find that a Cabinet Minister would be set over him to control him, as one was set to control the Court of Directors; and the nominal head administrator being only one person, and that one of inferior official rank, would have no power of resistance, and would sink into a mere Deputy. Would this be any improvement? I have always myself thought that a Board or Council for India, with a Cabinet Minister to control them but not to sit among them, was the really best system for India, and I have given my reasons for this in the concluding chapter of my book on Representative Government. It is, however, impracticable to go back to this, and under the present system I think your own opinions will lead you to the conclusion that the Secretary of State must necessarily change with the Government, and that the real knowledge of India which you hope to obtain in him by making him permanent can only be found in a Council of advisers with at least as great powers as the present Council. It is quite another question whether the

1869 — Aetat. 62. Council ought not to be more rapidly renewed. I am much disposed to think with you that its members should only be appointed (and should, *exceptis excipiendis*, only hold their seats) for five years; but I think they ought to be fully as numerous as at present, that all the different systems of administration in India may have somebody there who knows them well enough and has sufficient sympathy with them to correct any misunderstanding to their disadvantage.

. . . . . .

You see that, in order to find fault with anything, I have very soon got down to extremely small points, or to such as have very little to do with the general scope of the work. If there is any criticism of a somewhat broader character that I could make, I think it would be this—that (in speaking of the physical and moral characteristics of the populations descended from the English) you sometimes express yourself almost as if there were no sources of national character but race and climate, as if whatever does not come from race must come from climate and whatever does not come from climate must come from race. But as you show in many parts of your book a strong sense of the good and bad influences of education, legislation, and social circumstances, the only inference I draw is that you do not perhaps go so far as I do myself in believing these last causes to be of prodigiously greater efficacy than either race or climate or the two combined.

To Pasquale Villari,

sympathising with him on the death of his mother.

Blackheath Park, *le* 19 *mars* 1869.

J'avais remarqué, mon cher M. Villari, que depuis longtemps je n'avais pas de vos nouvelles; cette intermission n'est que trop expliquée par la lettre que je viens de recevoir. La sympathie la plus vive et la plus sincère ne peut presque rien pour consoler dans un si grand malheur. Dans l'affreuse souffrance des premiers temps c'est presqu'une moquerie que d'en offrir. Maintenant le temps est venu pour vous de ce profond abattement, cette perte de tout intérêt dans la vie, que je comprends si bien, et qui serait presqu'aussi dur à supporter, s'il n'y avait un moyen un seul, de soulagement, pour celui qui est capable de trouver un attrait dans le travail désintéressé pour le bien des autres. Ceux qu'une grande douleur privée a degoûtés de tous les intérêts personnels, ont souvent fini par trouver une véritable consolation et un renouvellement d'energie dans la concentration de leur sensibilité et de leur intelligence sur des travaux ayant pour but l'amélioration morale, intellectuelle ou physique de leurs semblables. C'est là ce que j'espère pour vous. Vous êtes un homme très précieux pour votre pays, tres supérieur par la pensée et par les talents au niveau commun des hommes dans quelque pays que ce soit. Nul pays plus que le vôtre n'a besoin de ces qualités dans ses citoyens, et aucun n'offre un champ plus vaste et plus propice pour les exercer. Vous avez un amour de votre pays qui, je suis sûr, n'a pas sombré dans le naufrage de votre bonheur personnel. Tout ce qu'il y a de soulagement possible dans un malheur comme le vôtre, vous l'éprouverez quand vous vous sentirez capable de vous remettre à quelque travail important pour le bien général, et de nature à exiger toutes vos forces intellectuelles.

1869 — Aetat. 62.

Vous trouverez peut-être que je parle bien à mon aise de travail à un homme accablé de douleur étant moi-même dans un état de contentement personnel que je n'avais éprouvé de longtemps. En effet, je suis comme un soldat licencié qui retourne à ses foyers pour y jouir de plus grand privilège qu'une vie de travail puisse offrir, le libre choix de ses occupations. Pendant que j'étais député je ne jouissais cette liberté que pendant trois ou quatre mois de l'année. Pendant ce temps je vaquais à mes études philosophiques, et j'avais préparé une nouvelle édition du grand traité de psychologie de mon père, avec des notes par moi-même et par d'autres de ses successeurs dans la même école philosophique. Cette nouvelle édition vient d'être livrée au public, et l'exemplaire que je vous avais envoyé avant de recevoir votre lettre, vous parviendra, j'espère, en peu de

1869 — Aetat. 62. jours. Maintenant je vais publier un travail où la question des femmes est traitée avec plus d'étendue que dans tout ce qui a paru jusqu'ici en faveur de leur affranchissement. Cette cause fait ici un progrès très rapide, et un si grand nombre de femmes, et des plus distinguées, ont répondu à l'appel qui leur a été fait, que le succès, bien qu'encore éloigné, ne me le paraît plus autant qu'il y a trois ans. Ce petit traité vous parviendra, j'espère, peu de temps après l'autre.

Je tiens plus que jamais à avoir de vos nouvelles, et je vous prie de m'en donner fréquemment. De mon côté j'espère avoir à l'avenir plus de loisir pour vous écrire.

To Henry Fawcett,

in reply to a request from him for Mill's view on " Mr. Gladstone's scheme for the appropriation of the revenues of the Irish Church."

Blackheath Park, *22nd March* 1869.

Dear Mr. Fawcett,—I have considerable difficulty in judging from outside any question of political tactics during the present transitional state of politics. And the questions you put to me are essentially questions of tactics, for on the substantial issues there can hardly be any difference of opinion. The landlords undoubtedly get what they have no right to; for though they are charged a fair price for the tithe, the State, in one sense of the word, pays that price for them by lending them the money at a much lower rate than they themselves can borrow at; just as it lends them its money or credit for the improvement of their land. Thus it undoubtedly makes a present to them; but as that present costs itself nothing, consisting only in giving them the benefit of its better credit, the Government may be right, as a matter of tactics, in granting them this advantage, which costs nothing to anybody. Again, to employ the resumed national property or a part of it in education would be a far better application of it than the one proposed; but the measure would then no longer tend towards a reconcilement of religious differences. The application of any of the money to the Queen's colleges or to undenominational schools would be vehemently opposed by the whole Catholic party. The battle of unsectarian education will have to be fought, but we may hope to fight it with better support if this measure has first passed, retaining completely the character of a healing measure. It seems to me, too, that Ireland has a just claim upon the general taxation of the empire for all that it requires in the way of education; and inasmuch as unsectarian education is contrary to the wish of the great majority of the Irish people, *that* at least can with much greater propriety be charged upon general taxation, than upon a fund belonging to Ireland as the Church property does. What can be said on the other side of both these points will occur to yourself; and I am by no means against criticising these provisions of the Bill in a speech. With regard to any directly hostile movement against them (which would certainly be unsuccessful), I doubt if any advantage would arise from it equivalent to the bad effect of an apparent want of unanimity in the Liberal party in carrying through this measure. I do not feel able to give a more positive opinion on the subject.

My daughter desires to be kindly remembered to Mrs. Fawcett and yourself.

To A. H. Louis,

on a proposal to form an Academy of Moral and Political Science.

BLACKHEATH PARK, *22nd March* 1869.

DEAR SIR,—The idea of an Academy of Moral and Political Science has often presented itself to my mind; as it could hardly fail to present itself to any one who has been all his life speculating and thinking on social questions and who has studied the institutions and ideas of foreign countries. But the result of the thought I have given to the subject has always been unfavourable.

The Society, or Academy, would either be a public

1869 — Ætat. 62. body or a mere private association. If a public body, the original members would be named by the Government; subsequent vacancies might be filled up, as in France, by the votes of the body itself. If the Government acted honestly in the matter, which we will suppose it to do, it would appoint the persons of highest reputation as writers or thinkers on moral, social, and political subjects without (it is to be hoped) any regard to their opinions; for to pay any regard to these would simply mean to exclude all whose opinions were in advance of the age. This, then, being supposed, what sort of a body would be the result? An assemblage of persons of utterly irreconcilable opinions, who would hardly even be sufficiently unanimous on any question to exercise, as a body, any moral or intellectual influence over it; while amidst this medley of opinions there would be an assured majority in favour of what is conservative and commonplace, because such is invariably the tendency of the majority of those whose reputation is already made. In consequence, the subsequent elections by the members, to fill vacancies, would be decidedly worse than we are supposing the original choice to be, for men of the highest eminence would often not be elected if any of their opinions were obnoxious to the *arriéré* majority. Guizot, Thiers, and Cousin while he lived, ruled the French Academy of Moral and Political Sciences, and very few who were not of their opinions were, or now are, admitted into it. The Académié Française rejected Littré, the man who by his single efforts was doing admirably the whole work which the Academy was especially appointed to do. Even Academies of Physical Science, in which there is less difference of opinions, always consist in majority of trained mediocrities, while the men whose footsteps mark the great advances in science often do not succeed during their whole lives in obtaining admission. Originality, scientific genius, is in general looked shyly upon by the majority of scientific men; and it is of the majority that academies, however honestly constituted, will be the representatives.

If, on the other hand, the Society was not a public and organised body, but was composed of volunteers rallying round some common standard, it would not materially differ from any voluntary association of persons agreeing in some of their opinions, and would carry no more weight than any other set of men who unite to assist and back one another in the propagation of their particular doctrine. 1869 — Aetat. 62.

It does not seem to me possible, by any combination, to make the collective force of scientific thought available as a power in social affairs. The French academies never have been such a power: the Academy of Moral and Political Sciences is neither consulted, nor, as a body, puts forth any opinions, or exercises any moral or political action, except by offering prizes for essays. Its transactions, consisting of the papers read before it, are published, but one seldom sees them quoted or referred to. Its individual members have such influence as their talents or character may give them, but collective influence it has none.

Having given you the reasons which made me fear that the results you anticipate from the formation of an Academy of Moral and Political Science would not be realised, allow me now to express the great pleasure which our short conversation gave me, and the satisfaction I should have in co-operating with you on the subject of the Alabama claims, and I doubt not, on many other important matters. There is such a lack of energy and earnestness in all classes above manual labourers; and those who have any wish or capacity for improved ideas are so shrinkingly afraid of what will be said of them, and so daunted by the smallest obstacle, that it is a *dies albo notandus* on which one meets with any man of intelligence who feels and thinks as you did both in the Commons Society, in our conversation afterwards, and now in your letter.

To Lord Amberley.

Blackheath Park, *9th April* 1869.

Dear Lord Amberley,—It gave me great pleasure to hear from you, and to find my anticipation confirmed,

1869 — Aetat. 62. that you would enjoy your liberation from trammels as much as I do myself. There certainly is no blessing in human life comparable to liberty, for those at least who, having any good use to put it to, can indulge themselves in it with a good conscience. I envy you the pleasure of having got to a Latin classic. I hope to be able to give myself the same satisfaction by-and-by. I have not read a Greek or Latin book for at least half-a-dozen years with the exception of Plato, whom I read right through preparatory to reviewing Mr. Grote's account of him. Cicero's philosophical writings are very pleasant reading, and of considerable value historically, as our principal authority for much of the speculations of the Greek philosophical sects, and a brilliant specimen of the feelings of the best sort of accomplished and literary Romans towards the close of the Republic; but as philosophy they are not worth much, and I like his orations and letters better. It is true I am much interested in everything that relates to that great turning-point of history, the going out of what was left of liberty in the ancient world, and that calm after the storm, that tragical pause at the beginning of the downhill rush, which is called the Augustan Age—so solemn in its literary monuments, so deformed by the presence of Augustus in it. No historian has treated that cunning, base, and cruel adventurer as he deserved except Arnold in the "Encyclopædia Metropolitana" and Ampère in "L'Empire Romain à Rome," merely because Virgil and Horace flattered him.

But this kind of reading after all is but recreation, unless one is making a particular study of history in order to write it, or for some philosophical purpose. Psychology, ethics, and politics, in the widest sense of the terms, are the really important studies now, both for one's own instruction and for exercising a useful influence over others.

The Endowed Schools Bill will do a great deal of good if the proper use is made of the powers which it assumes, and Foster's speech shows that he at least intends to do the best. Let us hope that he will have sufficient firmness of his own and sufficient support from others not merely to carry the Bill, for that is little, but to work it according to the recommendations of the School Inquiry Commissioners. I honour Dr. Temple and Acland for producing so good a report, for I have no doubt it is mainly their doing.

1869 — Aetat. 62.

It will be very pleasant to see you and Lady Amberley in autumn at Avignon, if we do not sooner.

To A. Lalande,

on Mr. Lowe's Budget proposal to abolish the shilling duty on corn.

Avignon, *2nd May* 1869.

Dear Sir,—Your letter has followed me here, and I have read it with great interest. As a piece of English composition, it is quite remarkable as the production of a foreigner, and I agree in a great part of its substance. Mr. Lowe has certainly much exaggerated the strength of the case against the shilling duty on corn. I, however, differ from you on one of the leading points of your argument, viz. where you aim at proving that the price of corn would not fall by the whole amount of the duty taken off, but by a smaller amount, dependent on the degree in which the importation of corn may be increased by the abolition of the duty. This argument was urged formerly, during the discussions which preceded the repeal of our corn laws, and I had occasion to contest it at that time. It seems to me that your argument errs by stopping short at demand and supply as the final regulations of price, without going on to that which, in the last resort, adjusts the demand and supply to one another, viz. cost of production (including all cost necessary for bringing the article to the place of sale). If from any permanent natural calamity smiting the soil with sterility the cost of the production of wheat were increased by a shilling a quarter, I apprehend that the price of wheat would rise by that amount, *plus* the

1869 — Aetat. 62.

ordinary profit upon it, even if there were no diminution of supply. Whether the supply would be finally diminished or not would depend on whether the rise of price caused a falling off in the consumption. But the conditions of production having been altered, the average price (that which the producer looks forward to and calculates upon) must accommodate itself to the new conditions. And the same thing happens if, instead of a natural calamity, we suppose the artificial burthen of a tax, which, though levied only on a part of the corn consumed, enables all the remainder to command on the average the higher price necessary for bringing in that part. Supply and demand determine the perturbations of price, but (when the article admits of unlimited increase) not the permanent or average price.

I think, therefore, your argument fails in one important point; and though some of your other arguments remain valid notwithstanding, I do not think them sufficient to outweigh the advantage of getting rid of the last remaining shred of Protectionism.

But I do not therefore dissuade you from publishing your paper. It is written in a way to command attention, and so many intelligent persons will think your opinion correct and mine erroneous, that it is right that the opinion should have a fair hearing. The only newspapers, however, which would be very likely to insert such a paper would be the Conservative journals, *Standard*, *Herald*, &c., and with them I have no relations. Probably it would have a better chance either with them or with the *Times* if sent by yourself.

To Edwin Chadwick,

on Lord Russell's Bill for the Creation of Life Peerages.

Avignon, 2*nd May* 1869.

Dear Chadwick,—Lord Russell's Bill, and its favourable reception by the Lords, was no otherwise of importance than as showing the need which the Lords feel of strengthening their position. So small a number of life members would do little good even if they were always honestly selected, which they will not be. A few good names may be put in at first, but as a rule the life peerage will be a refuge for the mediocrities of past administrations. If now and then a thoughtful and vigorous man gets in, he will no doubt have the means of publicly speaking his thoughts, but to an inattentive audience; for the peers are too stupid and too conservative to be moved except by a party leader who they think will carry obstructiveness to the utmost limits of practicability; and the public pay little attention to speeches in the House of Lords. I doubt if a second chamber can ever again carry weight in English politics unless popularly elected. I feel sure, at all events, that nothing less than what I proposed in my book on Representative Government will enable it to do so. These are my opinions, but I do not wish to throw cold water on anything which acknowledges an evil and points in the direction of improvement.

1869 — Aetat. 62.

I should not at all wonder if Gladstone, in what he said to you, did hint at a life peerage: though perhaps what he meant was to hold out hopes that you might be supported by the Government in a future candidature for the House of Commons. I should be more glad if it were the last, but I do not mean that I should advise you to refuse the former, for as it would be obviously a tribute to your legislative capacity, it would doubtless increase your weight.

To T. Cliffe Leslie,

who wrote to Mill about his difficulties in getting his articles accepted.

Partly by Helen Taylor.

Avignon, 8*th May* 1869.

Dear Mr. Leslie,—You should not take the editors and their ways so much *au sérieux*. You must remember

1869 that your writings are intended for the public good, and
—
Ætat. 62. that the editors are not half such good judges of that as you are. Consequently it is for you to make them take your articles just as you would make them take medicine, without any *amour propre* at having made it up for them yourself, and so put in a little sugar now and then if need be. Now, having made a real success with your amusing as well as useful articles of travels, the editors ask you for more of the same, and you should give it them, wrapping up good doctrine in this form. You should be no more on your dignity with them than with children. To a man like yourself most of them are children, as regards their motives and the objects they have in view. Morley indeed is better, but I dare say he is a good deal bothered, and he probably thinks that Chauffard's Mittermaier is a subject that can wait better than most. I should be vexed if the paper you wrote to oblige me should have any unpleasant effect on your relations with him. . . .

To A. M. Francis, of Brisbane, Queensland, on various political questions.

Avignon, *8th May* 1869.

Dear Sir,—I have received your letter, and I will answer its different points seriatim.

1. My letter to Mr. Holden has been much misunderstood if it is supposed to indicate any change whatever in my opinions on the sphere and functions of Government in the economical affairs of societies. The only opinion I intended to withdraw was that which recommended, in certain cases, temporary Protective duties in new countries to aid the experimental introduction of new industries. And even on this point I continue to think that my opinion was well grounded, but experience has shown that Protectionism, once introduced, is in danger of perpetuating itself through the private interests it enlists in its favour, and I therefore now prefer some

other mode of public aid to new industries, though in itself less appropriate. 1869 — Aetat. 62.

I quite agree with you that in Australia there are many important requisites of prosperity which the Government ought not to consider it beyond its province to provide. One of these is the one you mention—works of irrigation. I have long looked forward to the time when Australia would feel the need of tanks like those of Southern India, to retain through the dry season the surplus rains of the few rainy months. This, however, is a work on a great scale, requiring combined labour, and therefore difficult to accomplish with your present population.

I took no part in the discussion about the purchase of the telegraphs, because it was a mere experiment of which I do not foresee the result. I should object to the purchase of the railways until the smaller measure shall have approved its policy by its success. And in no case does it seem to me admissible that the Government should *work* the railways. If it became proprietor of them it ought to lease them to private companies.

2. With regard to lands, I am still, like yourself, in favour of the Wakefield system. I should, however, highly approve of selling the lands subject to a land tax, if the Government is in a condition to enforce its payment without a cost exceeding the worth; a difficulty which seemed fatal to this plan when Wakefield wrote.

3. On the importation of Polynesian labourers I am afraid we differ more widely. If the South Sea islanders came to Queensland spontaneously, the province would have every reason to welcome their coming. But I have the most deep-rooted distrust of plans for sending emissaries to induce them to come, even by no worse means than brilliant representations. And I do not believe that any laws, which it is possible to enforce among an English population, will protect ignorant and uncivilised strangers, living with them as servants, against outrageous abuses of power. If the experiment ever answers, it is probably with Chinese, who are a more fearless and vigorous race, and are able to make themselves very unpleasant to those

1869 — Aetat. 63.

who ill-treat them. But the common English abroad—I do not know if in this they are worse than other people—are intensely contemptuous of what they consider inferior races, and seldom willingly practise any other mode of attaining their ends with them than bullying and blows. I therefore most positively object to putting such victims in their power. If there are no other means of preventing labour from being over scanty, then I am afraid the inconveniences of the climate must be taken with its advantages. But I should think that the agricultural population of England would furnish (agreeably to one of Wakefield's principles) a sufficient number of young married couples to supply in a moderate number of years the labour required.

If in the expression of these opinions I have been rather brief and abrupt, I beg that you will attribute it to my occupations, and to the haste with which they oblige me to write.

To A. Lalande,

on the Budget proposal.

Avignon, 24*th May* 1869.

Dear Sir,—I have read your letter of the 18th inst. with attention and interest, and I am much inclined to think with you that the effect of so small a duty as one shilling a quarter on wheat is not sufficient to make it certain that any perceptible relief will be obtained by taking it off. Still, we must reason about small effects on the same principle as one does on large ones. The duty gives a premium of a shilling in cost of production to home-grown corn over imported. This must naturally cause a certain quantity more to be grown at home and a certain quantity less to be imported, and every additional quantity grown at home in a given state of agriculture is grown at a proportionally greater cost. The average price, therefore, must rise sufficiently to remunerate this greater cost, but it will not rise by the full amount of the duty; otherwise it would not have the effect of reducing the quantity imported. Thus the average price of corn will, I conceive, be raised by an uncertain amount short of one shilling a quarter. But this increased price the consumer has to pay on *all* corn, home grown as well as imported, and from this he will be relieved by taking off the duty.

1869 — Aetat. 63.

To P. A. Taylor, M.P.,

on the Bill brought into Parliament for the purpose of degrading Mr. O'Sullivan from his office of Mayor of Cork, on the ground of the support which he gave to the Fenian movement.

Avignon, 28*th May* 1869.

. . . I cannot but think that the dropping of the Bill against O'Sullivan has saved the British democracy from a most perilous snare. It seems to me that the distinction between a government by general laws and one of arbitrary edicts is the broadest in all politics, and absolutely essential to good government under any institution, for the reason long ago assigned by Aristotle, that government by law is guided by general considerations of permanent feelings, while government by special decree is guided by the passion of the moment. And it is most especially necessary that this distinction should not be tampered with in a popular Government, for most other Governments are under some check from fear of the majority; but when the majority is itself the Government, the check is only in its own breast, and depends on a strong conviction in the popular mind of its necessity, which conviction is enfeebled by every instance of violation. I think it would be a fatal notion to get abroad among the people of a democratic country that laws or constitutions may be stepped over instead of being altered; in other words, that an object immediately desirable may be grasped directly in a particular case without the salutary previous process of considering whether the

1869 — Ætat. 63. principle acted on is one which the nation would bear to adopt as a rule for *general* guidance. I have always admired Lincoln, among other reasons, because even for so great an end as the abolition of slavery he did not set aside the Constitution, but waited till he could bring what he wanted to do (by a little straining, perhaps) within the license allowed by the Constitution for military necessities.

To Dr. Cazelles,

on his French translation of the "Subjection of Women."

Avignon, *le* 30 *mai* 1869.

Cher Monsieur,—Je crois en effet que quelques pages préliminaires à la traduction de l'Assujetissement des Femmes seraient très utiles et je trouve les vôtres excellentes. Je vous soumettrai cependant deux ou trois observations.

1. D'abord il me semble que vous ne rendez pas pleine justice aux St. Simoniens et aux Fourieristes, que vous désignez clairement sans les nommer. Je condamne comme vous beaucoup de leurs doctrines et surtout le gouvernementalisme à outrance des St. Simoniens. Cependant je trouve que les uns et les autres ont rendu de grands services : et notamment sur la question des femmes, le St. Simonisme surtout ayant jeté dans les hautes régions de la vie intellectuelle et pratique, un grand nombre d'esprits supérieurs, désabusés aujourd'hui de ce qu'il y avait de faux ou d'exaggéré dans leurs systèmes, mais conservant ce qu'ils avaient de bon, y compris l'égalité des femmes. Les St. Simoniens avaient d'ailleurs le bon esprit de déclarer toujours qu'on ne peut prononcer sur la fonction des femmes sans elles et que la loi qui les doit régir ne peut être donnée que par des femmes ou par une femme. Ils n'ont donné leurs propres idées sur ce sujet que comme des hypothèses. Il est vrai que, comme il arrive le plus souvent, on leur a tenu très peu compte de cette réserve.

2. D'un autre côté tout en traitant Proudhon avec une juste sévérité vous me semblez lui avoir fait la part trop belle en disant qu'il a rendu de grands services à la course du progrès. Je puis me tromper, mais il m'a toujours semblé que Proudhon a été très nuisible à la cause du progrès. D'abord personne n'a tant fait pour provoquer la réaction de la peur, qui a eu et qui a encore des effets si funestes. Ensuite je ne vois dans ses écrits rien de sincèrement juste et progressif. Ce qu'il y a chez lui de plus puissant c'est sa dialectique subversive, mais c'est une dialectique d'un mauvais aller ; une vraie sophistique, car elle s'attaque au bien comme au mal, et au lieu de se contenter de dire ce qui peut se dire avec vérité contre la meilleure cause, elle entasse contre chaque côté de la question pêle-mêle avec les bonnes raisons, tous les sophismes et même les calomnies qu'on a jamais débités de part et d'autre. Cela brouille les esprits et fausse les idées, tandis que la bonne dialectique les éclairerait.

3. Tout ce que vous avez écrit à l'endroit de Lanfrey est parfaitement bien pensé et dit. Seulement il me paraît douteux si nous faisons prudemment de rompre en visière avec lui. C'est un homme qu'on peut toujours espérer de ramener aux idées vraies, et si on s'attaque aux gens, on risque d'intéresser leur amour-propre à persister dans la voie qu'ils ont une fois prise.

4. Je voudrais qu'il fût vrai qu'en Angleterre les esprits eussent été déjà préparés en 1851 à la discussion de l'émancipation des femmes, et que le temps où l'on pouvait s'en tirer par le ridicule était déjà passé. Cela est vrai aujourd'hui, mais ne l'était pas alors. La discussion n'a été réellement entamée en Angleterre que dans cette année-la, par l'article de ma femme que vous avez lu dans le 2me volume des Dissertations.

Il y a à la page 6 une expression qu'il serait peut-être bien de modifier : c'est là où vous dites "Il ne s'agit plus de changer les relations sociales de sexes." Je sais bien ce que vous avez voulu dire, mais ce qui est proposé dans mon petit livre serait certainement regardé comme un grand changement dans les relations sociales des sexes.

To Alexander Bain.

Avignon, *7th June* 1869.

1869 — Ætat. 63.

Dear Bain,—Mr. Veitch sent me a copy of the "Life of Hamilton." His replies to my strictures are so very weak (Mansel and water, with an infusion of vinegar), that I shall hardly feel any need of giving them the distinction of a special notice; except that I am bound to admit that the passage of Aristotle which Hamilton seemed to have misunderstood was not indicated by any reference of his own, but only of the editor's. That is quite sufficient for my purpose, since Mansel at least has learning, and that passage of Aristotle was, I suppose, the nearest he could find to bearing out what Hamilton said. But after all, Hamilton must have known what Aristotle meant by *ἐνεργεια*. I agree with you as to the general impression which the book gives of Hamilton. Only, as it shows advantageously a side of his character which I had no knowledge of, that of his private affections, the general result rather raised him in my eyes.

I am glad to be confirmed by you in my impression that nothing in my notes to the "Analysis," on the question of Belief, is incompatible with your theory of it. I shall be very glad to see your last views of the subject more fully developed. Cairnes, who had not previously studied psychology very seriously, but who has now been reading both the "Analysis" and our notes with full appreciation and great edification, seems to feel a need of some further explanations on the doctrine of Belief as connected with the Will, and what a man of his practised intelligence wants is likely to be wanted by most others. As far as we two are concerned, it is very unlikely that any difference of opinion between us should develop itself when your doctrine is explicitly worked out.

The Lords have done all the mischief they could to the Scotch Education Bill. One would have thought the unanimous recommendations of a Commission, partly Tory and fairly representative of all sections in Scotland, might have passed their ordeal. But they will no doubt, as you say, revenge themselves for having to eat their leek (if they do eat it) in the Church question by spoiling other Bills. They are becoming a very irritating kind of minor nuisance.

To J. E. Cairnes.

AVIGNON, *23rd June* 1869.

DEAR MR. CAIRNES,—I have had so much to do and so many other letters to write that I have delayed till now thanking you for your most acceptable letter of 23rd May, and especially for the sifting which you have given to my review of Thornton. You may imagine how gratifying it is to me that you give so complete an adhesion to the views I take of the wages fund. In regard to the general subject of demand and supply, I think there is not, at bottom, any considerable difference between us. My object in the *Fortnightly* was to show that the cases supposed by Thornton do not contradict, and invalidate, as he thinks they do, the equation of supply and demand. In this you agree with me, and you do not think the doctrine incorrect. The amount of its value, either scientific or practical, is a different question. But while I admit almost all that you say, I think that the proposition as laid down is something more than an identical proposition. It does not define —nor did it, as I stated it, affect to define—the causes of variations in value. But it declares the *condition* of all such variations and the necessary *modus operandi* of their causes, viz. that they operate by moving the supply to equality with the demand or the demand to equality with the supply. The numerous considerations which you notice as influencing the minds of sellers are all of them considerations of probable future demand and supply, modifying the effect which would take place if nothing but present facts were considered. Now it appears to me important to point out that these prospective considerations operate by inducing the sellers either to convert a

1869 — Aetat. 63. possible present supply into an actual one, or to withdraw an actual present supply into the region of merely possible ones, and that in either case the relation of the price to the actual supply and demand is constant, *i.e.* the price is that which will make them equal. If this statement does no more than give a distinct scientific expression to what is already implied in the terms used, still it is not unimportant to evolve and make explicit what the facts of purchase and sale and a market price really involve.

I am delighted that you have derived so much pleasure and advantage from the "Analysis." That alone is enough to satisfy me of the great good likely to be done by its republication. With regard to the difficulties you have found in some of Bain's notes, he is aware that his doctrines respecting Belief and Volition require further explanations and developments. I am myself not always sure that I am able to follow him on every detail, though I do not think that any of my views clash with his. I am, however, inclined to agree in what I think is his opinion, that volition is not a name for a peculiar state of feeling or phenomenon of mind, but only a name for the immediate and irresistible sequence between the specific action of the efferent nerve fibres as effort, and the internal cause which produces it, and which is either an idea or desire or (as explained for the first time by Bain) the spontaneous activity of the nervous system under the stimulus of nutriment.

Pray thank Mrs. Cairnes very warmly for her kind letter. I hope to be able to talk over with her and you any remaining difficulties she may feel. I wish the opportunity were nearer than it is likely to be, for Penzance and Blackheath are very far apart. But if Penzance aids your restoration to health I shall be very grateful to it. We were happy to hear good accounts of you from those who saw you in your passage through London. Helen desires her kind regards to you and Mrs. Cairnes.

To Alexander Bain,

in reply to a highly appreciative letter from him about "The Subjection of Women."

Blackheath Park, *14th July* 1869.

Dear Bain,—I am very glad that you are so well pleased with the new book. With regard to the single point on which you are doubtful, my defence is this. The policy of not laying down wider premises than are required to support the practical conclusion immediately aimed at was a wise policy ten years ago. It was the right policy until the women's suffrage question had acquired such a footing in practical politics as to leave little danger of its being thrown back. But the question has now entered into a new and more advanced stage. The objection with which we are now principally met is that women are not fit for or not capable of this, that, or the other mental achievement. And though it is a perfectly good answer to say that, if this be a fact, things will adjust themselves to it under free competition, and also that without free competition we cannot know whether it is a fact or not, many will ask and many more will feel, "Why make a great change and disturb people's minds, only to give women leave to do what there is no probability that they either can or will do? Why make a revolution on the plea that it will do no harm, when you cannot show that it will do any good?" Even if on no other account than this, it is thoroughly time to bring the question of women's capacities into the front rank of the discussion.

1869 — Aetat. 63.

But there is a still stronger reason. The most important thing women have to do is to stir up the zeal of women themselves. We have to stimulate their aspirations—to bid them not despair of anything, nor think anything beyond their reach, but try their faculties against all difficulties. In no other way can the verdict of experience be fairly collected, and in no other way can we excite the enthusiasm in women which is necessary to break down the old barriers. This is more important now than to conciliate opponents.

1869 — Ætat. 63. But I do not believe that opponents will be at all exasperated by taking this line. On the contrary, I believe the point has now been reached at which, the higher we pitch our claims, the more disposition there will be to concede part of them. All I have yet heard of the reception of the new book confirms this idea. People tell me that it is lowering the tone of our opponents as well as raising that of our supporters. Everything I hear strengthens me in the belief, which I at first entertained with a slight mixture of misgiving, that the book has come out at the right time, and that no part of it is premature.

One effect which the suffrage agitation is producing is to make all sorts of people declare in favour of improving the education of women. That point is conceded by almost everybody, and we shall find the education movement for women favoured and promoted by many who have no wish at all that things should go any further. The cause of political and civil enfranchisement is also prospering almost beyond hope. You have probably observed that the admission of women to the municipal franchise has passed the Commons, and is passing the Lords without opposition. The Bill for giving married women the control of their own property has passed through the Commons, all but the third reading, and is thought to have a good chance of becoming law this session.

To Professor John Nichol, of Glasgow,

in reply to a letter from him about "The Subjection of Women."

Blackheath Park, *18th August* 1869.

Dear Sir,—I have been long without acknowledging your letter of 20th July, because there were several points in it on which I wished to make some remarks, and I have not had time to do this sooner. Even now I am unable to do it at any length. You have, I doubt not, understood what I have endeavoured to impress upon the readers of my book, that the opinions expressed in it respecting the natural capacities of women are to be regarded as provisional; perfect freedom of development being indispensable to afford the decisive evidence of experiment on the subject: and if, as you truly say, conventionalities have smothered nature still more in women than in men, the greater is the necessity for getting rid of the conventionalities before the nature can be manifested. I have, however, thought it indispensable to weigh such evidence as we have and examine what conclusions it points to, and I certainly think that, in all matters in which women do not entirely lean upon men, they have shown a very great command of practical talent. I do not read the new evidence respecting Queen Elizabeth as you seem to do. She was already known to have had weaknesses of vanity and temper, but with the means of realising her position now afforded to us by the mass of contemporary documents transcribed by Froude, I confess she seems to me to have taken, on the whole, more just views of general feeling than her critics. For example: with the very small pecuniary resources she had (a thing generally forgotten), the economy absolutely indispensable could only be enforced by making those whom she employed (every one of whom was always in great need of money for the purposes of his department) feel constantly extreme difficulty in getting it, and the strongest motive to do without it if he could. Again, with half or more than half her subjects Catholics, herself under the ban of the Pope, and with a Catholic competitor for the throne, was it not wise in her to take advantage as long as she could of the real indisposition of the powerful Philip (an indisposition never fully known till now) to drive her to extremities? We are bound to remember that, after all that is said of the danger to which she exposed England and Protestantism by her parsimony and over-caution, the event has justified her; England and Protestantism survived the risk, and came out with greatly increased power and éclat.

1869 — Aetat. 63.

If you have read Mr. Motley's last two volumes,[1] you will have observed a great change in his tone respecting Elizabeth. There are no more of the disparaging com-

[1] ["History of the United Netherlands."]

1869 ments of his earlier volumes; but, on the contrary, her abilities are always spoken of with great respect.

— Ætat. 63.

As you truly say, queens, and kings too, are now superfluous; but the experience which women have given of themselves as queens is not obsolete. They are not now wanted as queens, but the qualities which made them successful as queens are still the conditions of success in all the practical affairs of mankind.

I thought it best not to discuss the questions of marriage and divorce along with that of the equality of women; not only from the obvious inexpediency of establishing a connection in people's minds between the equality, and any particular opinions on the divorce question, but also because I do not think that the conditions of the dissolubility of marriage can be properly determined until women have an equal voice in determining them, nor until there has been experience of the marriage relation as it would exist between equals. Until then I should not like to commit myself to more than the general principle of relief from the contract in extreme cases.

To G. Croom Robertson,

in reply to a letter from him, praising "The Subjection of Women."

Blackheath Park, *18th August* 1869.

Dear Mr. Robertson,—Want of time has prevented me from sooner thanking you for the very interesting letter you wrote to me on the subject of my little book. On the few points which you criticise, you show so clear a discernment of both sides of the question that there is little need or scope for answering you. Only on the smallest of them, the good government of Indian princesses, do your remarks present anything to be corrected. In an Asiatic principality good government (even comparative) is never obtainable by letting alone. It is obtained by an ever-watchful eye and a strong hand, depending as it does upon a rigid and vigorous control of the subordinate agents of government, whose power of plunder and tyranny, if left to themselves, is irresistible. The rulers who do let things alone are those whose affairs fall into disorder, and their countries into anarchy, through their supineness and self-indulgence; and these are generally male rulers. The measure of good government in the East is the closeness of the ruler's application to business; and it is really remarkable that the instances of this should be so preponderant in the temporary rule of women as regents.

1869 — Aetat. 63.

The comparison of women to slaves was of course not intended to run on all fours. I thought the differences too obvious to need stating, and that the fundamental resemblances were what required to be insisted on. But a different judgment coming from you cannot but be valuable to me.

The most important of your points is the suggestion of a possible turning of what is said about the usefulness of the present feminine type as a corrective to the present masculine, into an argument for maintaining the two types distinct by difference of training. You have yourself gone into considerations of great importance in answer to this argument, all of which I fully accept. I should add some others to them, as, *first*, it is not certain that the differences spoken of are not partly at least natural ones, which would subsist in spite of identity of training; *secondly*, the correction which the one type supplies to the excesses of the other is very imperfectly obtained now, owing to the very circumstance that women's sphere and men's are kept so much apart. At present, saving fortunate exceptions, women have rather shown the good influence of this sort which they *might* exercise over men, than actually exercised it.

To Mrs. Beecher Hooker,

in reply to a letter from her, praising "The Subjection of Women."

Avignon, 13*th September* 1869.

Dear Madam,—I beg to acknowledge, with many thanks, your letter of 10th August.

1869 — Ætat. 63.

You have perceived, what I should wish every one who reads my little book to know, that whatever there is in it which shows any unusual insight into nature or life was learnt from women—from my wife, and subsequently also from her daughter.

What you so justly say respecting the infinitely closer relationship of a child to its mother than to its father, I have learnt from the same source to regard as full of important consequences with regard to the future legal position of parents and children. This, however, is a portion of the truth for which the human mind will not, for some time, be sufficiently prepared to make its discussion useful.

But I do not perceive that this closer relationship gives any ground for attributing a natural superiority in capacity of moral excellence to women over men. I believe moral excellence to be always the fruit of education and cultivation, and I see no reason to doubt that both sexes are equally capable of that description of cultivation. But the position of irresponsible power in which men have hitherto lived is, I need hardly say, most unfavourable to almost every kind of moral excellence. So far as women have been in possession of irresponsible power, they too have by no means escaped its baneful consequences.

To Andrew Reid, of the Land Tenure Reform Association.

5th October 1869.

Dear Sir,—Your letter of 29th September has just reached me. I am very glad to hear of so many and such good adhesions. It is a proof that many have arrived at the conviction that the time has come for making some improvement in the land laws. But the subject has been so little discussed that there is sure to be great difference of opinion as to what that improvement should be. I myself agree in principle with Mr. Odger and his friends; but if the Association were to adopt as its purpose the resumption of all the land from its proprietors, it could not hope for any support except from a portion of the working classes. The proposal is entirely new and startling to all other classes, and a great deal of preparation will be required to induce them even to listen to it patiently. An association to agitate on a question is seldom timely or useful until the public have first been to a certain degree familiarised with the subject, so that hopes may be entertained of making at once a considerable show of strength. We are certainly very far from this point in regard to the question of taking possession of all the land and managing it by the State; I say nothing at present of the reasonable doubt which may be entertained whether we have yet reached such a degree of improvement as would enable so vast a concern to be managed on account of the public without a perfectly intolerable amount of jobbing. I must say that the general mind of the country is as yet totally unprepared to entertain the question. It is possible that the active spirits in the working classes may think nothing worth trying for short of this, and may consequently withhold their support from the Association. I think this would be a great mistake; but we must be prepared for the possibility of it. . . .

To T. Cliffe Leslie;

the first paragraph by Mill; the rest by Helen Taylor.

Avignon, *5th October* 1869.

. . . It seems to me that whatever can be justly said against women's fitness for politics, either on the score of narrowness or violence of partisanship, arises chiefly, if not wholly, from their exclusion from politics. Their social position allows them no scope for any feelings beyond the family except personal likings and dislikes, and it is assumed that they would be governed entirely by these in their judgment and feeling in political matters. But it is precisely by creating in their minds a concern

1869 — Aetat. 63.

for the interests which are common to all, those of their country and of human improvement, that the tendency to look upon all questions as personal questions would most effectually be corrected.

My daughter thinks the opinions expressed by the ladies you mention very natural for French men and women and those whose ideas have been most formed by French literature, for two reasons:—

1. The peculiar bringing up of women has on the whole, from a multiplicity of causes having to do with the history of the nation, and also with race peculiarities, tended in England to make women both weaker and gentler than men; in France, to make them more energetic and passionate. This passion and energy is chiefly used up in rivalry with other women, and a habit of fierce passionate contest between women as individuals is acquired. What helps to this is that energetic Frenchwomen are apt to be less domestic than energetic Englishwomen, partly on account of the smaller families, partly of the custom of sending the children out to nurse and to *pension*. Their energies are thus devoted in greater proportion than in England to rivalry with other women in dress, in love affairs, and in social success; so that being at once more energetic and more given to using their energies in specific contests for superiority with other women, they are more disposed to personal enmities.

2. It is probably true that women, on the average, are more what the French mean by *jealous* than men; it is certainly true that the less civilised people are more jealous in this sense than the more civilised; probably on this account it is that women are more jealous than men, as certainly the French are more jealous than the English. There seems, however, good reason to think that one of the specific benefits of political freedom is that it diminishes this moral vice of *jalousie*, to which the French are more subject than any other people I know, in private affairs, although not more so than the Spaniards and Greeks in politics. You have evidently seen the true answer when you say that the habit of

combination for common objects, which is always induced by political freedom, is the cure for the passionate and self-willed disposition of which the French accuse women, and other nations accuse the French. . . . 1869 — Aetat. 63.

To Frederi Mistral,

who had written to Mill acknowledging a copy of the French translation of "The Subjection of Women," and saying that he had been converted by it.

Avignon, *le* 6 *octobre* 1869.

Cher Monsieur,—Parmi toutes les adhésions qui ont été données à la thèse de mon petit livre je ne sais s'il y en a aucune qui m'ont fait plus de plaisir que la vôtre; et cela non seulement à cause de l'influence que donne à vos opinions votre position si importante dans le monde des lettres mais encore plus par la confirmation de ma conviction que les âmes poétiques, lorsqu'elles sont jointes à une intelligence éclairée, ne verront rien qui leur répugne dans la modification que la justice exige dans les relations sociales entre les deux sexes. En effet, dans toute société qui n'est pas profondément démoralisée il n'y a pas à craindre que l'homme ne cherche pas à idéaliser la femme. La nature l'y portera toujours: mais ici comme dans tout le reste, il s'agit pour l'idéal de ne pas trop s'écarter des conditions de la réalité. Autrement on aurait d'une part un idéal incompatible avec les conditions de la vie, et d'autre part une vie réelle toute prosaïque dans laquelle on retomberait toujours. Il en est ainsi de l'idéal que beaucoup de poètes ont voulu établir pour les femmes. Ils se sont figuré un être tout de fantaisie, qui aurait besoin pour exister d'un monde aussi imaginaire que lui; ils ont proposé aux femmes cet être-là pour modèle, et quand elles tâchent de s'y conformer, elles se heurtent contre les dures exigences de la vie réelle qui s'opposent invinciblement à la réalisation. Qu'on s'efforce tant qu'on veut à écarter de la vie des femmes ces exigences, on n'en vient jamais à bout: d'abord, pour la très grande majorité du sexe

1869 feminin c'est matériellement impossible; et chez le petit
Aetat. 63. nombre des privilégiées il en reste toujours assez pour les rendre dures, égoistes et cruelles, à moins d'en être préservées par une culture morale qui serait tout aussi efficace dans un état de choses plus naturel. Il me semble que l'idéal propre à l'existence humaine serait tout autre que cet idéal de fantaisie, sans être pour cela moins poétique; ce serait l'idée d'une personne complète dans toutes ses facultés, propre à toutes les tâches et à toutes les épreuves de la vie, mais qui les remplissait avec une grandeur d'âme, une force de raison et une tendresse de cœur très au-dessus de ce qui a lieu maintenant, sauf peut-être chez les plus admirables caractères dans leurs moments de plus grande exaltation. Si cet idéal a jamais été offert au genre humain c'est dans le Christ, et je ne sais pas ce qu'on pourrait demander de mieux soit à un homme soit à une femme sous le rapport de perfectionnement moral, que de lui ressembler. Or ce caractère-là est aussi profondément réel que poétiquement élevé et émouvant.

To Mrs. P. A. Taylor, Secretary of the London National Society for Women's Suffrage.

7th October 1869.

Dear Mrs. Taylor,—One of my working-men correspondents, and the most thoughtful and intelligent of them, Mr. William Wood, of Hanley, Stoke-on-Trent, who has lately enrolled himself as a member of the London Woman Suffrage Society, is very desirous of having a public meeting, or, if that should be impossible, a lecture in his borough, and offers to take upon himself the work of making the arrangements; but he considers it a *sine qua non* that "one at least of the ladies who are the glory and no small part of the strength of the movement, be present to speak to us in its advocacy." . . .

I have written to propose to Mrs. Fawcett to take up the project; if she does not, would it be impossible for you to do so? It would be unfair to ask you, who have so much on your hands in the central direction of the movement, to work at the outposts when the work can be done by anyone else, but we rely so much on your public spirit that we cannot help looking to you as a reserve when others fail. The cause has now reached a point at which it has become extremely desirable that the ladies who lead the movement should make themselves visible to the public, their very appearance being a refutation of the vulgar nonsense talked about "women's rights women," and their manner of looking, moving, and speaking being sure to make a favourable impression from the purely feminine as well as from the human point of view.

To W. T. Thornton.

By Helen Taylor.

Avignon, *23rd October* 1869.

Dear Thornton,—We are most happy to hear that you have had such an interesting holiday, and that both the weather and your health and spirits were so favourable to enjoyment. I am much obliged to you for your observations on the peasant proprietors. We must try to find out whether the farms which pleased you so much in North Holland are the property of the farmers. With regard to the internal discomfort of the houses in other places, it is probably a consequence and sample of the general habits of the country. In most parts of the Continent the taste for what we call comfort is much less developed than in England, and peasant properties, by the prudential and calculating habits which they foster, promote frugality as well as industry. The peasants (preferring saving to enjoyment) often exhibit a very meagre state of living when the means are, as in the case you mention of the widow near Darmstadt, ample. Helen says too that to understand this subject one must distinguish between comfort and neatness, although neatness is no doubt an essential to comfort in our eyes. There would almost seem something of race in the care for

1869 — Aetat. 63. neatness, which Helen says does not follow at all, as one might suppose, the variations of climate. Some Oriental peoples are very neat, as are the Spaniards (in the parts of Spain we have visited), and the Greeks. In Greek and Spanish rooms, where the furniture is poor, and there is substantial dirtiness, if vermin may be so called, the neatness is often charming, and most refreshing to the eye and spirits, while in French rooms of the same class the building will be more solid, the bedding comfortable and irreproachably clean, and yet the dust and untidiness will be repugnant and wretched to an English eye. Some of the same curious differences may be noticed in different parts of Germany, and Helen says that for many years she has tried to find any general rule which will explain these variations. She is inclined to think that it may perhaps prove that this pleasant tidiness of the home to the eye depends upon whether the women work out of the house or not, and may have nothing to do with race, climate, civilisation, or wealth. This, however, is still a mere hypothesis in her mind.

We too have made an excursion of about ten days in the Alps. We established ourselves in the inn on the top of the pass of Mont Cenis, 6000 feet above the sea, and greatly enjoyed walks among the neighbouring heights. We had at first splendid weather, but as it seemed to be changing we went off to some little-travelled parts of the Lower Alps, south of Grenoble, where we had again beautiful weather and much enjoyment. We have since had a still pleasanter, though shorter, excursion in the mountains of the eastern part of our department, in which last excursion we walked upwards of fifty miles in three days. The improvements in our own little place are now nearly completed, but until they are quite finished they continue to give Helen a great deal of troublesome occupation. I have no report to make as yet of work done, except what can hardly be called by that name—bringing up arrears of general reading—but I hope to have a better account to give in a little while. About Carlyle I agree both with you and with Hill. It is only at a particular stage in one's mental development that one benefits much by him (to me he was of great use at that stage), but one continues to read his best things with little, if any, diminution of pleasure after one has ceased to learn anything from him.

1869 — Aetat. 63.

To Dr. Cazelles,

(1) concerning an article in the *Revue des Deux Mondes* by M. Janet on the Philosophy of Hamilton; (2) concerning M. Charles Renouvier's views; (3) on Huxley's criticisms of Comte.

Avignon, *le* 23 *octobre* 1869.

Cher Monsieur,—Je vous remercie de m'avoir envoyé le *Journal des Débats*. La notice par M. Taine dépasse beaucoup en louanges, et ce qui vaut mieux, en adhésion, tout ce qu'on pouvait espérer. J'ai lu dans la *Revue* [*des Deux Mondes*] l'article de M. Janet. J'ai lieu de lui savoir gré encore plus que vous, des égards qu'il nous montre. Quant à la substance de l'article, mon appréciation diffère peu de la vôtre. La tentative qu'il fait de prouver l'existence objective des corps par un argument semblable à celui dont je me sers pour établir la réalité d'autres êtres sentants et pensants, est ingénieuse mais sans valeur aucune. Son exemple des deux lutteurs ne prouve que ce qu'on ne songe pas à nier, savoir que les possibilités permanentes de sensation qui sont de la catégorie de ce que nous nommons résistance, se trouvent quelquefois liées à une conviction rationnelle d'une autre sensation de résistance hors de nous, à quoi l'on peut ajouter que leur réalisation dépend quelquefois d'une volonté hors de nous. Tout cela n'a aucune difficulté dès qu'on admet la réalité de sensations et de volitions autres que les siennes propres.

Quant au problème général, M. Janet le déplace complètement. On lui dit que la force n'est qu'un phénomène, et il vous répond en prouvant la force, comme si vous aviez dit qu'elle n'existe pas.

1869 — Aetat. 63. Je viens aussi de lire l'opuscule de M. Renouvier. Sauf la question du libre arbitre, que du reste il a pu poser plus nettement et d'une manière plus rationnelle qu'on ne la pose ordinairement, parcequ'il a renoncé à sauver la prescience divine; sauf cette question, dis-je, il ne me semble pas qu'il y ait beaucoup de différence entre ses opinions et les miennes, sur les grandes questions de la métaphysique. Il nie la substance, il réduit les corps à des groupes de phénomènes. Il croit à la vérité me dépasser lorsqu'il nie l'infini, et il pense qu'en soutenant l'intelligibilité non de l'infini abstrait mais de l'infini *quoad hoc* j'ai voulu laisser une ouverture pour des spéculations transcendantes. Il n'en est rien: mon but était pratique, et surtout moral; j'ai voulu montrer que s'il existe un être possédant un attribut quelconque porté à l'infini, cet attribut doit être qualitativement identique au même attribut s'arrêtant au fini; que, par exemple, un Dieu infiniment bon ne peut être bon que de la bonté humaine. Ma controverse avec Mansel aurait dû prouver à M. Renouvier la grande importance morale, dans un milieu croyant, de cette thèse.

La réponse de M. Huxley à M. Congreve a déjà paru, dans le même recueil périodique que la conférence. Par un heureux accident j'ai conservé cette réponse et je vous l'envoie par la poste. C'est une critique amère de Comte, parfois juste, plus souvent injuste ou exagérée, et qui me paraît dans son ensemble extrêmement faible. Pour rendre justice à Huxley il faut se rappeler que le volume le plus imparfait et surtout le plus arriéré de la Philosophie Positive est celui qui traite de la chimie et de la biologie, et que ces deux sciences sont justement celles que Huxley connaît le mieux. Je ne lui crois pas de grandes connaissances dans les sciences qui dépendent de la mathématique: lorsqu'il se hasarde à contester les généralisations de Comte sur la philosophie générale des sciences, tout ce qu'il dit est tellement superficiel que le moindre disciple de Comte n'aurait pas de peine à le réfuter.

To Henry Fawcett.

Avignon, *24th October* 1869.

. . . I, like you, have a rather strong opinion in favour of making parents pay something for their children's education when they are able, though there are considerable difficulties in authenticating their inability. At all events, I would have it left an open question ; and because they refused to leave that and other secondary questions open I did not join the [Education] League. But I think you are quite right in overlooking this consideration and acting with the League in order to form a strong party in the House for the principle of universal and compulsory unsectarian education. . . .

1869 — Aetat. 63.

I do not know whether to be glad or sorry for the separate organisation which has been started by some leaders of the working men for a much more radical alteration of the land laws. The furious and declamatory violence of their resolutions and some of their speeches seems to show that they would have been a very intractable element in the other association, and that it is well rid of them. One thing I see clearly, that there will be more difficulty than ever in preserving the commons. The working-class speakers are filled with exaggerated ideas of the value of the waste lands for cultivation, and apparently do not care at all for the preservation of natural beauty; and if they make any way with their agitation the landlords will throw over the commons to save their estates. Our best chance of avoiding this will be the progress of education in all classes, and unfortunately it is much easier to improve education in quantity than in quality. It is no new thing that all good depends on work; but in the present state of matters the work of the more advanced minds, over and above its inherent difficulties, has the additional one that it is, in a certain degree, working against time. But there would be little to fear if there were a tolerable number who worked with the energy of spirit that you do.

1869 — Aetat. 63. Women's suffrage will help us in this as in so many other things, for women will be much more unwilling than men to submit to the expulsion of all beauty from common life.

To a Correspondent,

who asked Mill's advice as to whether he should desert his mercantile pursuits for a literary career.

AVIGNON, *24th October* 1869.

DEAR SIR,—I have received your letter dated the 18th inst. I need hardly say that I sympathise in your preference of literary to mercantile occupation; but all experience proves that of these two, considered as professions, the latter alone is to be depended on as a means of subsistence, and that the former can only be prudently taken up by persons who are already in independent circumstances. It is a rare good fortune if an author can support himself by his pen, unless as an editor or sub-editor of a newspaper or other periodical; and I suppose there is not in our day a single instance in which it has been done by poetry of any kind. All my experience of life confirms the advice which Coleridge, in his "Biographia Literaria," gives to writers even of the greatest genius—to let, if possible, their regular business, on which they rely for support, be something foreign to their favourite pursuits, reserving these as the consolation of their leisure hours. In that case, success, and the favourable estimation of others, are not a matter of necessity to them; if they produce anything worthy of being remembered, they can wait for it to be appreciated, or can be content with the pleasure of the occupation itself. My own conviction is that to be independent of immediate success is almost an absolute condition of being able to do anything that greatly deserves to succeed. Many of the meritorious literary men would feel themselves saved from lifelong disappointment if they could exchange their position for one of assured though moderate income in the vocation which you are so desirous of quitting for theirs. 1869 — Aetat. 63.

With regard to the publication of your work I hardly know what advice to give. It is easy to obtain a publisher if you are able and willing to take on yourself the risk of pecuniary loss. But it is difficult to find a bookseller who is willing to venture anything on the success of a dramatic poem; there are so many writers of dramatic poems, and so few buyers of them; and whatever may be the merit of yours, there is no certainty of its becoming known to the public. Even if an author has friends who are connected as writers or editors with the literary periodicals, which people consult to know what books to order from Mudie's, or the circulating libraries, he has but a precarious chance, for people have learnt to distrust the praises of periodicals. Authors often build hopes on recommendations to a publisher from some person who is considered a good judge, but these are so often given from mere good-nature that they carry little weight; nor do publishers consider the merit of a work as sufficient guarantee of its pecuniary success. For myself I have no means of aiding you in any of these ways. Even if authority carried greater weight than it does with publishers, I am not an authority on these subjects.

What I say to you I have said to many others who have made applications to me of the same kind, and I sincerely regret that I have nothing more satisfactory to offer.

In short, I see but two alternatives for a young author. He can test the probable popularity of his work by offering it to publishers and editors, who, whether rightly or not, are practically the judges of this; and if their decision is unfavourable he must either resign literary work, or content himself with working merely for the love of his work, accompanied by any such hopes as he may still venture to entertain of better success in the future.

To James M. Barnard, of Boston.

Avignon, *28th October* 1869.

1869 — Aetat. 63.

Dear Sir,—I thank you and Mrs. Barnard heartily for your kindness to Mr. Kyllman. I hardly know your equal in eagerness to do kind offices to your friends or to your friends' friends, while from your manner of conferring a favour any one would suppose that you were receiving one.

I have not written anything on the subject of police. What you have heard of is doubtless a private letter to one of my active supporters in Westminster, who asked my opinion on the proposal to place "habitual criminals" under police surveillance, a proposal since embodied in an Act of Parliament, some of the provisions of which appear to me very estimable. The letter, though signed by me, was written by my daughter, who has thought more or to greater purpose on these questions than I have. It was not intended for publication, but was sent without my permission to a newspaper. The date of the letter was 14th December 1868, but I have not a copy of any newspaper containing it, and I do not remember the date of publication.

The multiplication of casts of the finest works of ancient sculpture is very useful as one among many means of educating the public eye. Both in art and in nature a certain degree of familiarity is necessary not merely to the intellectual appreciation, but to the enjoyment of the higher kinds of beauty. Every one who takes pleasure in a simple tune has the capacity of fully enjoying Weber and Beethoven, but very often he derives little or no pleasure from a first hearing of them. It is a great mistake to think that children are not benefited by living and growing up among models of beauty. They are, on the contrary, more benefited than any one else, though not, at the time, conscious of the benefit. I can trace a great influence in my own development to the accident of having passed several years of my boyhood in one of the few old abbeys which are still inhabited, instead of a mean and graceless modern house, and having at the same time and place been familiar with tapestries from Raphael's cartoons, which peopled my imagination with graceful and dignified forms of human beings. There is a great want of this training of the perceptions and taste in our modern societies; but it is not by any one help or stimulus that the want can be supplied. The great desideratum in America—and though not quite in an equal degree, I may say in England too —is the improvement of the higher education. America surpasses all countries in the amount of mental cultivation which she has been able to make universal; but a high average level is not everything. There are wanted, I do not say a class, but a great number of persons of the highest degree of cultivation which the accumulated acquisitions of the human race make it possible to give them. From such persons, in a community that knows no distinction of ranks, civilisation would rain down its influences on the remainder of society, and the higher faculties, having been highly cultivated in the more advanced part of the public, would give forth products and create an atmosphere that would produce a high average of the same faculties in a people so well prepared in point of general intelligence as the people of the United States.

I have given an introduction to you, and to two or three of my other friends in America, to a correspondent of mine in Scotland, Mr. D. Watson of Hawick, who is anxious to obtain information that can be depended on (but is under the necessity of asking for it by letter) respecting the practical operation of Vote by Ballot in the United States. The example of America is often cited in favour of secret voting and sometimes against it, but there is a great deficiency of real information as to how it works in America, and even as to whether there is real secrecy at all. My correspondent and some of his friends are, like myself, unfavourable to secret voting, but they are anxious to obtain whatever light American experience can throw on the practical question.

To J. E. Cairnes,

who had asked Mill to look over some writings which he proposed to publish on Political Economy.

Avignon, *16th November* 1869.

1869 — Ætat. 63.

Dear Mr. Cairnes,— . . . Your letter made me rather ashamed of myself from the belief it showed that I must be very busy. Since I have been here this time I may almost call myself idle, having done little but to bring up old arrears of general reading. And I am seldom for long together too busy to spare time for anything *you* ask me to do, especially anything so pleasant as to read any of your writings. I beg that you will never allow any scruple to prevent your applying to me when you think I can be in any way useful, and with respect to the very interesting book you think of writing (I well remember how highly I thought of its precursor), I should be only too happy to read in the MS. either any part or the whole. Indeed, if I were to see all of it that relates to the French political economists as well as to Comte, I should be better able to compare your impression respecting them with my own. I believe we think pretty much alike about them. French philosophic writers seem to me decidedly inferior in closeness and precision of thought to the best English, and more in the habit of paying themselves with phrases and abstractions. The French political economists share largely in this defect. It should be remembered, however, that there is a much greater number of them than of English, unless to make up the equality we descend to English writers so bad as almost to turn the average the other way. There are also more exceptions than you perhaps know to the general vagueness and looseness of thought of French economists. Besides Say, and Turgot, of which last Courcelle-Seneuil says, with some reason, that it is harder to say what of the truths of the science he did not anticipate than what he did, there are some now living who have formed themselves very much upon the stricter and more precise English model—Joseph Garnier especially, in his treatise on Political Economy; Garnier is an exception to their false conception of the method of the science. Courcelle-Seneuil, whom I just mentioned, and who has written a book of considerable merit, "Traité Théorique et Pratique d'Economie Politique," is also to some extent an exception. A. E. Cherbuliez, of Geneva (who lately died), published in 1862 a "Précis de la Science Economique et de ses Principales Applications," which I thought favourably of. The last two of those treatises I have here, and can send to you if you would like to see them. I think both Reybaud and Michel Chevalier unfavourable specimens of French economists as to close thinking, and the former is besides of a narrow and prejudiced school. Bastiat shines as a dialectician, and his reasonings on free trade are as strictly scientific as those of anyone, but his posthumous work, "Harmonies Economiques," is written with a *parti pris* of explaining away all the evils which are the stronghold of Socialists, against whom the book is directed. The *Journal des Economistes* you will find in the London Library. A course of that gives a more correct idea than anything else of the general characteristics of French economists; the more as they occasionally carry on controversies with one another in its pages which bring out their several types of thought. They are divided by two broad lines: into Malthusians and anti-Malthusians, and into Utilitarians and anti-Utilitarians; this last distinction extends even to political economy, in consequence of the prevailing French habit of appealing to intuitive principles of *droit* even in economic subjects.

Your news of the Fawcetts is pleasant. I have a high opinion of Mrs. Fawcett's capabilities, and am always glad to hear of any fresh exercise of them. Respecting the Irish Land question, I hardly think it possible that you and I should not agree entirely when discussion has thrown sufficient light upon the details of the question. I feel with you that the reasons for fixity of tenure apply chiefly to *ryots*, or labourer-farmers, and not to capitalist-farmers,

1869 — Aetat. 63.

for whom leases suffice; and I feel also that, by making these last actual proprietors, a fresh agrarian question may be raised up on the part of the labourers whom they employ. The chief difficulty, I feel, is the practical one of having different laws for large and for small tenants; though I myself, in my speech in 1868, suggested as a possible expedient to make a distinction between arable and grazing farms. *A propos*, there has been a call from Ireland for a reprint of my two speeches on the land question, together with the chapters on that subject in my "Political Economy," and this is now being printed. Is it not curious that the plan in my pamphlet is almost always spoken of as a simple proposal to buy out the landlords and hold all the land as the property of the State? though it is palpable to every one who looks at the pamphlet that my proposal was simply a permanent tenure at a fixed rent, and that I only offered to any landlord who disliked this, the option of giving up his land to the Government instead. Mr. George Campbell sent me his paper before it was published, and I quite agree with you as to its great merit. He has since informed me that he has published it in an enlarged form and has sent me a copy. This is at Blackheath, and will be in the first parcel that comes.

To the Employés of Messrs. Brewster, of New York.

11th December 1869.

DEAR SIRS,—I have had the pleasure of receiving your letter of 12th November.

The plan of industrial partnership seems to me highly worthy of encouragement, as uniting some of the advantages of co-operation with the principal advantages of capitalist management. We should hope, indeed, ultimately to arrive at a state of industry in which the workpeople as a body will either themselves own the capital, or hire it from its owners. Industrial partnerships, however, are not only a valuable preparation for that state, and transition to it, but might probably for a long time exist by the side of it with great advantage; if only because their competition would prevent co-operative associations of workmen from degenerating, as I grieve to say they often do, into close joint-stock companies, in which the workmen who founded them keep all the profits to themselves.

The proposal of Messrs. Brewster is in some important respects a considerable improvement on the English industrial partnerships of which I have any knowledge; because it takes the employés themselves into council to determine the share of profit to which they shall be admitted, instead of fixing its amount by the sole will of the employers, and because it gives to a council, elected by the employés, an important share in the government of the workshops, even to the extent of allowing them, by a two-thirds majority, to overrule the wishes of the employers.

I have no such knowledge of the details of the subject as would enable me to make any suggestions that would be useful to you to receive. But I will show your letter and the printed plan of Messrs. Brewster to those of my friends who have more information on the subject and are more capable of making useful suggestions than I am myself, especially Mr. Hughes and Mr. Ludlow, both of whom have had an intimate connection with co-operation in England almost from its infancy. Only one point in Messrs. Brewster's plan occurs to me as open to criticism: that which provides that those who leave the employment voluntarily shall forfeit their share of profits for the current year. It seems to me that the boards to whom so many other powers are entrusted, might be the judges to decide whether in the particular circumstances of each case the share of profit should be forfeited or not.

To the Princess Royal of Prussia,

who sought an interview with Mill, and proposed to come to Avignon for the purpose.

Avignon, *26th December* 1869.

Madam,—I am most highly honoured by the message which I have received this morning from your Royal

1869 — Aetat. 63.

Highness, but I regret to say that being at present under medical treatment I am not in a condition to avail myself of the honour intended me. Indeed, I have scarcely the use of either hand, and have difficulty in even writing these few words.—I am, Madam, with the greatest respect, your Royal Highness's faithful servant, J. S. Mill.

JOHN STUART MILL
From a Cameo

CHAPTER XIII

1870

To Sir Robert Collier (afterwards Lord Monkswell), who was then Attorney-General.

Avignon, *11th January* 1870.

My dear Sir,—I take the liberty of enclosing to you the newspaper report of a matter in which I feel a painful interest, and in which I am anxious to obtain the aid of your influence towards mitigating the hardship of what seems to me an extremely hard case. On the 24th of December, a policeman named William Smith was charged before Mr. Benson the magistrate with an assault upon a labouring man. The evidence proved that the policeman saw the man knock down a woman (his wife, as it turned out) in the street at one o'clock in the morning and interfered for her protection, and in doing so struck the man with his staff—which assault on the man, Mr. Benson said, was "unprovoked, brutal, and unjustifiable," and sentenced the policeman to a month's imprisonment and hard labour. I learn from inquiries which I have since caused to be made, that the man, though of unblemished character and three and a half years' service, has been dismissed from the force and deprived of his livelihood.

1870 — Aetat. 63.

Now the only thing in which this poor man had exceeded his duty—the only point in which his conduct was not meritorious—was the blow with his truncheon; and in that he did what any man, not a police officer, might justly have been proud of doing, but which a policeman should not have done if he was able to take the man into custody by a less employment of force; which, however,

1870 — Aetat. 63.

is uncertain, as the man was evidently in an excited and violent state.

I am not a partisan of the police; on the contrary, I greatly distrust them, and think that magistrates rely too much on their evidence, and often treat instances of bribery, perjury, and other highly criminal conduct on their part with most undue lenity. But on this very account can there be a worse lesson to the police, or to the public, than that when so many are retained in the force after flagrant misconduct, one poor man, against whom there is no other charge, is dismissed for a little excess of zeal in protecting a woman against gross ill-treatment? Policemen will think twice before they will interfere again to protect men's wives, or any other women, against brutality when they find that any hurt they inflict on a brute of this description is declared from the seat of justice to be not only "brutal and unjustifiable," but "unprovoked," knocking down a woman in the street being no provocation to a bystander, even to an appointed and paid preserver of the peace—that, in short, a woman is a creature whom it is safe to knock down, but most dangerous to defend from being knocked down by another man.

The policeman's sentence will shortly expire and he will be released from prison. Would it be possible to prevail upon the Home Office to restore him to the force? He has surely been punished enough for the worst that he can be charged with—over-zeal in the performance of an important duty. I think it would be possible to get a well-signed memorial presented to the Home Office, praying for his reinstatement; but it would be better that it should be done by the spontaneous act of the Home Secretary, as it might perhaps be, if you would interest yourself in the matter. I write by this post to Sir John Coleridge and Mr. Russell Gurney, and would write to Mr. Bruce[1] if my acquaintance with him was sufficient to warrant it.

[1] [Home Secretary.]

To Pasquale Villari,

on the education of women.

Avignon, *le* 12 *janvier* 1870.

Mon cher M. Villari,— . . . Vous me demandez mes 1870
idées sur l'instruction des femmes, mais puisque vous Aetat. 63.
approuvez mon livre je crois que vous les connaissez déjà et que ce sont les vôtres. Vous savez que je ne voudrais nulle distinction dans l'instruction donnée aux deux sexes. Dans mon opinion l'instruction générale doit être la même; quant à la professionnelle, elle dépendra de la destination sociale de chaque élève, mais celle-là aussi doit être ouverte aux jeunes filles comme aux jeunes gens. Je crois que l'on finira par n'avoir que des écoles communes aux deux sexes. Après cela il va sans dire que la connaissance du milieu social de l'Italie doit décider de l'approche qu'il est aujourd'hui possible de faire à cet idéal. Le plus grand danger à craindre c'est que tout en faisant faire les mêmes études, on ne s'efforce pas à les faire faire aussi solides par les jeunes filles ; et qu'on se contente de quelque chose de plus superficiel, ne visant guère qu'à l'amusement ou à l'agrément. Ce danger cessera du moment où il sera compris que l'instruction des femmes est tout aussi importante aux intérêts sociaux que celle des hommes. Dès que cette idée-là se sera emparée des esprits, la cause sera gagnée. Et le gouvernement fera déjà beaucoup de bien en faisant voir que c'est là son intime conviction.

To Mrs. Charlotte Manning,

in acknowledgment of her book "Ancient and Mediæval India."

Avignon, 14*th January* 1870.

Dear Madam,—I have delayed very long to thank you for kindly sending me your book, the reason being that I have only just now found time to read it. Nothing can be more laudable than your purpose in writing the book, that of inspiring greater respect for the people of India in the

1870 — Aetat. 63. minds of those who are appointed to govern them. That respect, for the most part, exists in the experienced men who know the natives from a long course of service in India; but nothing can be more disgusting than the feelings and demeanour towards them of numbers of the raw young Englishmen who go out, and I am afraid this is an increasing evil, since the substitution of the Queen's army, who detest the country and only remain a few years in it, for a force of which the officers passed their whole career in India, and since the great increase of private adventurers, who are not even under that imperfect control from superiors, to which the military and the civil officers of government are subject.

I think you have done good service by putting within reach of the English public, in the compass of a single work, so much knowledge, both in the shape of information and of specimens of the thoughts and intellectual productions of the Hindoos. Opinions will differ as to the merits of these productions, and of the state of civilisation which they indicate; but they are an authentic and interesting product of the human mind; they deserve to be known, and anyone may now know where to find such a selection from them as is sufficient to give a correct general notion of their kind and quality. This could not, as far as I know, have been obtained before, without at least dipping into many books.

You ask me for information respecting the administrative capacity shown by so many ladies of ruling families in India, and especially whether these ladies are Hindoos or Mahomedans. They are almost all Hindoos. The case can seldom arise in a Mussulman principality, as by Mahomedan law the mother is not regent for her minor son, whereas among Hindoos the mother by birth or adoption is regent of right. One of the most remarkable, however, of these ladies, the late Sekunder Begum of Bhopal, was a Mahomedan. She was the only child of the ruler of the country; and at his death, according to the custom of the people, she could transmit the chiefship to her husband, but could not exercise it herself: she was, however, so much the stronger mind, and the most popular too, that the people obeyed her in preference to her husband; and after his death, which was an early one, she was allowed to govern the country, at first nominally for her daughter, but latterly in her own right. She was a most energetic, prudent, and just ruler, and her daughter, who has now succeeded her, and who has been carefully trained by her to public business, is expected to tread in her footsteps. Her own mother, too, was a remarkable woman. As the Native States were in my department in the India House, I had opportunities of knowing all that was known about the manner in which they were governed; and, during many years, by far the greater number of instances of vigorous, forceful, and skilful administration which came to my knowledge were by Ranees and Raees as regents for minor chiefs. . . .

To Judge CHAPMAN,

then a judge in New Zealand.

AVIGNON, *14th January* 1870.

DEAR CHAPMAN,—I am much obliged to you for your interesting letter on the colonial question, and all the more as your early departure will prevent me from having any opportunities of talking over with you the new aspects of the subject.

The causes you mention are, no doubt, those which have chiefly contributed to the indifference of official people in England about retaining the colonies. I suspect that separation would still be a great shock to the general English public, though they justly dislike being taxed for the maintenance of the connection. For my own part I think a severance of it would be no advantage, but the contrary, to the world in general, and to England in particular; and though I would have the colonies understand that England would not oppose a deliberate wish on their part to separate, I would do nothing to encourage that wish, except telling them that they must be at the charge of any

1870 — Aetat. 63.

wars of their own provoking, and that though we should defend them against all enemies brought on them by us, in any other case we should only protect them in a case of extremity, such as is not at all likely to arise. I have always thought, however, that we ought to have softened the transition in the case of New Zealand by guaranteeing a loan to enable the colony to maintain for a few years a sufficient force of its own raising without taking away the industrious population from the labours on which the very existence of the colony depends.

I do not see my way to any practicable mode of federal government for communities so widely scattered over the world. And I have attended sufficiently to colonial affairs to be aware that the colonies will not allow us to cart out our paupers into them. But emigration of able-bodied agricultural labourers who are not paupers I suppose they would welcome, and this would be very useful to us. Our having given up the unoccupied lands to the colonial governments creates many difficulties. I thought at the time that it was an error; that the lands ought to have been retained as the common inheritance of the whole people of the United Kingdom and the colonies taken together, and the first-comers having no just claim to the disposal of more than they could themselves occupy. But in this matter *jacta est alea*, and we have only to make the best arrangement we can with the colonists for the reception of such emigrants as they are willing to take.

To William Malleson, on the Contagious Diseases Acts. By Helen Taylor.

AVIGNON, *18th January* 1870.

. . . Not only do I object altogether to the extension of the Contagious Diseases Acts, but I have seen the passing of them, as they at present exist, with great regret, and should be extremely rejoiced if they could be repealed;

since not only do I object to them altogether on principle, but I think that in the long run those measures are likely rather to increase than diminish the evil they are intended to attack. Moreover, I fully agree with you in thinking that opposition to those Acts is more particularly incumbent on the defenders of the interests of working men, because working women are likely to be the greatest sufferers by this system of legislation, and, if it is to be carried out with anything like efficiency, it could only be by an enormous expenditure, which of course would fall in the long run upon the great mass of the taxpayers. Of course one need scarcely say that to any man who looks upon political institutions and legislation from the point of view of principle, the idea of keeping a large army in idleness and vice, and then keeping a large army of prostitutes to pander to their vices, is too monstrous to admit of a moment's consideration, while the safety of the country could be provided for by the military education of all classes, or until after every possible experiment with married soldiers had been tried and failed. I therefore do not think that this system of legislation, which I think utterly depraving to the mass of the population (not to speak of its gross inequality between men and women), is in any way specially necessary for the army and navy. It is a monstrous artificial cure for a monstrous artificial evil which had far better be swept away at its root, in accordance with democratic principles of government. . . .

To Lord Amberley,

in reply to an account of an interview which he had had with Mr. Lecky.

By Helen Taylor.

Avignon, *2nd February* 1870.

Dear Lord Amberley,—Mr. Lecky's state of mind on the subject of prostitution is characteristically conservative. He thinks that since it has not been reformed up to

1870 — Ætat. 63. this day it never can be. This is the true conservative standpoint. Whatever reforms have been already effected are well enough; if they were effected long enough ago they are even excellent. As to any reforms in the future, though they might be desirable in themselves, they are sure to bring with them greater evils than they can remove; and then come those jeremiads, more or less eloquent and touching, which we are so accustomed to both in politics and morals, about the fearful consequences to society of attempting to do anything that has not been done already. It would be hardly possible to support any opinion by flimsier reasons than these particular ones of Mr. Lecky.

Are we to consider what the Church accomplished in the Middle Ages as the extreme limit of the moral improvement possible to mankind? Are the violent appetites and passions of half-tamed or not even half-tamed barbarians a measure of the obstacles to be encountered in educating the young of a cultivated and law-observing community? The Church strove with sincerity and earnestness in the Middle Ages to suppress private war and the abuses of military violence, with very little success; but what could not be done then, has been found quite practicable since and has been actually accomplished.

It is of more importance, however, to consider Mr. Lecky's doctrine than his reasons. He considers prostitution as a safety-valve to prevent the propensity to which it ministers from producing worse evils. Now, in the first place, I believe that the propensity has hitherto been fostered, instead of being weakened, by the tendencies of civilisation (which has been a civilisation left mainly to the influence of men) and by the teaching of the Catholic Church, which, in order to add to the glory of the "grace of God," always has exaggerated and still does exaggerate the force of the natural passions. I think it probable that this particular passion will become with men, as it is already with a large number of women, completely under the control of the reason. It has become so with women, because its becoming so has been the condition upon which women hoped to obtain the strongest love and admiration of men. The gratification of this passion in its highest form, therefore, has been with women conditional upon their restraining it in its lowest. It has not yet been tried what the same conditions will do for men. I believe that they will do all that we wish, nor am I alone in thinking that men are by nature capable of as thorough a control over these passions as women are. I have known eminent medical men, and lawyers of logical mind, of the same opinion.

1870 — Aetat. 63.

But in the second place, supposing that Mr. Lecky is right in thinking, as he apparently does, that men are not capable of efficient control over this propensity, I should still differ from him when he thinks that prostitution is the best safety-valve. I, on the contrary, think that with the exception of sheer brutal violence, there is no greater evil that this propensity can produce than prostitution. Of all modes of sexual indulgence consistent with the personal freedom and safety of women, I regard prostitution as the very worst, not only on account of the wretched women whose whole existence it sacrifices, but because no other is anything like so corrupting to the man. In no other is there the same total absence of even a temporary gleam of affection or tenderness; in no other is the woman to the man so completely a mere thing, used simply as a means for a purpose which to herself must be disgusting. Moreover, so far from thinking with Mr. Lecky that prostitution is a safeguard even to the virtuous women, I think it cuts at the core of happiness in marriage, since it gives women a feeling of difference and distance between themselves and their husbands, and prevents married people from having frank confidence in one another. Marriage has not had a fair trial. It has yet to be seen what marriage will do; with equality of rights on both sides, with that full freedom of choice which as yet is very incomplete anywhere, and in most countries does not exist at all on the woman's side, and with a conscientious scruple, enforced by opinion, against giving existence to more children than can be done justice

1870 — Aetat. 63. to by the parents. When marriage under these conditions (and with such means of legal relief in extreme cases as may be adopted when men and women have an equal voice) shall have been tried and failed, it will be time to look out for something else; but that this something else, whatever it may be, will be better than prostitution is my confirmed conviction. The fact I believe to be, that prostitution seems the only resource to those, and to those only, who look upon the problem to be solved to be, how to allow the greatest license to men consistently with retaining a sufficient reserve or nursery of chaste women for wives. Their problem is not, as yours and mine is, how to obtain the greatest amount of chastity and happiness for men, women, and children. . . .

To Horace White, of the *Chicago Tribune*; on Chinese labour.

AVIGNON, 13*th February* 1870.

DEAR SIR,—I presume I am indebted to you for sending me the number of the *Chicago Tribune* which commented on my supposed opinions respecting Chinese immigration. Nothing could be clearer or fairer than the editorial statement of the reasons which, in my opinion, *might* justify the exclusion of immigrant labourers of a lower grade of civilisation than the existing inhabitants. But I never said that in America, and in the present circumstances of the case, it ought to be done. My letter on the subject, to a Californian citizen who had asked my opinion, has been so much misunderstood that I cannot but think the copy of my letter which I understand appeared in the newspaper, must have been a mutilated one. I distinctly declared that in my opinion the right course to be adopted is to endeavour by education to bring the rising generation of Chinese up to the level of Americans. If there is little or no rising generation (the Chinese not being permanent settlers), I said that in that case their coming could be no such evil to the labouring classes as to justify its prohibition; while the opportunity it gives of carrying the ideas of a more civilised country into the heart of China is an advantage to the people of China of which, I said, I do not think it would be right to deprive them. The only mode of immigration which I said that I thought should be prohibited, is the bringing over Chinese as coolies under engagements to work for particular persons; which is a form of compulsory labour, or, in other words, of slavery.

1870 — Aetat. 63.

To Alexander Campbell, of Glasgow.

Avignon, *28th February* 1870.

. . . I agree with you that the land ought to belong to the nation at large, but I think it will be a generation or two before the progress of public intelligence and morality will permit so great a concern to be entrusted to public authorities without greater abuses than *necessarily* attach to private property in land. Meanwhile we should try to go on limiting the power of individuals over land by imposing more and more conditions on behalf of the people at large.

To Sir Charles Dilke,

on a resolution passed by the London branch of the Education League, that national education should be purely secular.

Avignon, *28th February* 1870.

Dear Sir,—I most heartily agree with the resolution of the London branch, which I had already seen in the newspapers, and I am delighted that the Education League is preparing for a struggle. For myself I would rather, and I should think that the intelligent part of the working class would rather, have no National Education Act for the next five years, than one which should empower the State to establish schools on the denominational system. All other objections, strong as some of them are, might be waived in order to get a beginning made of a national system, but

1870 — Ætat. 63. that all schools *founded* by the Government, either general or local, should be purely secular is a point on which, if I were in Parliament, I should make no compromise, but if it was not conceded would do what I could to defeat the bill. Ever since I saw that the League was going to make a stand on this point I have been desirous of helping it by some expression of opinion, but I have not yet made up my mind how I can best do so. . . .

TO FANNY LEWALD-STAHR,

in acknowledgment of her book, "Für und wider die Frauen."

AVIGNON, *1st March* 1870.

DEAR MADAM,—I beg to return you my sincere thanks for your kindly sending me your excellent series of letters on the Women question. It is a real honour to have my name inscribed at the beginning of such a volume. Your book is both convincing and persuasive, and is singularly free from the two contrary defects, one or other of which writings for the cause of women so often exhibit, of indiscreet violence and timid concession.

So competent a testimony as yours is well fitted to make me think that I have been at least apparently unjust to German women in the remark I made in my little book on the insufficiency of their education. When I referred to this as being inferior to what it is in France, I did not so much refer to the ordinary character of the schools for young women, which, I believe, is much worse in France than in Germany, but to the much smaller number of women who, like yourself and a few others, have qualified themselves by their studies and acquirements for distinction and usefulness as writers. The average education of German ladies may be much superior (at least as to languages) to that of French ladies, but there appears to be as yet a much smaller number who stand out from the general level, and take a more or less high rank either in the literature or in the various discussions of their country.

To Sir Robert Collier.

AVIGNON, *3rd March* 1870.

My dear Sir Robert Collier,—Allow me to thank you for your kind attention to my letter, and for the interest you have taken in the case of the dismissed policeman. 1870 — Aetat. 63.

Undoubtedly, if the man has really been guilty of falsehood he ought not to be reinstated; but that he persists in his story is all he can do if he is innocent. Of course, in a case like this, in which the magistrate has shown such gross incapacity, there ought to be some independent examination of the worth of the evidence of the witness whose story was at variance with that of the man Smith. I should have supposed that it would have been within the province of the head of the police to have made such an examination; for however much respect is due to a magistrate's decision, magistrates are after all fallible (unhappily, in the case of Mr. Benson, apparently very fallible), and then it seems to lie with the Home Secretary and the immediate superiors of any one who has been aggrieved to redress the injury as well as they can in the absence of any Court of Appeal.

I hope you have by this time quite recovered from your unfortunate and troublesome accident, which I much regretted to hear of.

To Mr. (afterwards Sir) Arthur Helps,

in acknowledgment of his book, "Casimir Maremma."

BLACKHEATH PARK, *28th March* 1870.

Dear Mr. Helps,—Your letter was forwarded to me at Avignon, but I delayed acknowledging it until I should have an opportunity of reading your book, which was waiting for me here.

If, as you intimate, my review of your first publication had any share in procuring for the world the series of works which I and so many others have since read with so

1870 — Aetat. 63.

much pleasure and instruction, far from regarding this exploit of mine as a sin to be repented of, I should look upon it as a fair set-off against a good many sins. This most recent of your works is as full of valuable and happily expressed thoughts as any of its predecessors, while as a story it is far more successful than "Realmah," though perhaps not more interesting to a psychologist. With regard to its practical object, emigration, I should like very much to see the experiment tried in the manner you proposed, of founding beyond the seas a new community complete in all its parts. But the conditions of a new country produce of necessity a state of society so much more democratic than our own, that it is only very exceptional persons in our higher or middle classes that could either reconcile themselves to it or have the foresight and mental adaptability required for guiding and organising the formation of such a community. And considering the great addition made annually to the poorer part of our population, the scheme would have to be executed on a vast scale indeed if it is to clear out the bad quarters of our towns and leave them a *tabula rasa* for reconstruction on better principles; not to say that the inhabitants of those quarters are far from being, in general, good material to colonise with.

I am very happy that you go so far as you do with those who are seeking to remove the civil and political disabilities of women. Since you think women should have the suffrage, surely you should join the Suffrage Society, which claims nothing whatever but that independent women with a due property qualification should be allowed to vote.

To Mrs. Hickson,

on the death of her husband, William E. Hickson, the educational writer.

Blackheath Park, *28th March* 1870.

Dear Madam,—Before receiving your sister-in-law's letter, we had learned your irreparable loss from one of those who most loved you and Mr. Hickson, our friend Miss Lindley. My first thought on hearing the sad news was of you. I know too well that there is no consolation for a calamity like yours. But nothing can deprive you of what comfort there is in a knowledge of the deep respect which was felt for your husband, and will continue to be felt for his memory, by those who have known him as long and as well as I have. Mr. Hickson was one of the small number of those who, with no personal ambition to gratify, have laboured from an early age first to acquire the powers necessary for enabling them to render services to mankind, and then to use those powers to the utmost extent of their opportunities ; and he was, in no ordinary degree, successful in both objects. I have from an early period been accustomed to look upon him as in many important respects an example of what men should be. The loss of every such man makes the world poorer, and is to be lamented even by those who had not the privilege of his personal friendship—how much more by all who had.

To H. Taine,
on Frenchwomen.
By Helen Taylor.

Blackheath Park, *le* 21 *avril* 1870.

Monsieur,—Je suis bien aise d'apprendre que je n'avais pas negligé de vous envoyer le livre de mon père. Ce livre parut dans le moment le plus extrême de la réaction soi-disant spiritualiste, et il a manqué par là un éclatant succès tout en contribuant beaucoup à sauver un certain nombre de bons esprits. Réimprimé dans un temps plus propice à la philosophie inductive de la nature humaine, il tiendra à fortifier cette bonne tendance, sans jeter ses lecteurs dans les défauts que vous reprochez avec quelque raison à l'école matérialiste.

Quant à la question des femmes ; vous n'êtes pas le premier qui m'a fait à peu près les mêmes observations

1870 — Aetat. 63.

sur le caractère des françaises. J'ai été souvent frappé de l'espèce de mépris avec lequel les Français parlent souvent des Françaises, et (puis-je le dire?) il me semble que les Françaises ne manquent pas de rendre ce mépris même avec intérêt. Il est sûr que les hommes et les femmes en France ne s'estiment pas réciproquement; ce qui est, par parenthèse, assez souvent la conséquence de trop de galanterie dans les mœurs. Cependant j'ose dire que, comme beaucoup de Français et surtout de Parisiens et surtout encore des hommes de la classe aisée, vous ne connaissez pas toutes les belles qualités des Françaises. Il n'y a pas au monde de femme qui sache mieux "s'ennuyer, sans s'amortir ou s'éteindre" que la Française provinciale rangée et vertueuse de quelque rang que ce soit, et il n'y a pas de meilleure femme d'affaire ni de personne plus réfléchie, plus sobre (d'esprit), que les paysannes françaises, et encore beaucoup de femmes de la classe artisane quand elles ne sont pas écrasées par les souffrances dont leurs maris les abreuvent. Et même pour les jolies femmes et les Parisiennes, c'est un peu la légèreté des hommes français qui est cause que les femmes françaises ne leur présentent que les côtés fourbes de leur caractère. Quand ces mêmes femmes d'apparence frivole ont à faire avec des femmes anglaises, il arrive quelquefois qu'elles font voir un fonds de sérieux et d'amertume que se trouverait rarement peut-être même parmi ces Anglaises que vous croyez si sérieuses. Ce caractère sympathique qui est si gracieux, si aimable et dans les Français et dans les Françaises, fait que les femmes se montrent banales et frivoles quand elles croient voir que les hommes attendent d'elles la banalité et la frivolité. C'est à vous hommes intelligents de la France, à montrer que vous croyez les femmes capables des idées sérieuses et des goûts élevés, et je me trompe beaucoup si vous ne verrez pas bientôt se dévoiler une intelligence et une élévation dont vous ne surprenez pas encore l'existence.

To a Lady,

who sought Mill's advice as to whether she should separate from her husband, on grounds of incompatibility of temperament.

AVIGNON, *1st May* 1870.

DEAR MADAM,—You greatly overrate the qualities required for writing such books as mine, if you deem them to include that of being a competent adviser and director of consciences in the most difficult affairs of private life. And even a person qualified for this office would be incapable of fulfilling it unless he possessed an intimate knowledge of the circumstances of the case, and the character of the persons concerned. It would be a long and a difficult business to define, even in an abstract point of view, the cases which would justify one of two married persons in dissolving the contract without the consent of the other. But as far as I am able to judge from your own statement, yours does not appear to be a strong case, since your husband has still an affection for you, and since you not only do not complain of any ill treatment at his hands, but have so much confidence in his goodness and high feeling, as to feel sure that even in case of your leaving him without his consent, he would not seek to withhold any of your children from you. 1870 — Aetat. 63.

If I could venture to give any opinion, it would be that if the only bar between you and such a man is a difference in your "ways of thinking and feeling," unfortunate as such a difference is in married life, the mutual toleration which we all owe to those who sincerely differ from us forms a basis on which the continuance of your union may be made endurable, and the differences themselves, when nothing is done to exasperate them, may, as is usually the case between persons who live intimately together, tend gradually to an approximation.

To Alexander Bain,
on his work on "Logic."

Avignon, *17th May* 1870.

1870 — Ætat. 63.

Dear Bain,—I have now finished a careful reading of your book. When I compare it with my own mode of treating the subject I am much struck with the combination of nearly perfect agreement in the *fond* of our opinions on every part of it, with so much originality in the manner in which you have presented many of them. This, if it stood alone, would make the book very valuable, for there is no more important service to any set of thoughts than to vary their expression, and to deduce them from one another in different ways. But in addition to this, by varying the modes of statement you have illuminated points and aspects of our common doctrine which the previous exposition had left more or less in the shade, and you have followed out some of the principles into consequences not previously drawn.

I find little or nothing, relating properly to Logic, from which I dissent; but a good many apparent conflicts between your mode of expressing and presenting technical details, and mine; in most of which cases I still prefer my own. This applies chiefly to the first volume, and even that exclusive of its concluding chapters. When I next revise my "Logic" I shall carefully collate each chapter with the corresponding chapter of yours: but in general, instead of trying to incorporate your new matter, I think it will be both better in itself, and fairer to you, to refer to what you have done, give a brief account of it, and direct the student to your fuller exposition. Of course I cannot dispense with adapting the statement of the theory of Causation to the Correlation of Force; but your book has confirmed me in the opinion I had formed, that but little adaptation is required. In making that little I shall be greatly helped by the clear light in which you have placed the distinction between the two sorts of antecedent conditions, the conditions of Force and those of Collocation. 1870 — Aetat. 63.

Respecting the Conservation theory itself, you have given by many degrees the clearest explanation of it that I have ever met with, and I now seem to myself to understand the *facts* of the case pretty completely. But about the mode of expression of the facts I still boggle, and have a stronger impression after reading your exposition than I had before, that the men of science have not yet hit upon the correct generalisation, though they may be at no great distance from it. I am so anxious to understand this matter thoroughly that I write down my difficulties in hopes that you will help me to resolve them.

In the first place, you exclude from the theory two of the principal forces, Gravitation and Molecular Adhesion, expressly distinguishing these from the "correlated forces." Of course you do so because there is at present no proof of the convertibility of the other forces into these; and you do not take any notice of the hypothetical explanation of gravitation by molecular motions, given by Tait (I believe) and others, which so strikingly resemble the argument of Descartes to show that his vortices might generate a tendency to a centre. But though gravity does not take its place in the theorem of Conservation, motion generated by gravity does. Suppose, then, a weight suspended by a string over the shaft of a mine—suppose that the string breaks, and the weight falls, with rapidly increasing velocity, to the bottom. Here is a positive addition to the active force at work in the universe, which, when it ceases its mechanical motion, remains in the form of heat or in some other of the correlated forms. Now, at the expense of what pre-existing energy has this force been generated? The conservationists are obliged to say, out of potential energy. A given portion of potential energy has become actual; and if the weight is hoisted up again the power expended in raising it is so much taken back from the sum of actual energy and restored to the sum of potential.

Now I want to analyse the meaning of this phrase, "potential energy." It seems to signify some force actually

1870 — Aetat. 63. residing in the suspended weight. But it is nothing of the kind. There *is* a force actually residing in the weight—a force actually measurable : viz. the downward pressure with which it pulls at the string, and by which it is able to neutralise an equal weight at the other end of a lever. But this force is limited to that with which the body would commence falling if the string broke, and is far short of the vastly accelerated force with which it would reach the bottom of the mine. When we are bid to say that this augmented force existed previously as potential energy in the weight, this potential energy is not to common sense and logic anything which really existed, but is a mere name for our knowledge that a force *would* be created if the body began to fall.

I am discussing the expressions, not denying any of the facts. When force is expended in placing a weight in a "more advantageous position," as you express it (*i.e.* in a place from which it has further to fall in order to reach its centre of attraction), when it does fall to the depth from which it has been raised, it will reproduce the exact amount of force expended in raising it (making allowance for any part which may have been transformed into heat). The expression "potential energy" is no doubt adopted to enable us to say that the total amount of force in all Nature can neither be increased nor diminished, the sum of the actual force *plus* the sum of the potential being a constant quantity. But this only means that there is a vast reserve of force not existing in any shape now, but which gravity could call into existence, and that this not actual but possible quantity of force has an extreme limit, viz. the whole of the motion that would be generated by the rushing together of all the gravitating bodies in the universe until they could not possibly get any closer together. From time to time a little of this possible force gets itself created, and in that case it requires that an equal force should be expended if the effects produced are to be counterbalanced or undone.

It seems to me a bad and misleading form of expression to ascribe the motion, which would be gradually acquired by gravitating bodies if the obstacles which keep them apart were removed, to an energy of equivalent amount residing in the body before it begins to move.

1870 — Aetat. 63.

But if this objection could be overruled, a greater remains behind. You say (and this is a point quite new to me) that force may be, and is, expended in merely altering the collocation of bodies, without generating even potential energy. This, I suppose, is the case when force is expended in destroying molecular adhesion. But if this be so, how can the indestructibility of force be maintained? The sum of actual force *plus* the sum of potential is in that case diminished.

When you have time, perhaps you will kindly explain to me how the theory of Conservation, as at present expressed, can stand with this fact.

There are some questions in physical science which I should like to ask of you, but this can be done *viva voce* at some future time. In particular I was not aware that chemical combination *always* produces heat. I will ask you, some time or other, to tell me the explanation of the apparent exceptions—freezing mixtures and the like.

Among the differences of mere language between your book and mine there is only one which I much care about; your use of the word "elimination." In mathematics we eliminate what we want to get rid of: we eliminate y to obtain an equation containing only x. Of late careless writers in newspapers, &c., having picked up the term, have taken to using it in a sense the reverse of this: they eliminate not what they turn out but what they keep in: they eliminate the truth out of conflicting stories, &c. In your book you employ the term in both ways: whenever a separation is effected between essentials and non-essentials you speak indiscriminately of "eliminating" either the one or the other. Is this mode of using the term adopted from a deliberate choice? and what are the advantages that recommend it to you?

To Sir Charles Dilke,

on the position of the Women's Suffrage movement.

Avignon, *28th May* 1870.

1870 — Aetat. 64. Dear Sir Charles Dilke,—It seems to me that the position of the Women's Suffrage question is immensely improved by what has taken place in Parliament. You yourself a few weeks ago could not count as many as 100 members of Parliament who were known to be in our favour, and there are now, including pairs and absentees, 184, considerably above a fourth part of the House, of whom 29 voted in the second who had not voted in the first division. The amount even of Tory support was most promising, including some of the most prominent members of the party below Cabinet rank, and, among others, both the Whips. We knew that we had not a majority in the House, and that when the thing looked serious our enemies were sure to rally and outvote us unless the Government took up the cause, which the time had certainly not come for expecting. The rally is the first proof we have had that the thing is felt to be serious. I am in great spirits about our prospects, and think we are almost within as many years of victory as I formerly thought decades.

But I think it would be a great mistake to merge the women's question in that of universal suffrage. Women's suffrage has quite enemies enough without adding to the number all the enemies of universal suffrage. To combine the questions would practically suspend the fight for women's equality, since universal suffrage is sure to be discussed almost solely as a working men's question; and when at last victory comes there is sure to be a compromise by which the working men would be enfranchised without the women, and the contest for women's rights would have to be begun again from the beginning, with the working men inside the House instead of outside, and therefore with their selfish interests against our cause instead of with it. Thus women's enfranchisement would be thrown back for a whole generation, for universal suffrage is not likely to be obtained in less time than that; and at the end of the generation we should start again in a more disadvantageous position than we are in at present. . . .

1870 — Aetat. 64.

To Ch. Le Hardy de Beaulieu, the Belgian economist, on restrictions on child and woman labour.

Avignon, *le* 21 *juin* 1870.

. . . Quant à la question du travail des enfants, l'opinion générale comme celle des hommes éclairés en Angleterre se prononce de plus en plus pour la limitation légale, accompagnée du système *half-time*. On étend cette législation de plus en plus, en sorte qu'elle s'applique maintenant à presque toutes les industries qui ne sont pas purement domestiques, sauf l'agriculture qui jusqu'ici fait exception. L'expérience a prouvé que la loi peut seule faire face à l'intérêt combiné des fabricants et des pères des enfants à exploiter le travail de ces infortunés aux dépens de leur éducation et même de leur développement physique, et cette expérience a graduellement prévalu sur les idées de liberté individuelle. En effet la liberté individuelle n'est sacrée que dans ce qui ne regarde, au moins directement, que l'individu, et ne peut être invoqué pour l'exercice illimité d'un pouvoir quelconque sur les autres, dont les abus sont toujours dans le domaine légitime des lois. Cependant je suis tout à fait d'accord avec vous en ce qui regarde le travail des femmes, qu'en Angleterre on a soumis à quelques-unes des mêmes restrictions légales que celui des enfants. Vous savez combien je condamne les iniquités de la position actuelle des femmes dans la famille et dans la société, mais cette habitude de les traiter comme des enfants me semble contraire à leur véritable intérêt. Je voudrais qu'en les protégeant beaucoup mieux qu'à présent contre les abus

1870 — Aetat. 64.

de la force physique, on les reconnût comme moralement capables de se conduire et de s'engager par elles-mêmes, et qu'on ne fît acune différence quant à la liberté des contrats, entre elles et les hommes.

S'il vous serait agréable de posséder les dernières enquêtes parlementaires sur le travail des enfants j'aurai grand plaisir à les procurer et à vous les envoyer après mon retour en Angleterre, qui aura lieu dans le commencement de juillet. Je vous serais de mon côté très reconnaissant de tout renseignement sur le succès du système *half-time* en Belgique, système qui en Angleterre rencontre encore quelque opposition.

Je regrette que vous soyez du nombre considérable des hommes distingués dans les lettres ou dans les sciences qui dans notre siècle comme en d'autres ont été privés de la vue. Cette privation vous est commune avec mon ami M. Fawcett qui de tous nos hommes publics d'aujourd'hui s'est le plus occupé de cette question du travail des enfants. Comme vous il se soutient noblement contre ce découragement ; il ne se relâche en rien dans les travaux qu'il s'était proposés comme l'occupation de sa vie et dans lesquels il promet à sa patrie une carrière aussi utile que distinguée.

To George Adcroft,

in acknowledgment of a tract by him.

Avignon, *21st June* 1870.

Dear Sir,—I have read your little tract with interest, but I perceive that you have either published or intend to publish another pamphlet containing the remedies you propose for the evils you so justly denounce. In the meantime I will only say that I think you underrate the power of trade unions to raise wages; and that I differ from you when you say that a general rise of wages would be of no use to the working classes, because it would produce a general rise of prices. A general rise of prices, of anything like a permanent character, can only take place through a general increase of the money incomes of the purchasing community. Now a general rise of wages would not increase the aggregate money incomes, nor consequently the aggregate purchasing power of the community; it would only transfer part of that purchasing power from the employers to the labourers. Consequently a general rise of wages would not raise prices, but would be taken out of the profits of the employers; always supposing that those profits were sufficient to bear the reduction.

1870 — Aetat. 64.

The case is different with a rise of wages confined to a single, or a small number of employments. That rise, if taken out of profits, would place a particular class of employers at a disadvantage compared with other employers; and as soon as they ceased to hope that the loss would be only temporary, they would withdraw part of their capital, or at all events, all new capital would avoid those trades and go into others. Consequently the supply of these particular articles would fall short, and their prices would rise so as to indemnify the employers for the rise of wages. But this would not happen in case of a rise of all wages, for as all capitalists would be affected nearly alike, they could not as a body relieve themselves by turning their capital into another employment.

To Charles Eliot Norton, on the Land Question.

AVIGNON, *26th June* 1870.

DEAR SIR,—I have had the pleasure of receiving your letter of 17th June.

I agree, in the main, with all that you say respecting the limitation of the right of property even in movable wealth. I never meant to say that this right should be altogether unlimited, nor to ascribe to it sacredness in any other sense than that all the necessary conditions of human happiness are sacred. I do not indeed quite

1870 — Aetat. 64. agree with your friend Mr. Wright, when, in the passage quoted and concurred in by you, he seems to say that, from the utilitarian point of view, the right of private ownership is founded *solely* on the motives it affords to the increase of public wealth; because, independently of those motives, the feeling of security of possession and enjoyment, which could not in the state of advancement that mankind have yet reached be had without private ownership, is of the very greatest importance as an element of human happiness. But this is probably a difference rather in expression than in opinion between us.

There is, however, this great difference between the case of movable wealth and that of land, that so long as land is allowed to be private property (and I cannot regard its private appropriation as a permanent institution), society seems to me bound to provide that the proprietor shall only make such uses of it as shall not essentially interfere with its utility to the public; while in the case of capital, and movable property generally, though society has the same right, yet the interests of society would in general be better consulted by laws restrictive of the acquisition of too great masses of property, than by attempting to regulate its use. I have, in my "Political Economy," proposed limitations of the right of ownership so far as the power of bequest forms part of it, on the express ground of its being injurious to society that enormous fortunes should be possessed by gift or inheritance. . . .

The death of Dickens is indeed like a personal loss even to those who knew him only by his writings.

To Col. T. A. Cowper,

on the case of the Bombay Bank.

AVIGNON, *26th June* 1870.

MY DEAR COWPER,—I knew before reading your pamphlet that the Bombay Government, having by the constitution of the Bank the appointment of three of the nine directors, was morally responsible, not necessarily for the strict prudence of all the Bank's transactions, but at all events for their not being in violation of the admitted and generally practised rules of safe and legitimate banking. I knew also that those rules had, by the directors of the Bank, been flagrantly and systematically violated. But even after all I had read, my idea of their misconduct fell short of what it is shown to have been by your detailed history of their proceedings; and the many years during which I knew, studied, and profited by the work you did for the Bombay Government, have taught me to repose great confidence in any statements of yours, which, moreover, in the present case rest upon, and can be easily collated with, the report of a Government commission.

It is hardly possible for abuse of trust to be carried to a greater pitch in the forms of banking than it was by the managers of the Bombay Bank, when, to omit many other disgraceful facts, nearly half the capital of the Bank passed, on nominal securities, into the hands of a speculator who was himself one of the directors, or into those of friends recommended by him, generally for the purpose of puffing up his own special actions; when the secretary, Mr. Blair, who was allowed to lavish the funds of the Bank without check or control, received large pecuniary favours from this person; and when two even of the Government directors, one of whom was long President of the Bank, realised large sums by the sale of allotments which they received from speculative companies to whom loans were made by the Bank: the case was certainly one which, in a good system of commercial law, would come within the definition of criminal bankruptcy, and if justice were done, the chief culprits would be expiating their guilt by fine and imprisonment. Now I find that the Government, through the whole course of the Bank's misconduct, were as utterly regardless of their obligation to watch and control its management as if no such obligation had existed. They gave no in-

1870 — Ætat. 64. structions to the Government directors. They allowed the Bank to be carried on under the new charter without even any by-laws to govern and direct its management. And they neither obtained nor sought from their representatives on the Board any information respecting its proceedings. The great pressure of public business on an Indian Government might be some, though a very insufficient excuse for this quiescence as long as there was nothing to excite suspicion. But the quiescence continued after the mismanagement and embarrassments of the Bank were so notorious even in England as to alarm the Secretary of State, who felt it his duty to warn the Bombay Government. After this the conduct of the Government was, if anything, more discreditable than before. Their unwillingness to admit that anything was seriously amiss almost amounted to complicity. To the warnings and questionings which they now frequently received from their superiors in England and at Calcutta, they answered smooth things, extenuating to the utmost the amount of mischief, abetting the directors in withholding information demanded of them, and acting as if it were their deliberate purpose to screen the misconduct of the Bank, though probably only desirous of screening their own neglect of the duty of supervision. It is shown that had the Bombay Government, even after they had become aware of the evil, done their duty in preventing further malversation, the Bank, notwithstanding the great losses already sustained, might have been saved from insolvency, and the property of the shareholders might have been in great part preserved to them. By not having done this, even if by nothing else, the Bombay Government made itself morally a party to the misconduct of the directors, and responsible for it to the sufferers.

It may be said that the majority of the directors, including those most certainly guilty, were elected by the shareholders. But considering the extreme difficulty under which shareholders labour, as well in England as in India, in choosing trustworthy directors or in controlling them, it is certain that the shareholders placed

(as they had every reason to think themselves warranted 1870
in placing) their principal reliance on the Government; —
whose representatives on the Board, themselves high in Aetat. 64.
the public service, must, if they did their duty to Government even as the largest shareholder in the Bank, take care that its interests, in common with those of the other shareholders, should receive ordinary and decent regard from those to whose charge they were entrusted. The shareholders would have had no claim to indemnity from the Government for ordinary losses, or for such as were occasioned by irresistible circumstances, or even by ordinary and venial mismanagement. But they have a just claim *in foro conscientiæ* to reparation from the Government for loss sustained by gross and criminal violation of duty on the part of its agents. An able speaker in the House of Commons who was master of the facts, could make a speech on them which would resound through the whole country, and which would be damaging to any Government that resisted the claim.

You are at liberty to make use of this opinion of mine in any quarter in which you think it would be of service. If it goes to Mr. Gladstone or the Duke of Argyll, I would rather it should be as an enclosure in your letter than directly from myself. But though I think well of the intentions of both those ministers, I think them sufficiently like ministers in general to be much more certainly influenced through the press than by any representation addressed to themselves. I could put your pamphlet into the hands of the writers of several newspapers, and could probably induce them to pay some attention to the subject. How far they might be willing to proceed in what might be opposition to the Government I cannot tell.

There are several courses to choose from, and it is for you to consider which of them you prefer. One is to defer any appeal to Parliament or the public until it is certain that your application to the authorities is unsuccessful. Another is to endeavour to get a motion made in the House of Commons. And if this be deter-

1870 — Aetat. 64. mined on, the question occurs whether it should be done in the present session, or early in the next, the public mind being in the meantime acted on as much as possible through the press. If you decide for this session, I will when I return to England, which will be in about a fortnight, consult with my Parliamentary friends and try to find some one in the House willing to take up the subject, and capable of doing it with effect. There should, if possible, be simultaneously an organisation through the press; and any influence I have with editors I will most gladly make use of, but, as I have said, I do not know how far it is likely to be effectual. . . .

To H. Taine,

in reply to a letter from him thanking Mill for a favourable notice of his book, "De l'intelligence," which Mill had written in the *Fortnightly Review*.

Blackheath Park, *le 22 juillet* 1870.

Monsieur,—Je me félicite de ce que vous avez bien voulu exprimer une opinion favorable de la notice que j'ai publiée de votre très remarquable ouvrage. Je sais combien cette notice est insuffisante mais j'ai voulu, au premier moment possible, attirer l'attention des hommes éclairés sur un livre dont la publication en France me paraît destinée à faire époque. Votre livre n'a pas besoin d'être interprété. Il suffit qu'on le lise, car vous possédez parmi tant d'autres qualités, le génie de la clarté.

Quant à notre différence d'opinion, pour l'approfondir il faudrait entrer très à fond dans la théorie de ce qu'on peut nommer l'idéalisation d'une conception d'expérience; comme une ligne droite géometrique est l'idéalisation des lignes droites de nos sens. Cette conception idéalisée n'en est pas moins, comme vous l'admettez, un produit de l'expérience; mais vous dites qu'elle ressemble aux produits chimiques et que ses propriétés ne peuvent être connues que par l'observation directe. Je pourrais, peut-être, contester cela, et soutenir que c'est là l'une des différences entre une conception idéalisée et une conception composée : mais même en admettant votre opinion, on peut dire que cette observation directe ne pourrait vous révéler que les propriétés du produit regardé comme conception mentale, c'est à dire des faits psychologiques, et qu'elle ne nous dit rien sur les lois générales de l'univers.

1870 — Aetat. 64.

To J. Boyd Kinnear,

who had resigned from the Land Tenure Reform Association on account of its adoption of the principle that it is permissible for the State to purchase land, for letting as small holdings; as also of the principle of the taxation of unearned increment.

Blackheath Park, *22nd July* 1870.

My dear Mr. Kinnear,—Though I regret very much that you do not sufficiently agree with the articles of the new programme, to feel justified in remaining a member of the Association, it is not without deliberate consideration that I have concurred in a course of policy for the Association which we knew would prevent many persons whose support would have been valuable from joining it. We had to choose, however, between losing their adhesion, and depriving ourselves of all support whatever from the working classes : and we might still hope that those who had accepted our fresh programme would co-operate with us from without on the important points on which they agree with us, while as an Association we should have no power of usefulness whatever unless we could enlist in our support the most intelligent part of the working classes; who are very generally adopting as their creed the entire resumption of the land from private hands into those of the State. We thought it the wisest course, therefore, instead of limiting our demands so as to obtain the greatest attainable amount of adhesion among the

1870 — Aetat. 64. higher and middle classes, to go as far towards the demands of the working classes as we conscientiously could, provided that by this means we could induce them to support us and act with us; and the conference with some of their leaders, at which you were present, showed that they were willing to do so.

The provision for the purchase by the State of land in the market, would be chiefly applicable to neighbourhoods in which there are neither common lands, nor lands belonging to public bodies, sufficient to give a fair trial to small holdings and to co-operative agriculture. I quite agree with you that public bodies ought not to hold lands; but I think it quite worth trial how the State could manage landed property (which is a great part of its business in India); and of one thing I feel certain, that nothing but a trial on a large scale, and for a considerable period, would convince the working classes that such a system would be unsuccessful or injurious.

The article asserting the right of the State to the "unearned increase," &c., is not so worded as to imply that landowners are to be dealt hardly with in this respect. Its purpose is simply to assert the legitimacy of special taxation on land, in consideration of the special property it possesses, in a prosperous country, of continually rising in value. No doubt, as you say, this rise could not have been so great as it has been and is, had there been no improvements in agriculture, because, without those improvements, the growth of wealth and population could not have reached anything like the same extent. The improvements, however, arise in great part from the improved skill, and knowledge, and exertion of the tenants, not the landlords. And, for what the landlords have done, they would be indemnified by the option allowed them (and now inserted in the programme) of resigning their land to the State at the market price. It is probable, as you say, that the price of wheat is not now higher, proportionally to other things, than it was many years ago. But I apprehend that this is owing to foreign importation, and that nearly all other agricultural produce, especially cattle, meat, and dairy produce, have risen in an extraordinary degree. 1870

Aetat. 64.

Other property than land may, no doubt, rise in value without any exertion on the part of the owners. But I do not know of any other kind of property of any importance, which rises in value from generation to generation in every improving county by a sort of natural law, the exceptions to which are rare and only temporary. Not to mention that land being the gift of nature, and of limited quantity, a system of landed property which was just and reasonable so long as land was obtainable by all, is fairly liable to reconsideration as soon as the land has become insufficient in quantity, and has been engrossed by a small number of proprietors.

I hope your visit to the Channel Islands will accelerate the restoration of your health, which, I was very sorry to hear, stood so much in need of recruiting.

To H. K. Rusden, of Melbourne, on the Marriage Laws.

Blackheath Park, *22nd July* 1870.

Dear Sir,—I have received and read the essays which you did me the honour to send. I am quite of your opinion as to the usefulness, in the present stage of human improvement, of speaking out, without reserve, whatever opinions one has deliberately formed on topics important to mankind, subject, of course, to the duty of satisfying oneself by calm consideration that one knows, and has taken into account, such qualifications and counter considerations as may be necessary to make one's opinion a fair expression of the truth. I do not, however, blame a person who stops short of the complete public expression of unpopular opinions, when it would involve serious danger of the loss of his means of subsistence; for though it is often a merit, it is only in peculiar cases a duty, in any one to be a martyr for his opinions.

You are mistaken in thinking that I have purposely

1870 — Aetat. 64. withheld, in my book on "The Subjection of Women," any opinions which I thought relevant to the subject. The purpose of that book was to maintain the claim of women, whether in marriage or out of it, to perfect equality in all rights with the male sex. The relaxation or alteration of the marriage laws, in any other respect than by taking away all vestiges of the subordination of one sex to the other, is a question quite distinct from the object to which the book is devoted, and one which, in my own opinion, cannot be properly decided until that object has been attained. It is impossible, in my opinion, that a right marriage law can be made by men alone, or until women have an equal voice in making it. You say in one of your essays that my book recommends that marriage should be dissoluble at the will of either of the parties. Now I carefully avoided giving any opinion as to the conditions under which marriage should be dissoluble, for the very good reason that I have not formed, and do not consider either myself or any one else capable at present of forming, a well-grounded opinion on the subject. I, of course, accept your proposition that human freedom should not be interfered with, except by such precautions as are necessary to prevent injury to society; but what those precautions are, in this particular case, is precisely the question to be discussed, and it can only be determined justly or expediently by the joint experience, and with the full force and well-considered concurrence, of both sexes.

To Henry Fawcett, on the Franco-Prussian War. By Helen Taylor.

Blackheath Park, *26th July* 1870.

Dear Mr. Fawcett,—Sir Charles Dilke ended the note in which he told me of your wish to make a public demonstration on the war, by asking me, if I disapproved of it, to write to you, and therefore I have not written to you.

I highly approve of having a demonstration, and I hope there will be many of them. For myself, I do not wish for the present to appear in any way in the matter. A time may come when it will be the duty of every one to speak out. But while I do all I can in private, I think it best for the present, both for public and for private reasons, that my name should not appear. This letter therefore is confidential. In the meantime, I think the points of most importance are, that the English public should know, and show that it knows, that this war has been brought on wholly by Napoleon; that the Prussians are fighting for their own liberty and for that of Europe; that England is bound to protect Belgium; and that our utmost efforts can only, if Napoleon lives, defer war, not prevent it. Our turn must come. Therefore, that our people ought to arm at once, taking the responsibility off the Government, which is right to be prudent and silent. The volunteers ought to be armed with the newest and best rifle by public subscription. It is not a time for talking about peace and the horrors of war when our national existence may be soon at stake. At the same time it is wrong to attribute this war to France. Neither in justice nor in prudence ought we to do so. The Germans are right in saying that it is Napoleon and not France they are fighting, and Napoleon, if he lives, and is successful in humbling Prussia, will attack England, the fourth of the great powers that fought at Waterloo.

To Henry Kilgour,

acknowledging a pamphlet by him, written to advocate the formation of a joint committee of colonial legislatures for the consideration of imperial affairs.

Blackheath Park, 15*th August* 1870.

Dear Sir,—I beg to acknowledge your letter of 10th August, and the pamphlet to which it refers.

I am entirely in favour of retaining our connection with the colonies so long as they do not desire separation. And

1870 — Ætat. 64. I think the nation is of the same opinion, and would not tolerate, in the Government, any conduct which is believed to proceed from a desire to break the connection. But I confess I do not think it likely that a periodical meeting of delegates from all the colonies and dependencies, with no substantive powers, merely for the purpose of discussion, would excite sufficient interest in those countries to become a useful institution. What a colony desires from the mother country is generally something having reference to its own special wants, and which it would probably, in general, prefer to discuss singly with the Government, which has the power of decision. The participation of numerous delegates from other communities, with no interest in the particular question, communities whose wants are different and who have little fellow feeling, would, I should think, be more likely to be felt as an incumbrance than desired as a help.

Allow me to express my surprise that one who attaches so much importance as you do to the mere public discussion of subjects by those who are specially interested in them, should see no use in the admission into the House of Commons of representative working men. Their presence there seems to me indispensable to a sufficient discussion of public interests from the particular point of view of the working classes; which assuredly is not less worthy of being considered, nor has fewer truths mingled with its errors, than the points of view of the other classes now so superabundantly represented in Parliament. The "Parliamentary tone" does not seem to me to be at present so elevated as to be in any danger of being lowered by the admission of such men as Mr. Odger into a House a majority of whom seem to me to be abundantly endowed with all the characteristics you ascribe to him, except the "considerable mental vigour" for which you give him credit. The result I should expect from bringing contrary prejudices face to face, and compelling them to listen to one another, would be a great improvement on both sides: and in my own experience, the working classes are not those who have shown least willingness to be improved by such collisions.

To P. A. Taylor,

concerning the apprehensions which were entertained lest Mazzini, who had been taken prisoner by the Italian Government, might be secretly murdered.

By Helen Taylor.

22nd August 1870.

Dear Mr. Taylor,—I have the highest admiration for Mazzini, and although I do not sympathise with his mode of working, I do not take upon myself to criticise it, because I do not doubt that to him is mainly owing the unity and freedom of Italy. Nor do I in the least doubt the reality of the danger your letter speaks of. But the real safeguard against that danger lies in the fact that the whole Italian people, friends and enemies, are assuredly fully aware of it, and that the Italian Government must be fully aware that if any mischief happens to Mazzini while under their custody no one in Italy will attribute it to natural causes. On the other hand, nothing whatever would persuade any but a few scattered English people that any such danger exists at all. To say so would simply be to expose oneself in England to the imputation, fully believed by those who make it, of being a rabid and fanatical partisan; whereas in Italy the mildest and most moderate people will believe it even if it is not true. Hence I am sure that it would be impossible to bring the influence of English public opinion to bear in this matter. To attempt to do so would simply be to call forth such honest and genuine expressions of incredulity as might even convince the Italian Government of what they would otherwise never suspect—that if Mazzini dies in prison the English public may really not be sure that he was poisoned.

1870 — Aetat. 64.

The safety of Mazzini depends on the fear that his death might arouse feeling in Italy dangerous to those in whose hands he is. As I believe this to be the case, I think in all human probability the Government will be very desirous

1870 — Aetat. 64. of avoiding anything of the sort, and of setting him free as soon as they conveniently can. Some action on the part of English Liberals to request his liberation on grounds of humanity, his age, his health, &c., might, a little time hence, give an excuse to the Government they might be glad to take, to set him free. At present I fear they would not think it prudent to do it.

Were I an English personal friend of Mazzini I should certainly endeavour to obtain access to him, for I think the greatest danger at present is of his fretting himself into an illness, which in the hands of Italian doctors might naturally terminate fatally. The presence of a real friend might be of great use to him, and as English people's word is generally believed, the Italian Government might more easily permit English than Italian friends to see him, since they might trust them better to do nothing that they undertook not to do.

To Gustave d'Eichthal.

Blackheath Park, *le 27 août* 1870.

Mon cher d'Eichthal,—Merci d'avoir pensé à moi dans un temps si douloureux.

Depuis longtemps je suis arrivé à la triste conviction que, malgré l'incontestable réalité des progrès modernes, nous ne sommes pas encore à l'abri des grands malheurs et des grands crimes que notre siècle se flattait d'être parvenu à bannir de la terre. Je plains profondément le peuple français qui n'est pas responsable de tout ceci, qui n'aime pas et n'a pas voulu la guerre, et qui est condamné à la payer du meilleur de son sang et peut-être d'une humiliation nationale la plus difficile à supporter ; pourvu que l'Europe, et surtout la France, apprenne de ces tristes événements que, lorsqu'un peuple abdique la direction de ses propres destinées et se résigne à ce qu'un gouvernement fasse de lui un simple instrument de sa volonté, il est condamné à supporter toutes les conséquences de ce qu'il a laissé faire en son nom ; et qu'un gouvernement qui par les conditions de son existence a besoin de tout ce qu'il y a de plus malhonnête et de plus corrompu dans le pays, finit par être trompé par eux au point que même son appui de prédilection, l'administration militaire, se trouve pourrie et en décomposition au moment du besoin. 1870 — Aetat. 64.

Quelles que puissent être pour la France les suites immédiates de ces événements, il ne lui faudra pas beaucoup d'années pour redevenir tout aussi grande qu'auparavant; mais elle devra se contenter d'être l'une des grandes puissances de l'Europe, sans prétendre d'être la seule ou même la première: il lui faudra reconnaître pour les relations internationales comme pour celles de la vie civile la règle de l'égalité. La prétention d'un pays quelconque à être tellement au-dessus des autres pour que rien d'important ne se fasse sans le consulter, ne peut plus se soutenir aujourd'hui; et la France devrait voir dans la répudiation universelle d'une telle prétention, le triomphe du principe qui fait sa propre gloire.

J'espère qu'au moins vous n'aurez pas d'autres malheurs que le désastre public à déplorer et que la guerre épargnera toute votre famille.

Je suis arrivé ici huit ou dix jours avant la déclaration de guerre, alors qu'un pareil coup semblait presque aussi peu probable que la destruction de Paris par un tremblement de terre. La rapidité foudroyante des grands événements d'aujourd'hui n'est pas ce qu'ils ont de moins étonnant.

To Mr. (afterwards Professor) JOHN WESTLAKE.

BLACKHEATH PARK. *7th September* 1870.

DEAR SIR,—The question respecting the expediency of making the sale of instruments of war by neutrals to belligerents an offence against the law of nations is a difficult one, and though I have given it some consideration I cannot say that I have arrived at a positive opinion. Your paper will probably assist me in forming one.

About one thing I feel quite clear; that the matter ought not to depend, as it does by our present laws, on the discretion of the executive. For the sake both of principle and of policy the question should be determined by law.

1870 — Aetat. 64. And it cannot well be determined by law without a previous agreement among the principal nations; since otherwise we should either be adjudging to ourselves rights which might not improbably be disputed, or acknowledging obligations which might not be reciprocated.

On the rule itself, there is a conflict of considerations. On the one hand, real neutrality seems to me to consist in not aiding either side with means of carrying on the contest: including under "means," any articles of which the sole, or at all events the principal use, is for warlike purposes. On the other hand, it is generally, though not universally, true that the party most benefited by, because most needing, supplies from neutral countries, is the weaker of the belligerents, who is the more likely to be the oppressed or injured party; including, among the rest, all who are in arms, on however just provocation, against their own government. It is significant that the only case in which the power given to our own executive in this matter has been acted on (the case of the Greeks and Turks) is of this last description.

A further consideration is the difficulty of preventing exportation to the belligerent countries without stopping exportation altogether. It would be of little use to prevent guns being sent out to Dunkirk if they can be sent to Ostend, and from thence find their way into France. But this only amounts to saying that it is of no use for one country to act on the rule unless it is adopted generally. If it were so adopted the Belgian Government would be responsible for preventing the guns exported to Ostend from entering France.

On the whole, I incline most to leaving the exportation free, but not without misgiving; for when the access to foreign supplies operates, as it generally does, unequally upon the two belligerents, it seems to me hardly possible that the public opinion of the party suffering should not regard the professing neutral as substantially an ally of the enemy; and perhaps with still greater resentment as one who, without any ground of quarrel, seeks to make profit by a neighbour's misfortunes.

There is but too much ground for your apprehensions as to the feelings likely to be left by this war; but if it had been unattended with a great and decisive success on either side, it would probably have been much more prolonged, and the case is pre-eminently one in which the shortest evil is the best. Then, too, it was important that a striking retribution should fall on the aggressor in an unprovoked war. It is the justice of their cause which has roused the whole German people, and given them this irresistible might. But it is deplorable to think that the French nation may, from a false point of honour, persist in an unjust war which they neither originated nor desired.

To Sir Charles Dilke,

firstly, on the question of recognition of the French Government of National Defence; and secondly, as to whether a protest should be made against the transference of territory to the Germans, without obtaining the consent of the inhabitants.

Jointly by Mill and Helen Taylor.

Blackheath Park, 30*th September* 1870.

My dear Sir Charles Dilke,—On the first of the points mentioned in your note, I think that the Government of National Defence, being to all appearance obeyed as the Government of the country by all parts of France which are not in the power of a foreign army, ought to be recognised officially (it is already recognised semi-officially) as the *de facto* Government by Great Britain; which recognition I understand to consist in giving to our ambassador new credentials addressed to the new authorities. I think that what was done in the case of the Provisional Government of 1848 should be done in the present case; but after Gladstone's answer to the deputation, I do not think that there is any chance of inducing him to do this.

The second point I cannot see in the same light. The Germans have a very strong case. One of the wickedest

1870 — Aetat. 64.

acts of aggression in history has been by them successfully repelled, but at the expense of the bitter suffering of many thousand (one might almost say million) households. They have a just claim to as complete a security as any practicable arrangement can give against the repetition of a similar crime. Unhappily the character and feelings of the French nation, or at least of the influential and active portion of all political parties, afford no such security. I feel with you a strong repugnance to the transfer of a population from one government to another, unless by its own expressed desire. If I could settle the terms of peace, the disputed territory should be made into an independent self-governing State, with power to annex itself after a long period (say fifty years) either to France or to Germany; a guarantee for that term of years by the neutral powers (which removes in some measure the objection to indefinite guarantees), or, if that could not be obtained, the fortresses being meanwhile garrisoned by German troops. But there may be many objections to this which I do not see; and, at all events, our Government would probably urge it in vain. Our Government is not likely to have the smallest influence at present with Germany. English public opinion might perhaps have some little influence. But all demonstrations of the kind seem only likely to encourage France in a hopeless struggle.

If Gladstone had been a great man this war would never have broken out, for he would have nobly taken upon himself the responsibility of declaring that the English navy should actively aid whichever of the two powers was attacked by the other. This would have been a beginning of the international justice we are calling for. I do not much blame Gladstone for not daring to do it, for it requires a morally braver man than any of our statesmen to run this kind of risk.

I have willingly given you my opinion on the points on which you ask it, but I do not wish any public use made of it with my name, as I have no desire to push myself or to be put forward in the matter; for public opinion in England appears to me, on the whole, so reasonable and well-intentioned on the subject as to be likely ultimately to arrive at a right conclusion, and I am not sure whether we have really yet sufficient data as to the mere facts to enable us to form a very definite opinion.

1870 — Aetat. 64.

To Jean Arlès-Dufour, on the Franco-Prussian War.

Blackheath Park, *le* 29 *octobre* 1870.

Cher Monsieur,—Je n'ai pas eu le cœur de répondre à votre lettre du 26 septembre, parceque je ne pouvais vous rien dire de consolation dans l'immense malheur qui pèse sur la France.

Aujourd'hui votre voeu pour une médiation anglaise semble être exaucé, dans la mesure de ce qui est possible.

Ici la sympathie pour les malheurs de la France est grande, et le désir est général qu'elle sorte de cette crise aux conditions les plus favorables que comportent les circonstances, mais on ne pense pas moins qu'elle doit une grande réparation à l'Allemagne pour les vastes sacrifices de son sang le plus précieux qu'une agression injuste lui a imposés. Et l'on craint que cette facilité à croire ce qui est agréable, et à résister à l'évidence des faits, qui est propre aux habitudes du Français, ne leur fasse refuser des propositions supportables, pour être réduits à subir plus tard des conditions encore plus rigoureuses. Si le patriotisme éclairé de tout ce qu'il y a de meilleur en France pouvait décider les classes lettrés de la nation à voir dans les sacrifices qui sont devenus inévitables, une leçon pour ne plus jamais se laisser aller à préférer des rêves d'agrandissement au-dehors, à la recherche de la liberté et du progrès moral et social au-dedans, et pouvait décider l'immense majorité de la nation à ne se laisser gouverner que par eux-mêmes, alors on pourrait espérer que les tristes événements de cette année, quelque puisse être leur dénouement, deviennent la date d'une véritable régénération pour la France.

Je n'ai guère besoin de vous dire, cher monsieur, à quel point moi-même je partage votre douleur, et combien ma

1870 — Aetat. 64. sympathie est profonde pour tous les Français qui n'ont à se reprocher ni le commencement de cette déplorable guerre ni sa prolongation.

To Frederic Booker,

in reply to a question as to how working men should be supported, if elected on to the School Boards; it being supposed that these duties would consume their whole time.

By Helen Taylor.

Blackheath Park, 31*st October* 1870.

Dear Sir,—I have not a copy of the Act by me, but I have always understood that the prohibition of payment had reference only to payment out of taxes, rates, or any public fund. I do not believe that there exists any legal obstacle to payment of the representatives by their constituents, as the trades unions pay their officers and delegates. It would not cost the trade societies of Manchester much to pay, if necessary, to those working men whom you may succeed in electing, the weekly wages which they would earn if they worked at their ordinary employment. There appears to me, however, a more serious difficulty. If really, as you say, the working men will not have confidence in any man as a real working man who has saved enough to be independent, or who can spare even a portion of his time from earning his daily bread, it would appear that the moment they have elected a man they must lose confidence in him if he is to be supported by subscription, since from the moment when he is so supported he ceases to be a working man. I should have thought it had been the first object of all who have the interest of the working classes at heart that some among the working men, whose talents or good fortune enable them to be pecuniarily better off than the majority of their companions, should continue to be, and to be considered, still members of the working classes. But if they are to be looked on with suspicion and dislike this cannot be the case. It has always been my hope that the working classes might come to have a moderate portion of leisure, and I should regard it as a great misfortune if, the moment a working man is able to attain this, he should lose the confidence of his fellow-workmen unless he is dependent on their bounty. It cannot be impossible that a working man should retain the principles which are honestly entertained by so many individuals among the richest classes of the country merely because he has been able to become a master workman or a writer, &c., &c.; and as he will, if he has been born and has generally lived among the working classes, understand and sympathise with them better than most persons of other classes can do, I think such a man should be trusted till he has proved himself unworthy of trust. Doubtless many men will do so, as many men in every rank show when put to the test that their real motives for entering into public life were vanity or self-interest; but I cannot believe that a larger proportion of men mainly inspired by such unworthy motives would be found among the self-raised men of the working classes than among the self-raised men of the leading mercantile, manufacturing, literary, and others.

1870 — Aetat. 64.

To Mr. John Morley, on the Franco-Prussian War.

By Helen Taylor.

November 1870.

Dear Mr. Morley,—I am glad to see you have not yielded to the utterly false and mistaken sympathy with France, and indeed I go further than you do in the other side. Stern justice is on the side of the Germans, and it is in the best interests of France itself that a bitter lesson should now be inflicted upon it, such as it can neither deny nor forget in the future. The whole writing, thinking, and talking portion of the people undoubtedly share the guilt of Louis Napoleon, the moral guilt of the war, and feel neither shame nor contrition at anything but

1870 — Ætat. 64. the unlucky results to themselves. Undoubtedly the real nation, the whole mass of the people, are perfectly guiltless of it; but then they are so ignorant that they will allow the talkers and writers to lead them into just such corners again, if they do not learn by bitter experience what will be the practical consequences of their political indifference. The peasantry of France, like the women of England, have still to learn that politics concern themselves. The loss of Alsace and Lorraine will perhaps be about as painless a way of learning this lesson as could possibly be devised.

To Mr. John Morley,

on Russia's action in breaking the treaty of 1856 respecting the neutrality of the Black Sea.

By Helen Taylor.

Blackheath Park, *18th November* 1870.

Dear Mr. Morley,—We congratulate you very heartily upon your marriage, of which it gives us great pleasure to hear. Home life is the best possible *milieu* for work, and I hope you will be able to subordinate your work to the claims of your health, a task, however, which is found very difficult by everybody who can and will work well.

I am very anxious just now that there should be some proper protest against the infatuation of our press on the Russian question. I can compare it to nothing but the infatuation of the French press, which we have all been wondering at. Almost in the same breath in which our journals tell us only too truly that we are utterly unprepared for war, nay, unprepared for the most essential defence, they call upon us to declare war with one of the most powerful military empires of the world—a naval power too—and that at the very same time that our quarrel with America is still pending. So much for their common-sense. As for the rights of the question, it is doubtful whether they are not substantially on the side of Russia. At all events we are not bound in honour to attempt to carry out the treaty when our most important co-signatory can give no help. Least of all are we bound in honour to insist upon the perpetual adhesion to a treaty which in all probability we ought to be ready to abrogate. As for the argument that Russia is simply casting off all treaty obligations, that simply points to the fact that all such obligations always have been disowned directly the party unwillingly bound by them perceives a relaxation of force in the powers which attempted to bind it. This will always happen so long as treaties are made in perpetuity. Were they terminable, as they might be, those who object to them would have a rational hope of escape in some more moral way than an appeal to the same brute force which imposed them. It points also to the inherent weakness of the scheme of joint treaties and guarantees which must of their own nature fall to pieces directly there is any great change in the conditions or the relations of the joint powers. This treaty of 1856 should have been allowed to fall into disuse. That it has not been so allowed is a legacy of the evil Palmerstonian days. Now, I conceive that the only dignified thing for us to do is to let the treaty be abrogated by Russia, with a protest reserving our own liberty of action. The way in which Guizot dealt with the annexation of Cracow is a case in point, and would form a very good precedent for us in this matter.

1870 — Aetat. 64.

We shall hope to see you on Tuesday next, as you say, in the forenoon. There is a train at 35 minutes past 12 from Charing Cross, by which perhaps you can come and take luncheon with us.

To Henry Fawcett,

on Russia's action.

Blackheath Park, 18*th November* 1870.

. . . The newspapers are raging and blustering on the subject of Russia in a manner which will be very dangerous if the Government and the House of Commons think that

1870 — Aetat. 64. their ravings express the opinion of the country. Writers who for many months have never ceased sounding an alarm about our total want of preparation for a war even of self-defence, telling us that we have neither troops, nor horses, nor guns, nor officers, nor organisation, nor men capable of giving us these things—all, I believe, too true—now demand that we should instantly say to Russia, Retract that declaration of war; and when Russia refuses (as what power in such a case would not refuse?) we are to go to war with Russia at once, and, as they themselves think not improbable, with Prussia too. And all this for what? Because Russia shakes off an obligation which, though it may sometimes perhaps be rightly imposed as a temporary penalty for unprovoked aggression, no nation can ever be expected permanently to submit to. One would think such a thing had never happened before, as that a nation on whom hard terms had been imposed by victorious enemies has ever treated them as no longer binding after she had recovered her strength. The truth is, such things are often happening, and must often be submitted to, when the object itself is not worth a war; and so it will be until treaties are concluded as they ought to be, for terms of years only, instead of affecting to be perpetual. Will any one pretend that a nation can bind its posterity for all time by the conditions to which it has been forced to submit at a moment of difficulty? If not, such stipulations, unless they still remain in themselves desirable, must be allowed to become obsolete, and the only questions are after what lapse of time and under what conditions; questions which no one, I believe, is yet prepared to answer. Strength and opportunity have always decided them hitherto.

When one considers that England ought to have done the inestimable service to mankind of preventing the present terrible war if we had chosen to run a very slight risk of being involved in it ourselves, the proposal that after shrinking from this we should rush precipitately into war to limit the number of Russian ships of war in the Euxine shows a degree of criminal fatuity almost greater than that of Louis Napoleon and his advisers four months ago.

To Mr. Leonard Courtney,

on Russia's action.

Blackheath Park, 19*th November* 1870.

Dear Mr. Courtney,—I thank you very much for your kindness about my letter.

I perfectly understand that what you and other thoughtful men regard as the important point in the matter is the declaration of the Russian Government that it intends to throw off one of the obligations of the treaty without asking the consent of the other contracting parties. My position, however, is that it is not every breach of treaty that requires to be, or that ought to be, resented by war. The *fons et origo mali* is the great error of concluding treaties in perpetuity, instead of only for a term of years, which, by making it inevitable and sometimes even a duty to break treaties, creates that conflict of possible obligations which both fosters and shields unconscientiousness. No treaty is fit to be perpetual. When, however, a treaty is an amicable contract between nations for their joint advantage, it is in most cases possible to get necessary modifications effected by joint consent. But it is not, and never has been, thought to be so in the case of treaties which are real capitulations—terms of peace imposed by victors on the vanquished expressly because known to be disadvantageous to them. Even such treaties, if they were temporary, might be kept. But when no term is fixed for their expiration these treaties—those conditions of them especially which directly restrain the freedom of action of the country—always have been, and always are, violated as soon as the nation on whom they are imposed is able and willing to risk another war. And such violation is habitually condoned, unless the other parties to the violated treaty think the particular object worth a war. Was there ever a more direct violation of a treaty, to which all the powers of Europe were parties, than was committed by France when she placed another Bonaparte on the throne? But what country dreamed of going to war with France

1870 — Aetat. 64.

1870 — Aetat. 64. to prevent or chastise that breach of engagements? Instances more or less similar are too frequent in recent history for it to be necessary to enumerate them; but there is one worth mentioning, because it affords a precedent applicable to the present case. When Russia, Austria, and Prussia combined, in violation of treaties, to destroy the Republic of Cracow and annex it to Austria, Guizot was Foreign Minister of France. He made a public declaration, I do not remember if it was by a circular to his diplomatic agents or by a speech in the Chamber, or by both, that France took notice of this breach of treaties, that she did not intend to take any active measures in opposition to it, but that she reserved to herself the exercise of all such rights as the violation, without her consent, of a treaty to which she was a party, in her judgment restored to her. It seems to me that something similar to this is the only wise and dignified course for the English Government to take; unless, indeed, the repudiated engagement be such as it would enforce *de novo* if the thing were *res integra*, and that, too, at the cost of a war under the most disadvantageous and perilous circumstances; but as you, in common I should think with all rational persons who know anything of the subject, totally reject this supposition, I need not discuss it.

To W. T. Thornton.

Blackheath Park, *21st November* 1870.

Dear Thornton,—I am very happy that you so entirely agree with me about this insane clamour for war. I think there is a great deal in your argument, and even were there no other reason, the total inability of the most powerful of the parties to the treaty to do anything towards enforcing it, goes a very great way indeed to release the others from any obligation they might have contracted to do so. Will you not write a letter on the subject to one of the newspapers? Every additional protest at this particular time is of great value, by showing that Englishmen are not all mad together; and that those who determine future opinion will pass a severe judgment on a Government which should sacrifice the safety of England to mere bluster and brag. To do the present Government justice, however, it is my belief that they only want support from the public to show themselves yielding and conciliatory; and therefore we ought all the more to give public expression to this point of view. Those who pretend that we are bound by our engagements to go to war, rely chiefly on the tripartite treaty of England, France, and Austria. I send a page of the *Economist* which contains it. By the first article those powers guarantee jointly and severally, not the treaty with Russia, but the integrity of the Ottoman dominions. It cannot be pretended by any one that this guarantee comes into force until Turkey is attacked. By the second article they engage to consider any infraction of the treaty as a *casus belli;* and, if there are causes, to determine with Turkey and with one another what it has become necessary to do. This merely promises that when a case has arisen which gives them a right to go to war, they will take counsel together whether to do so or not. But a still plainer point is that by this treaty the three powers did not bind themselves to Turkey at all. Turkey was not a party to the treaty. They bound themselves only to one another, and can therefore release one another from the engagement. More, since one of the three, France, cannot possibly fulfil that engagement, it cannot require the others to do so, nor is there the least probability that Austria will make any such requirement from us; while even if she did, the practical impossibility of attaining the end without the aid of France would be a full justification for non-compliance, even in the case of the first article, much more in that of the second. It is perhaps also worth mentioning, for the sake of the completeness of the argument, that this very condition of the neutralisation of the Black Sea has been already broken through by the United States, and that on that occasion none of the contracting parties to the treaty thought fit even to protest.

1870 — Aetat. 64.

With regard to Utilitarianism, you have not said anything yet which would give to the most irrational or most

1870 — Aetat. 64.

irritable person living anything to "forgive." But were you to attack my book or my arguments with any amount of severity I should only see in the attack, coming from one of whose friendship I am so certain, an additional proof of friendship. Of course one is more glad when a person agrees with one in opinion than when he differs, unless he brings one over to his opinion. This you have not done, as yet. I think you will find all your arguments answered in Bentham's Introduction to the "Principles of Morals and Legislation," or in my father's fragment on Mackintosh, long before I wrote anything on the subject.

To Mr. John Morley,

offering to relieve him for a while of the duties of editing the *Fortnightly Review*, to enable him to recruit his health.

By Helen Taylor.

Blackheath Park, 28*th November* 1870.

Dear Mr. Morley,—I have been thinking much over our conversation when I last saw you, and I feel so very strongly how wrong it is that your health should be seriously risked, as I fear it is being, by the impossibility of putting the *Fortnightly Review* aside for a time, that if you cannot find any other friend to whom you would like to confide it, and if you think it would be possible for me to do it for you in a satisfactory manner temporarily, I should be very happy to do what I can. We do not intend in any case to leave England until my daughter has finished, or very nearly finished, her task with Mr. Buckle's MSS.,[1] and as her health only permits her to work very slowly, she has no expectation that this will be for many months. The books and MSS. she is obliged to refer to are so voluminous that they cannot well be carried about. They must be worked at at home, and as the stoppage

[1] [Buckle's "Miscellaneous and Posthumous Works," edited by Helen Taylor. 1872.]

or uncertainty of the French posts debars her from doing it at Avignon, we intend to remain here till it is done. It would be some satisfaction if this circumstance should enable me to be of use to yourself; at all events should other motives induce you to accept my proposal, you need have no scruples on the score of keeping us in England. I presume that the business part of the *Review*—money matters, advertisements, printing, &c.—are or could be deputed either to the publisher or to some one who could act as man of business; and I should think that whoever this may be, might, in the event of my undertaking the temporary editorship, write, under my directions, any letters that might be absolutely essential to contributors, and might receive and send on to me letters and articles. I could in that case undertake to read and judge of the articles and take upon myself the literary editorship, and either forward the letters to you or read them and forward only such as I might think your ought to see. What I myself should most shrink from in undertaking such a thing, would be not the work of editing itself, but the enormous increase of unnecessary correspondence which I fear I should incur if it were generally known that I had undertaken it, and on this account I think it would be best for letters to be sent to the publisher or some man of business, and for some one, other than myself, to be the ostensible name in such correspondence as could not be carried on by yourself. If you still continue to feel that an interval of at least comparative leisure would be of benefit to you, and can make no more satisfactory arrangement for the *Review*, I beg that you will not scruple to avail yourself of any help it is in my power to give.

1870 — Aetat. 64.

I returned the proof of my little article yesterday to the printers.

In reply to this letter, Mr. Morley wrote thanking Mill warmly for his offer, but saying that he had been able to make other arrangements for the conduct of the *Review*.

To Alexis Muston.

Blackheath Park, *le* 9 *décembre* 1870.

1870 — Aetat. 64. Monsieur,—Pardon du retard que j'ai mis à répondre à votre lettre, et qui ne fut causé que par le manque de temps. Ce fut un véritable rafraîchissement pour moi de recevoir de vous une pareille lettre au milieu d'événements si malheureux, comme ce doit être pour vous même une grande consolation que de pouvoir dans le malheur public vous rejeter sur la paisible étude des grandes questions qui importent tant aux intérêts permanents du genre humain.

J'ai très bonne opinion de l'ouvrage de M. Taine sur l'Intelligence, sauf les derniers chapitres où il me semble renier ses principes en croyant pouvoir étendre les généralisations de l'expérience humaine à des régions étrangères à cette expérience. Quant à la doctrine communément dite matérialiste, c'est à dire que toutes nos impressions mentales résultent du jeu de nos organes physiques, je trouve comme vous que jusqu'ici ce n'est qu'une hypothèse, puisqu'on n'a pas pu remplir la condition qu'exige une bonne logique inductive dans la recherche des causes, en établissant que, la cause donnée, l'effet a lieu. Pour cela il faudrait pouvoir fabriquer un organisme et essayer si cet organisme pense et sent. Dans ce cas-là on saurait si les conditions organiques que nous savons être nécessaires à la pensée, sont suffisantes pour la produire, si enfin ce sont de véritables causes, ou seulement des accompagnements obligés.

Quant à la question du moi, je ne puis rien ajouter à ce que j'ai dit là-dessus dans le livre sur Hamilton. Je doute si cette question comporte dans l'état actuel de nos connaissances une solution complète. Je suis allé jusqu'où je pouvais aller, et j'ai indiqué le point où s'arrête mon analyse. Pour la question du sentiment moral il en est autrement, et je crois que l'association en rend compte. Ce sentiment me paraît un résultat très compliqué d'un grand nombre de sentiments plus élémentaires. Mais la discussion de cette question serait impossible dans les limites d'une lettre. Je pourrais vous nommer des livres anglais ou elle est bien traitée, mais ils ne sont pas encore traduits. J'en ai touché un côté dans un petit livre qu'on a traduit en français "L'Utilitarisme": je ne me souviens pas si je vous l'ai envoyé. Sinon, veuillez me le dire et je vous ferai parvenir cette traduction lorsque les communications avec Paris seront rouvertes.

1870 — Aetat. 64.

To Professor J. Nichol, of Glasgow, on the Contagious Diseases Acts.

By Mill and Helen Taylor.

29th December 1870.

Dear Sir,—The chairman of the late meeting on Women's Suffrage had already conveyed to me the invitation which I have been honoured with to attend and address a meeting; but though it would give me much pleasure to do so, I have been obliged to answer that my engagements do not permit of my visiting Glasgow this winter.

I do not care much to discuss the Contagious Diseases Acts with yourself because, being willing as you are to allow women their fair share in electoral representation, you hold a perfectly defensible position when you differ from them on a point of legislation which concerns them. The position of those men, however, who, while they refuse women any share in legislation, enact laws which apply to women only, admittedly unpopular among women, is totally different from yours, and appears to me as base as it is illogical, unless, indeed, they are prepared to maintain that women have no other rights than the cattle, respecting whom a kindred Act has been passed. I fully agree with you that the true fundamental point to be set right is the franchise. I will, however, without referring to all the points in your argument which I disagree with, note down one or two of my reasons for differing from you on the main question.

1870 — Aetat. 64.

1. There is very strong evidence that in the country (France) where legislation similar to the Contagious Diseases Acts has been long in force and its full effects have been produced, it increases the number of the class of women to whom it applies. The comparative safety supposed to be given increases the demand, and the number of women temporarily removed from the market makes vacancies in the supply which has to be, and are, made up. This is not necessarily shown by statistical returns, inasmuch as those can take no account of the great mass of clandestine prostitution practised in evasion of the law, and which, if prevented, could only be so by a still more tyrannical use of the powers given to the police, and by exposing respectable women to a still greater amount of injury and indignity than at present.

2. No reason can be given for subjecting women to medical inspection which does not apply in a greater degree to the men who consort with them. The process is painful even physically, and sometimes dangerous, to women—not at all so to men; and it is idle to say that its application to men is impracticable—the same kind and degree of espionage which detects a prostitute could equally detect the men who go with her. The law being one-sided, inflicted on women by men, and delivering over a large body of women intentionally, and many other women unintentionally, to insulting indignity at the pleasure of the police, has the genuine characteristics of tyranny. You say that you think there is no weight in the objection that the law applies to one sex only, inasmuch as enlistment does the same. To this I think you will see that my replies are unanswerable. In the first place, the laws that represent enlistment are not made by women only, themselves not liable to it, and then applied to men only who have no voice in making them, as is the case in those penalties or discipline proposed to be applied to prostitutes by a legislature which neither consists of, nor is elected by, any proportion of women. Moreover, so long as women who offer them-

selves as soldiers are not accepted, the being a soldier must be taken as a privilege, and not a penalty, of sex. If women were only not soldiers because they are incapable of the fatigue and labour, then those women who in men's clothes have proved themselves capable would not be ejected on their sex being discovered. So long as this is the case military service is as much a privilege of our aristocracy as it is in Mahomedan countries where Christians are not allowed to serve. And the discipline to which this aristocracy voluntarily submits itself through the voice of a legislature which itself elects, cannot be compared to the discipline inflicted by those who do not share it without the consent of those who alone are exposed to it. Secondly, if it was impossible for any man to expose himself to military discipline without a woman as his companion, and if he only was liable to the discipline or punishment, the case would be more nearly parallel. You must remember that no woman can render herself liable as a prostitute without a man for her accomplice; yet when it comes to the punishment, or, if you prefer so to consider it, to the discipline, we hear no more of him. Thus the man only is a soldier, and he subjects himself voluntarily to the discipline; a man and a woman must be associated in prostitution, the woman only is subjected to discipline, and that without her own consent.

1870 — Aetat. 64.

3. There are important medical opinions against as well as in favour of the Acts. If the preponderance is in favour this carries no weight with me, for professional men look at questions from a professional point of view, it being a medical man's professional duty to ascertain disease as early as possible and put it under treatment at once. The professional association is quite sufficient to account for a medical bias. I suppose medical men would desire to place men also under the discipline, which would then be decidedly less odious and more effectual. We cannot take their authority for the half and then refuse it for the whole. Some of the warmest medical advocates for the Acts admit that their operation can never be satis-

1870 — Aetat. 64.

factory till men also are submitted to them, which they say they know men will never consent to.

4. With regard to those who object to the Contagious Diseases Acts as encouraging vice, I do not undertake to defend all that they say, but I think them so far in the right that even if there were the strongest reasons of other kinds for the Act, it would to soldiers and ignorant persons always have this for one of its drawbacks, and it cannot but seem that legal precautions taken expressly to make that kind of indulgence safe are a license to it. There is no parallel case of any indulgence or pursuit avowedly disgraceful and immoral for which the Government provides safeguards. A parallel case would be the supplying of stomach-pumps for drunkards, or arrangements for lending money to gamblers who may otherwise be tempted into theft in moments of desperation, and throwing out their wives and families. We have no such parallels by which to prove to men of lax habits in this matter that we disapprove of while taking care of them. It is tolerably plain, therefore, that as a matter of fact the legislature does regard this with less disfavour than any other practice generally considered immoral and injurious to society, and the public evidence of its doing so must of necessity tend to remove feelings of shame or disapprobation connected with it.

CHAPTER XIV

1871

To Edwin Chadwick,

on voluntary enlistment for the army.

Blackheath Park, *2nd January* 1871.

I do not think it safe to trust entirely to voluntary enlistment for the large defensive force which this and every other country now requires. The perfection of a military system seems to me to be, to have no standing army whatever (except the amount required for foreign possessions) but to train the whole of the able-bodied male population to military service. I believe that with previous school drill, six months' training at first and a few days every succeeding year would be amply sufficient for the infantry. This would not take away the young men from civil occupations to any material extent: the six months would be taken at the very beginning of active life; and there would be at once the greatest amount of force possible, and the strongest security against its being called out unnecessarily; for a service from which no one would be exempt would inevitably be unpopular unless the cause were one for which the nation at large felt a real enthusiasm. Any military force composed by voluntary enlistment, even under the improved circumstances contemplated by you, would have in a greater or less degree the inconvenience of a standing army: it would consist principally of the more idle and irregular part of the population, it would acquire a professional military spirit, and it would have time to learn habits of passive and active obedience to its commanders which would make it, if of any conceivable magnitude, an apt instrument of despotism.

To Mr. John Morley.

Blackheath Park, *6th January* 1871.

1871 — Ætat. 64. Dear Mr. Morley,—I rejoice to hear that your short visit to the seaside has somewhat improved your health, but I am afraid that its permanent re-establishment will be much retarded if you work up to the utmost limits of your strength. I hope that you will consider my proposal as still holding good, and that you will have recourse to it at once if you find that your health does not continue to improve.

If I were to write on the attitude which England ought to take in regard to the war, without entering into the subject of the war itself, what I should have to say would be soon said, for my answer would be, no attitude at all. It does not seem that there is any urgent necessity for saying this, as there is at present no danger that England will interfere in any way. There is not likely to be any party in Parliament for going to war with Germany in support of France. I greatly regret to see the political leaders of the working classes led away by the Comtists and by the mere name of a republic into wishing to drag England into fighting for a Government which dreads to face any popular representation, and is forcing the French peasantry, by the fear of being shot, into going up against their will to place themselves under the fire of the German armies; but there is not the slightest shadow of a probability that such counsels will be listened to by the Government or by any party in Parliament. The really vital subject of debate will be the necessity of strengthening ourselves for military purposes; and the subject on which Cairnes is writing seems to me to be that which, at the present moment, it is of real importance to take up energetically.

If, on the other hand, the question to be written about is the war itself, and its probable or desirable issues, I would rather that this work should devolve on any one than on myself. It is only an evident call of duty that would make me willing to write and publish all I think about the conduct of the French from first to last and about their claim, aggressors as they were, and defeated as they are, to dictate the terms of peace. 1871 — Aetat. 64.

Any one who writes on the subject might make good use of a remarkable pamphlet by Count Agénor de Gasparin, in which he proposes as the only right condition of peace the erection of Alsace and German Lorraine into an independent neutralised republic. I do not know if the most useful thing that you could publish at this moment on the subject would not be a short analysis of this pamphlet with copious translated extracts. I am afraid the French authorities by their obstinacy have let the time go by when the German people might have been induced to content themselves with this amount of concession. But it is really, though not unattended with difficulties, the only settlement that would be just to all parties; and by bringing it forward the minds of some readers might perhaps be put upon a right train of thought, and even the newspaper writers would have an idea suggested to them, their advocacy of which would make the nation less contemptible than they are making it at present.

If you would like to use M. de Gasparin's pamphlet for this or any other purpose, my copy is at your service.

To Mrs. Halsted,

an American lady resident in Florence, on a federation of the countries of Europe.

Blackheath Park, *19th January* 1871.

Dear Madam,—I have had the honour of receiving your letter of 29th December.

Your idea of a general federation of United States of Europe has occurred to many people, and has been a good deal talked and written about of late years among advanced philanthropists, especially on the Continent; indeed, there

1871 — Aetat. 64. can be no advanced philanthropist who does not look forward to something of the kind as the ultimate result of human improvement. But a great many things have to be got rid of, and a great many others to be created, before it will begin to be useful to pursue this federation as a practical object. Such a federal system supposes a very great degree of mutual trust on the part of the communities which comprise it, in at least the good intentions of one another. This trust substantially exists between the States of the American Union (with the temporary exception of the relations between North and South), but the States of Europe do not trust one another, and none of them really trusts its own Government, much less the Governments of the other States. There is, moreover, such a want of homogeneity among them, such differences in their opinions, their institutions, their education, and among some of them there is still so much mutual antipathy that none of them would choose to give up so much of its power over its own affairs into the hands of the others, as your scheme would require. Every improvement, however, which takes place either in the internal government or in the education of any of them, tends to diminish these obstacles and to bring universal peace, grounded on federal institutions, so much the nearer; and it is to such improvements we must trust for bringing about that and all the other salutary changes in human affairs which philanthropists look forward to.

To C. L. Brace, of New York.

Blackheath Park, 19*th January* 1871.

My dear Sir,—It is always a pleasure and advantage to hear from you, for your letters always contain, however briefly, valuable information which the ordinary sources do not give, respecting the various important movements going on in the United States. It is most interesting to have news of the struggle which you and others are making against the characteristic evils of the city of New

York, and when I hear that your efforts to extend education among the dangerous classes have already had a perceptible influence in the amount of juvenile delinquency, as shown by the prison records, I congratulate you most heartily; for success of that kind goes nearer than any other to the root of the mischief, and every step made renders further progress easier. It is also most gratifying to hear that there is an increased feeling for the reform and purification of the Civil Service. That the cause of free trade was greatly advancing we already knew; but that is a small thing compared with the other: besides, a people like the Americans, who really attend to their own public business, *must* find out that what is called protection is an organised system of pillage of the many by the few, and the different classes of the pillaged must soon see that the remedy is to put an end to the pillaging and not to ask to be compensated by permission to pillage somebody else, with an ultimate result like placing all Americans in a circle each with his hand in the pocket of his right-hand neighbour. The economic loss and waste of all this is tremendous, but the resources of your country and the facilities of living in it are so great that you can bear this waste for a time as no other country could do. But the corruption of your politicians is a far more serious matter; it saps the very roots of free government; and the triumphant success of villainy, by corrupting your legislatures and even the bench of justices, cannot go on without demoralising the whole nation. As you truly say, the only remedy is in awakening the public conscience. The still uncorrupted rural population, Mr. Disraeli's "territorial democracy," who have so often come forward and saved the country when it seemed on the brink of being led by the professional politicians into some great folly or iniquity —have to be awakened to the disgrace and danger of leaving the affairs of the country in the hands of men who care for them only as a source of corrupt profit. They have only to refuse their votes to these men and the evil is at an end.

You wish that our writers would discuss the idea of an

1871 International Court of Arbitration. They do discuss it; more has been said and written on the subject in the last year than ever before. But how little prepared the European world is for the realisation of the idea may be seen in the fact that the leaders of our working classes, who have been more zealous for peace than any other class, and who at the beginning of this war made a strong demonstration against allowing ourselves to be drawn into it, are now, at least many of them are, loudly demanding that we should go to war with Germany in behalf of France. I believe that the conditions of a settlement of differences by arbitration do exist between Great Britain and the United States; because in the first place, as I believe, there really exists in both countries a sincere repugnance to going to war with one another; and besides, the ostensible causes of our disagreements are always the real ones. But how could the quarrel between France and Germany have been referred to arbitration? The pretended grievance was a mere sham; the cause of war was that France could not bear to see Germany made powerful by union. If such a war could have been prevented it would not have been by a judicial process, but by a possible interference of neutrals to aid the party attacked. So with the Crimean war: the real question was not about any special ground of quarrel; it was, whether Russia should be allowed to conquer Turkey or not, which question did not admit of being referred to arbitration. When the nations of Europe shall have given up national hatreds and schemes of national aggrandisement, and when their institutions shall be sufficiently assimilated to prevent any of the governments from seeing in the greatness and prosperity of another state a danger to its power over its own people, they will probably be all so sincerely desirous of peace that they will never dream of any other than an amicable settlement of any accidental differences that may still arise. And every step taken in the improvement of the intelligence and morality of mankind brings this happy result a little nearer.

Ætat. 64.

There is a sort of stagnation just now in our internal politics, as the public can hardly feel interested in anything but the war. The bringing of the new Education Act into force is, however, one exception; the elections of the School Boards for London and other places have excited great interest, and there will probably be a great extension of instruction in reading and writing among the children of the poor. How much more will be taught or how well time must show; but no real friend of popular education regards this Education Act as a final measure. The right of women to a voice in the management of education has been asserted by the triumphant return of two ladies as members of the London School Board, and of several others in different parts of the country.

You ask if we are prepared for the tremendous collapse of the French military system. Nobody, I suppose, expected it to be so sudden and complete, but to those who knew France there was nothing surprising in it when it came. I hope it will tend to dispel the still common delusion that despotism is a vigorous government. There never was a greater mistake. When a Government is continually requiring its functionaries to commit rascalities for its sake, they will go on committing rascalities for their own, and as there can be no publicity and no effectual system for the detection of abuse when the Government itself has an interest in concealment, the funds intended for the service of the State find their way into private pockets, and all who want to get rid of onerous public obligations are able to buy them off. No doubt even Frederic II. and the first Napoleon were often cheated by their officers; but an indolent man like the present Napoleon, who, moreover, by the circumstances of his usurpation could get few honest men to serve him, was peculiarly exposed to have the whole of his administration one mass of profligate malversation. His folly was such that he does not seem to have had any suspicion of this, but rushed into war in reliance on ground which was completely rotten under his feet.

To the New York Liberal Club,

on being elected a corresponding member of that body. In response to a hint from the Secretary, Mill responded by a letter on Protection.

20th January 1871.

1871 — Aetat. 64.

DEAR SIR,—I have had the pleasure of receiving your letter of 11th November transmitting the diploma by which the New York Liberal Club do me the honour of signifying my election as an honorary member of their body. What you tell me respecting the origin and purposes of the Liberal Club reflects great credit on its founders. There cannot be a higher or more important aim than that of asserting and maintaining individuality of thought and character, together with its necessary complement, the fullest latitude of mutual criticism. Such associations are a means of making head against the greatest danger of a settled state of society, the danger of intellectual stagnation, and help towards raising up men qualified to speak to the public with decisive effect on those political and social questions which are continually presenting fresh demands on the collective thought and intellectual discernment of the nation.

You intimate that it might be acceptable if, in acknowledging your communication, I was to take the opportunity of expressing my opinion on the desirableness of a Free Trade policy for America. I cannot suppose that those who have thought me deserving of the distinguished honour conferred on me can have anything to learn respecting my opinion on a question of this nature. But I should not be doing justice to my sense of that honour, or to the interest I feel in the objects and in the prosperity of the club, were I not to comply with the wish expressed by you in its behalf.

I hold every form of what is called Protection to be an employment of the powers of Government to tax the many with the intention of promoting the pecuniary gains of a few. I say the intention, because even that desired object is very often not attained, and never to the extent that is expected. But whatever gain there is, is made by the few, and them alone; for the labouring people employed in the protected branches of industry are not benefited. Wages do not range higher in the protected than in other employments; they depend on the general rate of the remuneration of labour in the country, and if the demand for particular kinds of labour is artificially increased, the consequence is merely that labour is attracted from other occupations, so that employment is given in the protected trades to a greater number, but not at higher remuneration. The gain by Protection, when there is gain, is for the employers alone. Such legislation was worthy of Great Britain under her unreformed constitution, when the powers of legislation were in the hands of a limited class of great landowners and wealthy manufacturers. But in a democratic nation like the United States it is a signal instance of dupery, and I have a higher opinion of the intelligence of the American many than to believe that a handful of manufacturers will be able to retain by fallacy and sophistry that power of levying a toll on every other person's earnings, which the powerful aristocracy of England, with all their political ascendancy and social prestige, have not been able to keep possession of.

The misapprehension and confusion of thought which exist on this subject—misapprehension and confusion quite genuine, I allow, in the Protectionist mind—arise from a very small number of oversights, natural enough perhaps in those who have never thought on the subject.

1. When people see manufactories built and hands set to work to produce at home what had previously been imported from abroad, they imagine that all this is fresh industry and fresh employment, over and above that which existed before, and that whatever increased production takes place in these particular trades is so much additional wealth created in the country. The oversight is in not considering that this additional labour and capital to which this production is due are not created, but withdrawn from

1871 — Ætat. 64.

other employments in which they would have added as much to the wealth of the country; and not only as much, but more, since they would not have needed a subsidy out of every consumer's pocket to make their employment remunerative. That the apparent increase of employment produced by Protection is a mere transfer from one business to another is true everywhere, but is particularly obvious in America, since no one will question that labour and capital in the United States are in any danger of not finding employment, or that the time is at hand when they will even be obliged to submit to any diminution of wages or of profits.

2. There is a widely diffused notion that by means of protecting duties on foreign commodities a nation taxes not itself but the foreign producers. Because foreign nations can really be made to suffer by being deprived of a beneficial trade, it is imagined that what the foreigners lose one's own country must gain. But this is a complete misunderstanding of the nature and operation of Protection. Duties on such foreign commodities as do not come into competition with home productions sometimes do fall partly on foreigners, unless the effect is frustrated by a similar policy in the foreign country. Such duties do not destroy any wealth, and may alter its distribution. But such is not the case with any duties so far as they have a protective operation. For their protective operation consists in causing something to be made in one place which in a state of freedom would be made in another, and whatever does this diminishes the total produce of the world's labour; for in a state of freedom everything naturally tends to be produced in the places and in the ways by which the cost incurred in labour and capital obtains the largest return. If this working of the ordinary motives to production is interfered with, and producers are bribed at other people's expense to produce an article where they would not otherwise find it for their interest to do so, there is a loss to the world of a portion of its annual produce, which would have been shared in some proportion or other between the importing and the

exporting countries. America can in this way damage foreigners, but she cannot tax them, for she cannot avoid largely sharing their loss. 1871 — Aetat. 64.

3. A notion very powerful in the minds of some Americans is that if they let in the competition of what they call the pauper labour of Europe they would reduce their own labourers to similar pauperism. Let me observe by the way, that the labour which produces the exportable articles of Europe, and especially of England, is not pauper labour, but is generally the most highly paid manual labour of the country. But it is of course true that the general wages of labour in America are above the English level, and if these high wages were the effect of Protection, I for one should never wish to see Protection abolished. But it is not because of Protection that wages in America are high, it is because there is abundance of land for every labourer, and because every labourer is at liberty to acquire it. As long as this abundance of land relatively to population continues, wages will not decline. These high wages are not a special burthen upon the New England cotton-spinner or the Pennsylvanian iron-master, but have equally to be paid in agriculture and in those numerous branches of manufacturing and other industries (the building trades, for example) which every country necessarily carries on for itself. If those employments which form the bulk of the industry of the country can pay the high American wages and yield besides the high American profits, and if there are other branches of manufacture which cannot do this unless the people of the United States consent to pay them a subsidy in the form of a large extra price, the former class of employments yield a greater return to the labour and capital of America than the latter, and it is for the interest of American production on the whole that the labour and capital of the country should be diverted from the employments which require to be subsidised to those which can maintain themselves without.

4. An argument in favour of Protection which carries weight with many Americans who are not deceived by the economic fallacies of Protectionism, is that it is an evil

1871 — Aetat. 64. to have the population of a country too exclusively agricultural, and that the interests of civilisation require a considerable admixture of large towns. I acknowledge that there was no little force in this argument at a much earlier period of American development. But the time has surely gone by when the growth of the towns in the United States required any artificial encouragement. Even in those parts of the Union in which little or no protected industry is carried on, towns spring into existence and into greatness with a rapidity more marvellous than even the extension of the cultivated area of your territory. The necessity of centres both for internal and foreign trade, the multitude of occupations which from the nature of things are not exposed to the competition of distant places, and the many kinds and qualities of manufactures which are kept at home by the natural protection of cost of carriage, ensure to the United States a town population amply sufficient for a country in which to be an agricultural labourer does not mean, as it has hitherto meant in England, to be an uneducated barbarian. I believe the most enlightened Americans are generally of opinion that at present it is the rural much more than the town population which is both the physical and the moral strength of the country.

To these various considerations I might add that the protection lavished upon some favoured classes of producers is even from the Protectionist point of view a serious injury to other producers who depend on those for the materials or the instruments of their several businesses, and that the attempt to remedy this injustice by distributing protection all round exhibits American producers in the ludicrous light of attempting to get rich by mutually taxing one another. But these points have already been placed in so strong a light that it is quite superfluous for me to insist on them. Rather would I endeavour to impress my conviction that the evils of Protection, though they may be aggravated by the details of its application, cannot be removed by any readjustment of those details; and that any Protection whatever, just in so far as it *is*

Protection—just in so far as it fulfils its purpose—abstracts in a greater or a less degree from the aggregate wealth of mankind, and leaves a less amount of product to be shared among the nations of the earth, to the necessary loss of all nations whose industry is forced out of its spontaneous course by preventing them either from importing or from exporting any article which they would import or export in a state of freedom.

To J. K. H. Willcox, of New York,

in acknowledgment of some papers by him on the Women question.

Blackheath Park, *20th January* 1871.

Dear Mr. Willcox,—I duly received your writings on the Women question. I had already, with much pleasure, remarked some of them in the journals devoted to that cause. I have long been of the opinion expressed by you "that the cause of over-population," or at all events a necessary condition of it, "is woman's subjugation, and that the cure is her enfranchisement." It is one of the endless benefits that will flow from that greatest and most fundamental of all improvements in human society.

To T. Cliffe Leslie,

on compulsory military service.

Blackheath Park, *5th February* 1871.

. . . It does you great honour to have taken up the Swiss system, so early, as the example to be followed in reforming our own. Many thoughtful people are now coming round to the Swiss system (of which Chadwick's school drill forms a part), but the majority even of army reformers are still far behind. They are prejudiced against making military service within the country compulsory on the whole male population, chiefly because, for want of knowledge of facts, they have a most exaggerated idea of

1871 — Aetat. 64. the time which would have to be sacrificed from the ordinary pursuits of life. It is to be hoped there will at least be some few persons in Parliament who will resist the attempt likely to be made by the Government to satisfy the demand for an increased military force without making any fundamental change in the old system. It will be an uphill fight to get a really national defensive force, but it may be a question of life and death to this country not only to have it, but to have it soon. I do not know which are most smitten with imbecility, those who are for trusting our safety solely to our navy on the speculation that no foreign army can land in England, or those who, after crying at the top of their voices that we are utterly without the means of facing an enemy in the field, turn round next day and demand that we should instantly go to war with Russia for the Black Sea or with Germany for France.

To Pasquale Villari.

Blackheath Park, 16*th February* 1871.

Dear Mr. Villari,—It was a real pleasure to hear from you again. It is, as you say, a long time since any letters have passed between us, and the momentous and most unexpected events which have succeeded one another so rapidly during the time make it seem longer than it is. Among all these events there is but one which we can regard with unqualified satisfaction. The acquisition of Rome by Italy is now an accomplished fact, and I hope it will be an example how great the power of an accomplished fact is. But Italy will have to look to her strength. If either the Legitimist or the Orleanist party gets the upper hand in the struggle for power which will now take place in France, they will certainly ally themselves with the clergy. How hostile both those parties have always been to the cause of Italy we know; and when the French begin to aim at recovering their military reputation and some part of their influence in Europe, they are much more likely to make their first trial of strength with Italy (and indeed with any of the neutrals) than with Germany. This is one of the most serious dangers impending over Europe, though apparently one of the least thought of, at least in England. 1871 — Aetat. 64.

With regard to the present war, there now seems to be good hope that the National Assembly will put an end to it. The time for the neutral powers to have interfered was before hostilities had begun. I did not see this at the time, but have been converted to it now. I now believe that there would not have been any war, if even England alone had declared that it would send its fleet to act against whichever side began the attack. But there has been no time since, at which neutrals could have interfered to any good purpose. Armed interference was out of the question, for not having opposed the French aggression, they could not go to war to shield France from the penalties of failure; and for mediation there was no room so long as the French Government insisted that France alone of all nations may gain territory by successful war, but must not lose territory by the most thorough and most just defeat. Even now, when that pretension will probably be abandoned, things have gone too far, and the public opinion of Germany as to the only safe terms of peace has become too decided, to make it conceivable that the counsels or opinion of neutrals will be at all listened to by the German Government.

I regret for the sake of Italy that you no longer occupy your position in the Ministry of Public Instruction, though I hope for a large compensation in the use you are making of your leisure to write a book on Macchiavelli. You were, of course, quite right to resign rather than be the instrument of a policy you do not approve. Doubtless, a rigid economy in expenditure is at present indispensable to Italy; but education is the last of the public interests which should be the subject of any other economy than that which consists in making every *lira* spent go the farthest possible towards the attainment of the end. Unfortunately the economy of most governments consists in starving useful service and spending the money of the public in political or private jobbing; and I suppose Italy has its share of those costs like other countries.

To Mr. Mark H. Judge,

in reply to a request for Mill's opinion on the proper relation of trade unions to their members.

By Helen Taylor.

Blackheath Park, 21*st March* 1871.

1871 — Ætat. 64.

Dear Sir,—I have understood that the expediency of making the contract between a trades union and its members legally binding and enforceable by the tribunals, has been much discussed among trades unionists, and that the prevailing opinion among them is adverse to giving force of law to the engagement. I believe that one objection felt by the trades unionists to the establishment of a legal obligation, is that it would necessarily lead to the decision by the ordinary courts of law of the expediency of particular strikes, whenever funds have been prevented by such strikes from being forthcoming to meet the other liabilities of the unions. This appears to open up the question of how far it is well that the same organisation should provide for the trade interests as well as for the private interests of its members: and this is a question on which I am not at present prepared to give a decided opinion; for while, at first sight, the reasons against this combination appear extremely powerful, I am aware that there are others of very great weight in its favour. One of these reasons is that the fact that a trade union has other and pressing demands for its funds is likely to induce great caution, if not reluctance, to entering upon a strike; and the combination therefore is thought by many to have a tendency to diminish the number of strikes that will be undertaken by the unions.

To T. F. Kelsall.

Blackheath Park, 30*th April* 1871.

Dear Sir,—I thank you (though very tardily) for your very interesting letter, and I think your idea of making public access to parks (when beyond a small size) no longer optional with the proprietor, an excellent one; wholly right in principle, and more likely than anything else to reconcile the people to keeping up the parks instead of ploughing them up to grow corn, which I should much regret.

I agree with you that the State should prevent common land from being made the absolute property of individuals even with the consent of those who have common rights, and the programme of the association goes this length.

To William Martin Wood, of the *Times of India.*

AVIGNON, *24th August* 1871.

DEAR SIR,—I have just received your letter of 11th July. I cannot imagine how the passage quoted from my "Principles of Political Economy" can be supposed to give any support to the imposition of town duties. It is true I object to "calling" upon one tax to defray the whole or the chief part of the public expenditure; but the local expenses of the town of Bombay are a very small part of the share of public expenditure falling upon its inhabitants. A house tax appears to me one of the most equitable of all taxes, not only in so far as it falls on the occupier, but also (in a thriving town) as far as it falls on the ground landlord, from whom it merely intercepts part of the unearned increase of income which he derives from the general prosperity of the place. An octroi, on the contrary, must be levied on the necessaries of life or at least on articles generally used by the mass of the people, and is therefore one of the most unequal and most burthensome of all ways of raising a revenue. I do not say that in a country like India, where it is difficult to levy any tax to which the people are not used, financial security may not sometimes justify having recourse to such a tax, but I am sure it should only be adopted in extremity.

To Joseph Giles, of Westport, New Zealand, in reply to the question, "How far is a strict and logical philosophy consistent with religious faith?"

Avignon, *24th August* 1871.

1871 — Aetat. 65. Dear Sir,—From accidental circumstances your very interesting letter of 18th May 1870 has only just reached me. . . .

In regard to your question, whether an unverified hypothesis can rationally serve as a basis for expectation and action, I quite agree with you that it may do so to a certain extent; on subjects on which we cannot hope for knowledge, we may fairly choose among the various hypotheses which are neither self-contradictory nor contradicted by experience, the one which is most beneficial to our moral nature; provided we always remember that its truth is a matter of possibility and of hope, not of belief. Now the cultivation of the idea of a perfectly good and wise being, and of the desire to help the purposes of such a being, is morally beneficial in the highest degree, though the belief that this being is omnipotent, and therefore the creator of physical and moral evil, is as demoralising a belief as can be entertained. Both the copies of your lecture, I fear, have miscarried, but I am very happy to hear of its delivery, and to know that you take a view similar to my own of the most vitally important political and social question of the future, that of the equality between men and women.

I shall always be glad to hear from you, and to tell you my opinion on any subject interesting to you on which I have formed one.

To Emile Acollas, on the limits of the rights of majorities.

Avignon, *le* 20 *septembre* 1871.

Monsieur,—Je vous remercie sincèrement du don de la nouvelle livraison de votre "Manuel du Droit Civil." Je m'en promets beaucoup de plaisir lorsque j'aurai le temps de l'examiner particulièrement. En attendant je suis très content de posséder, dans un volume peu étendu, ce qu'il faut pour connaître et pour comprendre le droit français actuel en matière de mariage, présenté par un penseur qui ne cherche pas à en déguiser les injustices.

1871 — Aetat. 65.

Votre lettre, publiée dans le *Levant Times* n'a rien d'opposé à mes opinions, sauf peut-être quelques minuties de phraséologie. Du reste, les limites nécessairement étroites de la lettre ont dû restreindre le développement de votre pensée, qui se trouve plus pleinement exposée dans votre brochure "La République et la Contre-Révolution." Dans cette brochure il y a beaucoup de choses qui s'accordent avec mes plus fermes convictions, et quelques-unes qui indiquent des différences dans notre manière de voir. D'abord quant à la partie historique je suis entièrement de votre avis. Depuis ma jeunesse je n'ai qu'une même opinion là-dessus: en 1827 (alors même j'avais beaucoup étudié la Révolution française) j'ai publié un article dans la *revue de Westminster* où j'ai soutenu par des preuves irrécusables précisément votre thèse, savoir que l'attaque a toujours été du côté de la Contre-Révolution et que la Révolution n'a fait que se défendre. Quant à la partie philosophique, vous savez probablement par mon "Essai sur la Liberté," dans quel sens et avec quelles limites j'entends notre principe commun, celui de l'autonomie de l'individu. Je reconnais cette autonomie comme une règle rigoureuse dans les choses qui ne regardent que l'individu lui-même ou, si elles intéressent les autres, ne les intéressent que par l'influence de l'exemple ou par l'intérêt indirect que d'autres peuvent avoir au bonheur et à la prospérité de chacun. Par cette doctrine j'affranchis de tout contrôle, hors celui de la critique, le cercle de la vie individuelle proprement dite. Mais dans ceux de nos actes qui touchent directement aux intérêts d'autrui, il faut à mon sens une autre règle, celle de l'intérêt général. Par exemple je ne trouve pas comme vous que l'autonomie de la personne humaine exige que toutes les fonctions publiques soient électives. S'il y a (comme il y a assurément) des

1871 — Aetat. 65. fonctions importantes (celle de juge par exemple) qui exigent des qualités ou des connaissances qui ne peuvent être bien jugées que par des experts, je trouve que les citoyens peuvent sans compromettre leur autonomie individuelle confier à un ministre responsable la tâche de chercher et de trouver les hommes les plus compétents pour cette fonction. Pour parler plus généralement, je n'admets pas qu'une organisation politique quelconque soit de droit absolu. Je crois au contraire que des états de civilisation différents exigent souvent des institutions politiques différentes. Et même en admettant que, lorsque l'heure de la république est venue, la majorité n'a pas le droit d'imposer à toute la nation le gouvernement monarchique, j'y ajouterais qu'une minorité républicaine aurait encore moins le droit d'imposer la république à la majorité contre son gré; et que cette tentative ne peut aboutir qu'à une tyrannie, parcequ'elle ne peut réussir qu'en refusant à la plus grande partie du peuple les mêmes droits politiques qu'à la partie qui se tient pour plus éclairée, et en réprimant par la violence tout effort qu'elle peut faire pour revendiquer l'égalité de droits.

Malgré ces différences d'opinion je me réjouis grandement de votre puissante protestation au nom des droits de l'individu contre la prétendue souveraineté des majorités, idole auquel les démocrates français ont si souvent immolé, au moins en théorie, les principes les plus essentiels de la politique.

To C. L. Brace, of New York.

AVIGNON, *21st September* 1871.

DEAR SIR,—I thank you for your letter of 4th July. It gave me much pleasure to observe the more cheerful view you now seem to take of the moral and political prospects of the United States. This, in one so thoroughly alive to the evils and dangers which exist, can only arise from the increased energy of the struggle against them by the honest and intelligent majority of the nation; and to this your letter bears direct testimony. As long as there is "a deep well of conscience in the hearts of the people," no moral mischief will be able to get beyond a certain length without exciting a wide-spread determination to put it down; and where that is the case the future of mankind is safe even from very aggravated temporary evils. 1871 — Aetat. 65.

It is very gratifying also to hear from you that the condition of the labouring classes of the United States is highly prosperous. Statements have appeared in England which went to show that from the great increase of the cost of living in the United States, principally arising from the tariff, the wages of labour are no longer sufficient to give the labouring classes the comfort and well-being they have been accustomed to. This is not very alarming, for the tariff would in that case be swept away all the sooner; still one is glad to have it contradicted by such good authority.

In the old country there is all that uncertainty in the prospects of society for a generation or two to come, which there must be when new questions involving the whole structure of society have come to the front while even the advanced minds and *à fortiori* the minds of all classes are not yet prepared to take a rational and practical view of them. The leaders of the working classes have as yet very crude ideas on these questions, and our higher and middle classes have not yet got the length of seeing that the land question and the relation between labour and capital are the points on which the whole of politics will shortly turn; and that very soon no political question will cause any other strong interest than may be due to its bearing on these—with two exceptions, however: minority (or rather proportional) representation, and the condition of women, the last a still more fundamental question than even those others, and which may advance independently of them to the only admissible issue, complete social and political equality. It is much to be hoped that it will do so, for when women are free agents their weight is sure to be on the side of an adjustment of social difficulties, not by a fierce conflict, but by a succession of peaceful compromises.

1871 The arrangement made for the settlement of the Alabama dispute is as you say, most happy for both nations; and the new rules of international law, when generally adopted, will be very favourable to the general peace. The further advance you look for, the prohibition of all supply of munitions of war to belligerents by neutrals, has much to be said for it, but there are some things also to be said against it which have to be considered. Of these, that which weighs most with me is that the power of obtaining such supplies is favourable to the weaker belligerent, who is, in the great majority of cases, the one most in the right. It was not so in your slavery war, and it did not turn out to be so in the late war between France and Germany. But weak nations attacked by powerful despots, and above all, insurgent nations attempting to throw off a foreign yoke, would be placed at a sad disadvantage if thrown wholly on their own resources for the material instruments of warfare. . . .

Aetat. 65.

To William L. Robinson,

in reply to a letter from him.

Avignon, *9th October* 1871.

Dear Sir,—I have received your letter of 28th September, in which you do me the honour to ask my opinion as to whether it is right that the inmates of prisons should be employed in productive labour so as to defray wholly or in part the expense of their maintenance, or whether the objection frequently made to such employment, that it competes with free labour, is a valid objection.

In reply I beg to say that I hold it to be a sound principle, both economically and morally, that no person capable of work should be maintained in idleness at the expense of others, but that his labour should always be made available for or towards his own support. I also think that such labour judiciously employed is a most valuable instrument of prison discipline and of the reformation of offenders. It is, moreover, in my opinion an error to suppose that the employment of convicts in useful work diminishes the total amount of employment for free labour; since the funds which are employed in setting the convicts to work are not drawn from what would otherwise be paid in wages to free labourers, but from what would be levied in taxation to support the convicts in idleness or useless work. The only precautions to be observed are first, not to derange the labour market by a sudden irruption of a mass of convict labour into some one branch of industry; next, and chiefly, that articles produced by convict labour should be offered for sale at the market price for goods of the same quality, and not at a price reduced in order to force a sale.

1871 — Aetat. 65.

To John Stapleton,

in opposition to a suggestion from him for the nationalisation of the land.

Avignon, *25th October* 1871

Dear Sir,—I am glad that you have written out your opinion so fully on the various points connected with the land question. I cannot undertake to enter with equal fulness into all the considerations which your letter raises, but I will endeavour in a few words to show to you that the programme of the Land Tenure Reform Association would, if realised, accomplish much more good than you attribute to it.

You say it would not enable the working classes of the towns to obtain more space for their dwellings. But what prevents them from obtaining more space? Not the impossibility of getting land, for abundance of land in or near towns can be bought and is bought every year; but that the price of it is too high. And why is it too high? Because of the perpetual increase of its value. If this were taken by the State, there would be no motive to hold out for an extravagant price, and land could be obtained on much more favourable terms for the extension of building.

Besides, if suburban land for building were ever deficient, nothing hinders the State from compelling the sale of land

1871 — Aetat. 65.

for the extension and improvement of towns, just as it now does for making new streets and railroads.

With regard to rural land, you say that to take for the public only the "unearned increase" would not stop the population of the country districts from being drawn into the towns. If in this you refer to the conversion of agricultural land into deer forests as in the Scotch Highlands, this would be stopped by enacting that all tracts of land (above a certain small extent) which are left waste for more than a certain number of years shall revert to the State, for a compensation calculated on what the land brings in to the holder in its waste condition. There is nothing in the programme of the Land Tenure Reform Association which precludes this, and most of the members would probably be in favour of it.

But if you mean that private property in land causes a system of culture to be practised which diminishes the agricultural population, it is for you to show that the nationalisation of the land would not do the very same. If the land were managed as a branch of the public revenue, the tendency would be to manage it in the way which would bring in most rent, and nothing worse than this is done by a private proprietor. In fact, what you object to in this case, is the saving of labour in agriculture.

Those who support the nationalisation of the land are, I think, bound to state the plan on which they would have it managed for the public account. In the present low state of our political morality and of our administrative habits, I should expect that the land department would become a mass of corrupt jobbing, against which we see by the examples of New York, &c., that democratic institutions are not an effectual security; and that as a financial measure it would be a complete failure, the proceeds realised being probably not sufficient to pay the amount of compensation which even you would allow.

A few words on this subject of compensation. It appears to me that when a great alteration is made in institutions which have existed from a very early period of history with general approval, any expense, loss, or other inconvenience which has to be temporarily incurred cannot justly be laid on any one class, but ought to be fairly shared by the whole community who are to benefit by the reform. I have very radical notions as to what *is* the fair mode of sharing any burthen among the whole community. I would throw a very large proportion of it upon property—not all property, not property which has been earned by the industry of its present possessors, but property which has been inherited, and forms the patrimony of an idle class. But I see no justice in making those who happen to have inherited land bear more of the burthen than those who happen to have inherited money. I would lay a heavy graduated succession duty on all inheritances exceeding that moderate amount, which is sufficient to aid but not to supersede personal exertion. If the land were nationalised and the fund for compensating the holders were raised in this manner, the land-holders themselves would bear, I think quite fairly, a large share of the burthen.

You say, if it is not just to resume the land it cannot be just to take away the unearned increase of its value. I say so too, if it be taken without compensation; but the Land Tenure Reform Association proposes that the alternative should be allowed to the holders, of surrendering their land at its selling value; on which condition the legitimacy of the operation must be acknowledged by every one who ever voted for a railway Act.

To T. Cliffe Leslie,

on his proposal for the abolition of indirect taxation.

AVIGNON, *1st December* 1871.

DEAR MR. LESLIE,—It gave me great pleasure to hear such a good account of your improvement in health, and also to learn that you have been reappointed to the India Civil Service Examinership, and that the work is increasingly interesting to you.

I am much obliged to you for sending me your paper on Financial Reform. I need hardly say that I have

1871 — Aetat. 65.

read it with the greatest interest. You have made out a stronger case than I was aware could be made, of inconvenience and economic loss from the various restrictions on business necessitated by the existence of any cause or customs. Well, this does not decide the question, for every tax produces a great deal of incidental mischief, and the problem is to find which are those that produce the least. We have got to compare the evils of our remaining indirect taxes with those of the best substitutes that it is possible to provide in lieu of them. I cannot but think that to justify the entire abolition of indirect taxes there should be some better substitute suggested than a shilling income tax. You take no notice of the demoralising effect of a tax, of which the assessment depends on people's own returns of their income. I look upon this as a very serious matter indeed. One who knew City people very well, predicted, when the income tax was first laid on by Sir Robert Peel, that the consequence of it would be a great deterioration of commercial morality. Since then we have always been hearing complaints of the growth of mercantile dishonesty; the most flagrant instances of it have been detected where they were least looked for, and though, of course, it is impossible distinctly to trace the connection between this and the income tax, I have never doubted that the tax has greatly contributed to it. A false return of income tax has probably been in innumerable instances the first dereliction of pecuniary integrity. That this evil must be still further increased by every increase of the tax could only be doubted on the supposition that this dishonesty is now so widely spread as not to admit of any further increase. Besides, the evil would be actually added to by one of the most necessary improvements in the income tax, viz. that of requiring returns from those who at present have their income tax deducted from their income at the time of receipt. Nothing can be more unjust than to levy income tax from multitudes of people whose income is below the limit at which the tax professedly ceases, or at which the percentage is reduced, and throw upon them, poor, ignorant, and busy as the most of them are, the burthen of bringing evidence to get the money returned. 1871 — Aetat. 65.

I wish that you, and all the really enlightened enemies of indirect taxation, would turn your minds to contriving some less objectionable mode of direct taxation than the present. The house tax, considering that almost all our local taxes, at least in towns, are of that nature, cannot be much increased without making the overcrowding of dwelling-houses still more than it already is. The succession tax is a resource, but not an unlimited one, for that too, when the sum payable is large, is too easily evaded. A tax on total expenditure would be the best tax in principle, because it would exempt savings; but I do not see any mode of imposing it which would not depend on the returns made by the payers, not to mention that great objection would be made on the score of its falling most heavily on those who have many mouths to feed.

Your friends of the Financial Reform Association do not feel any of these difficulties, because what they desire —and what most of the advocates of exclusively direct taxation desire—is to throw the whole burthen on what they call realised property, that is to say, on savings; which is certainly the reverse of expedient, and is not just on any principles but those of Proudhon.

I have not insisted on the special reasons commonly urged for maintaining taxes on stimulants, because it is possible that there may be a satisfactory answer to them. Nor do I lay any stress on the utility of custom-houses, &c., for statistical purposes, because it may be practicable by a system of fines to induce importers or producers to make such returns as are required. These objections, though they have some weight, are plainly not decisive. But the moral objection remains, and until some mode is pointed out of raising a large revenue by direct taxation to which that objection does not apply, I must think that our indirect taxes had better remain, being only lightened from time to time as the prosperity of the country increases their productiveness.

Thanks for your kind inquiries about my health. My

1871 — Ætat. 65. indisposition was a good deal exaggerated, but has now quite left me. My daughter is still ailing, but has been rather better since the cold, dry winds set in.

To Charles Dupont-White,

on the condition of France.

Avignon, *le* 6 *décembre* 1871.

Cher Monsieur,—Merci de votre brochure. J'y trouve, comme dans vos autres écrits, des idées, des pensées, et ce qui est plus rare, surtout en France, l'absence de toute prévention de parti : ce qui fait que tous les partis y trouveraient quelque chose, que d'ordinaire ils négligent, en ne regardant pas assez. Quant à vos conclusions j'adhère complètement aux deux principales ; d'abord la république, c'est à dire l'élection seulement temporaire du pouvoir exécutif ; ensuite que cette élection ne soit pas faite directement par le suffrage universel. J'aurais désiré que vous eussiez exprimé une opinion raisonnée sur le mode d'élection. Un corps électoral spécial qui aurait le droit d'élire le président me semble à tous égards une mauvaise institution, à moins que ce corps ne soit lui-même nommé par le suffrage universel : encore faudrait-il qu'il ne fût pas nommé uniquement pour cela sous peine d'arriver au même resultat que celui des États-Unis, où les électeurs sont tous nommés avec mandat impératif de voter pour un tel, de sorte que le président est réellement élu par le suffrage populaire direct. Pour empêcher cela, il faudrait que les électeurs spéciaux cumulassent avec leur devoir électoral d'autres fonctions, assez importantes pour qu'en les nommant le peuple ne regardât pas exclusivement au choix du président. Je ne vois en France que les conseils départementaux et municipaux qui remplissent cette condition, et attribuer à ces corps l'élection du pouvoir exécutif pourrait être nuisible en faisant de toutes les élections à des fonctions administratives, encore plus qu'à présent, une pure affaire de parti politique. A tout prendre, le seul système qui me paraisse convenable est celui de l'élection du pouvoir exécutif par l'assemblée législative. C'est là de fait, bien que ce ne soit pas en théorie, le système anglais : et c'est le seul qui n'expose pas le pays à des conflits entre les deux pouvoirs—conflits qui pourraient paralyser le gouvernement pendant des années entières à moins d'un coup d'état de l'un ou de l'autre côté.

Je remarque qu'en concluant pour la république, vous vous servez principalement des arguments propres à la recommander aux classes supérieures. Cela est naturel et licite dans un écrit de circonstance.

Vous me demandez si je crois la France en décadence : C'est une question qu'on pourrait se faire aujourd'hui dans beaucoup d'autres pays. A mon sens la décadence morale est toujours la seule réelle. Qu'il y ait ou non décadence morale en France je n'oserais le dire. Il est certain que le caractère français a de très grands défauts, qui ne sont jamais plus montrés que dans l'année malheureuse qui vient de s'écouler. Mais il n'est rien moins qu'assuré que ces défauts n'ont pas existé au même degré dans ce qu'on appelle les plus beaux jours de la France. D'un autre côté les événements récents ont démontré un immense progrès, la disparition presqu'entière de la férocité. Il n'y en a là, que je sache, qu'un seul exemple bien caractérisé l'événement déplorable de la Dordogne. Du reste, nous sommes dans une époque où l'on doit s'attendre partout à un relâchement transitoire des liens moraux : attendu que les anciennes croyances qui créaient un idéal, une règle, et un frein, sont très affaiblies et que les nouvelles qui doivent les remplacer n'existent guère pour le grand nombre et ne sont pas assez affermies chez les esprits avancés, n'etant pas encore entrées dans l'éducation. Une condition nécessaire de progrès n'est pas une décadence, quoiqu'elle y ressemble quelquefois à beaucoup d'égards.

Ce qui m'inquiète davantage c'est l'insuffisance intellectuelle de la génération présente pour faire face aux difficiles et redoutables problèmes d'un avenir qui a l'air d'être très prochain.

Je crains aussi que la guerre civile de Paris ne soit fatale à la disposition d'esprit nécessaire pour juger con-

1871 — Aetat. 65. venablement ces questions épineuses ; et que l'exaspération mutuelle des deux partis n'éloigne plus que jamais chacun d'eux d'écouter ce qu'il y a de juste et de raisonnable dans les réclamations de l'autre. Quelque dangereuse que soit l'extrême crudité des idées des socialistes révolutionnaires, ce qui m'alarme beaucoup plus c'est l'effroyable abus de la répression par le parti aujourd'hui victorieux, aux yeux duquel il suffit d'avoir désiré le moindre des changements qui ont figuré dans le programme de la commune pour être un ennemi de la société, et qui semble vouloir massacrer ou déporter en masse, s'il est possible, tout le parti opposé. J'avoue que dans les dispositions actuelles du parti de l'ordre, l'unanimité politique des classes supérieures, que vous espérez obtenir par la république, ne me semblerait promettre qu'un effort violent pour tenir la classe ouvrière en sujétion par tous les moyens usités de la tyrannie monarchique—moyens qui seraient même portés à un plus grand excès par des classes dominantes que n'oserait le faire aujourd'hui un seul homme. Et si par ces moyens on venait à supprimer pour un certain temps toute tentative de résistance légale ou violente, on ne se servirait pas de ce répit pour mettre les questions sociales à l'étude dans le but de donner une satisfaction légitime aux aspirations naturelles de la classe ouvrière ; non, on s'endormirait comme sous le régime impérial, pour se réveiller au milieu d'un bouleversement général. Voilà ce que je crains pour la France, et à un moindre degré pour les autres pays de l'Europe.

Quant à la France j'avoue qu'en vue de l'avenir, et même d'un avenir proche, il me semble que la meilleure ressource serait dans le fédéralisme. Ce serait là le moyen d'adoucir la transition à une autre organisation sociale, en permettant aux novateurs de faire des expériences limitées, sans entraîner avec eux des masses de population qui n'en veulent pas et qui s'y opposeraient par la force si on tentait de les mettre en œuvre chez elles.

Ma fille se recommande aux bons souvenirs de Madame Dupont-White à qui je vous prie d'être l'interprète de mes hommages.

To Alexander Bain.

A paper on the Conservation of Force, written about the end of 1871.

I. *Potential Energy.*

It appears to me that this is a misnomer, and that it produces unnecessary obscurity in the theory of the Conservation of Force. The theory being that all force consists in motion, either molar or molecular, and that motion is neither created nor destroyed but only transferred, it seems as if the force said to be laid up, for instance, in the coal were a contradiction to the theory, unless one supposes that an undiminished quantity of molecular motion continues to take place in the coal during the whole interval between its first deposition and its extraction, and in that case one does not see why it should not produce heat. This difficulty is cleared up by the consideration that what is really potential is the motion. The motion, or other phenomena interchangeable with motion, which caused the formation of the coal, has not been stored up, but has ceased and been annihilated; but the coal which has been generated will, under suitable conditions, reproduce a quantity of motion or other equivalent phenomenon, which quantity not being indefinite, but exactly equal to the quantity previously expended, justifies the expression that a definite quantity of force has been stored up. Force, therefore, must be defined not as real motion, no more than as an occult cause of motion, but as a potentiality or permanent possibility of motion, just as matter is a permanent possibility of sensation. Hence it is not proper to speak of potential force or potential energy. Potential means (*vide* Hamilton) that which is not, but may be: but the energy *is;* that which sometimes is not, but always may be, is the motion itself; and instead of speaking of potential energy, we should define the energy itself as potential motion.

1871 — Aetat. 65.

II. *Gravitation.*

1871 — Aetat. 65.

The interchangeability, in the case of gravitation, of force not merely with other forms of force, but with what is called a "position of advantage," is a great puzzle, and seems to be so far a surrender of the theory of Conservation of Force. For the purpose of saving the theory it is denied that gravity creates any force, and even Mr. Bain accepts this doctrine, giving as the ground of it that "what is gained in power is lost in position; to restore the position would require the power to be given back." But surely this is merely the equivalent of what is true of all force. The force expended in chemical decomposition is restored in recomposition, and the power must be given back to replace things as they were before. The heat given out in freezing must be restored in melting. It seems to me that what requires force to overcome it must be allowed to be force. This difficulty, however, is removed by the change of language I have proposed. We should then say, as is usually said, that a stationary body resting on the earth exerts a present force equal to its weight; but besides an actual moving power equal to the weight necessary to balance it, it has a latent potentiality of motion equal to the whole of the motion which it would go through if it, with the whole earth, were to fall into the sun. Now when this body is lifted or thrown up to a higher position and remains there, it has added to its former potentiality of motion, in the direction of gravity, a quantity equal to the additional motion which it would have to perform in first falling back to its original position; and this quantity is exactly equal to the quantity of force which was expended in raising it. We may therefore say without impropriety that this amount of energy has not perished, but has been stored up in the body by the fact of elevating its position.

III. *Light.*

I do not see the difficulty which others appear to see in the relation of light to the theory of Conservation.

I do not see why that theory should make us expect that when a body by heating becomes luminous the light should be produced at the expense of heat. It ought to be so if light were itself a force; but my solution would be that light, like the *sensation* of heat, is purely subjective: what is objective, if the theory be true, is the vibrations of the medium. Now, though there are vibrations which produce only heat, or only chemical action, there are, if I remember right, none which produce only light; all the rays of the spectrum are, I believe, calorific, though in unequal degrees. I should therefore surmise that light is merely a concomitant, due to a physiological action of those vibrations, and that the chemical influence said to be exerted by light is really exerted by the vibrations themselves. Any other supposition seems inconsistent with the fact that there are rays, not luminous, which produce the chemical effect in a still higher degree than those which are luminous. Then, when a body is heated to luminousness, there would be an increased intervention of the form of force which is represented by heat, but no transmutation of any of it into another form represented by light; the sensation of light would be merely an individual effect on our optic nerve of the increased vibratory motion in the medium, and there would be no expenditure of force except what takes place at the transition from the ether to the optic nerve, which would be parallel with the similar expenditure of force that there must be in putting our nerves into the condition which gives the sensation of heat.

1871 — Aetat. 65.

IV. *Force expended without Result.*

Here seems still to lurk the only real imperfection of the theory. It appears that force expended in altering the mere allocations of objects, as in moving stones from the quarry to the place where they are to be used, is wholly lost, no potentiality of recovering equivalent motion being stored up. If this be so, then, according to the theory, the quantity of force in the universe must

1871 — Aetat. 65.

be constantly diminishing, since every change in the position of objects consumes some of it, and, unless when a "position of greater advantage" has been obtained, none is reproduced. This is a more serious matter than even the dissipation of energy by the solar radiation into space, since that is a transfer of the force to the interstellar ether, from which, for aught we know, it may be capable of being again collected about points. But if the Conservation theory be true, ought the force expended in altering allocations to be still preserved in a similar manner to the force radiated from the sun, viz. by being transferred to the ether? As a matter of fact, is not much of it converted into heat? I should much like to know what scientific authorities would say to this.

V. *Attraction and Repulsion.*

There still remain many questions, which may or may not have been settled, respecting the application of the Conservation of Force to those internal forces by which bodies are supposed to be held in their existing state, viz. molecular attractions and repulsions balancing one another. Here is apparently a vast store of potential motion, prevented from being actual by opposite potentialities. Is this store of latent force also derived from the sun? and if so, how? When air is condensed by pressure, heat is evolved. Is this heat a numerical equivalent of the motion, real or potential, which is expended? Take off all pressure and the particles of the air fly apart, until they are stopped by gravity: the expansive force, I suppose, is the force which was stored up in the air; but then air, in rarifying, absorbs a great quantity of heat. What is the explanation of this phenomenon by the Conservation of Force? It is not that the heat is transformed into expansive motion, as when heat applied to water converts it into elastic steam: on the contrary, the expansion comes first, and the absorption follows as its effect, just as if a vacuum had been made in the ocean of force and other force rushed

in to fill it; but this is not a transformation of force. 1871
I do not know whether these questions have been resolved, — Aetat. 65.
or what are the exact relations between the theorem of the Persistence of Force and these particular kinds of molecular action.

CHAPTER XV

1872–1873

THE following paper was sent by Bain, in reply to Mill's questions on the Conservation of Force, in February 1872:—

1872 — Ætat. 65. The phrase "potential energy" must not be too closely criticised. It covers a gap that at present we know not how to fill up. The difficulty does not occur in regard to the molecular force of chemical action, although the phrase is used for that case. The force supposed to be stored up in coal is not potential, but real movement existing in the oxygen. As compared with carbonic acid, oxygen contains in the shape of the high molecular movement all the force given out in combustion; and the lowered condition of molecular force in carbonic acid expresses the amount of change.

It is with gravity that the real difficulty occurs, in finding the suitable expression of equivalence. When force is expended to raise a body against gravity, we know only that the body, on falling again, would acquire the force equal to what had been expended, but we are unable to assign any molecular movement which represents the force expended, when the body has attained its height. If gravity could be explained in the form of some ethereal action of the intervening medium, doubtless the agitation of such a medium might be a molecular equivalent for the force expended in raising a body against gravity. But as this seems to be a hopeless attempt, we must just express the fact as we find it, and allow a break in the continuity of molecular and molar movement as respects force.

Another case very much resembling gravity is the action

of a spring, which is the case of attraction or repulsion in the small scale of molecules. This is equally heterogeneous with the idea of matter in motion as representing the type of force. At the present moment we must treat these attractions and repulsions exactly like gravity, as a break in the line of force considered as matter in motion. A distended spring is a position to attain which force is expended, and the recovery from which by molecular attraction restores the force into moving matter. But we cannot say the tension of the spring is itself moving matter.

In the case of the transference of bodies from one place to another, the force consumed all turns to radiant heat through the medium of friction or of collision. A heavy body set in motion would of course move for ever, and retain the force expended on it. It would go through space, and might be found, as it were, at all distances without any waste. That is the very nature of motion, to treat space and distance as nothing. But now, if we wish to arrest and to localise this body, we must apply a counter force to stop it. This counter force might be another body free to move, and to take on the equivalent momentum, so that nothing would be lost. But, in point of fact, we oppose bodies in motion by a dead obstacle, or a drag, which converts all the movement into sensible heat, raises the temperature of bodies, and, consequently, in cooling, all the heat and force are wasted by the usual mode of ultimate dissipation.

As to the question of light. The subjective aspect of the phenomenon does not exhaust its bearings. We must view light, as well as heat, both on the objective and on the subjective sides. Objectively, heat is supposed to be a mode of molecular motion capable of imparting motion, molar or molecular, at a definite rate of commutation. The difficulty lies in making good the same fact regarding light. No amount of mere light has ever yet been transformed into force in any of the other modes: yet light plays a part in the disturbance of molecular equilibrium. It is the occasion of combinations and of decompositions

1872 — Aetat. 65.

as in the well-known facts culminating in photography. As causing combination, it displays no molecular force in the sense of imparting a definite quantity of its own to another body. It merely puts the particles in a position to bring their own forces into play, and to begin a molecular change in the bodies combined. A mechanical disturbance and many other things would have the very same efficacy. The testing case of the transference of power is chemical decomposition. Heat is a decomposing agent because it can supply or restore the molecular power that was given forth when the elements first combined. Light is incapable of this. If it ever causes decomposition, it is in the presence of some other power that supplies the needful molecular force that was given out in the previous combination. The action of light upon the retina is apparently of this disturbing kind, and its great efficiency is due to the extreme instability of nervous matter.

The change of phrase from "potential energy" to "potential motion" is certainly an improvement, in respect of exchanging the vague word "energy" for the definite fact "motion," which is the word that is supposed to generalise, and at the same time embody, the fact called "energy" and "force." The gain of the new theory is from never losing sight of the "moving matter" as the cardinal circumstance, and the true meaning of what we call "force," "energy," "power," and the like.

To the Hon. AUBERON HERBERT, on working men.

ST. VÉRAN, *29th January* 1872.

DEAR MR. AUBERON HERBERT,—Your impression, as shown in your letter, of the mental state and tendencies of the working men, agrees very much with that which, with probably fewer means of knowledge than you possess, has grown up in my own mind. From the little experience which I have had, which chiefly relates to the more advanced portion of them, they seem to me to have but a narrow range of thought, but to be much more open than either the higher or middle classes to appeals made to them in the name of large ideas and high principles. I believe that they, less than any other class, turn away contemptuously from the supposition that life may be inspired by other objects than self-interest in the lower sense of the term: that they have a good instinct for discovering who are those that are really single-minded in their public professions and acts, and when they perceive this, will trust them not less but all the more for considerable differences of opinion on many matters. I also agree with you in the main as to the kind of cultivation which it is of so much importance, in a social and political point of view, to give to their moral nature. But it is not clear to me that this want can be supplied in the way that has presented itself to you. I am not sufficiently informed as to matters of fact, to know whether there is any considerable number of working people with active and inquiring minds who could be made to adopt as one of the great interests of life the learning and teaching of branches of knowledge unconnected with the political and social advancement of their class. My idea is (but I am open to correction) that, for some time to come, politics and social and economical questions will be the absorbing subjects to most of those working men who have the aspirations and the mental activity to which the appeal would have to be made, and that the moral lessons you wish them to learn can be most successfully inculcated through politics. You wish to make them feel the importance of the higher virtues: I think this can be most effectually done by pointing out to them how much those virtues are needed to enable a democracy, and above all any approach to Socialism, to work in any satisfactory manner. Again, they might, perhaps, be made ashamed of pursuing their political and economic objects from class selfishness instead of disinterested principle: they might, for instance, be shamed out of the exclusive regulations of many of the trades unions by inducing them to aim at the benefit of the entire labouring population in-

1872 — Aetat. 65.

stead of their own trade only; and it would be a vast moral improvement if this can be taught (for which the best of them, I believe, are now to a great degree prepared), to claim on principle for women all the rights which they demand for themselves. Then, again, the lesson of the great importance of other social functions than that of manual labour cannot be successfully impressed on them by any persons but those who enter into their own views of politics sufficiently to sympathise in the desire to get rid of any artificial privilege in favour of those social functions, and of any institutions that tend to limit the access to them to particular classes of mankind. Therefore, without doubting that the kind of associations you desire to encourage would be very beneficial in proportion as they could be realised, I should have more hope from teaching the same lessons in and through politics and economics, and from the acquisition of political leaderships of the working classes by persons who would make working-class objects their main business in politics, but who would pursue these on the strictest principles of justice, and with reference solely to the general requisites of social well being, and who would use all the influence they acquire with the working classes by advocating their cause to inculcate this as the only admissible mode of discussing and deciding social questions.

To Dr. W. B. Carpenter.

29th January 1872.

Dear Dr. Carpenter,—I am much obliged to you for sending me your two lectures and the paper on Common Sense, all of which I have read with much interest.

I have long recognised, as a fact, that judgments really grounded on a long succession of small experiences mostly forgotten, or perhaps never brought into very distinct consciousness, often grow into the likeness of intuitive perceptions. I believe this to be the explanation of the intuitive insight thought to be characteristic of women, and of that which is often found in experienced practical persons who have not attended much to theory, nor been often called on to explain the grounds of their judgments. I explain in the same manner whatever truth there is in presentiments. And I should agree with you that a mind, which is fitted by constitution and habits to receive truly and retain all the impressions made by its passing experiences, will often be safer in relying on its intuitive judgments representative of the aggregate of its just experience than on the experience that can be drawn from such facts or reasoning as can be distinctly called to mind at the moment. Now you seem to think that judgment, by what is called common sense, is a faculty of this same kind; and, so far as regards the genesis of it, I think you are right; but it seems to me that there is a very great practical difference. The reason why, in the cases I have referred to, the intuition is often more to be trusted than the reasoned judgment, is precisely (I apprehend) because it is not an affair of common sense but of uncommon sense; the perceptions and experiences which have culminated in the intuitive judgment were peculiar to the individual and cannot be recovered. If these evidentiary matters *could* be recalled, the superiority of deliberate over hasty judgment would reassert itself. Now, in the case of common sense, the very words imply that the evidences which are the real justification of the judgments are familiar to all mankind; and, if they are so, I apprehend that enough of them can always be recovered and put into a distinct shape to admit of subjecting the point to a real scientific test. Now, when this *can* be done, it always ought. For want of it, judgments by common sense are usually judgments by superficial appearances. Almost all false political economy, for instance, is made up of judgments by common sense.

On the physiological side of psychology your paper raises questions of great and increasing interest. When states of mind, in no respect innate or instinctive, have been frequently repeated, the mind requires, as is proved by the power of habit, a greatly increased facility of passing into those states, and this increased facility must be owing

1872 — Ætat. 65. to some change of a physical character in the organic action of the brain, whether in the organ itself we do not, I suppose, know. There is also considerable evidence that such acquired facilities of passing into certain modes of cerebral action can, in many cases, be transmitted more or less completely by inheritance. The limits of this power and transmission, and the conditions on which it depends, are a subject now fairly under investigation by the scientific world, and we shall doubtless in time know much more about them than we do now; but, as far as my imperfect knowledge of the subject qualifies me to have an opinion, I take much the same view of it that you do, at least in principle.

Your explanation of the self-delusion of the so-called Spiritualists is, no doubt, in many cases, a true one, but for my part I believe there is much more of absolute lying in their pretended experiences than people generally like to suppose. I am altogether incredulous as to any foundation of truth at all in it.

To Pasquale Villari.

Avignon, *28th February* 1872.

My dear Mr. Villari,—You needed no apology for not writing oftener; and if you did, I should need it as much. But our feelings towards each other do not require letters to keep them alive; and when, independently of other work, one has too many letters to write, one's surest friends are the most likely to be put off.

You judged truly that the loss of Mr. Grote leaves a great blank in my life. He was the oldest and, by far, the most valued of my surviving old friends. And though he died at a ripe age, he seemed to bear his years so well that I hoped that there might yet be a considerable prolongation of them. But if one lives to be old oneself, one is certain of losing those whom nothing can replace, and I have had too sad experience of this to feel the shock of a fresh instance very acutely. It is just so much taken from the value of life to me. It is pleasant to hear from you that he was so much appreciated, and is so much regretted in Italy. It is one of the signs which continually come unexpectedly of the hopeful course in which Italy is moving on. I fully appreciate the difficulties which you have so well pointed out. But it seems to me that there is a most encouraging mental activity among the (unfortunately too narrow) educated class in Italy, and there is, as there has always been, a foundation of practical common sense in the people, which is a safeguard against great and fatal errors such as, for instance, are so often committed by the French.

As you most truly say, the great problem is moral and intellectual rather than political; and you are probably helping on the improvement of your country still more by devoting yourself to authorship, in addition to the work of a professor, than by any administrative employment even in the department of public instruction, in which you would be dependent on a superior (and, what is worse, on a succession of superiors) for the power of carrying out your ideas. If you write what becomes the standard book on Machiavelli, you will do a service not merely to Italian but to European thought, and will help to train the thinkers of the time to come, which has become the chief thing that I also much care to do during such years of working power as remain to me. Mr. Grote's example is encouraging to this hope, for he worked at Aristotle up to his last illness; and his book, which is now printing, will, though not complete, be, I have no doubt, a most valuable exposition and appreciation of the more abstruse parts of Aristotle's philosophy. My own work lies rather among anticipations of the future than explanations of the past. I would gladly, if I could, contribute something in a more direct form than I have yet done towards rendering the great new questions which are rising up respecting life and society a little less difficult to our successors. But it is doubtful whether this can be done at present to much purpose (except in the negative way of dispelling actual error); for the impending transformation of society can only be tentative; the

1872 experience necessary for seeing far into it can only be obtained when the change is already in partial progress.

Aetat. 65.

We shall be at Avignon now probably for a considerable time, and I shall hope to hear from you there.

To Georg Brandes,

on Socialism.

Avignon, *le* 4 *mars* 1872.

Monsieur,—Je vous remercie de votre lettre du 9 janvier. Mon ignorance de la langue danoise me fermant tout accès direct au développement intellectuel de votre intéressant pays, je vous en ai d'autant plus d'obligation lorsque vous voulez bien me fournir des renseignements. Ceux que vous me donnez sur le progrès des idées libérales sont très encourageants. Je me réjouis du grand succès de vos leçons à l'Université. Je ne m'étonne nullement de l'opposition des professeurs de la faculté philosophique à votre placement officiel. C'est la répugnance bien connue des vieilles idées contre les nouvelles.

Vous me demandez mon opinion sur l'Internationale. Je crois que cette Association renferme une foule très diverse de représentants de toutes les écoles socialistes, tant modérées que violentes. Les membres anglais dont je connais personnellement plusieurs des chefs, me paraissent en général des hommes raisonnables visant surtout aux améliorations pratiques dans le sort des travailleurs, capables d'apprécier les obstacles, et peu haineux envers les classes dont ils veulent faire cesser la domination. Mais j'avoue que dans les débats de leur Congrès je n'ai guère trouvé quelque bon sens que chez les délégués anglais. C'est que mes compatriotes ont l'habitude d'attendre des améliorations plutôt de l'initiative individuelle et de l'association privée que de l'intervention direct de l'Etat. L'habitude contraire qui prévaut dans le Continent fait croire aux réformateurs qu'ils n'ont qu'à mettre la main sur les rênes du gouvernement pour arriver promptement à leur but; et non seulement les socialistes français

qui sont même peut-être plus modérés que beaucoup 1872
d'autres, mais plus encore ceux de la Belgique, de l'Allemagne et même de la Suisse, sous la direction apparente de quelques théoriciens russes, pensent qu'il n'y qu'à exproprier tout le monde, et abattre tous les gouvernements existants, sans s'inquiéter, quant à present, de ce qu'il faudrait mettre à leur place. Je ne les calomnie pas, je ne fais que répéter ce que j'ai lu dans leurs journaux. Je crois par conséquent que le bon côté de cette association consiste principalement dans les craintes qu'elle excite. Elle fait penser les classes, qui possèdent les biens de ce monde, au sort qui les attend peut-être dans l'avenir si elles n'arrivent à rendre l'état social beaucoup plus avantageux au grand nombre. Encore la peur est-elle une mauvaise conseillère comme on voit aujourd'hui en France. Pourtant un temps viendra où le danger sera regardé avec sangfroid et où les problèmes sociaux seront mis à l'étude avec une volonté réelle de trouver une meilleure solution que celle d'à présent. Il faut que les hommes éclairés s'occupent en attendant de préparer les esprits et les caractères.

— Aetat. 65.

Vous me demandez encore si on a écrit quelque chose de bon sur la question des femmes, ainsi que sur l'Utilitarisme. La question des femmes est entrée dans la discussion générale, mais ce qu'on écrit là-dessus depuis quelque temps n'a tout au plus qu'une valeur de circonstance. Quant à l'Utilitarisme on a publié dernièrement plusieurs articles contre mon livre, mais je n'y trouve jusqu'ici rien de neuf. Ce sont toujours les mêmes objections à peine rajeunies par le langage. Je n'ai jugé à propos de répondre à aucune de ces attaques: aux vieux arguments il suffit des vieilles réponses. Cette dispute pratique se décidera avec la dispute théorique, entre la métaphysique de l'intuition et celle de l'expérience: et sur ce champ-là le progrès scientifique assure la victoire à cette dernière. Cependant si on publie soit sur l'Utilitarisme soit sur la cause des femmes quelque chose digne de votre attention je vous en avertirai avec plaisir.

To Colonel T. A. Cowper, on Land Nationalisation.

Avignon, *21st April* 1872.

1872 — etat. 65. Dear Cowper,— . . . Mr. Newman is under some misapprehension as to the opinions I have professed: I do not say that "all the land of the country ought to be national." I think this a question of time, place, and circumstance, and I incline to Mr. Newman's opinion, that people should, at any rate, be allowed to own the houses they themselves live in, and even some space of ground, ornamental or other, adjoining. But his idea of aiming only at a maximum limit for landed property, though it might have been worth consideration in some former states of opinion, would now merely make the working classes hostile instead of friendly to us. Nor do I see that much would be gained by merely cutting up the great landed properties into estates of 5000 acres each. Mr. Newman's plan with respect to suburban land is the same as ours, with the addition that the power of compulsory purchase should vest in the municipalities instead of the State, a question of detail which we have left open. . . .

The following examination paper in Political Economy was drawn up by Mill, in response to a request from Miss Davies, of the College, Hitchin, that he should examine her pupils in that subject.

6th May 1872.

1. What is the distinction between Productive and Unproductive Labour, and between Productive and Unproductive Consumption?

2. Does all Productive labour tend to increase the permanent wealth of the country?

3. State any causes, in general operation, which tend to

increase the productive power of labour, and any which tend to diminish it. 1872 — Aetat. 65.

4. Explain in what sense the value of a commodity depends on supply and demand, and in what sense on cost of production.

5. What cost of production is it which determines the exchange value of the products of agriculture?

6. A state of free trade being supposed, can a country permanently import a commodity from a place where its cost of production is greater than that at which it could be produced at home?

7. What are the effects, first on the national wealth, and secondly, on the wages of labour, of a large government expenditure? and does it make any difference what the expenditure is upon?

8. In what respect are the interest of the labouring classes and that of the employers of labour identical? and in what respects, if in any, opposed?

9. What is the meaning of depreciation of the currency? and what are the principal causes of such depreciation?

10. By what means can a currency be protected against depreciation?

11. What is meant by the terms, a favourable and an unfavourable exchange? and is there any well-grounded objection to that phraseology?

12. How far, and in what respects, is the discovery of new and rich deposits of the precious metals a benefit to the national wealth?

13. Mention the principal circumstances that tend to produce either a rise or a fall in the rent of land.

14. State what are the known modes in which the produce of land, or the proceeds of the sale of that produce, are shared among the different classes of persons connected with the land, and state briefly the advantages and disadvantages of each.

To T. S. Barrett,

in acknowledgment of the book "New View of Causation."

Avignon, *6th May* 1872.

1872 — Aetat. 65.

Dear Sir,—I thank you for the copy of the second edition of your book on Causation. I quite agree in its leading doctrine, and have maintained the same in my System of Logic, viz., that there does not exist in nature any other necessity than the necessity of logical sequence, in other words, the certainty that a conclusion is true if the premises are true. But this definition does not explain to people the necessity which they fancy they find in the relation of cause and effect which they conceive, above all, not as a conditional but an unconditional, or absolute necessity.

I think this feeling of an imaginary necessity can be no otherwise explained than as I have explained it, namely, by the law of inseparable association, but that explanation appears to me sufficient. You are probably, however, right in thinking that the notion of physical necessity is partly indebted for the particular shape it assumes in our minds to an association of it with logical necessity. . . .

To Mr. John Morley.

Avignon, *11th May* 1872.

With regard to the Irish University question, my notion of a really national university for any country, but especially for a country divided between two different religions, would be a university in which instead of only one professor of history, of ethics, or of metaphysics, there should be several of each, so that as long as there are subjects on which interested people differ, they might be taught from different points of view; and the pupils might either choose their professor, or attend more professors than one in order to choose their doctrine: examinations and prizes being made equally accessible to all. If Trinity College

were reconstructed on this principle, there might be 1872
Catholic, Protestant, and freethinking professors of all these —
subjects, and in this way it seems to me that Catholics Aetat. 65.
would obtain all that they can justly claim; for their only tolerable ground for refusing to receive education along with Protestants is that Protestants and Catholics necessarily take opposite views of those subjects. Fawcett's bill certainly does not provide for this; but this I think would be its ultimate result; and I should be sorry to see any settlement of the question which would prevent this. Considering, moreover, how very noxious the higher instruction given by the Catholic prelates is sure to be, I think it right to avoid by every means consistent with principle the subsidising it in any shape or to any extent.

To Edwin Arnold,

who had sent Mill a leading article which he had written in the *Daily Telegraph* on "Science and Religion."

AVIGNON, *15th May* 1872.

. . . The article enclosed in your letter (which was sure to be, as you say it was, attacked and misrepresented) certainly does express a very general and most natural "longing" among those who have outgrown the old form of religious belief. I myself have more sympathy with the aspiration than hope to see it gratified to the extent of any positive belief respecting the unseen world; but I am convinced that the cultivation of an imaginative hope is quite compatible with a reserve as to positive belief, and that whatever helps to keep before the mind the ideal of a perfect Being is of unspeakable value to human nature. Only it is essential, to prevent a perversion of the moral faculty, that this perfect Being, if regarded as the Creator of the world we live in, should not be thought to be omnipotent.

To J. E. Cairnes.

Avignon, *15th May* 1872.

1872 — Aetat. 65. . . . I shall like much to read what you have written on the two points you mention in the theory of value. You say that on one of them our difference is merely verbal; I suspect it is so on both, relating only to the most convenient or most scientific mode of expressing the same doctrine. The two modes, which you contrast with one another, of expressing cost of production are, I imagine, both of them admissible, and both of them useful, as presenting different points of view. Of course, when we go down to the fundamentals of the matter, the cost to society, as a whole, of any production consists in the labour and abstinence required for it. But, as concerns individuals and their mutual transactions, wages and profits are the measure of that labour and abstinence, and constitute the motives by which the exchange of commodities against one another is immediately determined. That, at least, is my present view of the matter. . . .

To Pasquale Villari.

Avignon, *19th May* 1872.

. . . When I received your letter I did not possess, at Avignon, a copy of the tract on land tenure which you expressed a wish to see. I have now obtained one, and send it to you by this post. If it had been anything like what the *Revue des Deux Mondes* represented it to be, I should not have failed to send it to you. But it is a very slight thing indeed—neither a manifesto of the Radical party nor the programme of a new party. It is simply a few pages in explanation of the objects of an association founded for a special purpose, viz., to reclaim for the State whatever rights in the land it has not unconditionally parted with to private persons, including among other things the right to impose special taxation on landed property to the extent of the increase of value which it is continually acquiring in a prosperous country from the mere growth of wealth and population, without any labour or outlay by the proprietors. There is a party among our working classes who go much further, demanding the resumption of all land by the State, with more or less of compensation to the landholders. A time may come for something of this sort, but what is proposed by the Society is as much as I think desirable (not to say attainable) for a considerable time to come. I am sorry to say that the little tract has been reviewed in the *Deux Mondes* by a person so ignorant of my opinions as to call me a partisan of extreme centralisation. It is about the last reproach I should have expected. But a large class of French writers make assertions of facts with a levity almost incredible.

We are going very shortly to make a tour in Styria and other parts of the Austrian Alps, but letters addressed to me here will be forwarded. I hope to have a letter from you soon.

To Costantino Baer, on his book "L'Avere e l'Imposta" (Wealth and Taxation).

Avignon, *le* 30 *mai* 1872.

Monsieur,—Je vois avec regret et avec quelque surprise que depuis bientôt cinq mois j'ai reçu votre livre ("L'Avere e l'Imposta") sans vous avoir encore remercié de ce don et sans avoir obtempéré au désir flatteur que vous avez exprimé de connaître mon opinion sur vos conclusions. C'est que je n'ai trouvé que tout récemment le temps de donner à cet ouvrage la lecture sérieuse qu'il merite. Aujourdhui même je suis forcé d'abréger ce que j'aurais à dire sur votre livre.

D'abord en tant qu'ouvrage d'économie politique pure, je n'ai que des éloges à en faire. La seule critique que je crois pouvoir faire c'est qu'en traitant (page 83) de la manière dont un impôt sur les profits industriels et com-

1872 — Aetat. 66. merciaux retomberait sur le consommateur vous ne semblez pas peut-être distinguer suffisamment entre un impôt général sur les profits de tout capital productif et un impôt qui frappe seulement ceux de quelques branches de production. D'après les principes généraux de la politique la possibilité de faire retomber l'impôt sur les consommateurs me paraît manquer dès que l'impôt frappe toutes les industries sans distinction.

Comme ouvrage non pas d'économie politique abstraite mais de haute politique votre livre est plein de choses vraies et utiles; mais j'avoue que je n'en trouve pas la conclusion suffisamment établie. Vous soutenez que la règle de la justice en matière d'impôt, savoir que chacun doit payer en raison de son avoir, exige qu'il y ait deux genres d'impôt, l'un sur les dépenses improductives, et l'autre sur le capital; et que le possesseur d'un capital, après vous payer comme les autres sa part de tous les impôts de consommateur, doit payer en dessus un impôt proportionné à son capital productif. Or je ne suis pas ennemi de l'impôt sur le capital; je trouve assez probable, qu'à cause de l'incertitude et de l'effet si démoralisateur de l'impôt direct sur les revenus on viendra à imposer le capital comme moyen d'en atteindre les profits. Mais je ne trouve pas que dans le système que vous proposez chacun payerait proportionnellement à son avoir réel. Votre opinion me paraît ressembler à celle de quelques Socialistes, qui, parceque les profits du capitaliste et son capital sont tous deux compris dans son avoir légal, oublient qu'il ne peut réellement jouir de tous les deux, mais bien de l'un ou de l'autre à son choix. Il n'obtient ses profits qu'à condition de faire consommer son capital par d'autres: s'il s'en sert pour sa propre jouissance il renonce à en tirer du profit. Or l'égalité dans l'impôt me paraît consister en ce que chacun paie à proportion de ce qu'il peut appliquer à la satisfaction de ses propres besoins. Tant que son capital reste productif il n'en tire pas plus d'avantage personnel que si ce capital lui avait été confié par l'état, sauf le privilège qu'il n'aurait pas alors de le gaspiller sans être responsable à personne. . . .

To J. E. Cairnes.

2nd August 1872.

. . . I wish your letter had brought a better account of your health. I regret to have in that respect nothing to congratulate you upon, except the strength of mind with which you bear up against so serious a misfortune, retaining all your interest in the public, and seeking consolation in continuing to work for science and the general good. This is indeed only what might have been expected of you. I shall be very glad to see what you have written on the theory of value. Your decided opinion that the question between us is not chiefly verbal, or relating only to the best manner of setting forth the same truths, makes me think that I have still something material to learn from you on the subject, and I think it very improbable that on a question of abstract political economy, after full explanation, we should not agree. . . .

1872 — Aetat. 66.

Freeman belongs emphatically to what is called the historical school in politics and jurisprudence; he has the good qualities and the weaknesses of that school. Their error is, as is so often the case, a half truth giving itself out for the whole, for they are quite right in thinking that a good political institution is more likely to take a deep root when it has been called for by a felt want of the people, than when it has been set up by a king or a revolutionary leader on the strength of its general merits. But this truth is continually perverted into an attack on the use of reason in matters of politics and social arrangements, and Freeman does not sufficiently guard himself against this perversion.

To Costantino Baer,

a further letter on the taxation of capital.

Avignon, *le 22 septembre* 1872.

Monsieur,—Votre lettre m'est parvenue au milieu d'un voyage en Autriche et je n'ai pas pu lui donner une

1872 — Aetat. 66.

réponse immédiate. Je l'ai mise de côté avec le projet de vous écrire à mon premier loisir un examen détaillé de votre réponse à mes objections au sujet de l'impôt sur le capital. Cependant en relisant cette réponse il me semble que tout ce qu'elle contient avait été dit avec une très grande clarté dans votre livre même et que ce que vous ajoutez dans votre lettre n'est qu'un résumé des mêmes arguments. En tout cas vous n'avez pas ébranlé mon objection fondamentale, savoir que le capital, tant qu'il reste capital productif, n'a d'autre valeur pour le capitaliste que celle du revenu qu'il donne, et que par conséquent si on le fait payer sur le capital et aussi sur toutes ses dépenses il est en réalité imposé deux fois. J'accorde qu'on peut justement exiger de celui qui vit sans travailler sur le revenu de son capital ou de sa terre une plus grande contribution que de celui qui gagne un revenu équivalent en travaillant; aussi ai-je toujours demandé une réforme de l'income tax dans ce sens, mais cela est principalement vrai pour ceux qui doivent leur fortune à l'héritage et non à leur propre travail antérieur; aussi c'est surtout par l'impôt sur les successions que je voudrais rétablir, en cette matière, la justice sociale.

Quant à publier un article sur votre livre ce serait un plaisir pour moi, mais il est incertain si je pourrai disposer du temps nécessaire. J'espère pourtant que je pourrai écrire une notice raisonnée en deux ou trois pages et la faire insérer dans une revue où j'écris quelquefois. Si cela a lieu je me donnerai le plaisir de vous envoyer le numéro.

To Sir Charles Dilke,

in reply to a letter asking Mill's opinion whether anything could be done in the direction of obtaining State control over prehistoric and medieval remains.

Avignon, *22nd September* 1872.

Dear Sir Charles Dilke,—Excuse the delay in answering your letter, which was caused by my receiving it in the middle of a tour in the Austrian Alps.

I quite agree with you as to the importance of making some movement to prevent the destruction of natural or artificial objects of general interest. France has set us the example, by making a register of all Monuments Historiques, none of which, when so registered, can lawfully be destroyed or injured by a proprietor or by any local or merely departmental authority; though I have known a triumphal arch pulled down by the Ponts et Chaussées because it had not been entered in the Register. 1872 — Aetat. 66.

The cry of confiscation may be met, if the proposal is simply to make a list of all such interesting objects, Roman camps and Druidical circles included, and to provide by law that none of those may be destroyed or altered by the proprietor without his first giving the public the option of buying it from him for the equivalent of what it is worth to him in its existing state.

I perceive that Sir John Lubbock has given notice of a motion for next session for the preservation of pre-historic monuments. It will be a great advantage to be able to act in concert with him, and if his contemplated motion does not go the whole length of what is desirable, he might perhaps be induced to enlarge its scope.

To Lewis Sergeant,

of the Anti-Game-Law League;

in reply to an invitation to join the general committee of that body.

Avignon, *2nd October* 1872.

Dear Sir,—I thank you for the three numbers of the Anti-Game-Law Circular, which I have read with much interest. No one has a worse opinion than I have of the present Game Laws and their administration, and I would rather there were not a head of game left in England than that the existing injustice should continue. But I do not find in the papers you sent any clear and explicit statement of what, in the opinion of the League, the law on this subject ought to be. The opinions indicated are that there should be no laws whatever

1872 — Aetat. 66.

respecting game as game, and that wild animals, until taken or killed, should not be property, but when taken should be the property of whoever takes them. In the former opinion I am inclined to agree, but in the latter I am not satisfied. It seems to me just that wild animals should belong to those at whose expense they have been fed; the nearest practical approach to which is that they should belong to the occupier of the land on which they are taken or killed. Neither does it seem to me that the plan shadowed forth in the Circular would of itself terminate the evils arising from game-preserving. It is not, I suppose, intended to permit any one who pleases to kill game on other people's land without their permission. But if not, then until the lavish preservation of game comes to be stamped by public opinion with the disapproval and contempt which it deserves, it is likely still to go on; nor for this purpose should there be need of a new law of trespass: the more rigid enforcement of the existing trespass laws would suffice. There would be still more shutting up of paths and other thoroughfares than there is at present. The fields and woods would be as carefully guarded against trespassers as they now are against poachers, and the highways and such paths as could not be stopped would be shut in between fences, to the great loss of all wayfarers and lovers of rural walks. I presume all these points will be fully discussed in the Circular as it proceeds, but until I am satisfied respecting them I cannot, by joining the League, identify myself with the particular means by which they seek to attain our common object.

To the Secretary of the Nottingham Branch of the International Working Men's Association,

acknowledging a pamphlet by him entitled, "The Law of the Revolution."

AVIGNON, *4th October* 1872.

DEAR SIR,—I have to acknowledge your letter of 27th August, and to express, through you, my thanks to the Nottingham branch of the International Working Men's Association for the copies of their programme and of your able pamphlet which they have done me the favour to send. 1872 — Aetat. 66.

In the principles of the Association as set forth in the programme I find much that I warmly approve, and little, if anything, from which I positively dissent; though, from the generality with which those principles are laid down, it is impossible for me to say to what extent I should concur in the political measures which the Association would propose in order to bring the principles into operation.

A remark, however, is suggested to me by some part of the phraseology both of the programme and of the pamphlet, which I should think it wrong to withhold. What advantage is there in designating the doctrines of the Association by such a title as "the principles of the political and social Revolution"? "The Revolution" as a name for any sort of principles or opinions, is not English. A Revolution is a change of government effected by force, whether it be by a popular revolt or by a military usurpation. And as "the man" in English always means some particular man, so "the Revolution" means some particular revolution, such as the French Revolution, or the English Revolution of 1688.

The meaning intended to be conveyed by "the principles of the Revolution" can only be guessed at from a knowledge of French, in which language it seems to mean the political ideal of any person of democratic opinions who happens to be using it. I cannot think that it is good to adopt this mode of speech from the French. It proceeds from an infirmity of the French mind, which has been one main cause of the miscarriages of the French nation in its pursuit of liberty and progress; that of being led away by phrases, and treating abstractions as if they were realities which have a will and exert active power. Hitherto the character of English thought has been different; it has required propositions, not vague words, which only seem to have a meaning.

1872 — Aetat. 66.

There is no real thing called "the Revolution," nor any "principles of the Revolution." There are maxims which your Association, in my opinion, rightly consider to be essential to just government, and there is a tendency increasing as mankind advance in intelligence and education towards the adoption of the doctrines of just government. Those are all the facts there are in the case, and the more clearly and unambiguously these, and nothing but these, are stated, the better people will understand one another, and the more distinctly they will see what they are disputing about, and what they are concerned to prove. When instead of this men range themselves under banners as friends and enemies of "the Revolution," the only important question which is just and useful is kept out of sight, and measures are judged not by their real worth but by the analogy they seem to have to an irrelevant abstraction.

The otherwise very salutary intercourse which has grown up of late years between portions of the English and the French working classes, will be dearly paid for if it causes the advanced politicians of this country to abandon one of the best characteristics of the English mind, and replace it by one of the worst of the French.

I cannot conclude without expressing the great pleasure with which I have seen the full and thoroughgoing recognition by your body of the claims of women to equal rights in every respect with man, and of minorities, proportionally to their numbers, with majorities; and its advocacy of the Federal principle for the security of this last. As a further means to the same end, promoting at the same time other ends no less valuable, I would invite the attention of your Association to the importance of Proportional Representation.

To W. T. Thornton.

Avignon, *5th October* 1872.

. . . I have not yet begun to write on Mr. Grote's "Aristotle," not having yet received the book, but I am expecting it daily. In what I said about Lewes's book [Aristotle] I was purposely guarded, having hardly any knowledge of my own respecting those works of Aristotle to which he relates. I did not think it likely that any book by Lewes would be profound either in philosophy or scholarship; but it seemed to me on the whole a meritorious work, and this opinion was confirmed by Mr. Grote when I asked him what he thought of it. I cannot doubt, therefore, that if you wish to read respecting Aristotle's physical writings, the book must be worth your reading. 1872 — Aetat. 66.

I should like to have heard Louis Blanc expounding after his fashion the political state of France. We think with him that the French peasantry are becoming Republican; but we do not think that it is in an unintelligent way. Helen attributes it, I believe with reason, to the great desire of the peasantry for thorough education, and those perceptions from experience that lay schoolmasters teach better than clerical. The Republicans being the only party who do not want to give education into the hands of the priests, this more than anything else is making the peasants Republican.

To G. Croom Robertson,

on the Woman Suffrage Movement.

Chiefly by Helen Taylor.

Avignon, *5th November* 1872.

Dear Mr. Robertson,—You seem to us to underrate the value of a "pretty face" in a lecturer on women's rights. As my daughter says, it is not for the sake of effect on men that it is important, but for the influence it has on the younger women. It shows them that the championship of women's cause is not confined to women who have no qualifications for success in the more beaten track, and that they would not by joining in the movement forfeit their chance of the ordinary objects of women's ambition. This is an advantage which outweighs even some inferiority in lecturing powers. It is above all on

1872 — Aetat. 66.

the minds of women that we ought to work, for when the majority of them think the change right it will come.

We have a strong impression that money is more usefully expended on lectures in the provinces than in and about London. In London and the suburbs nearly all who are likely to come to a lecture have at least heard of the subject, and are already either favourable or hostile; but in country places the lecturer often pierces a quite fresh stratum of public opinion. It is often found that before any lecture had been delivered in a country town, nobody in the place had thought of the subject one way or the other, but that many are willing and ready to take the right view of it when presented to them. We should be sorry, therefore, to see provincial lectures neglected in favour of London ones. Indeed, our subscriptions to the former fund were made with the express view of lectures in the provinces. The general subscription rose out of my daughter's offering £100 to Mrs. Taylor for country lectures.

There is much to be said for your idea of addressing Mr. John Bright against the reintroduction of his Bill next year, and I should much like to see the sort of address you would think of sending, and if you would put it on paper in a rough way. It is important, however, not to include Mr. Eastwick in the same application with Mr. John Bright. You may remember that Mr. Eastwick said last session that he thought the parliamentary conduct of the question should be placed in other hands. Any address, public or private, should be made exclusively to Mr. John Bright. We think that the great motive, and it is a powerful one, for making some sort of an address to him is in order that we may influence members who are favourable to the suffrage to stay away in considerable numbers if Mr. John Bright insists on a division. This is the only way we can see of breaking the fall which is sure to come, and if Mr. John Bright knows that your committee recommends this policy, it will be more likely than anything else to check his folly—if anything would.

The decline of the annual subscriptions from £350 to

£217 is less than I should have expected, and not at all discouraging when we consider on the one hand the general tendency of subscriptions to fall off somewhat after the first year or two through negligence or forgetfulness, and, on the other, the subscriptions likely to have been drawn off by the rival committee and the general damp to the hopes of supporters by the unfavourable division last summer. 1872 — Aetat. 66.

To J. E. Cairnes.

Avignon, *9th December* 1872.

. . . There are two questions connected with the application of Political Economy on which I should much like to compare notes with you. Have you ever turned your attention to the merits and demerits of a tax on property, *i.e.* land and capital, realised or unrealised, as a substitute for an income tax? The pro's and con's are tolerably obvious, the pro's consisting rather in the demerits of other direct taxes than in the recommendations of this. My attention has been drawn to the subject by an Italian correspondent of mine, Costantino Baer by name, a clever and sensible man, well versed in the best English political economy, and who has published a little book recommending as the best system of taxation a tax on land and capital, of a percentage on their pecuniary value, combined with taxes on such modes of expenditure as may be a fair test of a person's general scale of unproductive expenses. I have written for the small print of the *Fortnightly* a short notice of this book, but I should much like to know your opinion on its main position.

The other subject is that which has given rise to a controversy between the *Times* and Fawcett—the expediency of requiring corporations and endowed institutions to sell their lands and invest in the funds instead. I suppose we are both agreed that bodies which are constituted for the performance of other important duties ought not to have their time and thoughts diverted from them to the management of landed estates, and it is perhaps not too

1873 — Aetat. 66. soon to begin teaching this doctrine. But I confess I should be sorry that the teaching should soon be successful. It seems to me that so long as it is certain that the lands, if brought into the market, would be almost all bought up and added to the possessions of wealthy landed proprietors, or made the foundation of new large private estates, it is better that they should remain as they are, at least until the programme of the Land Tenure Reform Association, or something like it, has become the creed of the Liberal party. Lands not yet appropriated by individuals should, I think, by no means be allowed to pass into private ownership, but should be sacred to public purposes, and made a means of trying all possible modes of collective management with a view of testing their practicability and the effects of those modes on the capabilities of collective management in general. It is well that there is such a resource for experimental purposes without meddling at all with private property in land until the advantage of doing so has been proved by sufficient trial. . . .

To Costantino Baer.

Avignon, *le* 8 *janvier* 1873.

. . . Les arguments que vous ajoutez dans votre dernière lettre à ceux qui se trouvent dans le livre, sont des *argumenta ad hominem,* se fondant sur une assimilation de l'impôt sur le capital à d'autres impôts que j'approuve, notamment aux impôts sur les *landlords* et à celui des successeurs. Il est vrai que j'approuve ces impôts-là, mais en avouant qu'ils sont contraires au principe financier de l'égalité. Je fonde mon approbation sur d'autres principes, qui, ce me semble, dans ces deux cas-là doivent primer celui de l'égalité. Quant aux impôts sur la terre, il me paraît juste (et je vois avec plaisir que vous êtes de la même opinion) de retenir pour l'état le tout ou une partie de l'accroissement de la rente qui a lieu par des causes naturelles ou sociales, indépendantes du travail ou des frais du propriétaire, tandis que l'intérêt du capital tend plutôt à baisser. Et quant aux successions, je ne reconnais aux héritiers, même directs, aucun droit moral à hériter au delà d'une légitime suffisante pour leur donner de bonnes chances dans la vie. Donc si la société permet d'hériter par delà cette limite, elle a le droit d'y mettre les conditions qu'elle veut; et elle peut user de ce droit dans le but de modérer l'inégalité de richesse, ce qui est moins permis lorsqu'il s'agit d'ôter aux travailleurs leurs propres gains. Par là vous verrez qu'au moins je ne suis pas en contradiction avec mes propres principes.

1873 — Aetat. 66.

To Mr. (now Sir) E. Ray Lankester,

who had invited Mill's adhesion to a scheme for securing certain reforms in the older universities.

8th February 1873.

Dear Sir,—I beg to acknowledge your letter of 8th January. I sympathise strongly with the desire to render the revenues of the universities more conducive than they as yet are to the purposes for which universities do or ought to exist, and I agree with you and your associates in thinking it a great defect in the mode of disposing of those revenues that no part of them is employed in making the universities places for the advancement of knowledge, while so very large a part of it is expended in giving incomes as reward for the mere acquisition of knowledge, unaccompanied with any obligation for extending it, for teaching it, or even for keeping it up. What would be the best system to adopt for the correction of this defect is a question which I am happy to see discussed, and which will probably require much discussion, but in the meanwhile I see very strong objections to some of the proposals mentioned in your letter. The abolition of the competitive examination for fellowships seems to me the reverse of an improvement. I quite understand that the object of this proposal is to prevent the appointments from being obtained by cramming. But it is not beyond the capacity of the universities to take sufficient security that success in the examinations

1873 — Aetat. 66. shall not depend on cram; nor is it understood that the high honours at either Cambridge or Oxford are generally so obtained. On the other hand, I have the greatest distrust of all schemes for disposing of high and well-paid employments by a nominating body. Such bodies, having only a collective responsibility, are often even more addicted to abuse their patronage than single functionaries: the members are apt to job for one another, and vote for each other's *protégés*. And even without the supposition of jobbing, a body like that which you have in view, composed indeed of scientific persons, but of persons whose position and reputation are already made, is not at all likely to look with favour on the striking out of new paths. Experience shows that academies, whether of literature or science, generally prefer inoffensive mediocrities to men of original genius. Cuvier was no ordinary man, but neither Geoffrey St. Hilaire nor Darwin would have had a chance of obtaining his vote for a professorship. As a previous knowledge of what is already known is now an indispensable requisite for carrying knowledge further, it seems to me necessary to retain a very strict competitive examination as the first condition for a fellowship. This would be no hindrance to requiring as an additional condition that the candidate should show, or have shown, by some original investigation, that he has powers which are worth securing either for teaching or for the advancement of science. Indeed, the nominating body, if it did its duty, would, I think, be obliged to institute some kind of competitive examination in order to ensure the possession of a sufficient quantity of positive knowledge by young men who could not in the nature of things have given as yet any considerable public proof of high scientific capacity.

The terms of the circular, which indicate the object you have in view without committing you to any particular plan, I have no fault to find with; and I agree in the main with the resolutions passed at the Freemason's Tavern, except that it appears to me desirable that the posts created for the prosecution of original research should generally or always have some amount of teaching duties also annexed to them. But even if I were much more confident than I am that my views would be in accordance with those of the majority of the association, I would rather not become a member unless I were able, which I am not, to take part in the proceedings, of which by joining the association I should assume a share of the responsibility.

APPENDIX A

Mill's Diary—January 8 to April 15, 1854

[On January 8, 1854, Mill tried the experiment of keeping a diary, in which he might commit one thought to paper each day. The diary ends abruptly on April 15.]

January 8.

THIS little book is an experiment. Whatever else it may do, it will exemplify, at least in the case of the writer, what effect is produced on the mind by the obligation of having at least one thought per day which is worth writing down. And for this purpose no mere speciality, either of science or practice, can count as a thought. It must either relate to life, to feeling, or to high metaphysical speculation. The first thing which I am likely to discover in the attempt is that, instead of one per day, I have not one such thought in a month; but only repetitions of thoughts, to us so familiar that writing them here would only expose the poverty of the land.

January 9.

What a sense of protection is given by the consciousness of being loved, and what an additional sense, over and above this, by being near the one by whom one is and wishes to be loved the best. I have experience at present of both these things; for I feel as if no really dangerous illness could actually happen to me while I have her to care for me; and yet I feel as if by coming away from her I had parted with a kind of talisman, and was more open to the attacks of the enemy than while I was with her.

January 10.

The English, looked at in one point of view, are certainly a remarkably stupid people. Looked at in another point of view they are continually striking one as a people among whom talent, of a certain sort, abounds. This strikes me often, for example, in reading Indian official documents, or in going through a number of a review or a magazine. The fact seems to be that there is a great amount of ability shown in the application of doctrines, while mere stolidity presides over the choice of the doctrines themselves. An Englishman's premises, the principles which he reasons from, or the rules of action which he is to apply, are all chosen *for* him. Somebody is supposed to have settled them long ago. The Englishman's ability consists in determining what ought to be done *supposing* that all these things have been settled rightly. But even when they have been settled rightly, he seldom knows or could prove it; he only firmly believes it. The maxims do not, in his mind, rest on evidence; their evidence, to him, is that they have, in a manner, grown into the mind itself.

January 11.

Those who think themselves called upon, in the name of truth, to make war against illusions, do not perceive the distinction between an illusion and a delusion. A delusion is an erroneous opinion—it is believing a thing which is not. An illusion, on the contrary, is an affair solely of feeling, and may exist completely severed from delusion. It consists in extracting from a conception known not to be true, but which is better than the truth, the same benefit to the feelings which would be derived from it if it were a reality.

January 12.

There is hardly a more striking example of the worthlessness of posthumous reputation than the oblivion into which my father has fallen among the world at large. Who was ever better entitled to take his place among the great names of England? He worked all his life long with complete disinterestedness for the public good; he had no little influence on opinion while he lived, most of the reforms which are so much boasted of may be traced mainly to him, and in vigour of intellect and character he stood quite alone among the men of his generation. Yet hardly one person who has grown to years of maturity since he quitted the scene seventeen years ago knows anything about him, even by name. It must be allowed, in part explanation, that the system of opinion with which he was identified has fallen much into the background of late years. The public has left behind both the good and the bad parts of it—if they can be called bad which are only omissions.

January 13.

The inferiority of the present age is perhaps the consequence of its superiority. Scarcely any one, in the more educated classes, seems to have any opinions, or to place any real faith in those which he professes to have. At the same time, if we compare the writings of any former period with those of the present, the superiority of these is unspeakable. We are astonished at the superficiality of the older writers; the little depths to which they sounded any question; the small portions of the considerations requiring to be looked at, which those writers appear to have seen. It requires in these times much more intellect to marshal so much greater a stock of ideas and observations. This has not yet been done, or has been done only by very few: and hence the multitude of thoughts only breeds increase of uncertainty. Those who should be the guides of the rest, see too many sides to every question. They hear so much said, or find that so much can be said, about everything, that they feel no assurance of the truth of anything. But where there are no strong opinions there are (unless, perhaps, in private matters) no strong feelings, nor strong characters.

January 14.

I sometimes think that those who, like us, keep up with the European movement, are by that very circumstance thrown out of the stream of English opinion and have some chance of mistaking and misjudging it. What is it that occupies the minds of three-fourths of those in England who care about any public interest or any controverted question? The quarrel between Protestant and Catholic; or that between Puseyite and Evangelical.

January 15.

It seems to me that there is no progress, and no reason to expect progress, in talents or strength of mind; of which there is as much, often more, in an ignorant than in a cultivated age. But there is great progress, and great reason to expect progress, in feelings and opinions. If it is asked whether there is progress in intellect, the answer will be found in the two preceding statements taken together.

January 16.

It is an immense defect in a character to be without lightness. A character which is all lightness can excite neither respect nor sympathy. Seriousness must be the *fond* of all characters worth thinking about. But a certain infusion of the laughing philosopher, even in his least popular form—an openness to that view of things which, showing them on the undignified side, makes any exaggerated care about them seem childish and ridiculous—is a prodigious help towards bearing the evils of life, and I should think has saved many a person from going mad. It is also necessary to the completeness even of the intellect itself. The contemptible side of things is part, though but a part, of the truth of them, and to be incapable of seeing and feeling that part with as much force and clearness as any other—to be blind to that aspect of things which was the only one the Cynics chose to look at—is to be able to see things only by halves. There always seems something stunted about the intellect of those who have no humour, however earnest and enthusiastic, and however highly cultivated, they often are.

January 17.

It is remarkable how invariably the instinct of the English people is on the side of the *status quo*. In all foreign wars, revolutions, &c., English opinion is sure to be against the side, be it king or people, that seems to be attempting to alter an existing order of things. All other nations admit that great political changes may be made, and even governments forcibly subverted, in order to improve as well as in order to preserve. The English allow this in theory, but their feelings never go along with it in any particular case.

January 18.

In the last age the writers of reputation and influence were those who took a side, in a very decided manner, on the great questions, religious, moral, metaphysical, and political; who were downright infidels or downright Christians, thorough Tories or thorough democrats, and in that were considered, and were, extreme in their opinions. In the present age the writers of reputation and influence are those who take something from both sides of the great controversies, and make out that neither extreme is right, nor wholly wrong. By some persons, and on some questions, this is done in the way of mere compromise; in some cases, again, by a deeper doctrine underlying both the contrary opinions; but done it is, in one or the other way, by all who gain access to the mind of the present age: and none but those who do it, or seem to do it, are now listened to.

This change is explained, and partly justified, by the superficiality, and real onesidedness, of the bolder thinkers who preceded. But if I mistake not, the time is now come, or coming, for a change the reverse way.

January 19.

I feel bitterly how I have procrastinated in the sacred duty of fixing in writing, so that it may not die with me, everything that I have in my mind which is capable of assisting the destruction of error and prejudice and the growth of just feelings and true opinions. Still more bitterly do I feel how little I have yet done as the interpreter of the wisdom of one whose intellect is as much profounder than mine as her heart is nobler. If I ever recover my health, this shall be amended; and even if I do not, something may, I hope, be done towards it, provided a sufficient respite is allowed me.

January 20.

Is it true, as Carlyle says, that nobody ever did a good thing by reason of his bad qualities, but always and necessarily in spite of them? Surely this can only be made true by an arbitrary limitation of the term "good" to *morally* good, which reduces the brilliantly sounding assertion to a mere identical proposition. Useful and even permanently valuable things are continually done from vanity, or a selfish desire of riches or power; sometimes even from envy or jealousy, and the desire to lower others. What is true is, that such good things would almost always have been *better* done, and would have produced greatly more good, if they had been done from a more virtuous motive.

January 21.

It is long since there has been an age of which it could be said, as truly as of this, that nearly all the writers, even the good ones, were but commentators: expanders and appliers of ideas borrowed from others. Among those of the present time I can think only of two (now that Carlyle has written himself out, and become a mere commentator on himself) who seem to draw what they say from a source within themselves: and to the practical doctrines and tendencies of both these, there are the gravest objections. Comte, on the Continent; in England (ourselves excepted) I can think only of Ruskin.

January 22.

In this age a far better ideal of human society can be formed, and by some persons both here and in France has been formed, than at any former time. But to discern the road to it—the series of transitions by which it must be reached, and what can be done, either under existing institutions or by a wise modification of them, to bring it nearer—is a problem no nearer being resolved than formerly. The only means of which the efficacy and the necessity are evident, is universal Education: and who will educate the educators?

January 23.

There is no doctrine really worth labouring at, either to construct or to inculcate, except the Philosophy of Life. A Philosophy of Life, in harmony with the noblest feelings and cleared of superstition, is the great want of these times. There has always been talent enough in the world when there was earnestness enough, and always earnestness enough when there were strong convictions. There seems to be so little talent now, only because there is universal uncertainty about the great questions, and the field for talent is narrowed to things of subaltern interest. Ages of belief, as Goethe says, have been the only ages in which great things have been done. Ages of belief have hitherto always been religious ages: but Goethe did not mean, that they must necessarily be so in future. Religion, of one sort or another, has been at once the spring and the regulator of energetic action, chiefly because religion has hitherto supplied the only Philosophy of Life, or the only one which differed from a mere theory of self-indulgence. Let it be generally known what life is and might be, and how to make it what it might be, and there will be as much enthusiasm and as much energy as there has ever been.

January 24.

The best, indeed the only good thing (details excepted) in Comte's second treatise, is the thoroughness with which he has enforced and illustrated the possibility of making *le culte de l'humanité* perform the functions and supply the place of a religion. If we suppose cultivated to the highest point the sentiments of fraternity with all our fellow beings, past, present, and to come, of veneration for those past and present who have deserved it, and devotion to the good of those to come; universal moral education making the happiness and dignity of this collective body the central point to which all things are to trend and by which all are to be estimated, instead of the pleasure of an unseen and merely imaginary Power; the imagination at the same time being fed from youth with representations of all noble things felt and acted heretofore, and with ideal conceptions of still greater to come: there is no worthy office of a religion which this system of cultivation does not seem adequate to fulfil. It would suffice both to alleviate and to guide human life. Now this is merely supposing that the religion of humanity obtained as firm a hold on mankind, and as great a power of shaping their usages, their institutions, and their education, as other religions have in many cases possessed.

January 25.

Vanity, in some persons, seems to be an intellectual defect; incapacity to appreciate qualities different from those they themselves possess; incapacity to feel the smallness of human affairs and capacities altogether; ignorance of the multitude of persons who have been or are superior to them, and the multitude of achievements superior to their little bit of attainment, &c. Accordingly this kind of vain persons equally exaggerate the merits and talents of their friends, or of any persons whom they like or admire. In others, again, vanity seems a moral defect; a form of selfishness; a dwelling on, and caring about, self and what belongs to it, beyond the just measure; especially what flatters its self-importance.

January 26.

Perhaps the English are the fittest people to rule over barbarous or semi-barbarous nations like those of the East, precisely because they are the stiffest, and most wedded to their own customs, of all civilised people. All former conquerors of the East have been absorbed into it, and have adopted its ways, instead of communicating to it their own. So did the Portuguese; so would the French have done. Not so John Bull; if he has one foot in India he will always have another on the English shore.

January 27.

Is composition in verse, as one is often prompted in these days to think, a worn-out thing, which has died a natural death, never to be revived? Only if Art, in every one of its other branches, is also destined to be extinguished. Verse is Art applied to the language of words; it is speech made musical; the most flexible and precise expression of thoughts and feelings, thrown into beautiful poems. Verse, therefore, I take to be eternal; but it ought, as well as every other attempt at public Art, to be suspended at the present time. In a militant age, when those who have thoughts and feelings to impress on the world have a great deal of hard work to do, and very little time to do it in, and those who are to be impressed need to be told in the most direct and plainest way possible what those who address them are driving at—otherwise they will not listen—it is foppery to waste time in studying beauty of form in the conveyance of a meaning. The shortest and straightest way is the best. The regeneration of the world in its present stage is a matter of business, and it would be as rational to keep accounts or write invoices in verse as to attempt to do the work of human improvement in it.

January 28.

A very useful periodical might be started, which should employ itself wholly in criticising the bad or foolish sayings of persons of note. Whenever a person of celebrity or importance made a speech containing appeals to bad feelings or encouragement to mischievous errors, it should show them up in detail; and when any such person wrote a book or pamphlet it should supply a thorough and minute criticism of it. Such a periodical would soon wield a great power if conducted ably, on principle, and without malice. It would inspire great awe in all persons whose names are before the public, and would make them fear to indulge in the truckling and feeding of every vulgar prejudice to which they now are, on the contrary, tempted by the instinct of seeking safety.

January 29.

That the mind of this age, in spite of its prosaic tendencies, is quite capable of and gifted for Art is proved by its achievements in music, in which it has excelled all previous times. Why, then, does it fail in all the other so-called fine arts? Because music, which excites intenser emotions than any other art, does so by going direct to the fountains of feeling, without passing through thought. It thus can be carried to any degree of perfection without intellect, or at least with only as much as is needed for mastering the technicalities of that as of any other pursuit. This is not true of any other of the arts; greatness in any of them absolutely requires intellect, and in this age the people of intellect have other things to do. In the ages of great architects, painters, or sculptors, these were among the men of greatest capacity whom the time produced; Leonardo was a great mathematician and discoverer in the sciences: Rubens was an ambassador; Michael Angelo was everything—poet, diplomatist, military engineer, as well as architect, sculptor, and painter; *all* were from their lives and circumstances obliged to be men of great practical address and ability, as may be seen from the life of such a man as Benvenuto Cellini. No such men now undertake the artist career, even in the countries in which the so-called arts are still honoured.

January 30.

When there is not time for real deliberation, it is generally safer to act on our first thoughts than on our second. For the first thoughts are likely to turn on the greater probabilities and more important points of the case; the second on some minor matter which qualifies and limits the former.

January 31.

A good practical idea, when once it has found anybody to stand up for it, certainly spreads nowadays with wonderful rapidity. When the India civil appointments were given up to competition, any one could see that the principle would in time be extended farther; but who would have expected that in the very next session of Parliament the Government would bring forward a plan for giving all the appointments in its own offices to the best-qualified candidates? Yet this, it seems, is to be the Queen's Speech this evening. It is curious to speculate on the change which a few years will make in English society, and even in English character, if once preferment is to go by real or even apparent merit, and no longer by favour.

February 1.

Nothing impresses one with a more vivid feeling of the shortness of life than reading history. The same man whom in one chapter we found entering on his career as a warrior or statesman, a few chapters farther on, when we are hardly aware of any lapse of time, we find old and dying. Like the tinge of melancholy in all biographies; the more we are interested in the hero, the sadder is our foreknowledge of the inevitable fifth act. One good effect follows from the dioramic passing before us of the long succession of historical characters who have "strutted and fretted their hour upon the stage"—an unbounded contempt for all those lives which make a great noise in their day, and leave the state of mankind in no respect better than they found it.

February 2.

It almost seems as if no strength of argument on subjects so abstract as the generalities of philosophy had the power of altering an opinion already formed. The partisan of the confuted doctrine not only is not convinced, but always finds some way of slipping his head out of the noose. But when we come to look into the matter, we find that this apparently unlimited possibility of raising counter-arguments against any argument, however conclusive, of which the subject is something at once highly abstract and extremely familiar, always depends on the great original error of thinking that an opinion deeply seated in the human mind proves itself. Until people can be untaught this cardinal error, they will never have any difficulty in persuading themselves of the truth of any doctrines which have long been part of the furniture of their mind. Phrases will never be wanting by which appeal can be made in some new form to the mind; habits of thought, in justification of any one of its thoughts: driven from one form of words, they will always find another in which to reproduce the same invariable inference that *so* the thing must *be* because it is the nature (*i.e.* the habit) of the mind so to conceive it. Yet, except in the logic, I know not where any real battle is kept up against this *fons errorum.* Every fresh edition is a renewal of the controversy.

February 3.

How many are there of the ways of the world, which, far from having been exaggerated by satirists, no satirist has dared to colour as highly as every-day fact would warrant. How far, for example, the stretch of invention in the way of malicious gossip transcends anything which we ever should or even *could* dream of the possibility of, until taught by experience. In youth the idea of liability to misrepresentation floats before the mind as a bare possibility, unlikely to be ever realised, and if realised, easily set to rights. As we grow older we learn that the most insignificant particulars in one's daily life, unnecessarily revealed, are very likely to be made the groundwork of a pile of *médisance* as mountain-like, and the top of it as distant from the foundation, as the Tower of Babel itself.

February 4.

The difficulty which writers have found in understanding the morality of Macchiavelli shows either great obtuseness, or extreme unacquaintance with the history of the period. It is scarcely credible that any one should ever have imagined the "Principe" to be a satire. It bears every mark of the most straightforward sincerity, as much so as the Florentine history, and the "Discourses on Livy." Modern writers, in their simple, not to say silly, conscientiousness, could not understand how a man, evidently of good purpose, could tolerate and even counsel crimes. But in the most flagitious of all recorded ages, when every one possessed of power, from the Pope, the King of France, and the Emperor to the smallest usurper of a petty Italian town or leader of a faction there, literally stuck at nothing—hesitated at no atrocity, no monstrosity of cruelty or perfidy, to forward even his smallest purpose—it might well be that even good men reserved their conscientiousness for the choice of ends, and thought that to be scrupulous about means was weakmindedness, and would place them at too great disadvantage in struggling with men who would reciprocate none of their forbearance, and who, in the degraded state of public opinion, would not even suffer much in character by availing themselves of every advantage given them. *Some* such arguing with themselves is incident to honest men in all ages—even in the present. The question what means are or are not immoral, always depends in part on the practice of the age; on what is done by other people. The radical and eternal distinction between vice and virtue is not in the means but in the ends. Macchiavelli was a man of real patriotism, a lover of liberty, and eager for the good of his country. But he saw no reason for fighting with foils against those who fight with poniards. And he had an artist-like admiration of perfection even in villainy; an intellectual respect for intellect and daring, though employed for ends which all his writings show that he disapproved.

February 5.

It is instructive to observe how exactly the same things admit of being said in defence of all religions. The first book of Cicero, "De Divinatione" (which contains the arguments to be afterwards refuted in the second), is an almost exact parallel to the writings in support of the Hebrew and Christian miracles. The quantity and quality of testimony produced in favour of oracles, omens,

&c., is overwhelming: and the arguments for the antecedent probability of such things, allowing that there are gods, and that those gods concern themselves about human interests, bear the closest resemblance to the arguments of Christian writers, and are quite as difficult to answer.

February 6.

Almost everything Carlyle says of Goethe appears to me to be mistake and misapprehension. But perhaps the greatest mistake of all is to imagine, as Carlyle does, that Goethe is the typical modern man; that he has shown to the modern world what it should be, and furnished the example by which modern life and the modern mind tend henceforth to shape themselves. To me it seems that nothing can be so alien and (to coin a word) antipathetic to the modern mind as Goethe's ideal of life. He wished life itself, and the nature of every cultivated individual in it, to be rounded off and made symmetrical like a Greek temple or a Greek drama. It is only small things, or at least things uncomplex and composed of few parts, that admit of being brought into that harmonious proportion. As well might he attempt to cut down Shakespeare or a Gothic cathedral to the Greek model, as to give a rounded completeness to any considerable modern life. Not symmetry, but bold, free expansion in all directions is demanded by the needs of modern life and the instincts of the modern mind. Great and strong and varied faculties are more wanted than faculties well proportioned to one another; a Hercules or a Briareus more than an Apollo. Nay, at bottom are your well-balanced minds *ever* much wanted for any purpose but to hold and occasionally turn the balance between the others? Even the Greeks did and could not make their practical lives symmetrical as they made their art; and the ideal of their philosophers, so far from being an ideal of equal and harmonious development, was generally one of severe compression and repression of the larger portion of human nature. In the greater huddle of multifarious elements which compose modern life, symmetry and mental grace are still less possible, and a strong hand to draw one thing towards us and push another away from us is the one thing mainly needful. All this is distinctly or obscurely felt by all who are entitled to any voice on such questions; and accordingly Goethe never influenced practical life at all, unless indeed by making scepticism illustrious; and his influence of any kind even in Germany seems to be now entirely gone.

February 7.

If it were possible to blot entirely out the whole of German metaphysics, the whole of Christian theology, and the whole of the Roman and English systems of technical jurisprudence, and to direct all the minds that expand their faculties in these three pursuits to useful speculation or practice, there would be talent enough set at liberty to change the face of the world. All other useless mental pursuits that I at present recollect give employment to few that are fit for anything else. But these still employ, and in a measure satisfy, here and there a man of nearly the first order of talent and a vast number of the second. The world had need be rich in intellect to be able to spare the immense amount of it which is now far worse than wasted.

February 8.

I would not, for any amount of intellectual eminence, be the only one of my generation who could see the truths which I thought of most importance to the improvement of mankind. Nor would I, for anything which life could give, be without a friend from whom I could learn at least as much as I could teach. Even the merely intellectual needs of my nature suffice to make me hope that I may never outlive the companion who is the profoundest and most far-sighted and clear-sighted thinker I have ever known, as well as the most consummate in practical wisdom. I do not wish that I were so much her equal as not to be her pupil, but I would gladly be more capable than I am of thoroughly appreciating and worthily reproducing her admirable thoughts.

February 9.

There are people who say that if you have but books in abundance you are independent of living sympathy, because you are in communion with the wise and good of all ages. Alas for such communion! The wise and good of all ages but the present —all those, at least, who have either written or been written about— can only by us of the present day be called wise and good with allowances. In the best of them we can discern what would *now* be great follies or prejudices and great moral faults. And so doubtless will posterity say, and truly, of those of the present time. If any in the past were wise and good in the full meaning of the terms, they were doubtless like the few who are so at present, never heard of, or not known for what they were, beyond a narrow circle into which they radiated good influences.

February 10.

The clergy, who in all the countries of modern Europe (except France and Germany in very recent times) have had education in their hands, and in England have it still as much as ever, have contrived to make discreditable all the branches of knowledge which they taught or pretended to teach. Thanks to them, Greek and Latin are commonly reckoned useless or worse, because they have taught them *minus* almost everything in them which is useful. Cambridge has brought discredit even upon mathematics, making it appear in practice to be a thing which narrows the mind, as it does whenever it is not taught with an express purpose of forming the intellect through it to things beyond it.

February 11.

It would certainly be unfair to measure the worth of any age by that of its popular objects of literary or artistic admiration. Otherwise one might say the present age will be known and estimated by posterity as the age which thought Macaulay a great writer.

February 12.

I suppose all things which are fundamentally true must, on the whole, produce by their promulgation (at least in the end) more good than harm; otherwise one would be apt to regret greatly the things which have been written in late times, as by Carlyle, in exaltation of the literary character, meaning thereby the office or function of literature—that it is the new priesthood, and so on. The consequence of the vulgarisation of these notions has been to make that very feeble and poor minded set of people, taken generally, the writers of this country, so conceited of their function and of themselves, however unworthy of it, and has at the same time made fine people think so much more of them, and admit them so much more easily to a distant participation of finery, under a polite show of equality of which they are invariably the dupes, that it has at once inflated their vanity and lowered their ambition. They aim at a sort of under-finery instead of aiming at things above finery. They would like to be indeed a priesthood, an aristocracy of scribblers, dividing social importance with the other aristocracies, or rather receiving it from them and basking in their beams. Why must it continue to be true of all professions and classes: "Starve them that they may work. Refuse them honour that they may be honest!"

February 13.

Many a man thinks himself, and in a certain sense truly, inaccessible to flattery, for no better reason than that his worst flatterer is himself. He holds himself so superior to others that their apparent estimation of him does not increase his own; or increases it only because the fact of his being admired affords fresh pabulum to his feeling of his own importance. This kind of self-conceited people are the most unamiable of all, for they do not even like other people for seeming to admire them.

February 14.

If human life is governed by superior beings, how greatly must the power of the evil intelligences surpass that of the good, when a soul and an intellect like hers, such as the good principle perhaps never succeeded in creating before—one who seems intended for an inhabitant of some remote heaven, and who wants nothing but a position of power to make a heaven even of this stupid and wretched earth—when such a being *must* perish like all the rest of us in a few years, and *may* in a few months from a mere alteration in the structure of a few fibres or membranes, the exact parallels of which are found in every quadruped! If, indeed, it were but a removal, not an annihilation—but where is the proof, and where the ground of hope, when we can only judge of the probability of another state of existence, or of the mode in which it is governed if it exist, by the analogy of the only work of the same powers which we have any knowledge of, namely, this world of unfinished beginnings, unrealised promises, and disappointed endeavours—a world the only rule and object of which seems to be the production of a perpetual succession of fruits, hardly any of them destined to ripen, and, if they do, only lasting a day.

February 15.

All things, however effete, which have ever supplied, even imperfectly, any essential want of human nature or society, live on with a sort of life in death until they are replaced. So the religions of the world will continue standing, if even as mere shells or husks, until high-minded devotion to the ideal of humanity shall have acquired the twofold character of a religion, viz., as the ultimate basis of thought and the animating and controlling power over action.

February 16.

Niebuhr said that he wrote only for Savigny; so I write only for her when I do not write entirely *from* her. But in my case, as in his, what is written for only one reader, that one being the most competent intellect, is likeliest to be of use to the many, readers or not, whose benefit is the object of the writing, though not the principal incentive to it.

February 17.

Every intellectual, or at all events every scientific, pursuit lies under the popular stigma of being unfeeling. This is partly the language of mere vulgar prejudice against the impassiveness essential to strictly rational enquiry, but it is also in some degree well founded, first, because persons of much feeling usually choose, by preference, other than scientific pursuits; and, secondly, because essentially solitary occupations, as scientific speculation usually is, do tend in some degree to deaden sympathy. For this, among other reasons, speculation never ought to be the sole and exclusive occupation of any one.

February 18.

Nine-tenths of all the true opinions which are held by mankind are held for wrong reasons. And this is one cause why the removal, now so constantly going on, of particular errors and prejudices does not much improve the general understanding. The newly admitted tenth commonly rests on as mistaken principles as the old error. What is the remedy? There can be none short of the reconstruction of the human intellect *ab imo*.

February 19.

Many books have been severely criticised for no better reason than that they did not satisfy the idea which the critic had formed from the title of what the book ought to contain; the critic seldom in these cases deigns to consider that all he says rather proves the title to be in the wrong than the book. So if a history or a biography professes, though but by implication, to tell anything, and then does not do so, but purposely keeps anything back, the writer may justly be blamed, not however for what his book is, but for what it professes to be without being. Goethe avoided this snare by calling his autobiography, which tells just as much about himself as he liked to be known, "*Aus* meinem Leben Dichtung und Wahrheit." The *Aus* even without the *Dichtung* saves his veracity.

February 20.

Whenever I look back at any of my own writings of two or three years previous, they seem to me like the writings of some stranger whom I have seen and known long ago. I wish that my acquisition of power to do better had kept pace with the continual elevation of my standing point and change of my bearings towards all the great subjects of thought. But the explanation is that I owe the enlargement of my ideas and feelings to *her* influence, and that she could not in the same degree give me powers of execution.

February 21.

So far are the contrivances in nature from being superior to those of art that when a delicate artificial instrument, a watch, for example, goes unaccountably wrong, it is then that we feel that it almost resembles a piece of nature's machinery, a living being.

February 22.

Carlyle is abundantly contemptuous of all who make their intellects bow to their moral timidity by endeavouring to believe Christianity. But his own creed—that everything is right and good which accords with the laws of the universe—is either the same or a worse perversion. If it is not a resignation of intellect into the hands of fear, it is the subornation of it by a bribe—the bribe of being on the side of Power—irresistible and eternal Power.

February 23.

Now when the superstition which prevented political changes is so much weakened, there is no solidity of conviction or force of conscience in our higher classes to resist the introduction of principles which if applied to their own case would deprive them of all they most value. Thus the present Governor-General of India, Lord Dalhousie, in his revenue administration, treats with contempt in theory, and tramples upon in practice, prescription as a foundation of property in land: prescription on which alone rests the title of most of the English and Scotch nobility and older gentry to their estates.

February 24.

Three-fourths of all the so-called philosophy, as well as all the poetry, spoken or written about Man, Nature, and the Universe is merely the writer's or speaker's subjective feelings (and feelings very often extremely unsuitable and misplaced) thrown into objective language.

February 25.

Two of the most notable things in the history of mankind are, first, the grossly immoral pattern of morality which they have always set up for themselves in the person of their Gods, whether of revelation or of nature; and secondly, the pains they have taken, as soon as they began to improve, in explaining away the detestable conclusions from their premises, and extracting a more tolerable morality from this poisonous root. For mankind are always growing better than their religion, and leave behind one after another of the more vicious parts of it, dwelling more and more exclusively on those which are better, or admit at least of a better sense. But this holding fast in theory to a standard ever more and more left behind in practice is one great cause why the human intellect has not improved in anything like the same ratio as the sentiments.

February 26.

Carlyle says of the English that they act more rationally than most other people, but are more stupid than almost any other people in giving their reasons for it. The second of these propositions sets a very narrow limit to the first. To act well without being able to say why one so acts is to act well only accidentally, *i.e.* because the natural or acquired instincts happen to set in a good direction. If the English in following unconscious instincts act better than other people, it can only be in so far as their much longer possession of a Government not arbitrary has made it an instinct in them to respect the rights of others, and as their greater political freedom has made them habitually look for success to "a fair field" rather than favour. And as a matter of fact, I do not think that the English do act more rationally than other people in any matters other than those to which the influence of these two causes extends.

February 27.

The doctrines of free will and of necessity rightly understood are both true. It is necessary, that is, it was inevitable from the beginning of things, that I should freely will whatever things I do will.

February 28.

In the moral and psychological department of thought, there is hardly an instance of a writer who has left a considerable permanent reputation, or who has continued to be read by after generations, except those who have treated or attempted to treat of the *whole* of some great department of speculation. Aristotle, Bacon, Hobbes, Locke, Hartley, Hume, Reid, Stewart, Brown, Descartes, Leibnitz, Spinosa, Kant, Condillac, Montesquieu, Adam Smith, Ricardo, Bentham, &c., &c. The only decided exceptions which I remember are Berkeley and Rousseau. Plato is an apparent exception, but really a striking example of the rule. Yet few of the systems of these systematic writers have any permanent value as systems; their value is the value of some of their fragments. But the fragments (the parts which are excellent in wholes which are inadmissible) if published separate would probably have attracted little notice. This is a tribute which mankind unconsciously pay to the value of theory and systematic thought; which they fancy they dislike, and are indeed never weary of decrying.

March 1.

The fanatical part of the English are just now very urgent for a parliamentary inquiry concerning nunneries, to ascertain whether young women are not detained in them against their will; and there have been in two successive Sessions majorities in the House of Commons against the Ministers for setting on foot this enquiry. Every word they say that has the least semblance of an argument is so literally applicable to marriage that the entire unconsciousness with which they triumphantly utter the most damning things is irresistibly ludicrous. One speaker said in yesterday's debate that a vow of obedience is contrary to the English Constitution and a violation of the personal freedom which is the right of every one. Another expatiated on the hardship of allowing young women under age to bind themselves by an irrevocable engagement when they cannot know what they are binding themselves to. What a sad absence of habitual reflection on the commonest human affairs is shown by its never occurring to these people how far *more* true all this is of marriage; and the marriage vow too is *legally* binding, which the other, in this country, is *not*.

March 2.

It is a common saying that the only true test of a person's character is actions. There is much error in this. Actions, even habitual ones, are as fallacious a test of character as any other. A person's actions are often an indication not so much of what the person is as of what he desires to be thought; or, in the case of a better sort of persons, of what he desires to think himself. Actions, no doubt, are the fittest test for the world at large, because all they want to know of a man is the actions they may expect from him. But to his intimates, who care about what he is and not merely about what he does, the involuntary indications of feeling and disposition are a much surer criterion of them than voluntary acts.

March 3.

One of the things which most require to be written about, and to be written much and well, is the perfect sufficiency of what is called materialism in theory, to supply the scientific foundation of idealism in feeling and practice.

March 4.

What is called morality in these times is a regulated sensuality; in the same manner exactly as the love of gain is regulated by the establishment of a law of property.

March 5.

Religion begins by being taken for granted; after a time, it is elaborately proved; at last comes a time (the present) when the whole effort is to induce people to let it alone.

March 6.

It is sometimes said that religion is the only preservative from superstition; that unbelievers and unbelieving times are the most indiscriminately credulous: "a godless Regent trembles at a star:" the popular delusions (Mesmer, Cagliostro, &c.) of the time preceding the French Revolution: mesmerism, table-turning, &c., at present. But the truth is, credulity and love of wonder are so natural to man that they always (hitherto) run riot when they have only reason to control them. Credulity has never yet been held in check but by a regulated credulity—a faith of some sort which excommunicates all wonders but those which it can use for its own purposes. Those who throw off this faith do not thereby become altered in the general texture of their understandings; they remain as credulous as ever, but being no longer preoccupied (and the appetite for wonder blunted) by one set of delusions, they are now open to all others.

March 7.

When the advocates of theism urge the universal belief of mankind as an argument of its own correctness, they should accept the whole of that belief instead of picking and choosing out of it. The appearances in nature forcibly suggest the idea of a maker (or makers), and therefore all mankind have believed in gods. The same appearances not only do not suggest, but absolutely contradict, the idea of a perfectly good maker; and accordingly mankind have never made their gods good, though they have always flattered them by calling them so.

March 8.

People who lead regular lives are often unable to conceive how it is that men with their eyes open do things which are obviously likely to bring them to ruin, ignominy, and perhaps suicide or the gallows. They account for it by supposing delusion, madness, the blinding influence of passion, &c., &c. They do not consider that the men who do the acts involving this ultimate extreme of failure in life are mostly men who are already in some position only one or two removes short of it.

March 9.

The characteristic of Germany is knowledge without thought; of France, thought without knowledge; of England, neither knowledge nor thought.

The Germans, indeed, attempt thought; but their thought is worse than none. The English, with rare exceptions, never attempt it. The French are so familiar with it that those who cannot think at all throw the results of their not-thinking into the forms of thought.

March 10.

Those who are in advance of their time need to gain the ear of the public by productions of inferior merit—works grounded on the premises commonly received—in order that what they may be able to write of first-rate value to mankind may have a chance of surviving until there are people capable of reading it.

March 11.

Thought and feeling in their lower degrees antagonise, in their higher harmonise. Much thought and little feeling make a mental voluptuary who wastes life in intellectual exercise for its own sake. Much feeling and little thought are the common material of a bigot and fanatic. Much feeling and much thought make the hero or heroine.

March 12.

As it is the best and not the worst people who suffer most from the pangs of conscience, so it is in our best moments that we feel the most bitterly the good that we are not. If I were wholly of a different nature from what I love and admire, I could with an untroubled mind enjoy and prize it like any other beautiful or precious thing that I could by no possibility myself have made. But when I am nearest to feeling in myself some likeness to the one being who is all the world to me, or when I make the greatest return of love for her most affecting love and kindness to me, then I am ready to kill myself for not being like her and worthy of her.

March 13.

An Englishman's writings on physical science never read like English writings, for they do not pare away and qualify. But compromise and halting half-way are so native to the English mind, that if an English mathematician had to argue his case in an assembly of his countrymen, one would expect him to say that in theory the three angles of a triangle may be equal to two right angles, but that in practice they are only equal to one.

March 14.

The way to be popular is to flatter everybody with being what he most wishes to be (or to be thought). This very undiscerning people do involuntarily, for they always take the will for the deed. A dull person cannot perceive real wit, but the man who is always straining for a joke passes for a wit in his eyes, because he blows a trumpet before his bad jokes and calls on everybody to listen to them. The rule holds even with respect to beauty: the woman who is thought handsome by silly people is always the one who *sets up* for being handsome, even if positively plain.

March 15.

The progress of opinion is like the advance of a person climbing a hill by a spiral path which winds round it, and by which he is as often on the wrong side of the hill as on the right side, but still is always getting higher up.

March 16.

It is part of the irony of life, and a part which never becomes the less affecting because it is so trite, that the fields, hills, and trees, the houses, really the very rooms and furniture, will look exactly the same the day after we or those we most love have died.

March 17.

When we see and feel that human beings can take the deepest interest in what will befal their country or mankind long after they are dead, and in what they can themselves do while they are alive to influence that distant prospect which they are never destined to behold, we cannot doubt that if this and similar feelings were cultivated in the same manner and degree as religion they would become a religion.

March 18.

In government, perfect freedom of discussion in all its modes —speaking, writing, and printing—in law and in fact is the first requisite of good because the first condition of popular intelligence and mental progress. All else is secondary. A form of government is good chiefly in proportion to the security it affords for the possession of this. Therefore mixed governments, or those which set up several concurrent powers in the State, which are occasionally in conflict and never exactly identical in opinions and interests, and each of which is interested in protecting the opinions and demonstrations of opinions which the others dislike, are generally preferable to simple forms of government, or those which establish one power (though it be that of the majority) supreme over all the rest, and thence able, and probably inclined, to put down all the writing and speaking which thwarts its purposes. It remains to be proved by facts (which in America are more promising than might have been expected) whether pure democracy is destined to be an exception to this rule.

March 19

The belief in a life after death, without any probable surmise as to what it is to be, would be no consolation, but the very king of terrors. A journey into the entirely unknown—the thought is sufficient to strike with alarm the firmest heart. It may be otherwise with those who believe that they will be under the care of an Omnipotent Protector. But seeing how this world is made, the only one of the works of this supposed power by which we can know it, such a confidence can only belong to those who are senseless enough and low-minded enough to think themselves in particular special favourites of the Supreme Power. It is well, therefore, that all appearances and probabilities are in favour of the cessation of our consciousness when our earthly mechanism ceases to work.

March 20.

A democratic revolution is one of the most unlikely of all events in England, for English working men are never likely to rise until they are starving, and they are not likely to be starving now for generations to come. But democratic institutions seem likely enough to be conceded, and that, too, more rapidly than is desirable, by the almost unasked liberality of the better part of the aristocracy. The Reform Bill of the present year and the plan of opening the Civil Service of Government to universal competition, are the most wonderful instances of unsought concession to the democratic principle—the former in its ordinary, the latter in its best, sense—which a reformer had imagined even in his dreams.

March 21.

Nothing so alleviates the smaller evils of life, and almost converts them into good, as the sympathy of those who love us and whom we entirely love. The very contrary is the case when the evil is great: the bitterest part of it is the suffering it causes to those whose life and happiness are bound up with our own.

March 22.

The upholders of the vulgar doctrine that women are not equal in intellect to men sometimes declare with an air of triumph that the writings of women are not original. The same thing is said of the Latin writers and for the same reason. The Greeks had written first, and the Romans, having received their whole literary education from them, remained to a certain extent their pupils. But if Roman civilisation had lasted a little longer, Roman literature would have outgrown its leading-strings. In the same manner women's literature is younger than men's. Men having long written, and written well, before women wrote at all, women naturally fell at first into the old paths which men had made, adopting men's opinions and men's forms of art. But before this is set down as want of originality, it should be known how many of the most original thoughts of male writers came to them from the suggestion and prompting of some woman.

March 23.

The only true or definite rule of conduct or standard of morality is the greatest happiness, but there is needed first a philosophical estimate of happiness. Quality as well as quantity of happiness is to be considered; less of a higher kind is preferable to more of a lower. The test of quality is the preference given by those who are acquainted with both. Socrates would rather choose to be Socrates dissatisfied than to be a pig satisfied. The pig probably would not, but then the pig knows only one side of the question: Socrates knows both.

March 24.

A person longing to be convinced of a future state, if at all particular about evidence, would turn with bitter disappointment from all the so-called proof of it. On such evidence no one would believe the most commonplace matters of fact. The pretended philosophical proofs all rest on the assumption that the facts of the universe bear some necessary relation to the fancies of our own minds.

March 25.

The only change I find in myself from a near view of probable death is that it makes me instinctively conservative. It makes me feel, not as I am accustomed—oh, for something better!—but oh, that we could be going on as we were before. Oh, that those I love could be spared the shock of a great change! And this feeling goes with me into politics and all other human affairs, when my reason does not studiously contend against and repress it.

March 26.

As I probably shall have no opportunity of writing out at length my ideas on this and other matters, I am anxious to leave on record at least in this place my deliberate opinion that any great improvement in human life is not to be looked for so long as the animal instinct of sex occupies the absurdly disproportionate place it does therein; and that to correct this evil two things are required, both of them desirable for other reasons, viz., firstly, that women should cease to be set apart for this function, and should be admitted to all other duties and occupations on a par with men; secondly, that what any persons may freely do with respect to sexual relations should be deemed to be an unimportant and purely private matter, which concerns no one but themselves. If children are the result, then indeed commences a set of important duties towards the children, which society should enforce upon the parents much more strictly than it now does. But to have held any human being responsible to other people and to the world for the fact itself, apart from this consequence, will one day be thought one of the superstitions and barbarisms of the infancy of the human race.

March 27.

Surely one of the most certain of the fruits to be expected hereafter from the progress of knowledge and good sense will be that nobody, unless killed by accident, will quit life without having completed the allotted term of threescore and ten.

March 28.

It is a loving wish to die before the one we entirely love, but a selfish wish to die before the one who entirely loves us. It is one of the most painful parts of our condition that, if we are fortunate enough to have a true friend, one or the other of these things must happen, unless, indeed, by a rare chance (as by shipwreck) both die suddenly, unexpectedly, and together.

March 29.

The passion for equality is an attribute either of the most high-minded or of those who are merely the most jealous and envious. The last should rather be called haters of superiority than lovers of equality. It is only the high-minded to whom equality is really agreeable. A proof is that they are the only persons who are capable of strong and durable attachments to their equals; while strong and durable attachments to superiors or inferiors are far more common and are possible to the vulgarest natures.

March 30.

When death draws near, how contemptibly little appears the good one has done! how gigantic that which one had the power and therefore the duty of doing! I seem to have frittered away the working years of life in mere preparatory trifles, and now "the night when no one can work" has surprised me with the real duty of my life undone.

March 31.

Apart from bodily pain, and from grief for the grief of those who love us, the most disagreeable thing about dying is the intolerable ennui of it. There ought to be no slow deaths.

April 1.

It is a happy effect of habit that the daily occupations, even when comparatively unimportant, which interested one during life continue to interest one, if one remains capable of them, even with the end full in view. I quite appreciate the wish to "die in harness."

April 2.

An experiment is now making in the altered state of human affairs, viz., whether a state of war will now, as formerly, interrupt internal improvement. There are already evident signs of its destroying in the public all active interest in improvement of institutions. But in this country ministries are now disposed to go on improving with less stimulus than heretofore from any opinion but that of the enlightened few. All that seems certain is that nothing will be done while the war lasts, which requires a strong popular impulse to carry it through the two Houses.

April 3.

The effect of the bright and sunny aspects of Nature in soothing and giving cheerfulness is never more remarkable than in declining health. I look upon it as a piece of excellent good fortune to have the whole summer before one to die in.

April 4.

Perhaps even the happiest of mankind would not, if it were offered, accept the privilege of being immortal. What he would ask in lieu of it is not to die until he chose.

April 5.

It is characteristic of the English that they have no trust in the attainment of any end by directly aiming at it. They think that if ends are ever attained it is by some indirectness or accident, in some way in which nobody would have expected it. Thus few of them believe that the plan for the reform of the Civil Service can answer, because they cannot persuade themselves of the possibility of discovering who is the ablest of a dozen men by bringing them all face to face to show what they can do. But they are perfectly satisfied with these they get now, by leaving the whole matter to chance.

April 6.

It is not surprising that in ages of ignorance the principal instrument of a magician's arts was supposed to be his books. Books are a real magic, or rather necromancy—a person speaking from the dead, and speaking his most earnest feelings and gravest and most recondite thoughts.

April 7.

Hero worship, as Carlyle calls it, is doubtless a fine thing, but then it must be the worship not of a hero but of heroes. Whoever gives himself up to the guidance of *one* man, because that one is the best and ablest whom he happens to know, will in nine cases out of ten make himself the slave of that most misleading thing, a clever man's twists and prejudices. How many are there of the most deservedly great names in history whom their contemporaries would have done well and wisely in implicitly following? One hero and sage is necessary to correct another.

April 8.

Moral regenerators in this age mostly aim at setting up a new form either of Stoicism or of Puritanism—persuading men to sink altogether earthly happiness as a pursuit. This might be practicable in the ages in which myriads fled to the Thebaid to get into any solitude out of such a world, but must be a failure now when an earthly life both pleasant and innocent can be had by many and might by all. What is now wanted is the creed of Epicurus warmed by the additional element of an enthusiastic love of the general good.

April 9.

All systems of morals agree in prescribing to do that, and only that, which accords with self-respect. The difference between one person and another is mainly in that with which their self-respect is associated. In some it is with worldly or selfish success. In others, with the supposed favour of the supernal powers. In others, with the indulgence of mere self-will. In others, with self-conceit. In the best, with the sympathy of those they respect and a just regard for the good of all.

April 10.

If mankind were capable of deriving the most obvious lessons from the facts before them, in opposition to their preconceived opinions, Mormonism would be to them one of the most highly instructive phenomena of the present age. Here we have a new religion, laying claim to revelation and miraculous powers, forming within a few years a whole nation of proselytes, with adherents scattered all over the earth, in an age of boundless publicity, and in the face of a hostile world. And the author of all this, in no way imposing or even respectable by his moral qualities, but, before he became a prophet, a known cheat and liar. And with this example before them, people can still think the success of Christianity in an age of credulity and with neither newspapers nor public discussion a proof of its divine origin!

April 11.

The Germans and Carlyle have perverted both thought and phraseology when they made Artist the term for expressing the highest order of moral and intellectual greatness. The older idea is the truer—that Art, in relation to Truth, is but a language. Philosophy is the proper name for that exercise of the intellect which enucleates the truth to be expressed. The Artist is not the Seer; not he who can detect truth, but he who can clothe a given truth in the most expressive and impressive symbols.

April 12.

In quitting for ever any place where one has dwelt as in a home, all the incidents and circumstances, even those which were worse than indifferent to us, appear like old friends that one is reluctant to lose. So it is in taking leave of life: even the tiresome and vexatious parts of it look pleasant and friendly, and one feels how agreeable it would be to remain among them.

April 13.

In how many respects it is a changed world within the last half-dozen years. Free trade instead of restriction—cheap gold and cheapening, instead of dear and growing dearer—despotism (in France) instead of liberty—under-population instead of over-population—war instead of peace. Still, there is no real change in education, therefore all the other changes are superficial merely. It is still the same world. A slight change in education would make the world totally different.

April 14.

The misfortune of having been born and being doomed to live in almost the infancy of human improvement, moral, intellectual, and even physical, can only be made less by the communion with those who are already what all well-organised human beings will one day be, and by the consciousness of oneself doing something, not altogether without value, towards helping on the slow but quickening progress towards that ultimate consummation.

April 15.

The remedies for all our diseases will be discovered long after we are dead; and the world will be made a fit place to live in, after the death of most of those by whose exertions it will have been made so. It is to be hoped that those who live in those days will look back with sympathy to their known and unknown benefactors.

APPENDIX B

Tract on Right of Property in Land

[This tract was written by Mill in April 1873, and was the last thing he wrote before his death. It was written for the Land Tenure Reform Association.]

RIGHTS of property are of several kinds. There is the property which a person has in things that he himself has made. There is property in what one has received as a recompense for making something for somebody else, or for doing any service to somebody else; among which services must be reckoned that of lending to him what one has made, or honestly come by. There is property in what has been freely given to one, during life or at death, by the person who made it, or honestly came by it, whatever may have been the motive of the gift—personal affection, or because one had some just claim on him, or because he thought one would use it well, or as he would most wish it to be used. All these are rights to things which are the produce of labour; and they all resolve themselves into the right of every person to do as he pleases with his own labour, and with the produce or earnings of his labour, either by applying them to his own use, or exchanging them for other things, or bestowing them upon other persons at his own choice.

But there is another kind of property which does not come under any of these descriptions nor depend upon this principle. This is the ownership which persons are allowed to exercise over things not made by themselves, nor made at all. Such is property in land; including in that term what is under the surface as well as what is upon it. This kind of property, if legitimate, must rest on some other justification than the right of the labourer to what he has created by his labour. The land is not of man's creation; and for a person to appropriate to himself a mere gift of nature, not made to him in particular, but which belonged as much to all others until he took possession of it, is *prima facie* an injustice to all the rest. Even if he did not obtain it by usurpation, but by just distribution; even if, at the first foundation of a settlement the land was equitably parcelled out among all the settlers (which has sometimes been the case), there is an apparent wrong to posterity, or at least to all those subsequently born who do not inherit a share. To make such an institution just, it must be shown to be conducive to the general interest, in which this disinherited portion of the community has its part.

The general verdict of civilised nations hath hitherto been that this justification does exist. The private appropriation of land has been deemed to be beneficial to those who do not, as well as to those who do, obtain a share. And in what manner beneficial? Let us take particular note of this. Beneficial, because the strongest interest which the community, and the human race, have in the land is that it should yield the largest amount of food, and other necessary and useful things, required by the community. Now, though the land itself is not the work of human beings, its produce is; and to obtain enough of that produce somebody must exert much labour, and, in order that this labour may be supported, must expend a considerable amount of the savings of previous labour. Now we have been taught by experience that the great majority of mankind will work much harder and make much greater pecuniary sacrifices for themselves and their immediate descendants than for the public. In order, therefore, to give the greatest encouragement to production, it has been thought right that individuals should have an exclusive property in land, so that they may have the most possible to gain by making the land as productive as they can, and may be in no danger of being hindered from doing so by the interference of anybody else. This is the reason usually assigned for allowing land to be private property, and it is the best reason that can be given.

Now, when we know the reason of a thing, we know what ought to be its limits. The limits of the reason ought to be the limits of the thing. The thing itself should stop where the reason stops. The land not having been made by the owner, nor by any one to whose rights he has succeeded, and the justification of private ownership of land being the interest it gives to the owner in the good cultivation of the land, the rights of the owner ought not to be stretched further than this purpose requires. No rights to the land should be recognised which do not act as a motive to the person who has power over it to make it as productive or otherwise as useful to mankind as possible. Anything beyond this exceeds the reason of the case and is an injustice to the remainder of the community.

It cannot be said that landed property, as it exists in the United Kingdom, conforms to this condition. The legal rights of the landlord much exceed what is necessary to afford a motive to improvement. They do worse; they tend in many ways to obstruct, and do really obstruct, improvement.

For one thing the landlord has the right, which he often exercises, of keeping the land not only unimproved, but uncultivated, in order to maintain an inordinate quantity of wild animals for what he calls sport. This right, at all events, cannot be defended as a means of promoting improvement.

Again, if the purpose in allowing private ownership of the land were to provide the strongest possible motive to its good cultivation, the ownership would be vested in the actual cultivator. But in England almost all the land of the country is cultivated by tenant-farmers, who not only are not the proprietors, but in the majority of cases have not even a lease, but may be dispossessed at six months' notice. If those lands are well cultivated, it cannot be in consequence of the rights of the landlord. If those rights have any effect on cultivation at all it must be to make it bad, not good. If farmers with such a tenure cultivate well, it is a proof that property in land is not necessary for good cultivation.

But, it will be said, if the mere cultivation can be and is satisfactorily carried on by tenants at will, it is not so with the great and costly improvements which have converted so much barren land into fertile. The returns to these improvements are slow, and a temporary holder, even if he has the capital, will not make them. They can seldom be made, and, in point of fact, seldom are made by any one but the proprietor. And as a certain number of landed proprietors do make such improvements, the institution of property in land is thought to be sufficiently vindicated.

Giving all the weight to this consideration which it is entitled to, the claim it gives to the landlord is not to all the possible proceeds of the land, but to such part of them only as are the result of his own improvements or of the improvements made by predecessors in whose place he stands. Whatever portion of them is due, not to his labour or outlay, but to the labour and outlay of other people, should belong to those other people. If the tenant has added anything to the value of the land beyond the duration of his tenancy, the landlord should be bound to purchase the improvement, whether permanent or temporary, at its full value. If the nation at large, by their successful exertions to increase the wealth of the country, have enhanced the value of the land independently of anything done by either the landlord or the tenant, that increase of value should belong to the nation. That it should do so is not only consistent with the principles on which landed property confessedly depends for its justification, but is a consequence of those very principles.

Now, the labours of the nation at large do add daily and yearly to the value of the land, whether the landlord plays the part of an improver or not. The growth of towns, the extension of manufactures, the increase of population consequent on increased employment create a consequently increasing demand for land, both for the habitations of the people and for the supply of food and of the materials for clothing. They also create a constantly increasing demand for coal, iron, and all the other produce of mining industry. By this increase of demand the landed proprietors largely profit without in any way contributing to it. The income from rural lands has a constant tendency to increase; that from building lands still more; and with this increase of their incomes the owners of the land have nothing to do except to receive it.

The Land Tenure Reform Association claim this increase for those who are its real authors. They do not propose to deprive the landlords of their present rents nor of anything which they may hereafter add to those rents by their own improvements. The future Unearned Increase is what the Association seeks to withdraw from them and to retain for those to whose labour and sacrifices from generation to generation it will really be due. The means by which it is proposed to accomplish this is Special Taxation. Over and above the fair share of the landlords in the general taxation of the public, they may justly be required to pay hereafter a special tax within the limits of the increase which may accrue to their personal income from causes independent of themselves.

Against this proposal it is objected that many landholders have bought the lands they hold, and in buying them had in view not only their present rental but the probability of future increase; of which increase therefore it would be unjust to deprive them. But the Association do not propose to deprive them of it without compensation. In the plan of the Association the landlords would have the right reserved to them of parting with their land to the State, immediately or at any future time, at the price for which they could sell it at the time when the plan is adopted. By availing themselves of this option they would not only get back whatever they had paid for the prospect of future increase, but would obtain the full price for which they could have sold that future prospect at the time when the new system was introduced. They would be left, therefore, in a pecuniary sense exactly as well off as they were before, while the State would gain the difference between the price of the land at the time and the higher value which, according to all probability, it would afterwards rise to. There would be no transfer of private property to the State, but only an interception by the State of an increase of property which would otherwise accrue at a future time to private individuals without their giving any value for it, since they would have been reimbursed whatever money they had given, and would even have received the full present value of their expectations.

There is another objection commonly made, which is disposed of by the same answer. It is often said that land, and particularly land in towns, is liable to lose value as well as to gain it. Certain quarters of London cease to be fashionable, and are deserted by their opulent inhabitants; certain towns lose a portion of their trading prosperity when railway communication enables purchasers to supply themselves cheaply from elsewhere. Those cases, however, are the exception, not the rule, and when they occur, what is lost in one quarter is gained in another, and there is the general gain due to the prosperity of the country besides. If some landlords for exceptional reasons do not partake in the benefit, neither will they have to pay the tax. They will be exactly where they are now. If it be said that, as they took the chance of a diminution they ought to have the counterbalancing chance of an increase, the answer is that the power of giving up the land at its existing price, in which both chances are allowed for, makes the matter even. Indeed, more than even. No one would benefit so much by the proposed measure as those whose land might afterwards fall in value, for they would be able to claim the former price from the State although they could no longer obtain so much from individuals. By giving up the rise of value they would obtain an actual State guarantee against a fall. And this would be no loss to the State, for every such fall in one quarter, unless owing to a decline of the general prosperity, implies a corresponding rise somewhere else, of which rise the State would have the benefit.

A third objection is sometimes made. Land, it is said, is not the only article of property which rises in value, from the mere effect of the advance of national wealth, independently of anything done by the proprietor. Pictures by the old masters, ancient sculptures, rare curiosities of all sorts, have the same tendency. If it is not unjust to deprive the landlord of the unearned increase of the value of his land, by the same rule the increase of value of Raphaels or Titians might be taken from their fortunate possessors and appropriated by the State.

Were this true in principle, it would lead to no consequences in practice, since the revenue which could be obtained by even a very high tax on these rare and scattered possessions would not be worth consideration to a prosperous country. But it is not true, even in principle.

Objects of art, however rare or incomparable, differ from land and its contents in this essential particular, that they are products of labour. Objects of high art are products not only of labour but of sacrifice. The pains, patience, and care necessary for producing works which will be competed for by future ages are far from being those from which the greatest immediate, and especially the greatest pecuniary, advantage is reaped by the artist. Such works almost always imply renunciation of a great part of the gains which might easily have been obtained by hasty and marketable productions; and often could not be produced at all unless the few purchasers who are able to distinguish the immortal from the ephemeral could feel that they might without imprudence pay a high price for works which would be a fortune to their descendants. The prospective rise in price of works of art is by no means an unearned increase; the best productions of genius and skill alone obtain that honour, while the increasing value of land is indiscriminate. Governments do not think it improper to disburse considerable sums in order to foster high art, and encourage the taste for it among the public. Much more then should they not grudge to the artist what may come to him spontaneously from the estimate which good judges form of what his productions may sell for, long after he is dead. I grant that in many cases the increased value does not reach the artist himself, but is an addition, and sometimes an unlooked-for addition, to the gains of a middleman, who may have bought at a very moderate price works which subsequent accident or fashion suddenly bring into vogue. This is a contingency to which artists, like all other workmen, are liable; if they are unable to wait they may be obliged to sell their future chances below the true value to somebody who can. But they obtain, on the average, a higher remuneration for their labour than they could obtain if they had no such chances to sell. And it must be remembered that, along with his chances of profit, the dealer takes the risk of loss. Changes in the public taste and judgment may take place either way; if some works which may have been bought cheap acquire a high value, others for which a high price has been paid go out of fashion, gradually or even suddenly. If dealers are exposed to the one chance they must have the benefit of the other. Were they deprived of it, their useful function, by which, until replaced by something better, artists are greatly benefited, could not be carried on.

Neither can it be said, as in the case of land, that receiving the market price of the day would compensate the holder for the chances of future increase. There is no market price of such things: it is a matter of individual judgment, and even if an average could be struck, it would not compensate any one for the disappointment of his own expectation. The objection, therefore, from the supposed parallel case fails in its application: the cases are not really parallel.[1]

Other objectors say that if it is allowable to take the unearned increase of the value of land, it must for the same reasons be allowable to take for the public the unearned increase of the price of railway shares. But the fallacy is here so transparent as scarcely to require pointing out. In the first place, every penny which is obtained by railway shareholders is, not the gift of nature, but the earnings and recompense of human labour and thrift. In the next place, railway shares fall in price as frequently as they rise, which is far from being the case with land. If it be said that the prosperity of the country tends to increase the gains of railway shareholders as well as those of landlords, the same national prosperity leads to the creation of competing railroads, and of new and comparatively unproductive branches, so as to take away from the old shareholders with one hand nearly if not quite as much as it bestows on them with the other. The two cases, therefore, differ in the essential point.

We have now, we think, exhausted the objections of principle which are usually made to the detention by the State of the unearned increment of rent. It has, we think, been shown that they are all of them such as a very little consideration of the subject is sufficient to dispel. But, besides these theoretical, there are practical objections, in appearance more formidable, but as we shall be able to show, quite as inconclusive.

It is alleged that, granting the justice of claiming the unearned increase for the State, there are no means of ascertaining what it is. It would be impossible (it is said) to distinguish the increase

[1] In so far as there does exist any parallelism, its consequences should be accepted. The right of property in things which, being unique, belong in some sense to the whole human race, assuredly ought not to be absolute. If a half-insane millionaire took it into his head to buy up the pictures of the great masters for the purpose of destroying them, the State ought to stop his proceedings, if not to punish him for the mischief he had already done. It may hereafter be thought right to require that those who possess such treasures should either open their galleries to public view, or at least lend the contents from time to time for the purpose of exhibition; and should allow to artists under reasonable restrictions regular access to them for the purpose of reproduction or of study. With regard to other possessions of public interest, such as architectural remains and historical monuments generally, they ought to be, if not acquired by the State, placed under State protection. The pretence of right to destroy them, or to make any change which would impair their historical interest, ought not for a moment to be listened to. The preservation of such monuments is one of the articles in the programme of the Land Tenure Reform Association. Had it been conceded fifty years ago, many interesting relics of antiquity would have been still in existence which are now irreparably lost.

of rent which arises from the general progress of society, from that which is owing to the skill and outlay of the proprietor: and in intercepting the former, there would be perpetual danger of unjustly encroaching upon the latter.

There would be some ground for this objection in a country of peasant proprietors. The improvements made by such a class of landowners consist more in the ungrudging and assiduous application of their own labour and care, and in attention to small gains and petty savings, than in important works, or in the expenditure of money. It would really be very difficult, if not impossible, to determine how much the proprietor and his family had done in any given number of years, to improve the productiveness or add to the value of the land.

But it is quite otherwise with the improvements made by rich landlords, like those who own nearly all the soil of the British Islands. What they do for the land is done by outlay of money, through the agency of skilled engineers and superintendents. It is easy to register operations (for instance) of thorough drainage, and to ascertain and record, as one of the elements in the case, the cost of those operations. Their effect in adding to the value of the land has a natural measure in the increased rent which a solvent tenant would be willing to pay for it; and the whole of that increase, whether great or small, we would leave to the landlord.

The possibility of a valuation of unexhausted improvements is assumed as a matter of notoriety in all the discussions, now so common, respecting Tenant Right. It is already a custom in many parts of England to compensate an outgoing tenant for these improvements; what is a custom in many places will soon, it is probable, be made a legal obligation in all; and among the objections made to its imposition by law, we are never told of the impossibility of doing it. But if it is possible to value the effects of temporary improvements, why should it be impossible to value the effect of permanent improvements? A Bill compelling a valuation of both, and giving compensation for both alike, has been introduced into the House of Commons by a high agricultural authority, Mr. James Howard, and has met with influential support.

Yet if this be possible, the object is completely attained, for there is no other difficulty. The fact of an increase of rent is easily ascertained. There is nothing needed but the trouble and expense of registering the facts. It might be necessary to have a survey of the whole country, ascertaining and recording the conditions of every tenancy, and to renew this operation periodically, say every ten or twenty years. This is not so difficult as the cadastral operations of some Continental countries, or the revenue surveys of British India; for these undertake to determine, by special inquiry, what rent each piece of land is capable of yielding. In the proposed survey it would suffice to record what it does yield; allowing the landlord, if he can, to prove that it is under-rented, in which case he ought not to suffer for his past moderation.

It should be understood also that no intention is entertained of paring down the increment of rent to the uttermost farthing. We assert in principle the right of taking it all: in practice we have no desire to insist upon the extreme right, at any risk of going beyond it. No doubt, the option allowed to the landlord of giving up the land at its existing value would secure him against pecuniary wrong; but we should be sorry to trade upon his reluctance to give up an ancestral possession, or one endeared to him by association. We would leave, therefore, an ample margin by way of insurance against mistakes in the valuation. We would not insist upon taking the last penny of the unearned increase. But we mention that within that limit, taxation on the land, in addition to the landlord's share of all other taxes, may justly be, and ought to be, imposed. We contend that a tax on land, not preceding but following the future increase of its value, and increasing with that increase, is a legitimate financial resource; and that it is for the individual landlord, by making an authentic record of what he does for the land, to preserve evidence that its increase of rent is the consequence and rightful reward of his own intelligent improvements.

This is the meaning of the fourth article in the programme of the Land Tenure Reform Association; and the reasons which have now been given are its justification. The more it is considered the more general, we believe, will be the adhesion to it of those whose regard for property is not a superstition but an intelligent conviction, and who do not consider landlords as entitled to pecuniary privilege but only to equal justice.

INDEX

S

T

THE END

Printed by Ballantyne, Hanson & Co.
Edinburgh & London

805423

Printed in Great Britain by
Amazon.co.uk, Ltd.,
Marston Gate.